BARBAROSSA
THROUGH GERMAN EYES

About the Author

Jonathan has an honours degree in History and served in the British Army, completing operational tours in Northern Ireland and Bosnia, and latterly acting as a military instructor to friendly governments in the Arabian Gulf. He has written extensively, although not exclusively, on the Second World War, specialising in the fighting on the Eastern Front, and non-Germans who served in the *Waffen-SS*. A regular expert contributor to all aspects of media, including TV and a range of magazines including *History of War*, *All About History* and *The Armourer*. He also often features on radio; BBC Radio 4, Talk Radio, Newstalk, and in a large number of podcasts, such as ww2podcast.com, History Hack and History Hit. His previous books include *Death on the Don: The Destruction of Germany's Allies on the Eastern Front* and the best-selling *D-Day Through German Eyes*.

Other books by Jonathan Trigg

Hitler's Legions series
Hitler's Gauls – The History of the French Waffen-SS
Hitler's Flemish Lions – The History of the Flemish Waffen-SS
Hitler's Jihadis – The History of the Muslim Waffen-SS
Hitler's Vikings – The History of the Scandinavian Waffen-SS

Hastings 1066
Death on the Don – The Destruction of Germany's Allies on the Eastern Front 1941-44 (nominated for the Pushkin Prize for Russian history)
The Defeat of the Luftwaffe – The Eastern Front 1941-45; Strategy for Disaster

Voices series
Voices of the Flemish Waffen-SS: The Last Testament of the Oostfronters
Voices of the Scandinavian Waffen-SS: The Last Testament of Hitler's Vikings

Through German Eyes series
D-Day Through German Eyes: How The Wehrmacht Lost France
VE-Day Through German Eyes: The Final Defeat of Nazi Germany
The Battle of Stalingrad Through German Eyes: The Death of the Sixth Army

BARBAROSSA
THROUGH GERMAN EYES

THE BIGGEST INVASION
IN HISTORY

Jonathan Trigg

AMBERLEY

*For Tim, the best friend anyone could hope for,
and for Mike – rest in peace.*

Half-title page: Soviet civilians watch the invaders as their village burns behind them. (Author's collection)

Title page: Invasion Day. Nerves taut, a German section crosses the river to begin the largest invasion in history. (Author's collection)

This edition published 2023

Amberley Publishing
The Hill, Stroud
Gloucestershire, GL5 4EP

www.amberley-books.com

Copyright © Jonathan Trigg, 2021, 2023

The right of Jonathan Trigg to be identified as the Author
of this work has been asserted in accordance with the
Copyright, Designs and Patents Act 1988.

British Library Cataloguing in Publication Data.
A catalogue record for this book is available from the British Library.

ISBN 978 1 3981 1551 4 (paperback)
ISBN 978 1 3981 0723 6 (ebook)

Typeset in 10.5pt on 13.5pt Sabon.
Typesetting by SJmagic DESIGN SERVICES, India.
Printed in India

Contents

Introduction

Midsummer 1941, Europe at war. Nazi Germany – the state that had started the conflict – had done what no other nation in history had ever accomplished, having conquered almost the entire Continent in a series of jaw-droppingly swift campaigns. After the crushing defeat of the First World War, an Austrian down-and-out jailbird turned demagogue had risen to power in Berlin and ordered Germany's new armed forces (the *Wehrmacht*) into action. Hitler's aggression saw Denmark, Norway, Belgium, the Netherlands, Luxembourg, Yugoslavia-as-was, and Greece all conquered in less than two years. Even once-mighty France – Germany's *Erzfeind* (arch enemy) – had fallen. Added to the list were Czechoslovakia and Austria – both swallowed up without a shot being fired – and proud Poland, carved up between Berlin and its newfound ally, the Soviet Union, less than twenty years after re-emerging as an independent country after centuries of suppression and partition. As for the rest of mainland Europe, Portugal and Nationalist Spain were neutral but friendly, while Hungary and the kingdoms of Italy, Romania and Bulgaria were allies. With the United States gripped by isolationism, only Great Britain and her Empire now openly opposed the Nazi dictator.

He'd won. Hitler now controlled the Continent in a way that not even Napoleon or Julius Caesar had. Many of his own people – including a significant number of senior military men – remembered the two million dead of the First World War, and had been horrified at Hitler's thirst for conflict, yet even they were now in thrall to a leader who had defeated almost the entire West at a blood price of just one-third of the losses sustained at Verdun back in 1916.

Now was the time for Hitler to consolidate his gains, to focus on beating the British, and then establish the Thousand-Year Reich he boasted of.

Instead, the inveterate gambler made the biggest bet of them all. Massing the largest invasion force ever seen in history of the world, he flung it at the largest country in the world – Joseph Stalin's Soviet Union. This was *Unternehmen* Barbarossa – Operation Barbarossa. Intended to be a lightning campaign lasting eight to ten weeks, Barbarossa foundered, and Nazi Germany and her allies were drawn into a blood-letting that had no parallel and ended in complete failure.

The reasons behind its failure centre on shockingly poor planning on the part of the Nazi state, and more specifically the German military, but the waters were muddied in the post-war period to protect a myth of Teutonic efficiency and instead create a very different narrative around Barbarossa, one that laid the blame for disaster squarely at Hitler's door alone. The leading proponents of this narrative included Franz Halder, Erich von Manstein and Heinz Guderian. These men were part of the senior leadership cadre for Barbarossa, and so had the most to gain by deflecting criticism away from themselves and onto a dictator who was conveniently dead, and had been laid bare to the world as the monster he truly was.

In very broad terms, the generals' narrative, to give it a name, was that upon invasion, the *Wehrmacht* had swept deep into the Soviet Union at a pace hitherto unknown in warfare, winning huge victories on the way and taking the Germans to within an ace of success, when Hitler – in a fit of near-lunacy – threw it all away by abandoning the all-important drive on Moscow, and instead diverted his forces to Ukraine. There, around the city of Kiev, they would win the greatest military victory ever, but one that was doomed to be pyrrhic. Guderian's own son – Hans Günther – loudly parroted this line as a senior officer in West Germany's post-war *Bundeswehr*: "All the senior officers at the time believed that the offensive on Moscow should continue. The turning point in the war was when the original plan to reach Moscow and take it was dropped by Hitler for something quite different."

The story continued that with winter fast approaching Hitler turned once more to Moscow. Now, the lack of time to capture the Soviet capital was compounded by the dictator's earlier decision to delay Barbarossa and first invade Yugoslavia and Greece. However, by an almost superhuman effort, the *Wehrmacht* thrust at the capital, winning more enormous victories before finally being forced to halt by the onset of Russia's General Winter, even with the onion domes and spires of St Basil's Cathedral tantalisingly in sight. A massive Soviet counter-offensive then put paid to any hope of German success and set the seal on Barbarossa's failure.

The generals' narrative also stated that, simultaneous to the invasion itself, in the newly conquered territories a coalition of SS death squads and local anti-Semitic collaborators carried out a campaign of mass murder that slaughtered well over a million Soviet Jews, Communist Party officials and ordinary civilians. Alongside this planned programme of extermination, a terrible accident – outside of the *Wehrmacht*'s control – was occurring as the millions of Red Army prisoners-of-war (POWs) captured by the Germans during their advance overwhelmed the material resources of their captors, leading to huge numbers of them tragically dying of thirst, hunger and disease.

In all of this, the German Army – the *Heer* – was not complicit. Its officers and soldiers were simply doing their duty at the front while the vastness behind them became a charnel house. When – much later – those same officers and soldiers were confronted with the reality of what had been going on, their response was shock and horror, swiftly followed by loud protestations of personal innocence; see no evil, hear no evil. As one former member of the invasion force said to his only son years later, "All that was out of our field of view. We didn't concern ourselves with it."

For a number of reasons – not least of which was the necessity to absolve the West German military of its failure and guilt and rearm the country to face the new Soviet Cold War threat – this narrative was accepted and became the *truth*. However, since the end of the Cold War, much of the prevailing orthodoxy about the invasion and its failure has come under intense scrutiny, as historians have challenged many – if not all – of the foundation tenets of the Barbarossa myth.

First and foremost, the idea that the German Army stood entirely separate from the Nazis' war of extermination in the East has been blown apart. An initial wave of books and memoirs released in the immediate post-war years pretty much parroted the line that sought to lay blame for Barbarossa's utter barbarity at Hitler's door alone. Those same works tried to sanitize ordinary soldiers' actions in the campaign, and if any references to atrocities were included they were couched in euphemisms; anyone executed or shot out-of-hand was a partisan or a bandit, never just a civilian, a Soviet Jew or a prisoner-of-war.

The first chinks in the wall of denial came from a second – much later – tranche of diaries and memoirs, written or released for publication decades after the events themselves, which didn't seek to whitewash the invasion and matter-of-factly described the looting, killing and sexual violence that was intrinsic to Barbarossa. For the first time, former soldiers who had taken part in the invasion began to speak out. Men like Ulrich de Maizière – at the time a young *leutnant* in the Army High Command's planning centre: "Of course the *Wehrmacht* was involved ... in shootings and deeds which contravened international law," and he was clear where he believed blame lay. "(The *Wehrmacht*) took part in an offensive war, a war which the highest levels of command had decided was to be one of annihilation..." The former *jagdflieger* (fighter pilot) Heinrich Graf von Einsiedel – a great-grandson of Otto von Bismarck – was equally clear when he was interviewed for the 2017 television documentary *Hitler's Holocaust*: "The majority of senior officers, generals and so on, that I met can purely and simply be described as Nazis ... the need for *lebensraum* ('living space'), our right to conquer ... all that went without saying." That isn't to say every soldier in the invading host indulged in a murderous rampage, far from it, but the dark side of the campaign – and by any measure it was incredibly dark – was part and parcel of it from the very first day.

The *Hamburger Institut für Sozialforschung* (Hamburg Institute for Social Research) then threw fuel on the fire when it opened an exhibition in 1995 entitled '*Vernichtungskrieg – Verbrechen der Wehrmacht 1941 bis 1944*' (War of Annihilation – Crimes of the *Wehrmacht* 1941–1944). To the consternation of many Germans and Austrians, the exhibition comprehensively demolished the concept of the clean *Wehrmacht*, using incriminating documents from the time and myriad appalling photos taken by the troops themselves. Despite often rowdy protests outside its venues, the exhibition was viewed by over a million visitors in thirty-three German and Austrian cities.

The second falsehood to be exposed was that Germany's armed forces were so powerful and her generalship so superior that Barbarossa should, indeed would, have succeeded, had it not been for Hitler's amateurish meddling. More and more studies have cast doubt on this supposition, citing instead the lack of troops, weapons and equipment available to the *Wehrmacht*, to make the case that the invasion force may indeed have been the largest ever assembled, but it still wasn't big enough for the job, regardless of anything the dictator did or didn't do.

This book seeks to take that argument one step further by trying to show that, barring a miracle, Barbarossa was doomed to fail from the outset, with the intelligence, the plan, the forces, and, crucially, the logistics never anywhere near the mark to deliver victory. Ulrich de Maizière acknowledged as much after the war: "The mistake underlying the whole operation was that the resources, the depth, the sheer size of the Soviet Union, and the number of men it could mobilise, was totally underestimated not only by the soldiers at the front but also by the higher levels of command."

A maxim in military circles is that an army is always ready to fight and win the last war, but never the next. The *Wehrmacht* fits the cliché to a tee. In essence, the German general staff – its famed professional officer corps – had designed and built a military that would avoid the bloody stalemate of the First World War's Western Front by smashing France with fast-moving armoured troops supported by the flying artillery of the *Luftwaffe*. The mass of the Army – still composed of marching infantry – would then use western Europe's dense and modern road network to consolidate and seal the victory that had eluded their forefathers in 1914. The generals were right, and German success in the summer of 1940 proved it.

Where they failed was in not applying the same principles to the war in the East.

In the First World War, the eastern theatre was not Imperial Germany's main effort, it was a subsidiary front left to their chief ally, Austro-Hungary. When Vienna and Budapest's staggering ineptitude forced Berlin to intervene to avert calamity, relatively meagre German forces proved the Russians' undoing. For Hitler, this led to a belief that the eastern behemoth was a paper tiger, and a western-style campaign would lead to a total collapse of the country and a swift victory – and his generals agreed with him. There was little or no understanding that twenty years of ruthless Soviet communism had forged a completely different state from the incompetent and decaying tzarist regime that preceded it. Consequently, the generals failed to organise, equip and man an army that could defeat this new enemy, and led the *Wehrmacht* to launch the sort of assault that triumphed against Paris, but would end in the east with exhaustion while still caught in the country's hinterland – in truth, 90 per cent of the Soviet Union would never see a German soldier, except as a captive. This was not just Hitler's doing, but a direct, collective failure of German military leadership.

The Barbarossa myth is also clear on the issue of time, or rather the lack of it after Hitler allowed himself to be distracted by the attacks on Yugoslavia and Greece, losing a month of excellent campaigning weather, further compounded by his folly in sending the cream of his armoured forces south to seize Kiev and Ukraine, wasting all of August when, instead, they should have been focused on Moscow. This squandering of two months and more meant the German offensive ground to a halt due to the inevitably worsening weather.

In truth, the German offensive was badly faltering *before* the turn south in August. The *Wehrmacht* had never fought a campaign lasting more than four to six weeks, and by the time the order came to strike towards Ukraine, after almost eight weeks in the field, it was nearing exhaustion. The battle of Kiev – far from being a milestone in the continuing rise of what was now the *Ostheer* (the German Army in the East) – was almost its undoing. The subsequent drive on Moscow by *Heeresgruppe Mitte* (Army Group Centre) – *Unternehmen Taifun* (Operation Typhoon) – was the last gasp of a punch-drunk boxer doomed to fall before the bell was rung. In that context, the loss of one or two months made no difference;

the *Wehrmacht* would have shot its bolt by September no matter when it had crossed the Soviet border.

It is for that reason that I finish the story of Barbarossa after the Kiev encirclement and before the beginning of *Taifun*. Almost all histories of the campaign take the Red Army's counter-offensive in front of Moscow on 5 December as the end of the invasion, but Kiev marked its real end. At that point the German plan for a giant three-pronged offensive across a broad front, aimed at winning the war before Christmas, was consigned to the bin by no lesser figure than Hitler himself, who instead signed off on a single thrust towards Moscow, while accepting that the Reich would still be fighting in Russia in 1942. Hitler's Barbarossa gamble had failed.

For the next three years and more, across a landscape of thousands and thousands of square miles, huge armies battled each other into the dirt and ice. In the end, the attrition was simply too great for Hitler's Germany to withstand, and Joseph Stalin would have the deep satisfaction of seeing his armies victoriously standing in the ruins of Berlin, even as the body of his nemesis was being burnt by his aides in the shell-pitted garden of the Reich Chancellery.

But back in the summer and autumn of 1941 it seemed to most that Adolf Hitler and his *Wehrmacht* were forging a very different history. The *Wehrmacht* seemed unstoppable, conquering the Baltic states, eastern Poland, Belarus, Ukraine, and marching to the gates of Leningrad and even Moscow itself.

The sheer scale of it all is difficult to comprehend, even today. Including allies, the invasion force would comprise almost four million men, well over half a million motor vehicles – and even more horses – over seven thousand artillery pieces, almost four thousand panzers and assault-guns, and close on three thousand aircraft; the list goes on and on. But what that list obscures is that all those men and women massed on the border – and their friends and families back home – had a name, a face, a story. Barbarossa would transform those stories – and end millions of them. It would end even more stories on the Soviet side, where the tragedy and suffering would be monumental, but this book is not about their tragedy, their suffering, it is about the invasion from the German point of view, and, distinctly, from that of the frontline soldier – the *landser* – his corporals and sergeants, and the junior and middle-ranking officers who would lead them in combat. The *feldmarschalls* and generals directed the fighting and would win the laurels, but this is the story of the campaign primarily from ground level, from the men who would fight it, and ultimately lose it.

One of those men was Hans Roth, a native of Frankfurt and an Army reservist in his early thirties. Married to Rosel, he'd completed his obligatory military service in peacetime, and had then concentrated on growing his successful graphic design business. Recalled to the colours on the outbreak of war, he left Rosel and their five-year-old daughter Erika and became an anti-tank gunner – a *panzerjäger* – in *Generalleutnant* Willi Moser's 299. *Infanterie-Division* (299. *ID*).

Newly formed from Thuringians and Hessians like Roth, the division had no great antecedents or military traditions, and wasn't filled with fanatical Nazis; it was just one of the ten new divisions established in February 1940 under the auspices of *Welle 8* (Wave 8). A *Welle* being the German designation for a group of infantry divisions raised at the same time with approximately the same structure, equipment and training. Most of the 299. *ID*'s ranks were filled with youngsters from the 1940 draft class, with relatively few being older men like Roth. Its commander, Willi Moser, was an artilleryman who had served in the First World War and whose first divisional command this was. Broadly typical of much of the German general officer class of the time, Moser was calm, competent and professional rather than a Caesar-in-waiting. After receiving their baptism of fire in France, Roth and his comrades were transferred to the western bank of the River Bug in occupied Poland in the run-up to the offensive. On being told of the planned invasion he was ecstatic: "Hurray! The greatest battle of all time will start the day after tomorrow! ... What luck we have! ... we will be part of the first wave! ..." He spoke of the huge build-up he saw around him: "The forest to our rear is filled with intense activity. Heavy artillery has been placed in position, our panzers have arrived, and flak cannons were set in place last night." Then, on the very eve of the attack, he tried to imagine the future:

> For the moment there is a quiet, wonderful, twilight peacefulness over the countryside. The huts in this village will be on fire in a few hours, the air will be filled with the howling and screeching of shells, and the impacts will tear apart the fields and roads ... what will the following weeks bring?

The shock of the invasion's opening bombardment awed him. It was "as if Armageddon had arrived. It is impossible to comprehend one's world in such an inferno."

Just two days later, the almost breathless anticipation Roth had felt before Barbarossa had been replaced by something of the savagery that would epitomise the Russo-German war, a savagery that he – despite being a loving husband and father – quickly embraced:

> Never have we experienced anything like this ... the village of Lokacze ... damn snipers! House after house has to be cleared out with hand-grenades. They fire at us until the roofs collapse on their heads and they

are buried under the rubble. Others escape at the last minute as human torches. They either fall dead in the street or we beat them to death.

Hans Roth would stay on the Russian front for exactly three years, before – on the very anniversary of the launch of Barbarossa – he and his entire division were annihilated in the great Soviet summer offensive of 1944 that immolated Germany's *Heeresgruppe Mitte.* His body was never recovered. There is no grave; the only memory his daughter had of him was a kiss goodbye as he went off to war: *"Auf Wiedersehen, liebling Erika."*

Roth was one of so very many lost in that dreadful campaign, his service at the front in many ways epitomising the conundrum of the German soldier: brave, dutiful, loyal, yet capable of barbarous inhumanity on an epic scale.

Now, eighty years on, this book is about all the Hans Roths lined up that fateful day in June 1941; their stories, their view of the fighting.

Notes on the Text

In the book I have adopted a number of devices which, in my view, both improve the text itself and help the reader with the ebb and flow of the story. I appreciate that some readers may not agree with one or more of these, but I ask for forgiveness if that is the case.

So, firstly, during the war most Germans used the term 'Russians' to cover everyone in the now-dissolved Soviet Union's Red Army and State, despite the multitude of nationalities and ethnic groups within it. For ease, I've done the same.

Many place names have changed since the war in the former Soviet Union and in regions that have since become part of other states, such as those parts of what was the Third Reich that are now modern Poland. I have applied a mix-and-match approach to this situation, with most place names given using their spelling at the time and then their modern name in brackets: e.g. Breslau (modern-day Wrocław in Poland). But I have also – to the annoyance of some, I accept – used modern-day names on occasion, for example the state of Belarus, which at the time of the German invasion was a Soviet republic called variously 'Belorussia', 'Byleorussia' or even more colloquially 'White Russia'. I have also adopted a similar approach to numbers.

Regarding German military units I have used German nomenclature, for example the 88th Infantry Division is written as *88. Infanterie-Division* or shortened to *88.ID*, and *kompanie*, *bataillon* for company and battalion when appropriate. German ranks are likewise; Captain is *Hauptmann*, etc. The exception is where the holders are *Waffen-SS* members, and there I've used that organisation's own designation of *SS-Hauptsturmführer* and so on. There is a table of comparative ranks in the appendix.

In researching this book I have been helped enormously by a number of authors who have come before me and written important, authorative, and enjoyable works. I am thinking in particular of Robert Kershaw's *War Without Garlands*, Michael Jones's books on the Leningrad and Moscow fronts, David Stahel's excellent tomes, and Sönke Neitzel and Harald Welzer's *Soldaten* – I have read them all with delight, and quoted from them with gratitude.

I have also quoted the many veterans I have interviewed with reference to their experiences on the Eastern Front – and to them I owe an enormous debt of thanks for re-living some of the most painful memories of their lives. Lastly, I cannot say enough about the generosity and support of the *Museumsstiftung Post und Telekommunikation Briefsammlung* – the letter collections of the Museum Foundation for Post and Telecommunications in Berlin. Their collection of German military *Feldpost* currently stands at over 120,000 and they have given themselves the mammoth task of digitising as much as they can obtain; and considering the amount of written correspondence between the homeland and soldiers at the front runs into the billions, I wish them well in their endeavour. In the meantime, the mountains of letters sent to friends and family by ordinary serving members of the *Wehrmacht* already available is a treasure trove, and one in which I have delved deep. Readers will notice that some of the letter authors are identified either by just their initials or their first names; this is according to their families' wishes.

As ever, in any such work there are bound to be errors, and I apologise for them, but where they have been made they are all my own.

1

Food & Hatred

On June 14 Hitler assembled all the *Heeresgruppen*, *Armee* and *Panzergruppen* commanders in Berlin to explain his reasons for attacking Russia ... His detailed exposition of the reasons that led him to fight a preventative war against the Russians was unconvincing ... the causes were insufficient to take such a drastic course of action, as were the ideological theories of National Socialist dogma and reports of Russian preparations to attack us.[1]

It was early summer 1941, and the above writer – Heinz Guderian – was attending a conference where Adolf Hitler, the dictator of Nazi Germany for eight years past, formally announced to his senior military commanders his intention to launch an attack that still shapes our world today. Guderian, a general and an Army brat from the German military's Prussian heartland, would play a leading role in the ensuing drama that would eventually destroy both his beloved Army and country. In some ways he would also typify the Germans who would fight this new war: experienced, well-trained, and accustomed to victory, yet naïve and arrogant to the point of blindness. He would glory in his successes before falling to his master's rage, and would stick to the mantra of 'see no evil' while profiting from barbarity – in his case via a stolen country estate and fat monthly cheques from a secret Nazi Party slush fund.[2]

With the war over, Guderian would set about writing his memoirs, which he subtly – and sometimes not so subtly – tailored to underpin the 'clean *Wehrmacht*' narrative and place the burden of military failure squarely on the shoulders of his late and unlamented boss. His comments about the 14 June conference are a case in point. He stated that at the meeting his strongly held view was that "Adolf Hitler's Germany was even less capable of fighting such a war than had been the Germany of 1914", and yet he uttered not one word in protest – and neither did anyone else. He recalled that "the assembled company listened to Hitler's speech in silence and then, since there was to be no discussion, dispersed, in silence, and with heavy hearts". The Prussian general shouldn't have been surprised at the manner in which such a momentous decision was communicated; the exact same scenario had played out the previous autumn when Hitler had announced to many of the same men that Nazi Germany would shortly attack in the West, even as the fighting in Poland was raging.

As for Hitler's decision to turn East once more, Guderian himself sent Hitler a memo in late 1939 that his *aide-de-camp*, *Major* Gerhard Engel, described thus: "(Guderian) reported very unfavourably about Soviet armaments and morale ... Especially tanks, old and obsolete. Signals also very backward." The panzer general was clearly critiquing the Red Army as a potential future enemy.

In fact, it is difficult to believe Guderian felt much else at the time of the conference besides a feeling of exhilaration at the opportunity Hitler had given him to fulfil his military ambitions. Those ambitions would ultimately prove costly in the extreme. For Guderian, they would see his hometown of Kulm in West Prussia become Polish Chełmno after almost two centuries of German rule, and what remained of his nation carved up between East and West. But on 14 June 1941 he had been given an order by his *Führer*, and he would carry it out; he would celebrate his fifty-third birthday three days later, and five days after that would step on Soviet soil as an invader.

Guderian didn't elaborate on what he thought Hitler's motivations were for war against the Soviet Union, choosing instead to simply explain them away as 'National Socialist dogma', when in fact the crux of the dictator's reasoning would be central to the direction of the ensuing campaign and the way it was fought. In reality the invasion was launched for two reasons: food and hatred. The former to fuel the Nazi aim of achieving global domination, and the latter the destruction of the enemies they believed stood in their way. The incubus of that all-consuming hatred of the Soviet Union didn't lie with Guderian and the mass of the German people but was overwhelmingly in the mind of one man, Adolf Hitler. The creator of National Socialism detested communism – bolshevism as he consistently called it – and had set his heart on destroying it years before he achieved power, its annihilation being at the heart of the Nazi world view, their *Weltanschauung*. This philosophy held that all human history was a war, with the world as the prize as well as the battlefield. In this ultimate contest, survival could only be achieved by winning, and that victory only achieved by the extermination of one's enemies. For Hitler those enemies were right in front of his eyes – the Jews and bolshevism. In his mind, the two were inextricably linked, so the destruction of bolshevism and the Jews were one and the same. As bolshevism was centred in the Soviet Union, and that same country had a population of millions of Jews, destroying the Soviet Union would achieve his ideological goals – hence Barbarossa.

No one knows definitively why Hitler hated the Jews as he did. Much of it probably originated from his time as an impoverished wannabe-artist in Vienna before the First World War, but it's impossible to say for sure. The same goes for his loathing of bolshevism, a credo that shared much of its philosophy with National Socialism. The English novelist Nancy Mitford – whose own sister Unity was vociferously pro-Nazi – thought the two ideologies closely related: "There's never been a pin to put between Communists and Nazis. The Communists torture you to death if you're not a worker, and the Nazis torture you to death if you're not a German." Barbara Runkle, a young American studying classical piano in Munich in the late 1930s, also recognised their common ground: "Slowly but surely I've grown to be a great enemy of National Socialism – oddly enough for the same reasons that turned me against communism; they're amazingly similar, which makes it almost unbelievably stupid that the next war will be between Germany and Russia, each ostensibly protecting their own 'religions'."[3]

Along with almost everybody else, Runkle took it for granted that the two states would at some point go to war, which made it all the more remarkable when, on 23 August 1939, Nazi Germany's Foreign Minister Joachim von Ribbentrop signed the Nazi–Soviet Non-Aggression Pact in Moscow. The treaty committed both sides to peaceful co-existence, provided for large-scale economic co-operation, and contained secret protocols designed to divide up Poland and the rest of eastern Europe into mutual 'spheres of interest'. The Pact dumbfounded the world, but in Germany was met with almost universal acclaim, including by those in Hitler's inner circle: "To see the names of Hitler and Stalin linked in friendship was the most exciting turn of events that I could have imagined" was the reaction of Hitler's favourite architect, Albert Speer. The urbane Speer was far from alone in his praise, as the young Prussian aristocrat Tassilo von Bogenhardt acknowledged: "Our Pact with Russia ... came as a complete surprise to everyone and was hailed as the *Führer*'s greatest triumph ... the thought that our eastern frontier was secure was a great relief to all."[4]

Von Bogenhardt may have been less gratified to hear his *Führer*'s own view when he declared to a small gathering of cronies at his Berghof mountain retreat that "war must come. This Pact is only meant to stall for time. We must crush the Soviet Union."

Hitler used that time to his advantage, destroying Poland, conquering most of Scandinavia, and then routing France and throwing Great Britain off the Continent. It was at that point in late summer 1940 that he secretly declared to a handful of his most senior commanders his intention to break the Pact and invade the Soviet Union.

In the utmost secrecy, preparations were begun. The *Oberkommando des Heeres* (OKH – Army High Command) Chief of Staff, Franz Halder, immediately began to draft a plan and requested a report on the Red Army from the Reich's Military Attaché in Moscow, *General der Kavallerie* Ernst-August Köstring. He and his deputy Hans Krebs wrote back stating that in their opinion Stalin's Great Purges had decimated the Soviet armed forces, and as a result the "officer corps especially was now poor" and that "it will be twenty years before they recover".

Walther Warlimont – the Deputy Chief of *Wehrmacht* Operations – was brought in on the secret while on the special train reserved for the Operations staff, and remembered that time with a mixed sense of immense personal satisfaction and surprise:

> After the French campaign and triumphant victory we were in a good mood since we believed that our boss Alfred Jodl [Chief of *OKW* Operations Staff] would come and announce promotions for his staff officers. But this assumption vanished when he arrived and ordered the dining car doors closed and sentries posted on them ... without any introduction he told us that Hitler had resolved to go to war with Russia. It was a great shock for all of us – there were three or four of us there – and we immediately began to raise objections ... he said 'We must understand that sooner or later it will be necessary to fight Russia to crush bolshevism, and it might as well be now when we are at the height of our military strength.'[5]

Generalleutnant Erich Marcks – Chief of Staff *18. Armee* and a noted military innovator – was put in charge of building on Halder's initial thoughts, and, with help from Warlimont and his team, in just five days at the beginning of August produced *Operationsentwurf Ost* (Operational Draft East), a report that quickly became known as the 'Marcks Plan'.

In it, Marcks significantly evolved Halder's initial work, stating first and foremost that the workaholic chief of staff's original estimate of a 100-division invasion force was far too small, and that no fewer than 180 would be needed, a force the *Wehrmacht* couldn't hope to field in the East with Great Britain still a threat in the West. Hitler's answer was simple: the Army would have to expand – massively and rapidly.

Marcks also set out how the Soviet Union's military defeat was to be brought about. Firstly, the *Schwerpunkt* – the main effort – would be made north of the gargantuan Pripet Marshes that effectively split the front into two zones, north and south. This main thrust would take advantage of the denser and more advanced road and rail network in the northern region to shatter and overwhelm the Red Army, while forces in the south would pin down enemy troops opposite the Romanian border. The main attack would push on to take Moscow – seen universally across the German senior officer cadre as the key to victory. The Germans would then leave a small force in the north as a hard shoulder to screen off Leningrad and protect a thrust to the south that would seize the riches of Ukraine. On reaching the shores of the Black Sea, the entire German force would then turn east once more and advance on a broad front to a line roughly Rostov–Gorki–Arkhangelsk. At that point it was envisaged that what was left of the Soviet Union would be unable to mount any sort of credible resistance and the campaign would effectively be over.

Hitler's response to this part of the plan was hostile. In his view Moscow was almost immaterial as an objective, while capturing Leningrad – as the so-called 'cradle of bolshevism' – was critical, and most importantly the seizure of Ukraine's wealth couldn't wait until the latter stages of the operation – in short, he fundamentally disagreed with the Marcks Plan.

Over the next few months – under Halder's guidance and with Hitler's urging – the plan morphed into something that was almost unrecognisable from its origins. There would not be a single, overwhelming thrust north of the Pripet but three separate assaults, with hardly any mutual support between them. They would attack more or less simultaneously, with the most northerly aimed at Leningrad, and its neighbour – Marcks's dominant force, now downgraded to just being the most powerful of three offensive strikes – tasked with conquering Belarus and Smolensk and then advancing towards Moscow, without having the capital as a specific objective. In the south, the original defensive shield was replaced with a huge array of forces whose job it was to capture Ukraine and the Donets, and thus provide the Reich with the food and raw materials it so desperately needed.

In operational terms, about the only fragment left of the Marcks Plan was the desire to destroy the Red Army on or near the frontier and prevent its withdrawal into the Soviet Union's effectively limitless interior. The overriding assumption was that the campaign would be decided in the border regions, where the *Wehrmacht* would smash the Red Army. This would inevitably lead to the collapse of the Soviet Union, whereupon the German advance would become little more than a triumphal procession.

So it was that just before Christmas 1940, Adolf Hitler sat at his enormous desk in the Reich Chancellery and individually signed nine numbered copies of the eleven-page *Führerbefehl Nr. 21 Fall* Barbarossa (*Führer* Directive No. 21 Case Barbarossa) in its distinctive scarlet cover with a diagonal yellow line, embossed on the front with 'Top Secret'.

The name – Barbarossa – was Hitler's choice. Fascinated by Germanic history and folklore – although not to the extent of his head of the SS, Heinrich Himmler – the Nazi dictator reached back to the Holy Roman Emperor Frederick I 'Barbarossa' (red-beard) whose exploits in the twelfth century ended with his drowning on crusade in the River Saleph in modern-day Turkey. After death he assumed a legendary status for Germans with the fable that he and his knights lie sleeping in a cave beneath the Kyffhäuser mountains in central Germany, and will rise again to restore Germany's greatness when the nation is most in need. Hitler thought the title apt for his most ambitious venture:

> The German *Wehrmacht* must be prepared, even before the conclusion of the war against England, to crush the Soviet Union in a rapid campaign ... The bulk of the Russian Army stationed in western Russia will be destroyed by daring operations led by deeply penetrating armoured spearheads, and the withdrawal of combat-capable units into the vastness of the Russian interior is to be prevented. The enemy will then be energetically pursued, and a line will be reached from which the Russian Air Force can no longer attack German territory. The final objective of the operation is to erect a barrier against Asiatic Russia on the general line Volga-Arkhangelsk. The last surviving industrial areas of Russia in the Urals can then, if necessary, be eliminated by the *Luftwaffe*.

Job done, Hitler left his office, strode through the ornate marbled corridors and down the steps of the Chancellery, acknowledging the salutes of the black-clad *SS-Leibstandarte* sentries before climbing into the Mercedes that would take him the short distance across the capital to the Sportpalast arena, one of his favoured speaking venues. There, as ever, he would appear before a hand-picked audience. The budding *Luftwaffe* officer Heinz Knoke was among them: "Three thousand keen young soldiers, nearly at the end of their training, who will soon go as officers to frontline operations ... 'Here comes the *Führer*!' It is a solemn moment. Then Hitler begins to speak." Knoke remembered the speech with quasi-religious intensity: "I don't suppose the world has ever known a more brilliant orator than this man. His magnetic personality is irresistible. One can sense the tremendous willpower and driving energy ... We listen to the spellbinding words and accept them with all our hearts ... Here and now every one of us pledges his life in solemn dedication ... It's a deeply moving experience. I shall never forget the expressions of rapture which I saw on the faces around me."

Hitler's speech consisted of many of his usual themes, majoring on Germany's greatness, and he talked at length about his belief that the

Germans needed *lebensraum* to allow them to fulfil their destiny as a master race. In his mind this *lebensraum* was to be found in only one place: the East. Outside, the weather was cold and overcast – it was 18 December 1940.

With the decision made, Directive No. 21 acted like a stone thrown into a pond with the ripples spreading outwards, bringing more and more senior soldiers, sailors and airmen – some two hundred and fifty in all – in on the secret. Amongst them were Heinz Guderian and two of his trusted lieutenants:

> My new Chief of Staff and my IA (Operations Officer), *Major* Bayerlein, were summoned to a conference by Halder where they heard for the first time about the proposed campaign against Soviet Russia – Operation Barbarossa. They returned … and spread out a map of Russia in front of me – I could scarcely believe my eyes … Hitler had criticised Germany's leaders in the first war for their failure to avoid a conflict on two fronts, so was he now, before the war against England had been decided, to open a second front against the Russians? … I made no attempt to hide my disappointment and disgust … my two staff officers were surprised by the vehemence of my language and explained to me that Halder had calculated that Russia would be defeated in eight to ten weeks … renewed study of the campaigns of Charles XII [King of Sweden whose army was defeated by Tzar Peter the Great at Poltava in 1709] and Napoleon I clearly revealed all the difficulties of the theatre to which we were threatened to be committed. Our successes to date … and in particular the surprising speed of our victory in the West, had so befuddled the minds of our senior leaders that they'd eliminated the word 'impossible' from their vocabulary.[6]

Even as Hitler set the wheels of invasion formally into motion – and Guderian and a coterie of other officers began beavering away on their plans – Moscow was transporting huge amounts of strategic raw materials and foodstuffs to Germany under the terms of a series of economic agreements signed after the adoption of the Non-Aggression Pact. The German industrialist Hans Kehrl – known as the Nazis' 'textile Pope' on account of his dominance of the sector – was a huge fan of the new economic partnership: "We had the greatest trade agreement we ever had … and from an economic point of view everything was in order. I personally negotiated with the Soviets to build a synthetic fibre mill in Russia."[7]

Kehrl was right, the agreement was a godsend for Nazi Germany and its struggling economy.

Germany had some natural resources; the smoke-stack cities of the Ruhr sat atop the second largest coalfield in the world and Silesia was almost built of the black stuff, but the country had no oil deposits, no iron ore, no copper, tungsten, bauxite, cotton or rubber, and the sheer size of the military consumed resources – and food in particular – at a prodigious rate, while doing nothing to increase supply. As the soon-to-be *Luftwaffe* fighter pilot Norbert Hannig said: "Goering stated openly that Germany's preference was for guns rather than butter ... there was work for all, and a sense of purpose and order was restored ... but for every metre of autobahn laid, how many shells were produced?" Hannig could see the reality of Nazi policy for himself. Germany's aggression on the world stage, and her accelerating rearmament, cut her off from global markets – food in particular – and necessitated the introduction of rationing in August 1939, with every German issued monthly colour-coded booklets with tear-off coupons called *Essenmarken*, which covered everything from milk, butter and cheese to meat, sugar, eggs, soap and even clothes. Those rations were not generous. German government guidelines stated that an average working adult needed 2,750 calories per day to stay fit and healthy, and at first the rations – at 550 grams of meat and 310 grams of fats (for example lard for cooking) per week – were set to deliver over and above that. However, although this was the maximum someone could buy, it was often unavailable as the supply chain broke down and the shelves emptied.

Germany wasn't helped by having the pig as the cornerstone of its national diet. Unlike Britons' beloved lamb and mutton, Germans' four-legged meat of choice didn't eat grass, but instead required much the same diet as humans – usually processed into animal feed. That same animal feed – overwhelmingly imported from the United States – disappeared as the British Royal Navy blockaded German ports and choked off imports following the beginning of hostilities. The blockade – so effective in the First World War – cut the tonnage of imports into Germany by more than two-thirds from pre-war levels, and drastically hit supplies in a country that previously bought in almost 20 per cent of its annual food consumption.

The result was an official takeover of the food supply system and a renewed push on the already-declared *Erzeugungsschlacht* programme (Battle of Production), with every farmer who worked more than 12.5 acres forced to register their landholding, crops and livestock. Micro-management was the order of the day, with draconian punishments for anyone who didn't follow the rules. In one horrific instance a farmer from the northern city of Rostock was convicted of butchering a pig without permission, and after being convicted, was beheaded as a warning to others. This, however, didn't stop a major official cull of the 23 million-strong national pig herd in the winter of 1939 as Germany's farmers struggled to feed them. Families began to rear their own pigs in gardens and allotments, until they were told by the authorities that such ownership disqualified them from the ration system. With pork increasingly scarce, the German *wurst* began to be bulked out with breadcrumbs and even sawdust – much to the disgust of the average *hausfrau* trying to feed her family.

Other staples fared just as badly, with one British traveller before the war noting that there was "no comfort to be found in the hotel dining room. The coffee is very weak, and the bread is no longer crisp as it's made from poor quality flour."[8] Not surprising given the traveller's coffee was more than likely made from chicory, or burnt wheat grains, and was officially called *Muckefuck* – although most Germans just called it *Ersatzkaffee* (substitute coffee). As for the bread, after the war a recipe was discovered deep in the bowels of Berlin's *Reichsnährstand* (RNS – Department of Food and Agriculture) on Wilhelmstrasse – labelled 'Top Secret' and dated 1941 – setting out the recommended composition of a typical loaf of bread: 50 per cent bruised rye grain, 20 per cent sliced sugar beets, 20 per cent 'tree flour' (i.e. sawdust), and 10 per cent shredded leaves and straw. Other pre-war visitors to the Third Reich noted how meals everywhere were never more than two courses and usually just the one, with "pancakes with jam instead of syrup … and just bread and butter sandwiches".

A paucity of commercial refrigeration facilities meant food couldn't be shipped across the country from where it was in surplus to where it was in deficit, and even when it was it often spoiled as very few German households had fridges. Charlotte von der Schulenberg was a German *hausfrau* struggling to raise four young children while her husband – Fritz-Dietlof – was away in the Army: "People needed ration and clothing cards … There were only a few vegetables and a little fruit around, and that was already coming from the garden." Those Germans lucky enough to live near a border and have friends and relations on the other side took advantage of the situation to travel over and eat the type of food that could no longer be found in the Reich. The Maegers, split across the Belgian–German border, were one such family: "Our relations on the German side were always highly delighted to be invited to come over for a good meal. Certain foods – chocolate, eggs with a strong golden yolk from poultry fed on maize, and above all prized Waldhorn butter – were especially praised."

With very few imports the German national diet soon became monotonous and based on thin soup, poor-quality bread, potatoes and preserves. Even then, the total volume of food available continued to shrink, with bread rationed for the very first time as early as 1940, and existing meat and fat rations reduced by almost a third the following winter, despite the victorious *Wehrmacht* requisitioning food from the newly occupied lands in the West and sending it home. Soon, the country's beef and dairy herds were in the same dire straits as their porcine brethren, the availability of milk dwindled and even the beer became noticeably thinner. A diner at a friend's house was surprised to be offered a pudding as "it was the first Sunday of the month, a day when all German citizens aware of their duty were urged to prepare only a stew ... pudding was an infringement, if only a minor one, against the principle of community spirit".

For a nation used to rising in the morning to the heady aroma of freshly brewed coffee and hot bread rolls, and working hard all day while munching sausage and ham, this was dire indeed – and a *Maß* of watered-down beer of an evening was no consolation. Hitler's war was forcing the Reich to go hungry.

Rationing wasn't the only challenge to German livelihoods as the war snowballed. The War Economy Decree increased taxes and working hours, froze wages, and cut overtime rates – all to help support the Nazi war machine. Public discontent – especially in working-class neighbourhoods – persuaded Berlin to reverse at least some of the measures around Sunday working and bonus rates, but overall, life became noticeably harder for most.

This was the national context into which Soviet goods trains rumbled; Soviet phosphate fertilizers enriched tired German soil, and Soviet foodstuffs disappeared into hungry German mouths. In return for advanced weaponry, manufactured goods and cold, hard cash, over an eighteen-month period Moscow shipped one and a half million tons of wheat, oats and rye, another million tons of soybeans, and five hundred thousand tons of phosphate fertilizers to the Third Reich. Also loaded onto the trains rolling west were two million tons of petroleum products, a hundred thousand tons of raw cotton and almost double that weight of manganese and chromium, the latter duo vital in producing weapons-grade steel. But it still wasn't enough. Raw material supplies dwindled, petrol was near to impossible to get hold of – even after the *Wehrmacht* seized over 90 per cent of French stocks – and the fear of mass food shortages and ensuing unrest began to stalk the corridors of the Chancellery. This was the Nazi conundrum writ large: the war Germany had started to make it a global superpower was slowly strangling it by denying the country access to the very resources it needed to win the war and feed its own people. With Britannia undefeated and ruling the waves, the war that would build the Thousand Year Reich looked like destroying that same Reich at birth. Hitler's new empire needed ownership of natural resources it could reach by land, away from British sea power.

The Nazi dictator thought he had been given the answer by his forty-four-year-old Georgian-born de facto Minister for Food and Agriculture, Herbert Backe: "The occupation of Ukraine would liberate us from every economic worry." The bespectacled Backe, a qualified agronomist and the brains behind *Erzeugungsschlacht*, had noted that 90 per cent of Soviet foodstuffs sent to Germany under the auspices of the Pact came from the incredibly rich 'black earth' soils of the southern Soviet republic of Ukraine, while most of the mineral wealth flowed from the mines of the Donets basin and the wells of the faraway Caucasus. He reasoned that seizure of these regions would give the Reich two things the Nazis desperately wanted: the economic self-sufficiency to insulate the Party from the popular discontent that Hitler and other senior Nazis believed had ultimately been responsible for Imperial Germany's defeat in the First World War, and the raw materials that would enable the Third Reich to challenge the global dominance of the British Empire and the US. Many ordinary Germans believed this argument. "Before long we would be producing all the raw materials we needed ... so no lack of foreign exchange or economic fluctuations from the outside world would affect us ... No-one was going to be able to make any money out of us – as they did in the bad old days."[9] Gerhard Kunde, a twenty-seven-year-old Berliner destined to take part in Barbarossa as a member of Georg Braun's *68. Infanterie-Division*, agreed: "More than fifteen years ago the *Führer* said in his book *Mein Kampf* that Germany must have colonial territory in the east to be able to live. He was clearly referring to Ukraine. Today, when we are practically cut off from overseas imports, not only does Germany need Ukraine, but also northern, central and western Europe, if it doesn't want to starve to death."[10]

Regardless of whether a huge land grab would bring an end to Germany's economic woes or not, rationing changed the national conversation. Food – the search for it, its amount and variety – very quickly became a mainstay of German conversation. Diaries, journals, letters and interviews with veterans and survivors of the time are literally full of references to what people ate – or didn't eat – and when. The unemployed merchant seaman and part-time Nazi brownshirt, Fritz Muehlebach, outlined his priorities when he received his eight *Reichsmarks* and forty *pfennings* weekly unemployment benefit:

I immediately spent one *Reichsmark* on eleven small sausages from a little stand outside the labour exchange ... you got eleven for the price of ten, and I ate the 'free' sausage straightaway. The rest I kept for breakfasts and suppers for the rest of the week ... I kept another *Reichsmark* and twenty pfennigs for buying bread ... and I was able to go to the Party café where for ten pfennigs you got a really good midday meal.[11]

Food became a national obsession, and an obsession that played a hugely significant role in Nazi Germany's reasons for launching Barbarossa, for how the operation was directed from the very top, and the way the men involved in it then fought.

2

The *Wehrmacht* – the World's Finest

By June 1941 the German *Wehrmacht* – comprising the Army (*Heer*), Air Force (*Luftwaffe*), Navy (*Kriegsmarine*) and Armed SS (*Waffen-SS*) – was the most feared military force on the planet. In remarkably short order it had conquered eleven countries – including the homeland of the second biggest colonial power on earth – and had humbled the largest empire in history. It had done all this while suffering relatively few casualties in comparison to the scale of its victories, and having had to rapidly scale up from its post-Versailles Treaty pygmy status. That treaty had declared Germany would have no air force, a mini-navy, and an army of just 100,000 men for a nation conditioned to having a barracks in every town with marching bands, military parades and uniformed fanfare. Indeed, Bismarck had used the Army to provide common ground to the various German ministates when they were merged together after unification in 1871. Even more than the explicit influence the military had on life in general, there was something deeper, something more innate, that tied German society and its military together, as Erich Dressler – a teenager at the time – instinctively realised: "A German boy would one day become a German man, and the German man is first and foremost a warrior. He must be hard, and he must know how to obey, and to obey is an important thing – one must learn to obey in order to command."

So, when Hitler came to power in 1933 and immediately began a rearmament programme, he was giving water to the thirsty. Striking a deal with the upper echelons of the armed forces, he demanded freedom of action to dismantle Germany's infant democracy and destroy his internal enemies, and in return he promised them glory, promotions and command of a leviathan. With a few notable exceptions, the generals jumped at the opportunity. In May 1935 the National Defence Regulations were introduced. The opening lines read: "Military service is a matter of honour for the German people. Every German is liable for military service. In time of war every German man and every German woman is obliged ... to render his or her services for the good of the fatherland."

In practical terms, the regulations reintroduced conscription and decreed that a man's liability for military service lasted from his nineteenth birthday up to the age of forty-five. On that basis, the Army – which had already trebled in size since Hitler's accession to power two years earlier – began a period of frenzied expansion.

Building on its regional structure – the *Wehrkreise* – the Army adopted the *Welle* system. The five *Wellen* in 1939 created sixty-two divisions, with another fifty-seven coming from the seven separate 1940 *Wellen*. By the time it invaded Poland the new Army had a strength of 3.7 million men. However, that figure needs some qualification. Over 700,000 of those men lacked anything other than the most basic training, and another million or so were ageing veterans of the First World War, making the trained fighting strength of the Army nearer the two million mark. Regardless, another 800,000 men were added for the campaign in the West, many being middle-aged reservists who were quickly demobilised and sent home after the fighting. Consequently, the Army actually reduced in size from 155 to 120 divisions, even as the Royal Air Force effectively sank German invasion plans in the Battle of Britain.

However, having taken the decision to invade the Soviet Union, and having seen the draft Marcks Plan, Hitler abruptly switched tack and ordered the huge increase in the Army's overall strength the bespectacled planner had asked for. Most significantly, the dictator decreed a doubling in the number of armoured divisions. As its use of armour was the greatest advantage the *Wehrmacht* had over its rivals, this revolution in Germany's panzer arm – the *panzerwaffe* – was to have a critical bearing on Barbarossa.

Most armies using tanks at that time had opted for a combination of weighty, 'pill-box-like' heavies, and light 'gallopers'. In the Soviet Red Army, the former was epitomised by models such as the behemoth T-100, all 58 tonnes of it, with a crew of eight and not one but two turrets, with twin cannon and no fewer than four machine-guns. At the other end of the scale was the minuscule T-38, just over three tonnes in weight, with a two-man crew and a single machine-gun. In short, the Soviets were experimenting. Red Army doctrine on the use of armour was in a similar state of flux. The Soviets first opted for massing armour together in powerful mechanized corps but had then gone in the opposite direction when Stalin had Mikhail Tukhachevsky – the architect of the mechanized corps concept – tortured and executed as the very first victim of the Great Purge. This meant Soviet thinking followed the Anglo-French model of spreading tanks out amongst the infantry, so failing to achieve overwhelming strength at any one point.

Only Nazi Germany had gone the whole hog and created armoured divisions designed to operate independently to provide a battle-winning advantage. It had been these new panzer divisions which had led the way in Poland, the Low Countries and France, a fact that didn't escape the Red Army generals who survived the bloody scythe of Stalin's paranoia. In something of a mad rush, they switched horses again, and reinstituted Tukhachevsky's previously discredited ideas. Rarely an organisation to do things by halves, the Red Army established nine mechanized corps in the summer of 1940 alone, and another twenty in the spring of 1941. Vehicle parks and testing grounds all over the Soviet Union were emptied to equip them, and there was no shortage of tanks, with Moscow's inventory running to an eye-watering 23,767 available by 22 June 1941. As ever with the Soviet Union, the bald numbers tended to hide – or at least obscure – the reality. In truth, design experimentation meant there was a multiplicity of models – with over fifteen thousand being obsolete BT-series and T-26s. The whole fleet was poorly maintained, with almost three-quarters in need of repair, with a lack of spare parts and maintenance facilities. There were also nowhere near enough trained crews to man all the available armour.[1]

However, all was not perfect on the other side of the fence either. Even after the laurels of the 1939–40 campaigns, the debate about the use of armour still raged on among the senior ranks of the German Army. Cheerleaders for the panzers, such as Heinz Guderian, Hasso von Manteuffel and Wilhelm von Thoma, believed them to be war-winners, but these officers were in a minority, and in a force still dominated by generals from the infantry and artillery most of the *Wehrmacht*'s upper echelons thought panzer tactics unproven and their commanders reckless; a view typified by Ludwig Beck, Halder's predecessor as Chief of the Army Staff, who believed that "a divisional commander sits back with maps and a telephone. Anything else is utopian!" After clashing with Guderian, the latter wrote that Beck "wanted the panzers to be employed primarily as infantry support weapons, and the largest unit he would agree to was the brigade, he wasn't interested in the formation of panzer divisions ... he created a barrier of reaction at the very centre of the Army". Beck wasn't alone. Many other generals remembered the Austrian *Anschluss* debacle when Guderian's new panzer force had broken down en masse and clogged up miles of Austrian roads, leaving the cavalry and infantry to triumphantly enter Vienna ahead of them.

With the two factions at loggerheads, Hitler's attitude was crucial; would he swing full square behind his young Turk panzer chargers, or err on the conservative side, as he had during the French campaign when he had halted the armour outside Dunkirk, inadvertently helping the British Expeditionary Force to escape? His decision was to compromise – which pleased no one. The great mass of the Army would remain as infantry divisions, while the *panzerwaffe* would double in size, but with no overall increase in tank numbers. Instead, each existing panzer division (numbered from 1 to 10) would hand over one of its two constituent panzer regiments to the ten new divisions, numbered 11 to 20. The result was the strength of a German panzer division fell from over three hundred tanks to less than two hundred, with serviceability issues usually keeping the number available for combat to around one hundred and fifty.

Partly, this policy of dilution was a matter of practicalities; German industry wasn't organised on a war footing, and in 1939 was only building an average of sixty-two panzers a month, a figure which rose to 182 in the latter half of 1940. This was risibly inadequate and was barely keeping up with battle casualties, with over six hundred panzers lost in France at a rate of over one hundred a week. With homegrown manufacture so slow, the *Wehrmacht* improvised, with a wholesale plundering of the advanced Czech armaments industry after the Germans marched into the rump of the country following the Munich agreement. This yielded enough tanks to equip no fewer than six of the new, scaled-down panzer divisions. The Germans would have pressed large numbers of the approximately 2,000 captured French tanks into the ranks as well, but the Gallic preference for one-man turrets was not suited to the German operational model, and so hundreds of them were instead relegated to occupation duties or handed over to allied armies.

Inadequate tank production wasn't the only laggard impacting the *panzerwaffe*'s ability to act as the Army's battle winner. The manufacture of anti-tank (*panzerjäger*) vehicles and integral artillery (*panzerartillerie*) carriages was decidedly sluggish too. Even more marked was the infantry problem. Operating with tanks is a complex and difficult job that requires infantry to be specially trained and equipped. It also requires mobility. The division's infantry needs to keep up with the division's tanks, and this means vehicles, and more specifically armoured vehicles to protect them from enemy fire as they manoeuvre around the battlefield. The German answer to this problem was the ubiquitous *SdKfz 251*, an open-topped half-track that carried a whole squad and was capable of being armed with a variety of weapons including on-board machine-guns. However, half-track production was even more anaemic than panzer manufacture, and would remain so throughout the war. In an army that seemingly prized mechanization, only 10 per cent of Germany's armoured infantry would ever go into battle in or on a half-track, and barely 15,000 of these workhorses were built in total. Trucks were press-ganged into service instead; fully half, of all the Reich's civilian fleet was forcibly seized by the state in 1939, but even then the problem was nowhere near solved – Germany simply didn't have enough, and production was way off the pace.

Once more, plundering became the *Wehrmacht*'s order of the day. First on the list were the riches of their newly conquered enemies, particularly the now-defunct French Army. The *Wehrmacht* had already bagged over 5,000 artillery guns and almost a third of a million rifles from the defeated *poilus*, and now it was time to pillage their vehicle parks. London's contribution was also gratefully received, with the 85,000 burnt-out, immobilised or abandoned motor vehicles left behind by the departed British picked through, with Bedford and Morris 15- and 30-cwt trucks particularly prized. Useful as these victors' spoils were, they were no panacea. Spare parts and servicing for so many different models was a quartermaster's nightmare, and all the captured vehicles were built to drive on the well-maintained metalled roads of western Europe, not the sand and dust of Soviet Russia's dirt tracks. Nevertheless, this tide of plunder flowed into the armouries and vehicle parks of the new divisions. Heinz Guderian was well aware of the problems they caused: "I concentrated especially on the training and equipping of the divisions for which I was responsible ... most of the vehicles in the new divisions which Hitler had ordered created, were French. This equipment was in no way capable of meeting the demands of warfare in the East, while German vehicle production was insufficient to meet our increased requirements, so we couldn't replace the palpably inferior *beutefahrzeuge* (booty vehicles) with German ones."[2] This led to the farcical situation of one of the new formations, *18. Panzerdivision*, fielding no fewer than thirty-seven different types of motorcycle, ninety-six types of infantry personnel carriers, and an eye-watering 111 varieties of truck.[3]

Regardless, Hitler believed that a doubling of the number of panzer divisions meant a doubling in their fighting power, and his views were supported by officers like Walther Nehring, who contradicted Guderian and von Manteuffel by insisting that the old 300-plus panzer formations were too unwieldy anyway and needed a reduction in strength to increase speed of action and operational flexibility. Somewhat ironically, Nehring was then given command of *18. Panzerdivision*.

In the end Hitler got his way. The *panzerwaffe* would grow to twenty divisions. Guderian tried to reconcile himself to all the changes: "The smaller numbers of panzers per division was compensated for – to a certain extent – by the fact that the old *PzKpfw* Is and IIs had almost completely been replaced by newer *PzKpfw* IIIs and IVs. We believed that we could rely on our panzers being technically better than all known Russian types, and we thought that this would more or less cancel out the Russians' vast numerical superiority." Guderian's assumption was a delusion. In the event some 1,100 of the 3,500 panzers deployed for Barbarossa would be obsolete *PzKpfw I*s and *II*s, and a further 760 were Czech *beutepanzers*. Only 1,400 of the fleet would be the heavier and better armed second-generation *PzKpfw III*s and *IV*s.

The *panzerwaffe* would also be short of tracked artillery and anti-tank vehicles, and their specialist infantry regiments would lack mobility, with many of the latter having to be ferried forward in trucks appropriated from standard infantry units, a robbing-Peter-to-pay-Paul approach that left the bulk of Germany's infantry divisions with even less motor transport than they were originally issued.

Filling all these new divisions in such a short period of time, both panzer and infantry, was a mammoth task. To physically provide the manpower, the Army drafted in the eligible age groups from birth years 1919, 1920 and 1921 – young men who had grown up under Nazi rule but were, as yet, without military experience. They would form much of the twelve *Wellen* of 1939–40, with large numbers of them only starting basic training in the summer of 1940 and completing it just one short month before Barbarossa. Their cadres of officers and NCOs would have some experienced soldiers among them, but not all, meaning large numbers of frontline divisions on invasion day were untested.

One new recruit in the summer before Barbarossa was eighteen-year-old Richard von Rosen. A scion of a Baltic German family with a faded aristocratic lineage, von Rosen volunteered in early 1940 and opted to join the panzers. "With an excited feeling in my stomach I reported to the officer of the watch at the panzer barracks ... forty-one eighteen-year-olds for training ... eight to a room, we sized each other up." Training was tough and relentless. "We were always on the go from six in the morning until curfew at ten, exercises and more exercises, a horde of instructors were let loose on us ... Two *Obergefreiter*, auxiliary instructors, were extremely sadistic – this period of our training was hellish as we were entirely at their mercy. Nobody dared complain ... these primitive beings had it in for me especially as I was a 'von'."[4]

Despite the tough time he was given, von Rosen wholeheartedly agreed with his compatriot Hermann Rothe – who would rise to the rank of *Oberst* during the war – that "being a member of a panzer crew was like being a member of a family". Rosen and Rothe also agreed on the pivotal role of the driver in every crew: "Driving the panzers required a lot of physical strength ... our instructors – all NCOs – made it very clear that it was unacceptable to stall the vehicles or, even worse, throw a track, the minimum punishment for which was to spend some time running behind the panzer as it drove across the training area!" Horst Reibenstahl also thought the driver was vital. "The skills of the driver were of huge importance ...

quite often the fate of the entire crew depended upon his skills." This meant that in action, as crews and commanders were sometimes juggled about, "a crew commander always tried to take his driver with him if he had to go to command another panzer for whatever reason".[5]

It wasn't just physically demanding either. The mental aspects of the training were just as important, and for the panzer crews this meant "cunning, resourcefulness and cool-headedness", as well as the more mundane aspects of maintenance as Rothe recalled: "The maxim was 'A vehicle or gun which is properly serviced never breaks down,' so we cleaned our panzers and their guns for endless hours."

As for the new infantry formations, they were classed as Type 1939 divisions, and were structured in much the same way as the recruits' fathers' First World War units, as one young draftee explained:

A *gruppe* [squad/section] consisting of ten soldiers was the smallest operational unit, and a *zug* [platoon] of four *gruppen* was the primary sub-unit of a *kompanie* [company]. A regular infantry *kompanie* contained about 180 men, though specialised *kompanien* could be significantly larger. Each *bataillon* [battalion] contained four *kompanien*, while each regiment included three *bataillonen* and two specialised *kompanien*. An infantry division was made up of roughly three infantry *regimenter* [regiments], an artillery regiment, a *bataillon* of anti-tank weapons, a reconnaissance *bataillon*, a headquarters and support troops, all told about 17,000 men.

The Type 1939 was a powerful creature, capable of putting up a tough fight, but it had an Achilles heel, one that would prove its undoing in the vastness of the Soviet Union – a lack of motorised transport. In fact, each Type 1939 division was only allocated 911 motor vehicles of all types, with most being two-wheel drive trucks. Those trucks were intended to ferry the division's heavy equipment and bulk stores such as ammunition, with almost everyone expected to march.

The *Wehrmacht* needed an answer to its transport problem, and its solution was the horse. The fields and stables of Germany and occupied Europe were ruthlessly raided and their occupants put in harness for the military. In total, each Type 1939 division was allocated an astonishing 5,375 horses, more than five for every motor vehicle. They weren't just for the heavy lifting either; they were ubiquitous. Every platoon had its own pair of horses and the standard *Hf. 177* cart they pulled, with each company also having two four-horse ammunition wagons, three more animals for the machine-guns and mortars, one for rations and two for the legendary German field-kitchen, the *Gulaschkanone* (goulash cannon), with its 200-litre cooking pot and 90-litre coffee kettle. The only nod to the modern era was that the *Hf. 177* cart had pneumatic tyres and not metal-rimmed wooden wheels.

Keeping this menagerie fit and fed was a manpower-heavy task, with twenty-one men in each 180-strong company dedicated to looking after their equine charges, on top of the integral divisional veterinary company. Wilhelm Lübbecke, a signaller in the newly raised *58. ID*, described the way it worked in his unit: "In our communications platoon there were about twenty-five men, all of whom had trained together ... Subtracting the soldiers in the platoon who drove the wagons carrying our communications gear and who took care of the horses, there were about fifteen of us left whose primary role was to set up communications."

Where possible, the Germans tried to use Pomeranian draught horses, noted for their pulling power and gentle temperament, but whose fodder consumption and general health requirements were prodigious. Grass alone being insufficiently nutritious, each horse was fed several pounds of grain per day, and every ten days they needed to rest for at least one. They also needed frequent veterinary checks and, regardless of all that care, were still prone to sickness and injury. All of this took time, and it's hard to see how a six-man operation taking almost half an hour to hitch up a single artillery gun to its horse team was going to be practicable for an invasion that relied above all things on the speed of advance.

Believing that horses would be a cheap and reliable form of transport in the less-developed east, the *Wehrmacht* wilfully ignored the huge costs of feeding, grooming, handling and caring for this travelling zoo. The German planners also conveniently forgot the lessons of Napoleon's *Grande Armée*, whose 200,000 European horses were almost all dead within six months of first stepping into Russia.

Their would-be opponent, meanwhile, was moving in the opposite direction. Prior to Stalin's forced agricultural collectivisation programme, the Soviet Union boasted 34,000,000 horses, but the widespread starvation and disruption caused by the ill-starred policy had seen that figure plummet to 21,000,000 before war broke out. With fewer horses available, the Red Army had little choice but to turn to motorised transport to fill the gaps, leading to the counter-intuitive situation where a standard Soviet 1941-era rifle division only had 3,039 horses, almost half the complement of its supposedly more advanced German counterpart.

Given the lack of motorised transport, and so many other vital categories of weaponry and equipment, the outlook for the Barbarossa invasion force was clear: if the *panzerwaffe* couldn't cause a total collapse of the Red Army, it was going to be down to the infantry to achieve victory. Those infantry divisions would be advancing at a pace of 60 centimetres per step – the same as a Roman legion 2,000 years before. This was not what Hitler or any of the Nazi high command envisaged, but it was the reality.

However, in Hitler's eyes any possible shortcomings could, and would, be overcome by one thing above all else: the innate racial superiority of the German fighting man. Knowing and understanding this fighting man was, and is, the key to comprehending Barbarossa in all its vastness and failure.

For most Germans – and many in the outside world – Barbara Runkle's description of Karl Maier – a young soldier she went out with a few times – typified the 5,000,000 men of the *Wehrmacht* in 1941:

> Absolutely moulded into his uniform, a clean, shapely head with crisp, closely cut chestnut hair, a straight little face, white teeth and darling wide smile ... a trustworthy soul, he was what you would term '*ein einfacher Mensch*' [a simple man] ... he was very proud, very sensitive, very amusing, very affectionate, could sing and play the guitar beautifully, and was an expert shot and skier. He was a typical soldier of the best kind; quick, clean, brave, proud, and he believed passionately that Germany should be proud and strong once more.[6]

While it is impossible to single out one soldier among so many to be in some way representative of the whole, twenty-one-year-old Wilhelm Lübbecke was as good an example as any of the young men who would fill the ranks of the invasion force. Young Wilhelm had been born on his family's modest 200-acre farm near the small village of Püggen, in the rolling hills of north Saxony-Anhalt. Like so many of his generation, he grew up combining school with work to help make ends meet at home. For him, that meant working on the farm; watching over his family's dozen or so cows, and helping with the harvests of apples, rye, potatoes and barley. He was the eldest of nine children born to his father, also called Wilhelm, and mother, Margarethe. Two of his siblings died from disease in early childhood – something that was depressingly common at the time. His upbringing was nothing out of the ordinary, he attended a single-class school in a nearby village, with life revolving around family, farm and church. A serial player of pranks, he struggled with his disciplinarian father and adored his devoutly religious mother. The trappings of modern life were pretty much non-existent on the Lübbecke farm: "Lacking trucks, tractors, or indeed any form of automotive vehicle, we did everything with manpower and our eight horses." Food was never plentiful, although the family did better than most city-dwellers. Every year his father would slaughter a proportion of their pigs for the family. "Due to the lack of refrigeration we had to preserve the majority of the meat by making it into sausage and bacon or by curing it."

While they were relatively well-off for the time, the Great Depression had a huge impact on the family, driving them into debt: "When my family couldn't pay our creditors on time, officers from the local court would come to our home. These visits were a humiliating experience, particularly for my father ... officers would affix Kuckucks (government repossession stickers) on two or three pieces of our best furniture ... My father's fine oak desk received a Kuckuck two or three times as we went in and out of debt." Not an overtly political family, they held many views considered mainstream at the time. "Most Germans did not accept that the nation had been truly defeated (in 1918) ... it was the revolutionary actions of left-wing Communists and socialists on the home front that had undermined the Army's morale." The Versailles Treaty was reviled for "unjustly holding Germany guilty for starting the war ... many Germans felt a lingering sense of grievance". Young Wilhelm ended up attending a few meetings of the right-wing ex-soldier *Stahlhelm* (Steel Helmet) organisation, although not from any ideological yearning: "They gave boys my age a chance to shoot their Mauser rifles on firing ranges. It was a lot of fun, even if the recoil left my shoulder sore for days."

The ushering into power of Hitler and his Nazi Party caused no real alarm in the Lübbecke household, indeed they saw the advantages the Nazis brought as the country climbed out of its economic turmoil: "Hitler began to mobilize the six million unemployed for projects like building the autobahns ... furthermore the Nazis introduced other programs ... for example they offered workers who joined the government's official labour union the chance to take discounted vacation cruises abroad, while rewarding high performing workers with completely free holidays." Hitler's foreign policy reinforced this sense of the nation getting back on its feet, as Lübbecke remembered when Hitler ordered the Army to march into the formerly demilitarised Rhineland in 1936: "There was a sense of pride among Germans at what was seen as a rectification of a wrong done to our country ... the operation increased Hitler's public support." Although, he also realised this show of military force was exactly that, a show. "Cousin Heinrich (serving in the Army at the time) later told me that his division's shortage of vehicles had required it to confiscate all the civilian trucks it could find to carry out the mission." Not especially academic – and definitely not interested in farming as a career – Wilhelm looked to better himself by becoming an apprentice electrician in the city of Luneburg.

More interested in pursuing girls than a career, he nevertheless read the tea leaves and avoided conscription by volunteering for the Army in 1939 aged nineteen. "Perhaps because I'd volunteered for the Army I was never drafted into the RAD [*Reichsarbeitsdienst* – Reich Labour Service] ... it operated along military lines, except its members carried spades rather than weapons ... it helped prepare young men for military service." Opting for the newly formed *panzerwaffe*, he was destined instead for *Generalleutnant* Karl von Graffen's locally recruited *58. Infanterie-Division*. Called up before he could complete his apprenticeship, he relished the tough training regime. "Our *kompanie* commenced its field training, which took place every day, regardless of rain or snow. It was about physical exercise to build our stamina and instruction in the use of weapons ... I found deep satisfaction in the discipline, camaraderie, adventure, and ascetic routine of soldiering." The young Saxon also recognised the respected role of the military in German society, and the ingrained sense of respect the majority of the populace felt for it and the other formal institutions of the state: "Long before the Nazis came to power, Germany's military internalized a culture of respect for order and authority that was rooted in every social institution; the family, the schools, churches, the law and everything else. When training for the Army our instructors drilled discipline and obedience into us. We obeyed the commands of our officers without question." His father understood what his eldest son was talking about, having fought and been wounded himself as a cavalryman in the First World War.

In the middle of his training, Lübbecke's new division was hastily filled with middle-aged reservists, and sent west to sit on the French border as the *Wehrmacht* devoured Poland. Months later, the division was brought home, the older men were released from duty, and Wilhelm and his fellow draftees took their places in the ranks. They had their first taste of battle a short while later when Germany invaded France and the Low Countries. After that campaign, his unit was designated as an assault division for Barbarossa in the soon-to-be-formed *Heeresgruppe Nord* – Army Group North. His experience of being sent east, with no idea as to why, was typical:

> We were in Belgium on occupation duties, then the whole division was told to pack up, we're moving, but no one knew where to ... organising the move was a time consuming task due to the number of horses and volume of equipment ... In two days we were all on trains heading east; through western Germany to Elbing where they put us in a barracks ... we still lacked any information about our destination. Not even our *kompanie* commander knew where we were headed. We asked ourselves what the hell were we doing there? What will happen next? ... The funny thing about military life is the prevalence and power of rumours ... various theories raced around about our mission ... some predicted 'We're headed to Finland', others with equal confidence said 'We're going to Sweden' and so on, and then in small steps of about fifty kilometres each time we moved towards the Russian border.[7]

Lübbecke's personal journey from poor farm boy to committed soldier was far from being the exception at the time. The Australian diplomat Arthur Yencken noted that "the whole population seems to have been spruced up. Young men no longer slouch ... they have recovered their self-respect."[8] Gisela Franz-Osterwald – a young red headed artist from Berlin – was clear that it was Nazism that had made the difference: "There were happy faces on the streets, people were beaming, somehow they now had a goal and ideals, and they felt there was a reason to live."

Max Kuhnert, a saddler and upholsterer originally from Dresden, who would end up serving in *1. Kavallerie-Division* during Barbarossa, expressed how he and so many young men of his generation felt on the eve of war: "Our energy unlimited, longing for excitement, and filled with a foolish desire to do something great ... we could all feel it deep down; something big was going to happen and we – our generation – were privileged."

Kuhnert could be forgiven for articulating the eternal yearning for excitement of every generation of youth, but there was no denying that he, Karl Maier, and the young men Arthur Yencken and Gisela Franz-Osterwald saw and talked about so approvingly had been through a system like no other in the world (except, ironically, for the one operating in the Soviet Union). The system was designed to produce soldiers – fit, ready and prepared to serve the Reich – and the Barbarossa invasion force was the zenith of that system.

Even before the Nazis' accession to power, youth groups, scouting and the like, were well-attended in Germany, but with Hitler's entry into the Chancellery, the entire structure was radically overhauled as a key part of the Nazification of German life. The main National Socialist youth organisation for boys, the *Hitlerjugend* (HJ – Hitler Youth) had been set up back in 1923 and had a respectable 26,000 members by 1930. This wasn't nearly enough for its leader, Baldur von Schirach, who noted with displeasure that the Lutheran *Evangelische Jugend*, for instance, had some 600,000 participants, so, after winning Hitler's backing, it was decreed that all existing youth groups were to be disbanded and their members compulsorily transferred to the Hitler Youth. This transformation wasn't welcomed by all. Heinz Knoke was ten in 1931 when he joined the *Pfadfinderbund* (Association of Boy Scouts): "We used to roam all over Germany, camping and hiking, developing a feeling of comradeship in sing-songs round the camp-fire." Knoke and his scouting brethren had run-ins with the Hitler Youth: "A special church service was held one Sunday for the various youth organisations ... coming out of the church into the market square we were set upon by members of the Hitler Youth, and a violent street-fight ensued – the police had to intervene." So, when the order came through in December 1936 that made Hitler Youth membership obligatory for all German boys, Knoke took exception; "The *Pfadfinderbund* was declared an illegal organisation, and we were collectively incorporated into the *Jungvolk*, a junior division of the Hitler Youth ... when I became eligible for full membership I refused."

Knoke was in a minority with his refusal – at a stroke there were now no fewer than 7,300,000 young lads in an organisation that was overtly preparing them for a military life, as the teenaged Erich Dressler recalled with glee: "We marched in formation, like soldiers ... on short marches we loaded our rucksacks with stones, for these marches weren't for fun but were meant to develop our toughness and powers of endurance."[9] Another youngster who would end up fighting in the East, Andreas Fleischer, remembered it as fun: "We had lectures two evenings a week, and at weekends we'd go to camps out in the countryside where we'd do a lot of sport, lots of marches, and at night we'd sit around camp-fires singing songs."[10] There were lessons, too, in basic field-craft, map reading and even elementary weapon handling, as well as propaganda sessions where the Nazis' poisonous racism was poured into young ears.

Erwin Bartmann, a young Berliner from a solidly working-class family living in the Friedrichshain district of the city, was nine years old when Hitler came to power in 1933. He initially joined the *Jungvolk*, and then when fifteen "I officially transferred from the Jungvolk to the Hitlerjugend, but was exempt from having to attend the frequent meetings because I was working long hours in a local bakery. I was, nevertheless, charged the same fees as other boys and was a sort of honorary member." The situation wasn't to Bartmann's liking: "I rather resented the fact that my job as a baker prevented me from becoming an active member of the *Hitlerjugend*," having always enjoyed the "communal singing and sports competitions at the weekend camps."

Alongside remembering tough field marches, Erich Dressler also proudly recalled taking part in November 1938's *Kristallnacht* pogrom (Night of Broken Glass) against German Jewish shops, businesses and synagogues. "The night was full of the music of smashed and splintering glass, and the chorus of our anti-Jewish songs – 'I am a Jew, do you know my nose,' and 'Ikey Moses has the dough.'" Bartmann remembered the pogrom too, his main worry being broken glass puncturing the tyres of his precious bicycle as he rode to work at four o'clock the next morning.

Girls weren't exempt from the Nazis' regimentation and militarization of youth. For them it was the *Bund Deutscher Mädel* or BDM (League of German Girls). Hildegard Trutz, a baker's daughter, was an enthusiastic junior leader in her local BDM. "I could never stick Jews ... I thought they were simply disgusting. They were so fat, they all had flat feet and they could never look you straight in the eye. I couldn't explain my dislike for them until my leaders told me it was my sound Germanic instinct revolting against this alien element." Trutz would go on to become a *Lebensborn* mother and marry an SS man.[11]

After finishing their time in the Hitler Youth, young men would transfer to the RAD to "provide honorary service to the German people" – in effect a compulsory work programme. Organised in local battalions along solidly military lines, and with a motto of *Arbeit adelt* (Work Ennobles), members would provide unpaid labour for six months or more, living in barracks, wearing uniform and working up to seventy-six hours a week to clear land, drain marshes, help with the harvest and work on construction projects such as road building. Max Kuhnert did his RAD service in 1937: "We helped the farmers on the land, cleaned river-banks, planted trees, did plenty of sport and had lots of fresh air. Most of all we had comradeship and learned discipline."[12] In short, he, like many other young German men at the time, enjoyed it. Karl Fuchs, another RAD draftee, wasn't so sure. "We have to get up at five o'clock every morning. After reveille we have fifteen minutes of morning callisthenics. In half an hour I have to be washed, dressed and have my bed space cleaned up ... If the bed is not made properly the inspecting officer simply throws the whole thing on the floor and you have to start all over again."

At some point during their RAD service the youngsters would receive their call-up papers and then report to a designated regional Army centre where they would begin sixteen weeks of basic military training including fire and movement drills, weapon handling and marksmanship, field-craft and additional physical fitness training, although after a stint in the Hitler Youth and then the RAD, most recruits were pretty fit anyway.

Not all of the youngsters serving in the RAD went into the Army. Friedrich Karl-Wacker was one who followed a different path: "I completed my six months compulsory service with the *Reichsarbeitsdienst* ... during this period we were visited by an SS recruiting official. He talked about how, if we joined the *Waffen-SS*, not only would we really feel that we had done our bit for the war effort, but, having served in the *Waffen-SS* at the front, we would enhance our status after the war."

The Army, however, did indeed take the vast majority of new recruits and put them through a tried and tested process. Tassilo von Bogenhardt recalled his own induction: "After fifteen minutes of early morning PT ... most of us had headaches which lasted for the rest of the day ... we shivered under a cold shower, were chivvied into our clothes and then through a hastily swallowed breakfast ... as time went on we did longer and faster route marches, ending up with 45 miles in 48 hours with full packs."

Bogenhardt wasn't alone, most young recruits found full-blown military training tough. One of them ruefully remembered his initiation:

As soon as we got to the camp gates all hell broke loose – 'You idiots! You assholes!' were the nicer words the instructors used on us. We all then had to crawl through the gate with our suitcases ... On day two we were woken up at 6am – not very gently as you can imagine – by whistles and shouts, we almost fell out of bed. Two men were picked to go get coffee and the morning ration of bread and jam and bring it back to the barracks as soon as possible. After breakfast everybody got into their uniforms and gear ... then the day started with marching and drill ... for lunch it was bean soup, three boiled potatoes and a piece of bread ... In the afternoon it was classes about weapons and tactics ... at 6 o'clock the classes were over.

Martin Pöppel recalled, "Our training was unbelievably hard, but basically fair. It passed quickly if only because we were drilled so hard from morning to night that we never got a moment to think."

Training was even tougher for those selected for NCO or officer training, as the eighteen-year-old Richard von Rosen discovered on his acceptance for the latter: "I spent more time on the ground than standing up ... after curfew one evening two of our instructors roused us from our beds in our pyjamas and made us crawl across the muddy village street where a herd of sheep had been that afternoon ... all because one of our comrades had a drop of coffee in his field flask at room inspection. When the light was put out and we lay on our straw sacks in our filthy pyjamas I drew the blanket over my head and howled in anger!" Von Rosen would spend between three and four months with a regular unit before studying at one of the Army's War Schools – *Kriegsschulen* – for a further two months, then four more months at a Special-to-Arm School – a *Truppenschule*. Not quite the finished article, the officer candidate, or *fähnrich*, would then serve eight weeks on field probation as an *Unteroffizier* before finally being commissioned.

For NCOs – the corporals and sergeants who were the backbone of any unit – there were two categories of entrant, the first being new recruits hoping to become career soldiers, and the second those who were selected while in service or who volunteered as such. The former would apply aged sixteen, enlist at seventeen and then serve a term of up to twelve years in uniform. The latter category would also serve up to a dozen years. Preparation was rigorous, with both cohorts doing up to a full year or more of normal service before attaining NCO rank. Wolfgang Reinhardt was a former member of the Hitler Youth who went through it all:

I was a recruit in the Army NCO School at Potsdam-Reiche – an élite school. Whoever went through its doors could be proud to have been there and walk three inches taller. All the training was geared to war, we were trained on mortars and machine-guns, made mock attacks on bunkers, and so on, although it wasn't all pretend as we used live ammunition. The training was tough ... I'll give you an example. There was a river in East Prussia called the Liebe, a small river perhaps one metre deep. Anyway, we were ordered to march into the Liebe, about turn and march out, and then about turn and march into it again, and so on, and all the time we had to hold our rifles and machine-guns out of the water.

Karl Fuchs agreed: "We have to learn and train until we perfect all our skills ... the intensity of training is tremendous and there is no rest for anyone." Martin Pöppel said of it, "Our arduous training continued. For example, we did a twenty-five kilometre march with full equipment and radio sets ... This was followed by night exercises including an orientation race using sketches and prismatic compasses ... In August we went to Wildflecken troop training grounds (on the border between Bavaria and Hesse). The marches, exercises, night alerts, the shooting and radio practices were all even worse than before. Every night we fell into our beds completely exhausted ... one of our mottos about the damn place was '*Lieber den ganzen Arsch voller Zwecken, als vierzehn Tage Wildflecken*' (Better an ass-full of nails than fourteen days at Wildflecken)." But Pöppel tempered his complaints: "In action later on we realised time and again how valuable this training was for us. Sweat saves blood was a truism that was often confirmed."

Rosen described the sort of leader this training regime produced: "Our *kompanie* commander, *Oberleutnant* von Cossel, was twenty-four years of age and for me embodied the ideal type of officer – we would all go through fire for him ... his bravery and calmness, even in critical situations, impressed me again and again. In every respect he was the model officer for me." As for Rosen himself, he was posted to 4. *Panzerdivision* and joined a crew in one of the newly issued *Panzer III*s. "I became the gunner in a Panzer III with a 5cm 38 L/42 main gun and two co-axial 7.92mm MG34s ... the firepower of a single panzer was impressive, besides which it was well-armoured and fairly fast." Rosen also noted that he and the other four crewmen had one sub-machine gun, five pistols and a number of egg and stick grenades between them, all bundled into the panzer. "It was extraordinary how much gear and equipment had to be put in a panzer, but as long as done properly it all fitted in."

The object of all this training was to produce confident, capable soldiers, who would be able to operate effectively with the minimum of supervision from superiors to achieve their missions. As one officer put it, "We apply simple methods to our leadership. You will find that our lower units are trained so that many men in them – besides the leader himself – are capable of taking command."

As for the personal equipment the mass of German soldiers would rely on for their lives during Barbarossa, it was a mixed bag. The infantryman's basic weapon, his rifle, was the *Kar98k* – often incorrectly referred to as the '*K98*' which was actually a Polish carbine. Accurate and reliable, the *Kar98k* was a bolt-action design from the First World War and was becoming outdated as modern technology was moving in favour of semi-automatic rifles to significantly increase each soldier's firepower. Instead, to achieve that increased weight of fire, the Germans opted for machine-guns: the iconic *machinenpistole MP38*, often wrongly called the *Schmeisser*, and the *MG34*. Distributed down to squad/section level, the MG34 was a high-performance machine-gun that spat out rounds at the rate of 900 a minute. Belt-fed and light enough to be carried by one man, it was a revolutionary weapon that gave German infantry a distinct advantage, especially when its Soviet soon-to-be opponents were still equipped with hugely heavy 63-kilo Maxims sporting protective steel shields and mounted on wheels or sleds. Nevertheless, this firestorm of a gun had its drawbacks. It was expensive and time-consuming to manufacture and was engineered to such a level that it was prone to jamming if not maintained to a high standard. Its barrel also had an alarming tendency to literally melt if fired at anything over 250 rounds a minute: "When it fired the barrel got so hot that we had to change it using heat resistant gloves." Regardless, with its mobility, and even at a reduced rate of fire, it gave the German infantry a tangible combat edge.

Away from his weaponry, many of the same flaws in-built into the *MG34* were prevalent across much else of the German infantryman's equipment. While British and Soviet uniforms were purposefully utilitarian and cheap to produce, the same could not be said for the attire of the average *Wehrmacht* soldier. Soldiers were typically issued half a dozen different uniforms on enlistment, most of which would be rarely worn, with the emphasis on looking the part rather than on utility or comfort. The most important item was the *feldbluse* – or field blouse – which was materially wasteful with pleats, cuffs, pockets and piping galore. Over the field blouse the webbing that every German soldier used to carry his personal kit was a composite of metal and leather – two materials the resource-poor Reich had precious little of. Even the legendary knee-length German jackboot used reams of quality animal hide when ankle-high boots would have done the job. The average soldier was then weighed down with a panoply of equipment of varying practical usage: "Fully loaded I carried two boxes with six mortar bombs, sixty rounds of ammunition for my rifle, a couple of hand-grenades, a collapsible shovel, a bread sack, a section of a canvas sheet, a trench knife, a gas tent and a gas mask – around 25 kilos of weight I had to lug around the battlefield." That gas mask container was a classic example of waste, precisely and expensively made from costly metal to hold a piece of equipment that almost no *Wehrmacht* soldier ever used. That same soldier declared, "They focused too much on small details and perfection … later when we came across Russian equipment it was very basic with no frills, but it worked." All of this would change as the war dragged on, but not before Barbarossa.

These were the soldiers who would line up in the East on invasion day – and they would be confident of victory, particularly given the conquest of France a few months previously, as trainee transport driver Benno Zeiser heard for himself: "The whole thing should be over in three or four weeks they said, others were more cautious and said two to three months. There was even one who said it would take a whole year, but everyone laughed at that: 'why, how long did the Poles take us? How long to settle the French eh?'"[13] The Army medic Stefan Thomas thought the same: "My father lay for three long years in the mud of Champagne in front of Verdun in World War One, and now in 1940 we saw France fall apart in three to four weeks of blitzkrieg."[14]

It is difficult to overestimate the impact the French victory had on Germany and its *Wehrmacht* – after it, anything seemed possible and for so many defeat was unthinkable. Germany had entered a new golden age, and young men like Leo Mattowitz believed in it wholeheartedly:

When Hitler took power in 1933 I was eleven years old and lived in the Ruhr, and we were poor and so was everyone else I knew. I went to school with a small piece of bread, my father was unemployed as was everyone else, we had no shoes, only wooden clogs in which I had to walk four kilometres to school through the snow and rain. I got my first real shoes from Adolf Hitler, and all of a sudden my father had a job, all our neighbours had jobs, so we all supported the Nazis.

However, not all of Germany's youth were as enthusiastic for Hitler and his war as Leo Mattowitz. Werner Harz was one such doubter: "In 1940 I was called up to Artillery Replacement Regiment 172 in Frankfurt – a gruesome and yet strangely interesting experience … In those early days I formulated my own personal objectives; I decided that this was a useless and hopeless conflict, and that at all costs I would try and keep myself out of it."[15]

All told, some three-quarters of the 1941-era German Army was destined to take part in Barbarossa, a proportion that was almost matched by the *Luftwaffe*. Of the three main branches of the *Wehrmacht*, the *Luftwaffe* was, arguably, the most Nazified in its composition and outlook. Banned by the Versailles Treaty from existing, Germany's infant air force had been surreptitiously created in the Weimar years under the auspices of the black *Reichswehr*, a cover name for a raft of paramilitary units. To help prepare for the day when it could be officially acknowledged, a whole series of glider clubs had been established across Germany to inspire and train a new generation of pilots and aircrew.

This was Norbert Hannig's introduction to military flying: "My flying career began in the upper fifth shortly after Easter 1940 ... with the Flieger-Hitler Youth, a branch of the Hitler Youth movement whose aim was to promote gliding as a sport among boys aged between fourteen and eighteen. Its members were taught to fly gliders free of charge by instructors from the Nationalsozialistisches Fliegerkorps (National Socialist Flyers Corps – NSFK)."

A number of early graduates from the glider clubs were then despatched to the Soviet Lipetsk air base for combat training, contrary to the stipulations of Versailles. Wolfgang Falck was one such pilot: "Everything was done in civilian clothing ... we flew Dutch aircraft, with all the writing on the plane in Spanish ... All the flight mechanics were Russian, but the supervisor was German. We were kept separate from the Russians, we had our own barracks, our own officers club and our own hangar. The Russians were very friendly, we had civilian friends and girlfriends too, but they weren't supposed to speak to us because we were evil capitalists!"

There at Lipetsk, and in Spain during the Civil War under the aegis of the Condor Legion, pilots like Falck formulated the tactics of aerial combat and ground support that would be the mainstay of the *Luftwaffe*'s role in Barbarossa. Headed by Hitler's designated successor – Hermann Goering – and with little in the way of pre-Nazi history or traditions, the new service was filled with eager young men drawn to its glamour and imbued with support for National Socialism. Rudolf Miese was such a recruit: "At age fifteen and sixteen we built models of gliders and took part in competitions. At age seventeen we built a model SG 9 – a glider for initial training ... after RAD service in the winter of 1938/39 I took part in pilot training at the school in Windelsbeiche near Bielefeld. It was a wonderful time."[16] Karl Born was another: "Flying was enormous fun and I was full of enthusiasm for it ... I had taken up glider flying in the Hitler Youth when I'd first joined in 1936 aged thirteen ... After my gliding days I volunteered as soon as I could, and then, when I was aged twenty in 1941, I went on my first mission."[17]

Men like Miese and Born had been intrinsic to the *Wehrmacht*'s successes since the beginning of the war, but theirs was a service designed for tactical supremacy and not strategic victory. The *Luftwaffe*'s goal in all its campaigns up to that point had been much the same. Firstly, destroy the enemy air force at the outset (preferably on the ground), and once air dominance had been achieved, act hand in glove with the Army as its flying artillery, hammering the enemy armies into shards. This operational concept had worked brilliantly. The only time the *Luftwaffe* had been asked to do anything different – to operate as a single strategic service during the Battle of Britain – it had failed. Unfortunately for the Germans, the *Luftwaffe* hadn't learnt the lessons from that defeat, nor made good the significant losses they'd incurred: some 1,977 aircraft and over 3,000 experienced aircrew, including a high proportion of well-trained multi-engine bomber crews. To compound the *Luftwaffe*'s post-Battle of Britain hangover, whilst they were still fighting over southern England, their brethren in the Army and *Kriegsmarine* were resting and recuperating after the summer campaigns. This nine-month hiatus was a boon that Germany's overstretched airmen simply didn't get, and now they were once more to be hurled straight into a battle that would test them to the very limit.

The one *Wehrmacht* service branch that was pretty much struck out of Barbarossa was its smallest, the *Kriegsmarine*. Always the Cinderella of Nazi Germany's armed forces, the navy was stuck fighting an internal battle over the very nature of its future role, with two factions battling it out, each determined their vision should predominate. The dominant clique was headed by Erich Raeder, commander of the *Kriegsmarine* and the first man to achieve the rank of *grossadmiral* since Henning von Holtzendorff back in the First World War. Raeder wanted to build a huge surface fleet to challenge the dominance of the Royal Navy and presented Hitler with a grandiose proposal called Plan Z, which called for one of the biggest naval building programmes ever seen. The other, far smaller, faction within the *Kriegsmarine*'s high command was led by Karl Dönitz, and saw the submarine, Germany's feared U-boat, as the key to victory. Initially, Hitler backed Raeder's vision, hooked on the idea of using the navy to secure the Reich's access to the world's resources, but when Herbert Backe proffered the potential bounty of the Soviet Union instead, the dictator – always a land animal and of course obsessed with bolshevism – dropped Raeder's massively costly Plan Z and turned his attention eastwards.

With no access for German vessels through the Mediterranean and the Turkish Dardanelles into the Black Sea, the only possible maritime area of action against the Soviet Union was the Baltic. This would relegate the *Kriegsmarine* to a subsidiary role at best in the forthcoming invasion. For the young enlistees in the Navy it meant a comparatively cushy number, as Heinrich Wendel admitted in a letter to his family in early 1941:

We received six weeks of basic training, I often cursed that I volunteered ... it was a constant grind from morning to evening. No trace of leisure at all. Well, that's finally over now. Here in Kühlungsborn [a seaside town near Rostock on the Baltic coast] we live a life like God in France. As I told you, we sleep in duvets. As far as food is concerned, I can only say that I have put on 21lbs in four months ... At the moment there is an uncanny heat; thirty-five degrees in the shade ... Every day we plunge into the cool waters of the Baltic Sea ... Then we lie on the beautiful beach in the sun, which has already made us look like negroes.

The only experience Wendel had of the war – outside of the odd sortie in his minesweeper – were a few air raids: "The only thing I notice here from the war are the visits from Tommy, which are not uncommon."

There was one other German military force which would take part in Barbarossa. Initially it would be a bit player, but over time its role in the Russo-German war would grow, and come, in many ways, to symbolise the struggle between the two dictatorships – the *Waffen-SS*. The *Waffen*, or *armed* SS, had been founded back in 1925 as a personal eight-member bodyguard for Hitler. Growing over time, in the autumn of 1934 the now-head of state decreed the creation of the three-regiment *SS-Verfügungstruppe* (SS Special Purpose Troops), or *SS-VT* for short. In effect, what had been a paramilitary Party organisation was transformed into a branch of the armed forces in its own right, albeit a minnow. Having fought in Poland, France and the Balkans, the *SS-VT* had metamorphosed into the motorised *SS-Reich Division* – the premier fighting formation of the infant force. It was joined in the spring of 1941 by Hitler's original bodyguard, now the *SS-Division Leibstandarte-SS Adolf Hitler* (*LSSAH*, or simply the *Leibstandarte*). Sometimes derided as little more than a ceremonial formation only suited to parade duty in Berlin, Hans-Gerhard Starck remembered the *Leibstandarte*'s training as being altogether more professional: "The days spent in training were long and hard. The training itself was always intense and repetitive, and very realistic. It was repeated until everything was done almost automatically … the instructors pushed us to the limits of our endurance and gave us tasks to prove our steadfastness." Another volunteer, Erwin Bartmann, remembered one such task he and his squad were given when they were marched to the barracks swimming pool: "The instructor trotted up the stairs of the ten-metre diving tower. He stopped for a moment at the edge of the uppermost platform before stepping out into the void and, feet first, plummeted into the water." Then it was the recruits' turn: "Bartmann, you're first." The young SS trooper couldn't swim. He jumped anyway.

Much SS training was modelled on comparable Army lessons, as Wolfgang Reinhardt would have recognised: "One day, for example, we were taken on a march carrying full kit and wearing gas masks. We reached the Dutzend-Teich, a large pond with water around five to six feet deep. We were ordered to march on, straight into the water, singing all the while. Nobody faltered. Then, at last, we were ordered to turn back when the water reached our necks." Recruits usually remarked on how rigorous their training was, and for most, like Herbert Maeger, it was a positive experience. "I found the harsh training excellent for my physical condition – never again in my life have I been as fit as I was then."

Alongside these two formations would be a further three SS divisions and a regimental-sized unit, all of differing origins and capabilities. *SS-Division Wiking* had been established in the summer of 1940 around a cadre from the *SS-Reich*. In what became a defining feature of the *Waffen-SS*, the bulk of its rank and file were meant to be composed of non-German foreign volunteers of impeccable racial heritage: Norwegians, Danes, Flemish Belgians and Dutchmen. One of the volunteers was a young Dane named Ivar Corneliussen: "Training was hard. One of my friends didn't look after his rifle properly so the instructor told him to hold it above his head and run around this field we were in again and again, and he had to shout all the time at the top of his voice – 'I must look after my rifle, I must look after my rifle.'" Another *Wiking* volunteer, Henk Kistemaker, an eighteen-year-old teenager from Amsterdam, remembered his own enlistment: "The physical tests for entry were very strict, and the doctor also measured my skull to figure out if I was Aryan enough." A former steelworker, Kistemaker found the training tough: "We had to march up a hill carrying a gun tripod that weighed 20 kilos. On its own 20 kilos isn't too bad, but marching uphill you felt every kilo believe me ... and they'd make you take cover and dive to the ground so that tripod would hit the back of your helmet. By the time we finished we were exhausted."

The two other SS divisions were decidedly different from these three élite all-volunteer formations. The *Polizei Division* wasn't actually a *Waffen-SS* unit at all. As its name suggests it was composed of policeman that Heinrich Himmler – as head of the Reich's multitudinous law enforcement services – had transferred en masse into an armed role. Its members wore police uniforms and insignia, but as they were rigidly under Himmler's control they were considered for all intents and purposes to be part of the SS; they would officially become a *Waffen-SS* formation in early 1942. The final division the armed SS would field for Barbarossa was the most controversial, the *SS-Division Totenkopf.*

Formed in late 1939 almost exclusively from former concentration camp guards, it was led by Theodor Eicke. Eicke was an organiser and administrator of immense talent. When given control over the Third Reich's new concentration camp system, he turned a chaotic, inefficient sprawl into a smoothly functioning system able to play a key role in Nazi plans. Talented as he was, Eicke was also sadistic, murderous, and brutal, and his division was much the same. Its training was tough, as the Danish ethnic German Andreas Fleischer recalled:

The training was hard, very hard, I can tell you. After the war I became a sergeant in the Danish Army and most of the men used to complain about the training, saying it was tough and so on, and I used to say to them, 'you know nothing, this training is easy compared to what I did during the war.' We were trained to follow orders, no matter what they were, we had to follow them, it was about discipline – that made training hard, so if we were told to jump down into the mud or into ditches full of water, then we did it. We were also trained never to leave a wounded comrade behind, we had to get them and carry them back to be treated, no matter what. And, we were told 'never steal, not ever'. I remember once an Army soldier came up to me and said 'Hey, I thought you *Waffen-SS* boys never stole anything, but you have, you've stolen from us.' I just looked at him – looked him in the eye and said, 'You better get away from me man, or there'll be trouble, we SS don't steal, so go away.' That was that, he went away.

The *Totenkopf*'s first taste of action was in France, where it came unstuck during the British counterattack at Arras on 21 May. As their anti-tank shells bounced off the heavy British Matilda tanks, some of its members fled in panic, much to Eicke's disgust and the Army's amusement. Six days later it committed the infamous Le Paradis massacre, shooting dead ninety-seven members of 2nd Battalion Royal Norfolk Regiment who had had the temerity to strongly resist the SS troopers before surrendering when their ammunition ran out.

Last, and definitely least, of the armed SS formations, was *SS-Kampfgruppe Nord*, a battle group of two-plus regiments hastily thrown together and sent north to the Finnish-Soviet border in the Arctic Circle.

A complex organisation, the *Waffen-SS* has sometimes been portrayed as the Nazis' ideological spearhead for Barbarossa, but it was simply too small in early 1941 to be anything other than an adjunct to what would be an overwhelmingly Army affair. That isn't to say that many, if not all, of its members weren't thoroughly committed to the idea of the destruction of the Soviet Union and bolshevism – they were – but perhaps the Nazi indoctrination that has become synonymous with them was not as all-pervasive as is often thought, as one young volunteer described: "We had a political lecture every Sunday about the Hitler Youth and all that sort of stuff, anyway our commanding officer would arrive and say 'Look here boys, I haven't got any magazines or books about political things. I don't have a radio and I don't much feel like it anyway, I've got enough to do during the week, so Heil Hitler, the session is over.'"[18]

Despite the flaws and problems that are synonymous with any military force, the *Wehrmacht* as a whole was a superb instrument of war as it prepared for the invasion, as one former member proudly declared: "I had received the best training there was and I was in the best army in the world."[19]

Veterans, just-trained draftees, reservists, ex-*Reichswehr* and *Freikorps* men; all told, the Germans would be able to mass well over three million men for the invasion. Staggering though this number is, they would still be outnumbered by a significant factor – the kiss of death for an attacker. Berlin needed to find more men, but from where? There were two alternatives. Nazi Germany could look again to its own resources, or it could cast its net out wider and do something it had never attempted before – work with allies. Heinz Guderian was clear about what he thought: "On 22 June 1941 the German Army consisted of 205 divisions: thirty-eight in the West, twelve in Norway, one in Denmark, seven in the Balkans, two in Libya, and 145 available for operations in the East. This dispersal of strength was unnecessary; thirty-eight in the West and twelve in Norway seemed particularly high."

As with many of the numbers involved in Barbarossa, the figures Guderian quotes are the subject of not a little controversy. Several other knowledgeable sources state that the *Wehrmacht* had up to 153 divisions to deploy in the East (including nine second-rate, so-called security divisions, designated to provide rear-area cover once the invasion got under way), but what isn't disputed is that Berlin did indeed leave significant forces positioned across its empire when it needed every man, panzer and gun it could get hold of for Barbarossa. The distinguished historian and former British Army officer Brigadier Peter Young said that of the German divisions left out of the Barbarossa order of battle, some thirty-two were so short of men and equipment as to be practically useless – and while that may well be an accurate assertion, it still leaves an additional twenty-eight deployable formations sitting more or less idle. This included *General der Artillerie* Hermann Tittel's 69. *Infanterie-Division* for example. Formed in August 1939, it first saw action in the invasion of Norway where it performed creditably, and was then assigned to occupation duties, ending up sitting there right up until the end of 1942. Tittel's men were joined in their unnecessary security duties by their comrades of the 199. *Infanterie-Division*. Its ranks were filled with older ex-*Landwehr* men, who, while not first-rate, could have just as easily fulfilled rear-area protection tasks in Russia as in Norway. The 205, 208, 302 and 304. *Infanterie-Divisionen* were much the same. Mostly filled with men from older age groups, these formations would sit out 1941 in comfort in barracks across France and Belgium even as their comrades in the East were crying out for reinforcements.

While a case could be made that divisions like these wouldn't have added a great deal of combat power to the original Barbarossa force, it is harder to claim that for a raft of other units. *Generalmajor* Hugo Ribstein's Silesian 81. *Infanterie-Division*, for example, had seen combat in the French campaign and was up to strength and well equipped, as were Joseph Lehmann's 82. *ID* and Kurt von der Chevallerie's 83. *ID*. All would spend Barbarossa in the West, guarding against a non-existent invasion threat from Britain. In that light, its hard to judge OKH's dispersal of troops the length and breadth of occupied Europe as anything other than wasteful to the point of stupidity, particularly when in the place of trained German soldiers with German equipment, German training and a common language of command, the alternative was allies of dubious quality.

The Nazis were never good at sharing. It wasn't in their nature. Throughout their short-lived and brutish history, they made no secret of seeing anything and everything that was non-German as inferior, and that did not make for strong alliance building. In fact, they seemingly went out of their way to act in an arrogant and high-handed manner towards their allies; even towards fascist Italy, which was initially the senior partner in the relationship and the first signatory of the Pact of Steel (*Patto d'Acciaio*).

However, utilising a mixture of threats and persuasion, by early 1941 Berlin had managed to assemble a motley collection of allied nations who would contribute forces to Barbarossa, including the kingdoms of Italy and Romania, the Roman Catholic clerical dictatorships of Slovakia and Croatia, and the right-wing authoritarian regimes of Hungary and Finland – the Kingdom of Bulgaria was also officially an ally but its wily Tsar, Boris III, would permit no active part for Bulgaria's military in the invasion.

The Finns had already fought the Red Army in the 1939 Winter War, and Helsinki was determined to recover all the territory it had been forced to hand over after Moscow's unprovoked attack. The Finnish leader, Marshal Carl Mannerheim, made two armies available for what the Finns would call the Continuation War. The 150,000 men of the South-Eastern and Karelian Armies would fight independently of German command, with the majority tasked with advancing towards Leningrad and liberating Finland's lost lands, while a small force would guard the far north of the country in concert with the four German divisions of the *Armeeoberkommando Lappland* (Army High Command Lapland). All in all, Finland would commit almost half its armed forces to the invasion, but would be a semi-detached ally at best.

Croatia's clerico-fascist Ustaše government would send a reinforced regiment, the *Verstärktes Kroatisches Infanterie-Regiment 369* (369th Reinforced Croatian Infantry Regiment), but it wouldn't start its move east until late August, so was discounted from the initial invasion roster. The Slovaks would make a better fist of it, sending two of the country's three infantry divisions – formed into the 42,000-strong Slovak Army Corps – accompanied by their most modern military formation, a mechanised brigade which contained their only armoured force, a meagre affair of former Czech Army *PzKpfw 38(t)s*, plus some *Strv m/41* light tanks manufactured for the Swedish government but never shipped.

Well trained, and mainly composed of former Czech Army men, the Slovaks' weaknesses were in mobility and firepower. The Corps only had 700 trucks – half that of the same-sized German formation – and a paltry fifty-four horse-drawn artillery pieces. Assigned to the southern area of operations, the Slovaks would stand alongside those most reluctant of German allies, the Hungarians.

Desirous of looking the part rather than playing it, Hungary's dictator – Admiral Miklós Horthy – proffered the grandly entitled Carpathian Group as Hungary's contribution to Barbarossa. Only 2,000 men stronger than the Slovak Corps, it was composed mainly of marching infantry with a dash of cavalry and mountain troopers, a few outdated artillery guns and a laughable collection of obsolete armoured vehicles including some 65 Italian-made *Ansaldo* tankettes.

That left the two kingdoms of Italy and Romania. Mussolini's Italy was in such a poor state economically that when asked by a somewhat exasperated Berlin what it required in terms of raw materials to wage war, Rome submitted a shopping list so gargantuan it was estimated that 17,000 railway wagons would be required just to transport it. Incredibly – given the Reich's own shortages of just such materials – Berlin did try to provide its ally with at least some of what it requested, but it wasn't enough to avert military ignominy for Italy in southern France and Greece. Rome was now in the process of adding to that miserable tally in north and east Africa, where British and Commonwealth troops were almost enjoying humiliating Italian forces wherever they met them. If Italy had any spare troops, Africa was surely the theatre they should have been committed to, but in the mind of a dictator like Mussolini military logic came a poor second to political expediency and spurious matters of national prestige, as he pointed out to one of his senior commanders when referring to Barbarossa: "I just need a few thousand casualties to justify my seat at the table afterwards."

Those *few thousand* sacrificial lambs were to come from the newly established *Corpo di Spedizione Italiano in Russia* – CSIR (Italian Expeditionary Corps in Russia). The CSIR would initially compose the 60,000 men of the 9th *Pasubio*, 52nd *Torino* and 3rd *Duca d'Aosta* Divisions. The first two were infantry units, the latter a mixed cavalry, light armour and infantry formation, every one undermanned and under-equipped like all their contemporaries in the Italian armed forces. Even the *Regio Esercito* (Royal Italian Army) considered itself not fit for purpose, a high-level internal report blithely stating that "our Army is antiquated in its training methods and concepts of war – as war moves from being static to being one of motion". The report's author could have thrown in any number of other flaws if he had wished, a point that the *Torino*'s Alarico Rocchi would agree with. "Our boots were hopeless and flimsier than ballerina shoes." The weapons furnished to Rocchi and his fellow Turinese were little better. Their rifles were First World War vintage 6.35mms, their anti-tank artillery was mainly 2cm cannons – useless against anything but the lightest of opponents – and even their grenades were dreadful, as demonstrated by one of their own general officers during a training exercise for the invasion. Holding one up, he explained to his audience: "The standard issue SRCM Model 35 grenade ... manufactured with precision and with a record of many years of use. It is equipped with safety devices that allow its safe transportation ... and will not allow it to explode even if the grenade itself is flattened." To prove its efficacy, the officer then proceeded to pull the pin and throw it as far as he could. Unfortunately, the general's pet German shepherd didn't understand the nature of the demonstration and bounded after the grenade to fetch it back. Returning it to his now panic-stricken master, a quick-acting NCO grabbed the saliva-drenched grenade and threw it away once more – this time making sure he kept hold of the animal as he flattened himself, and the frustrated canine, on the ground. He needn't have bothered – the grenade sailed through the air, landed, bounced, and didn't go off – it was a dud.

This wouldn't be much of a problem in the two cavalry regiments of the aristocratic *Duca d'Aosta*, where the officers acted like medieval potentates and the sabre was still very much the weapon of choice. The monocled and moustached Count Alessandro Bettoni commanded the *3° Reggimento 'Savoia Cavalleria'* of the division, and "was treated like a divinity, and surrounded by the greatest names among the Italian – and in particular the Roman – nobility".

Bettoni at least led his men from the front, not a common trait among much of the Italian officer corps, many of whose members were inadequately trained, ageing reservists. The preponderance of elderly officers was at its worst at the top of the Army, where the pre-war Chief of Staff, Pietro Badoglio, was seventy, and his successor Ugo Cavallero a sprightly sixty. By contrast, senior German commanders like Halder, Keitel and Jodl were all in their fifties. Age did not bring wisdom among Italy's senior military leadership either, with one of their number, Ettore Bastico, declaring that "the tank is a powerful tool, but let us not idolise it; let us instead reserve our reverence for the infantryman and the mule". Gifted with such remarkable insight, the sixty-four-year-old Bastico was perhaps not the obvious choice to be given overall command of the Axis North African campaign and Erwin Rommel's *Afrika Korps* – as he was a few short weeks after the launch of Barbarossa.

As bad as their elderly leadership, poor weaponry and interminable bureaucracy were, it was the *CSIR*'s lack of motorised transport – as with the Slovaks and the Hungarians – that would prove the Italians'

Achilles heel in the Soviet Union. Taking a leaf out of the Germans' book, the Corps' quartermasters turned to requisitioning civilian commercial vehicles and roughly painting over the company logos, as well as using horses and pack-mules, to try and bring an element of mobility to their desultory command. Almost symbolic of the organisational mire the *CSIR* was in, shortly before deployment east the Corps' designated leader, the bespectacled Francesco Zingales, fell seriously ill and had to be hurriedly replaced by a veteran of the ill-fated Balkans campaign, Giovanni Messe.

Romania, under the leadership of the young King Michael and his *Conducător* (a Romanian title comparable to the Italian *Duce*) Ion Antonescu, was the most enthusiastic of Germany's Barbarossa allies. Promised not just the return of its Soviet-annexed provinces of Bessarabia and northern Bukovina but also the over-lordship of a huge new Transnistria super-region between the rivers Dniester and Bug, Romania committed the 300,000 men of the *Armata a 3-a Română* and *Armata a 4-a Română* – the 3rd and 4th Romanian Armies. With their thirteen divisions and eight independent brigades this force comprised almost half the country's peacetime army. While not nearly as well trained or equipped as comparable German formations, nevertheless the Romanians constituted by far the largest contingent of allied troops for Barbarossa.

The Germans had mixed expectations of their allies. One officer described the Slovaks as "brave soldiers with very good discipline", but was less complimentary about the Italians. "They have big mouths, make a lot of noise and show off like they're Julius Caesar, but when push comes to shove forget it, they're useless." The armoured corps commander Erich von Manstein was more nuanced about the biggest allied contingent: "The Romanian soldier – who was normally of peasant origin – was modest in his wants and usually a capable, brave fighter, but the possibilities to train him as an individual fighting man who could think for himself in action – let alone as an NCO – were limited to a great extent by the low standard of education in Romania." Manstein was correct; literacy in Romania was only at 60 per cent, and far lower outside the big cities. It was nigh on impossible to train men for modern warfare when they couldn't read or write.

Taken together, there would be more than half a million allied soldiers joining the Germans on invasion day, increasing the assault force to nearer four than three and a half million in total. Those same allies would also add several hundred aircraft to the strength of the *Luftwaffe* – the Italian *Corpo Aereo Spedizione* alone was almost a hundred strong – but as with their ground contribution, the allied aerial forces lacked modern equipment and training and would be of limited use.

3

The Build-up

Even with the Barbarossa directive signed and planning going ahead full steam, for the bulk of the *Wehrmacht*, war with the Soviet Union was simply unthinkable. After the French campaign the cavalryman Max Kuhnert spoke for many: "I was quite confident that from now on everything was going to be fine, peaceful ... when someone mentioned Soviet Russia I could only smile. It was too preposterous to even think about."

Wilhelm Lübbecke agreed with his mounted comrade: "Most of us found it very difficult to imagine that Germany would attack Russia ... the scale of the Soviet Union tended to make the prospect of invasion difficult to conceive." Gerhard Kunde – down south with Rundstedt's army group – poured cold water on the idea of an invasion of the Soviet Union when he wrote to his mother: "We no longer take the rumours seriously, on the contrary, the announcement of such an idea results in us laughing out loud."

So, if the Soviet Union wasn't the target, why were so many soldiers being massed on the border? Panzer crewman Richard von Rosen was weighing up the options: "In the regiment rumours were rife ... either the USSR would allow us free passage into Persia or Iraq, or we were to relieve Rommel – nobody thought of an attack on the USSR."

Johannes Kaufmann was a Messerschmitt Bf 110 pilot: "We departed Lippstadt on 17 June 1941 and set course eastwards – we weren't told our ultimate destination ... the following day we arrived at our new base, the airfield at Radzyn, some 80 kilometres west-south-west of Brest-Litovsk." Kaufmann and his comrades were in the dark as to why they had been ordered to fly east:

Nobody knew the real reason for our transfer and so the rumours were soon flying thick and fast ... the favoured theory was that we were part of a gigantic pincer movement designed to trap the British and Free French forces operating in the Middle East. The southern arm of the pincer was to be provided by the German and Italian troops in North Africa ... all we were waiting for was for the Soviet authorities to grant us right of passage through their territory.[1]

Heinz Knoke – now a fully-fledged *jagdflieger* like Kaufmann – heard much the same: "No one knows what is happening. One rumour has it that the Russians will permit us to cross the Caucasus to occupy the oil fields of the Middle East and seize the Dardanelles and the Suez Canal." The idea of a giant left hook through a friendly Soviet Union and down into the rear of Great Britain's Middle Eastern command – unbelievable as it might sound – was widespread throughout the *Wehrmacht* at the time, as a young officer from *258. ID* wrote in a letter home in late May. "Some are saying that we've leased the Ukraine for the next ninety years and received permission to march through Turkey to Iraq ... every latrine rumour is closely followed by another."

Gefreiter Hubert Hegele of *1. Gebirgs-Division* (1st Mountain Division) put pen to paper in his diary to express his thoughts:

> Many rumours have been flying about recently ... to the right of transit through Russia in order to assist hard-pressed Iraq against its English attackers. An attack on the Soviet Union? Well, we don't believe that at all. First of all, Germany has a friendship pact and a non-aggression pact with the Soviet Union; and secondly – a battle against this vast empire? No, that won't happen. What is truth – what is rumour? What do we little wheels in this vast machinery of war know? Nothing, absolutely nothing ... That something is coming though, we surely know that.

Hegele was far from alone in believing a conflict with the Soviet Union was unthinkable. In June 1941 Otto Skorzeny was a young officer in the *SS-Wiking*. Destined to find fame later on in the war as the man who freed Mussolini from his captors after he was deposed in 1943, the towering Viennese would be described rather grandiosely by Churchill as *the most dangerous man in Europe* at that stage, but in 1941 he was just a junior officer with an impressive set of university duelling scars:

> We speculated about our next military objective, but none of us envisioned that we would soon embark on a war against Russia. To the contrary, the most persistent rumour was that our objective would be the oil fields of the Persian Gulf. Russia would grant the German Army free passage and we would march across the Caucasus into Iran

... Another rumour was that we would march via Turkey into Egypt and surround the English Near-East Army in a pincer action. As a result of this conjecture I took along the book *The Seven Pillars of Wisdom* by T.E. Lawrence. The tempting Orient provided us with many hours of conversation while we were transported in a wide arc around Bohemia and Moravia to reach Poland via Upper Silesia.

The idea of Moscow allowing safe passage across thousands of miles of its territory so that the Germans could defeat the British in the Middle East may seem ludicrously far-fetched now, but at the time was viewed by many German soldiers, sailors and airmen as entirely possible. Whereas, for those same servicemen – and indeed most of Germany – an attack on Stalin's empire seemed inconceivable. Alexander Stahlberg, a junior officer in *12. Panzerdivision*, definitely thought so: "Hadn't Hitler and Stalin ceremoniously signed a Non-Aggression Pact less than two years ago? Hadn't Hitler been visited by Molotov (the Soviet Foreign Minister) in November the previous year?" Josef *Sepp* de Giampietro, a special operations trooper in the *Bau-Lehr-Bataillon z.b.V. 800* (800th Special Duties Construction Training Battalion, better known as the Brandenburgers), agreed: "You'd even hear gossip about a war against Russia, but nobody took this very seriously." The young South Tyrolean had just fought against the British in Greece and considered a further move against them as the most likely option: "Our high command had planned a genius chess move; Russia would allow us to march through its territory ... across the Caucasus and into Iran ... where we would launch a surprise attack into the rear of the British who were fleeing from the *Afrika Korps*."

In the middle of all the rumours and gossip, German high command went about readying for the forthcoming invasion. On 7 August 1940 – four months before Hitler signed off on the Barbarossa plan – the Chief of the OKW (*Oberkommando der Wehrmacht* – *Wehrmacht* Supreme Command), Wilhelm Keitel, signed the '*Aufbau Ost*' directive (Build-up East), which called for a huge programme of infrastructure building and upgrades across East Prussia and occupied Poland in particular. With the majority of the *Luftwaffe* heading east, an additional 250 airfields needed to be fully refitted and expanded – or even built from scratch – in occupied Poland alone. Dozens more were built in Romania and East Prussia, and supplies of fuel, food, ammunition and spare parts were stockpiled.

The movement of troops and equipment east necessitated the total subordination of much of Europe's railway system to the needs of Barbarossa. Some 17,000 separate trains were used to move the assault divisions into place, starting with the first twenty-five in February, another twenty in March and April, a further thirty in May, and the last fifty-one in the first three weeks of June itself. Nineteen additional divisions were to be held back in *OKW* reserve until needed.

Work on such a gigantic project couldn't be kept completely quiet, and it wasn't long before the rumour mill sprang into action again, although the tale that now seemed to gain the most traction among service personnel and civilians alike was that all this activity was entirely defensive in nature against a possible Soviet attack on the Reich. Helmut Mahlke, a Stuka pilot, heard that tall story: "There were rumours of Soviet forces massing along the frontier, perhaps with the intention of attacking us from the rear." Unbelievably, these stories continued to do the rounds even after Barbarossa was launched. The *Kommodore* of *Jagdgeschwader 51 (JG. 51* – Fighter Wing 51), Werner Mölders, told his mother after the beginning of the campaign, "You must be thankful that we attacked Russia. Fourteen days later they would have attacked us and would have ended up in Berlin."[2] The Dutch SS volunteer Hendrik Verton firmly believed the story: "Stalin was about to attack Germany and everything was being prepared ... it was no coincidence that over two and a half million Red Army soldiers ... were stationed where they were in the western Soviet Union ... it was proof enough to convince every German soldier that Barbarossa was a preventative measure against an obvious act of aggression aimed at Germany."[3] Léon Degrelle, the Belgian Walloon Rexist leader who volunteered to fight in the German Army, was of the same view as his Dutch counterpart:

> Stalin stated his intent to come into the war when Hitler and the western powers have destroyed each other ... by 1941 Stalin had 17,999 tanks, and the next year he would have had 32,000 – ten times more than Germany, and their air force would have had a 10 to 1 superiority too. The very week he signed the Non-Aggression Pact he gave orders to build 96 airfields on the western Soviet border, with another 180 planned for the following year.

Clearly framed after the war with a very large slice of hindsight, Degrelle's comments do, however, contain a grain of truth. A draft plan for a pre-emptive strike against the Reich had indeed been drawn up by the Soviet high command, and Moscow did call up 800,000 reservists in May to increase its strength in the border regions to over four and a half million men. Moscow also significantly reinforced the western units of the Soviet air force, the *Voyenno-Vozdushnye Sily (VVS* – literally Military Air Forces). However, those same plans were never taken seriously, and Moscow had no intention of invading the Reich. Right up until the last, Stalin himself refused to believe the Nazis would attack.

As it was, the vast majority of German soldiers, sailors and airmen didn't have the faintest idea what was planned. The Dutch SS volunteer Henk Kistemaker remembered that "suddenly they woke us in the middle of the night and told us to be ready to leave in 30 minutes. The whole unit boarded trains and we were transported to Poland." Kistemaker's fellow *Wikinger* Eduard Jahnke was just as clueless: "There were some rumours around that perhaps we were going to go through Russia to British India ... but these were rumours, nobody believed them. We asked our commanders: 'Where are we off to?' – 'No idea!' was the response."[4] Kistemaker was not impressed by their new billets. "Poland looked untended and poor ... the barracks had no running water so we all had to wash in the nearby river – luckily it was June not December!" Richard von Rosen was also in the dark as his panzer regiment moved east: "We reached Siedlce, seventy kilometres from the Soviet-German border ... at 0700 hours we set off for the border. We were on the dusty Polish highway for half a day. For most of us what we saw was totally new ... the houses were all wooden with thatched roofs. There were no brick buildings at all ... it was a preview of what we'd see week after week in Russia ... we especially noticed the many Jews, identified by their yellow star."[5]

The American writer and political commentator Howard K. Smith was based in Berlin as a foreign correspondent in early June 1941. Every day he passed the front window of his favourite local book shop, noting the prominent display of a popular book of satirical Russian short stories. One day he walked by as usual, and to his surprise the book had disappeared and been replaced with a copy of *My life in the Russian Hell* – the book shop was next door to *Alois*, the restaurant owned by Hitler's half-brother. Smith wrote that this was the first time that he thought war against the Soviet Union must be imminent.

One man who did know what was happening was *Major* Karl Wilhelm Thilo, a staff officer based in France. Back in the autumn of 1940 he wrote in his diary, "Russia is to be photographed from the air up to 300 kilometres beyond its borders; preparations for invasion. I myself have to work on a mission for the German Military Attaché in Moscow to reconnoitre routes and communications for three spearheads."[6] German high command was familiar with much of the western Soviet Union; its geography, terrain, weather patterns and so on. After all, many of them had fought there in the First World War. However, that knowledge was not the same as detailed target mapping, particularly of the service arm they most feared – the Soviet Air Force.

Berlin knew that Moscow had invested heavily in aircraft design and manufacture in the 1930s, and they also knew that just as the *Luftwaffe* was perceived as glamorous among German youth, so much the same sentiment prevailed in the Soviet Union, with many of the best and brightest filling VVS flight academies. With the offensive predicated on a rapid destruction of the enemy air force to allow the switch of the *Luftwaffe* to its role of airborne artillery, it was seen as vital by the Barbarossa planners that the VVS's bases and overall strength be accurately mapped. They decided that the best way to achieve that was to initiate the first ever extensive aerial reconnaissance of a supposedly allied nation. It was this plan that Thilo was privy to. In order to carry out this most sensitive of tasks, the Germans turned to a forty-seven-year-old ex-Imperial Navy flyer from Lower Saxony: *Oberstleutnant* Theodor Rowehl.

Of medium height and build, Rowehl was unremarkable except in his passion for three things: his wife, his daughter,[7] and his absolute belief in the importance of aerial reconnaissance. Indeed, following the end of the First World War he had gone so far as to fly a private plane over the new German-Polish border to try and photograph evidence of fortifications – a mission he paid for out of his own pocket. Impressed by the results, German intelligence took him on, and now it was to him and his four squadron *Fernaufklärungsgruppe des Oberbefehlshaber der Luftwaffe (AufklGrp OB der Lw* – Reconnaissance Group of the Commander in Chief of the Air Force) that they turned. Specialists in high-altitude flying and target photography, Rowehl's men used upgraded Dornier Do 215-B2s, Junkers Ju-88Bs and Ju-86Ps, with pressurized cabins, auxiliary fuel tanks and powerful Zeiss cameras, to carry out around 500 separate flights over the western Soviet Union. Often reaching altitudes of 36,000 feet or more, the Germans were nevertheless spotted by Soviet aircraft and ground observers, but on Stalin's express orders were left unmolested to avoid provoking Germany. One bewildered VVS member recalled, "We were in a very silly situation. We saw German spy planes fly over our positions every day, but we were not authorised to oppose them. We couldn't even request them to leave! A Ju-88 would overfly us early in the morning, heading deep into Soviet territory at high altitude. In the evening he overflew us again on the return flight … on one occasion a pilot took off and chased a German plane. When he returned, he was immediately arrested."

On the list of what Rowehl was tasked to locate and map were military headquarters, barracks, rail and road systems, supply depots and such like, but above all, airfields. Fifty aircraft and 500 overflights may seem a great deal, but the area Rowehl was instructed to cover was some 579,150 square miles – more than twice the size of France. Even so, what they did find in that huge space should have given Berlin significant pause for thought as, to some extent, the western districts of the Soviet Union resembled a gigantic armed camp. There were extensive fortifications, large-scale troop build-ups, and the VVS forces in particular looked daunting. Rowehl's aerial reconnaissance seemed to show there were twenty-three VVS divisions in the west, equipped with around 7,300 aircraft. Berlin further estimated there were an additional 3,000 aircraft in the country's interior, and about 2,000 more in the Far East facing the Japanese.

The sheer numbers terrified Berlin – but they were woefully inaccurate.

In reality, there were seventy-nine VVS divisions in total, with close on 8,000 aircraft in the west, and almost the same again based in the interior. In what would soon become the immediate battle-zone the numbers were stacked against the Germans. Major-General Alexander Novikov's Leningrad District had 1,270 planes, his neighbour in the Baltic District, Major-General A. P. Ionov, had slightly fewer at 1,140, while Ivan Kopets and Yevgeny Ptukhin in the Western and Kiev Districts respectively had 3,144 between them. Feodor Michugin's Odessa District had the fewest at just under a thousand, and they were all backed up by the 1,346-strong long-range bomber force. Pitted against this behemoth would be anything between 2,232 and 2,598 frontline German aircraft – depending on serviceability – a third less than the *Luftwaffe* had for the campaign in the West the previous year, and fewer than it concentrated for the Battle of Britain. The German fliers would be hugely outnumbered in every category of aircraft: fighters, bombers, ground-attack, reconnaissance – even seaplanes.

The *Luftwaffe* pressed on regardless. Johannes Kaufmann and Günther Scholz were two of the pilots taking their aircraft eastwards: "Everything was ready for us on arrival, an advance party from our *Gruppe* had flown in earlier and they quickly guided us into the well-camouflaged dispersal areas hidden under the trees bordering the field ... a little distance away a hutted encampment served as accommodation." Scholz found the same: "After converting to the new model Me 109 F the *Staffel* moved to Schlossberg/Insterburg in East Prussia under strictest secrecy. We weren't allowed to fly at our field base and the aircraft dispersal points were fully camouflaged in forests and in the undergrowth."[8]

Both Kaufmann and Scholz would have cause to look back on those days of relative comfort with nostalgia, although at the time they were under strict security, as *Obergefreiter* Fritz Hild, a *pionier* (assault engineer) in *7. Infanterie-Division*, made clear in a letter home:

This morning we have arrived in our new accommodation. First, we needed to sit down to digest the shock. The village consists of just three uninhabited houses, where the battalion staff are now housed. Otherwise there is not a single building in sight. It is no wonder when you learn that we are only twenty kilometres from the Russian border and that we are in a former Lithuanian district ... Our beds are made of straw and hay ... The journey here went well. We boarded a train on Sunday at 7pm and then we went to Insterburg, where we got off. Then we had to drive another 180 kilometres to arrive at our new 'quarters' this morning at 5am. Now I must ask you to keep the strictest secrecy about what I have written here. We actually have to leave our mail open in the office so it can be checked before it's sent.

A junior NCO in *50. Infanterie-Division*, Hellmuth H., was under the same instructions as Hild when he told his wife in a letter just before the invasion, "For reasons of secrecy regarding where we are, our destination, etc., we have been ordered since yesterday to hand over our letters still open, so that the *kompanie* boss can see what we've written. I've got nothing against this, especially since our new boss is older and more fatherly than his predecessor." Hellmuth had already fought in Poland, France and Greece and was a Nazi Party member, and his coping strategy in such circumstances was to focus on the everyday aspects of life. "I received your letter number 34, thank you. Of course I agree with you buying the coats you found, it's clear that you needed them, and anyway I am amazed that you have managed to save up the money!"

Despite the best efforts of the censors and *Wehrmacht* security, news was bound to leak out given the enormity of preparations for the attack, as the aristocratic panzer officer Hans von Luck discovered for himself: "At the beginning of June, suddenly and without warning, our division was entrained in Bonn ... and detrained in Insterburg, East Prussia ... I used the opportunity to visit some friends on an estate nearby." The matriarch in charge of the estate asked him, "Now we're threatened with a long and difficult war with Russia ... what more does Hitler want? Is it this *lebensraum* he and Rosenberg (Alfred Rosenberg, the Nazi Party ideologue and standard bearer for the idea of eastern *lebensraum*) talk about so often?"[9]

Prussian *grande dames* weren't the only ones who'd tumbled to the truth. The commander of *Heeresgruppe Mitte* (Army Group Centre), Fedor von Bock, had been ensconced in his headquarters in Posen (modern Poznan) since the previous October, but two days before the invasion moved up to the village of Rembertov on Warsaw's eastern outskirts. He noted in his diary: "Today my Polish cleaning lady proved how hard it is to keep something secret in wartime; she asked me to see to it that she kept her position, as I was – after all – going away soon!"

The men Bock would lead into the coming campaign were also finally beginning to realise what was going on. *Infanterie-Regiment 40* – part of Hans-Jürgen von Arnim's newly created *17. Panzerdivision* – crossed the Oder River into occupied Poland in early June. Driving by truck and half-track along "poor, dusty roads" the regiment arrived by the middle of the month at Siedlce–Konstantinov, not far from the Russo-German frontier. There they prepared to attack:

> The Russians notice barely anything of our intentions to attack. On 16.6.41, the divisional order arrives for the regiment to move into the assembly area at Derlo – fifteen kilometres north of Brest-Litovsk ... Parts of *Kompanie* Nr. 3 take over surveillance and security along the Bug River, after men from our regiment, disguised in customs uniforms, have carried out reconnaissance and soundings on the Bug beforehand. Firing positions and observation posts for the heavy weapons are determined ... The remaining elements of the regiment arrive in the staging area by the evening of 21.6 ... The surveillance of the far bank provides a clear picture of the enemy.

The Germans went even further to prepare for the coming offensive. "Officers Bapst and Steiner swim across the Bug repeatedly and tap the Russian telephone lines. The sand on the Russian riverbank is regularly smoothed over in order not to leave any footprints."

The reality of what was about to happen was also beginning to dawn on von Arnim's neighbours to the north. Leeb's army group had the narrowest front and the smallest assembly area, and although it was the runt of the *Ostheer* litter in terms of size, with just 640,000 men and 600 panzers, it struggled to get into position on time without giving the game away to the Soviets. Georg-Hans Reinhardt's *XXXXI. Korps (mot.)* with its two panzer divisions and twin infantry divisions – one of which was motorised – found the whole operation especially troublesome, as 6. *Panzerdivision*'s Erhard Raus recalled:

> [We] assembled in the area around Osterode, Riesenburg, and Deutsch Eylau [modern Iława in Poland]. From this point the build-up for the attack proceeded in a succession of four separate night marches. The assembly movements proved very difficult because of the sheer mass of troops in *Heeresgruppe Nord* that were approaching the border, and their often conflicting routes of march. Crossing the Neman River turned out to be particularly difficult. Our lighter vehicles crossed at Schreitlauken on an auxiliary bridge over which a test run had only been driven at the last moment. Panzers and heavier vehicles moved across the Memel bridge at Tilsit, which also had to be used by 1. *Panzerdivision*, so that two parallel columns converged at a single point ... with all movements restricted to the hours of darkness and never allowed to extend into daytime.

One of *1. Panzerdivision*'s officers remembered the same series of events:

> All armoured units were ordered to only march during the night. Officer reconnaissance teams, clad like civilian hunters or farmers, were dispatched into the countryside to take a look at the area east and southeast of Tilsit and west of Tauroggen. However, the area west of the former German/Lithuanian border remained strictly 'off-limits' ... No armoured movements were permitted after the initial assembly of the division ... Now everything was thoroughly prepared and organised.

Much the same sort of covert reconnaissance was going on up and down the start line for the invasion, as *Obergefreiter* Alfred Opitz of *18. Panzerdivision* saw for himself as he sat and stewed in a humid forest. "The air was thick enough to stifle ... Last-minute reconnaissance of terrain and enemy forces beyond the frontier was carried out, with some of the reconnaissance teams going out to inspect border regions disguised as local hunters and farmers, and even carrying farm implements to complete the ruse."

For the mass of men now poised on the border, the hours crawled by interminably. The oppressive humidity also brought out a more immediate enemy than the Red Army, as one German soldier made clear: "Between the thickets of pine and fir trees we put up tents ... and camouflaged them. The region was dominated by an unimaginable plague of mosquitoes. Myriads of these blood-sucking pests could bring one to the point of desperation. These June days were hot and oppressive and, at least for me, filled with great worry and inner tension." A fellow *landser* in *20. ID (mot.)* found himself under the same relentless attack:

> We were surrounded by swamplands. It was very hot and humid. But the worst were the thousands of big mosquitoes infesting the area. There was not a single minute without several stings from these beasts. After about an hour my hands and face started to swell from all the bites, and so was it with my comrades. We saw no other way out but to build some fires and assemble around it in small groups ... It was a miserable night, and no-one could get any sleep.

Nazi Germany's military intelligence – the *Abwehr* – could be forgiven for enduring some sleepless nights themselves before the attack. Never the *Wehrmacht*'s finest service arm, the *Abwehr* was out of its depth in attempting to assess the Reich's soon-to-be enemy. Its grave errors regarding the strength and dispositions of the VVS was symptomatic of its failure across the board to understand and appreciate the economic, military and political might of the Soviet Union. It failed to acknowledge the massive industrial and raw materials centres in the eastern Soviet Union, it failed to accurately predict the depth of Soviet manpower – despite it being common knowledge that this reserve was huge – and it also failed to both analyse and then comprehend the rugged nature of the country's road network and the impact this would have on the German plan. All three issues would come to play a vital role in Barbarossa, as the bomber pilot and junior *Luftwaffe* staff officer Werner Baumbach put it: "Despite all our technological advances, Russia had remained a land power of the first order. Her inexhaustible reservoir of men and her vast distances are her weapons." Baumbach knew what he was talking about. In autumn 1940 he spent time at the German Embassy in Moscow, and had undertaken a fact-finding mission to the Soviet Far East. On his travels he saw for himself that the country with the largest landmass on earth could boast only 64,000 kilometres of hard surface all-weather roads, and just 82,000 kilometres of railway – railway utilising a different gauge to Europe, meaning German trains could not run on Soviet tracks.

As for industry and raw materials, the Marcks Plan upon which Barbarossa was originally based assumed that the Soviet armed forces could not afford to abandon their supply and production centres in the west, and would therefore have to fight to defend them rather than retreat into the country's cavernous interior. This would provide the *Wehrmacht* with the opportunity to annihilate them in situ. Baumbach's mission poured cold water on this theory:

> In the Kuznetsky basin there are coal deposits estimated at 400 million tons. The giant Stalinsk metal works is the pride of Soviet Siberia, and the black soil steppe region at the foot of the Altai is among the most fertile on earth, and barely inferior to the Ukraine ... There are few areas of the world in which such abundant resources of raw materials offer such prospects for the establishment and growth of important industries ... it is small wonder that the foundations of Russian heavy industry extend from the Urals to the Kuznetsky basin.[10]

Baumbach also recorded in his diary that "it is quite impossible to find out the size of the Russian army. If there are any tactical or strategic analyses of air force formations, they are out of date." His frustration at his own high command's refusal to face the military reality was palpable: "Sober reports (from the German Military and Air Attachés in Moscow) go into waste-paper baskets or are watered down before they reach Berlin." His conclusion was forbidding and unequivocal: "Russia cannot be conquered on land."

Twenty-six-year-old Anton Böhrer was not as well-travelled as Baumbach, in fact he was a simple gardener in his hometown of

Höpfingen until the Army came calling. Now, he was a senior NCO in the artillery regiment of Otto Gabcke's *294. Infanterie-Division*, and his view of the wisdom of invading Russia mirrored that of the *Luftwaffe* officer, as he wrote to his father on 11 June: "I am firmly convinced that nothing will happen in Russia … we cannot afford to go against such a huge country, whose soldiers, however, are not as good as we Germans … The country is so big that it would be as easy for us to get lost in it as it was for Napoleon."[11] Böhrer wasn't the only German to pause and remember Napoleon's 1812 disaster, *Leutnant* Axel von dem Bussche-Streithorst of *23. Infanterie-Division* mused on the same: "Funny, almost exactly 129 years ago, the Emperor Napoleon, supported by the Prussian corps under General Ludwig Yorck, started the great Russian campaign. We all know what happened to them – will we do better?"

Von dem Bussche-Streithorst, Böhrer and Baumbach – among many others – may have harboured doubts about an invasion, but they were probably in a minority. Hans von Greiffenberg was a vastly experienced general staff officer who had completed secondments with several foreign armies before studying at Fort Leavenworth in the US before the war. In early 1941 he was the Chief of Staff-designate for *Heeresgruppe Mitte*, and responsible for planning the proposed thrust towards Moscow via Smolensk. "We were following Napoleon's invasion route, but we didn't think that the lessons of the 1812 campaign applied to us in 1941. We were fighting with modern means of transport and communications – we thought that the vastness of Russia could be overcome by rail and motor-engine, telegraph wire and radio. We believed in the power of our battle-seasoned Army and its well honed coordination with the *Luftwaffe*. Above all, we had absolute faith in the infallibility of blitzkrieg." The preparations went on.

Richard von Rosen and his fellow panzer crewmen were driving ever further east when signalled off the road and into a forest near the Russo-German border. "Our readiness areas were precisely laid out, the endless great forests turned into one giant troop depot. Division after division lay here, completely camouflaged against air reconnaissance … on 16 June we loaded live ammunition, which took us all day. For each panzer we had to load aboard about 4,000 machine-gun rounds … also around seventy high-explosive and sixty armour-piercing shells … that same day we were immunized against cholera." Rosen and some of his comrades received some very basic instruction in Russian – which they took little notice of and quickly forgot. If they were then in any doubt as to what was about to happen, it was dispelled two days later when they were briefed that they would be the spearhead company of the regiment, with their initial objective being the town of Kobryn, some 60 kilometres across the border to the east. Final preparations were then made: "The day before the invasion we received our special rations ... three tins of rice or vegetables, five small sacks of bread, three boxes of Shoka-Kola ... this was in addition to our iron rations – none of it could be touched unless ordered."

Rosen now knew exactly what was about to happen, as did his fellow tanker Hans von Luck, whose unit had also been briefed:

> We were in a strange frame of mind ... the huge distances were beyond our mental grasp. The Ural mountains were nearly 2,000 miles away and they were merely the end of European Russia – beyond them lay the endless expanse of Siberia ... we weren't really afraid, but neither were we sure what our attitude should be towards an enemy whose strength and potential were unknown to us, and whose mentality was completely alien ... even the youngsters who'd grown up in the Hitler Youth fell silent – they doubted Russia could be defeated with idealism alone ... despite all our doubts and questions, we did what soldiers have done in every age; we set our minds on the present and prepared to do our duty.

Hubert Becker, an artillery *leutnant* on the northern section of the soon-to-be front, was in much the same frame of mind as Luck: "We didn't understand the Russian campaign from the beginning – nobody did. But it was an order, and orders must be followed to the best of your ability as a soldier. I am an instrument of the State and I must do my duty."[12]

The reticence Becker and Luck described was shared by many, and not just members of the Army. Surprisingly, even members of that most ideologically committed of all the Third Reich's armed forces, the *Waffen-SS*, felt a sense of disquiet at the enormity of Barbarossa, and what it could and would mean for them. An artillery officer in the *SS-Division Reich* remembered when he and his brethren were told of the impending operation:

> All unit commanders were called to a conference at Gmunden am Traunsee to be briefed on the upcoming war against Soviet Russia. There were no enthusiastic Sieg Heils for there weren't any of us who weren't concerned at the size of the landmass in which we were soon to operate. The rank and file weren't told what was going on, so when we moved east in June the wildest rumours began, including one about moving through Russia to attack the British in India. We unloaded in Lublin, passed through vast Polish forests until we arrived at last at the River Bug, where we bivouacked but weren't allowed to light fires ... *Untersturmführer* Kindl and a few men from battery headquarters moved into deserted farmers huts on the riverbank to carry out

observation of the eastern bank ... the battery survey troop began to
mark out gun positions and target maps were distributed.[13]

Not everyone was in the know at that point, however. Sigmund Heinz
Landau was a teenaged Transylvanian ethnic German – a *volksdeutsche* –
who had left his home town to enlist as a volunteer auxiliary in a
Luftwaffe anti-aircraft battery defending Romania's oil refineries.
Establishing himself as a valued and hard-working member of the team,
he was called into his commander's office in the second week of June.

"Landau, we're leaving the country any day now for an unspecified
destination. I can only tell you there will be fighting. You can leave us or
come along, the choice is yours."

"I'll come along sir."

"That's what I thought. Don't tell your parents or anyone else, now
back to your battery."

In two days he was on a train heading northeast, "with our guns
camouflaged". Landau would soon cross the Soviet border and begin
almost four years of brutal fighting.[14]

Saturday, 21 June 1941, was a gloriously warm and sunny day in
Berlin. Couples took advantage of the weather to stroll arm in arm in the
Tiergarten, and the cafés down the Ku'damm and Unter den Linden were
doing a roaring trade at their pavement tables. After what had seemed a
never-ending winter, people were glad that a long, hot summer seemed in
store.

At the last high-level command conference before the invasion, Franz
Halder noted sourly that despite the concentration of almost three-
quarters of all the *Wehrmacht*'s artillery in the east, the latest intelligence
estimates suggested the Soviets would still outnumber the German guns
in the frontier regions by several thousand. As a final piece of operational
security, mail censorship was officially increased to a full lockdown;.
"Embargo on feldpost letters from B+1 to B+5."

Following the conference, the *OKW* issued the codeword 'Dortmund'
to its three army group headquarters. They, in turn, then sent the assault
armies the signals 'Dortmund, Mohn, Kresse, Aster, Aster'. Dortmund
was the key – it confirmed H-hr as 03.15am, Sunday 22 June. If there
was any delay the *OKW* would issue the counter codeword 'Altona' – no
one expected that to happen. *OKW*'s war diary noted, "Thus, the start of
the attack is once and for all ordered for 22 June."

While Berlin was pleasantly warm that Saturday, out on the Russo-
German border it was stiflingly hot. Winter in Russia had gone on longer
than usual, and it had snowed just the week before in Moscow, but now
the more usual weather patterns had asserted themselves and the heat was
oppressive. Up and down the border well over three and a half million

Axis soldiers lay almost comatose in forests, encampments and deserted villages. After the war, veterans recalled how the forests stank of sweat, diesel fumes and horses' urine, and how soldiers' shelters seemingly took up every foot of space for mile after mile. It was a midsummer's day and there would only be a handful of hours of darkness; in Leningrad, famous for its' 'white nights' as they were called, it wouldn't get dark at all. The troops sat on their equipment, trying to doze, eating without any real appetite, and writing last letters home that would have to wait to be posted until after the embargo.

In a last flurry of activity those men who still didn't know what was going to happen were briefed. Johannes Kaufmann remembered being told the news: "The afternoon of 21 June 1941 finally brought an end to the speculation. All flying personnel were assembled for a short address by *Geschwaderkommodore Major* Storp, he revealed to us that hostilities against the Soviet Union could be expected to begin at any moment." Kaufmann's fellow flyer, Heinz Knoke of *JG. 52*, was also told. "21 June 1941 … We are now based at Suwalki (renamed Sudauen by the Germans in 1939), a former Polish Air Force station near the Russian border … in the evening orders come through that the airliner on the scheduled Berlin-Moscow run is to be shot down … 22 June 1941; general alert for all squadrons."[15]

Reactions to the announcement varied. On being told, Franz Siebeler, a former bank apprentice and now artillery gunner in *14. Panzerdivision*, wrote home to his parents with a mixture of relief and righteous determination:

> Tomorrow morning the dance will start here. Who would have thought that! But it is something that must be done, and long-term friendship with the Russian would not have been possible. They would have waited for the opportunity to attack us … I don't want to wage war against anyone, but these murderers and deniers of God must get their punishment. Let's hope that everything goes well. The enemy will probably be ready in large numbers, but that shouldn't be an obstacle for us. It won't be as easy as it was in Yugoslavia, but the Reds must be conquered … Include me in your prayers. Warmest greetings to all, especially the Warms family.[16]

Unteroffizier Wilhelm Prüller remembered the reaction upon being told of the impending invasion:

> Some of us simply gaped with astonishment, some took it with equanimity, some were horrified … Personally I think it's a good thing that we face the fight squarely and save our children from having to do it … in the long run it would have proved impossible for two such giant nations, living right next to each other and with completely different

ways of life, to exist side by side in peace and understanding. The fight between Communism, which is rotting so many peoples, and National Socialism was bound to come. And if we can win now, it's better than doing it later. And the *Führer* will know what he's doing. Above all, I'm sure it will end well.

Prüller was very far from being alone in believing a German victory was inevitable. One of his fellow NCOs – Eberhard Krehl – was an orderly on a senior artillery staff and recalled the hubris of the officers all around him: "Shortly before daybreak on 22 June 1941, *Oberleutnant* Wieland turned up in our quarters with the words: 'It's all kicking off against Russia. I've just come from a meeting with the generals of the panzer units. One declared, 'In five weeks I'll be in Moscow,' then the next: 'I'll be there in four at the latest,' then the last retorted: 'I'll make it in three.' So, it's going to go very quickly."

Writing in his diary, a young mountain trooper – a *gebirgsjäger* – could barely contain his joy: "Early tomorrow morning we're off against our mortal enemy bolshevism, thanks be to God. For me, a real stone has fallen from my heart. Finally this uncertainty is over, and you know where you are. I'm very optimistic ... and I believe that if we can take all the land and raw materials up to the Urals, then Europe will be able to feed itself and the war at sea can last as long as it likes."[17] One of the young *jäger*'s junior officers expressed much the same view: "It came as quite a surprise, but after the *Führer*'s explanation it's all become clear. Naturally, the question of food is important. With Russia we will be able to feed ourselves."

For many of the waiting men, the excitement was palpable. One such was Heinrich Haape, an *Assistenarzt* (junior doctor) with the veteran *6. Infanterie-Division*. "It all starts in a few hours! Our regiment is positioned right at the very front. The enemy's resistance must be broken, despite bunkers, hordes of men, and any amount of devilry. It is a war for Germany's greatness and future."

Oskar Scheja was not as confident as his erstwhile comrade: "I was in *5. Kompanie, II Bataillon, Regiment 525, 298. Infanterie-Division*. We had been camped on the River Bug in the town of Hrubieszow for the past few weeks ... That morning I was jarred awake by movement in our tent. The men were saying that our CO had summoned us to meet in a clearing ... it was very quiet for such a large group, partly out of fatigue, but mostly in anticipation of what we expected to hear ... The CO walked into the middle and announced that the time had come to move east into Russia. I had waited anxiously for this – we all had – but hearing the actual words gave me pause."

For many, the news spurred a last act of faith before the guns signalled the beginning of the most momentous campaign in the Third Reich's short and violent history, as the medic and Catholic priest Bernard Häring recalled; "The evening before the war with Russia began, we were all quite aware of its imminence. I was called by the official chaplain of the Division and asked if I would hear soldiers' confessions in one of the nearby churches. A great many soldiers made their confessions that evening."

For others, the news was doom-laden. *Hauptmann* Ekkehard Maurer was serving in the Prussian 23. *Infanterie-Division* at the time: "My battalion commander (*Major* Werner Heinemann) and I – I was his adjutant – were in our foxholes, and just before the artillery barrage began he whispered to me, 'Don't ever forget 22 June 1941 at 0315am.' Then he paused, 'well, I don't think I have to tell you not to because you won't forget it anyway, but at this moment, the worst disaster for Germany in many centuries is about to begin.'" Maurer would go on to win the German Cross in Gold for bravery and survive the war. His commander would do neither.[18]

The young infantry officer Hans Jochen Schmidt noted in his diary that night: "Each of us received sixty rounds of live ammunition. From that point forward our rifles stayed loaded. There could be no thought of sleep. But we had a radio, which unfortunately quit on us much too early. No-one suspected anything yet in the Reich and they were enthusiastically playing dance music, which we let trickle comfortingly over our souls ... At midnight the *Führer*'s proclamation was read out to us, and the tension became almost unbearable."

Wilhelm Lübbecke shuddered as he remembered being told of the offensive. "One night in the woods, we were told that 'tomorrow morning at 3am you are going to attack Russia.'" Now they all knew the truth of what was going to happen in a few short hours. The largest invasion force ever assembled stood ready.

One of them, *Gefreiter* Alfred Liskow, a *pionier* in Ernst-Eberhard Hell's 15. *Infanterie-Division*, made a momentous decision on being told the news – he would desert and warn the Soviets. Ghosting his way through the picket lines, he reached the River Prut, slipped into the water, and swam across to the eastern bank. There, he cautiously began to look for the Soviet troops he knew were around. He found a sentry and gave himself up. Taken for interrogation, he told his story. The information was passed up the line, and in the meantime Liskow was held under armed guard. Separately, and several hundred miles to the north near Kovel, another German soldier, Wilhelm Korpik, was doing the same as Liskow. He too deserted and went across the lines to warn the Soviets. In civilian life, the thirty-year-old Liskow had been a joiner in a Bavarian furniture factory, while Korpik had worked as a labourer in his native Berlin; both had communist sympathies and wanted Hitler stopped.

Paralysed with indecision and fear of retribution, local Red Army commanders waited for orders as to what to do with these two Cassandras. Maksim Purkayev, Chief of Staff of the Kiev Special Military District, telephoned his old boss – Georgy Zhukov, now the Red Army's Chief of the General Staff – and told him of Liskow's warning. Korpik's confirmatory information may have been discussed too, it isn't known. Zhukov subsequently met with Stalin in his Kremlin office at 2050hrs Moscow time, and discussed the deserter's information. Orders went out from the Kremlin to place Moscow's air defences on standby, and all western frontier districts were put on alert, but instructed very clearly that they were not to fire back even if fired upon. As for both Korpik and Liskow, they simply disappeared, almost certainly shot on the dictator's orders for spreading disinformation. As the clock ticked towards midnight, Stalin left the Kremlin and went to his country dacha just outside Moscow. Once there, he went to bed.

Back on the German side of the border, the *SS-Reich* – including its artillery – began to move forward. As the clock ticked down to H-hour, Heinz Guderian moved forward too. "At 0210hrs on 22 June 1941 I went to my command post located in an observation tower south of Bohukaly, 9 miles northwest of Brest-Litovsk. It was still dark when I arrived there at 0310hrs."[19]

Gefreiter Hubert Hegele of *1. Gebirgs-Division* waited impatiently for H-hour:

> Good Lord, the minutes pass by so begrudgingly today. Not a sound is to be heard. Only when you really prick up your ears can you detect some gentle whispering. We are just twenty metres from the border fence ... The Russian sentries standing on their observation platform haven't a clue. It's just two men, but they'll be the first to go down. 0306 hours. If I could only smoke a cigarette." With nothing to do but watch the minutes tick by, the young mountaineer became quite poetic. "The sky is now cloudless, and the stars are shining down on us insignificant souls with their cheerful splendour, but the silver grey of the morning intrudes ever more strongly in their twinkling magnificence. You cannot grasp hold of sober thoughts in these final minutes – but you hardly need to. I say a little prayer and ask the good Lord to stand by my side. 0310 hours. Still five minutes. The faces of my comrades look like grey masks. Their gaze is fixed straight ahead. The pounding in our chests grows louder and louder.

Heinrich Haape was with his battalion commander, Peter Neuhoff, as the final minutes ticked by. Having only recently finished his military training, Haape was almost hopping with excitement at the prospect of action: "Five minutes to zero hour! I am standing on the crest of a small hill on the south eastern border of East Prussia, the wide plains of Lithuania stretching ahead of us ... I know that a million other Germans are looking at their watches at the same time ... Three tremendous army groups and the *Luftwaffe* are poised for the mighty onslaught."

Helmut Pabst, a former law student and now a signaller attached to an artillery unit, was just as taken with the scene as his fellow invader. "The units moved up to their positions quietly, talking in whispers. There was a creaking of wheels – assault guns ... we were waiting for the infantry. They came up in dark, ghostly columns and moved forward through the cabbage plots and cornfields."[20]

The Prussian aristocrat and landowner Manfred von Plotho was with his beloved *71. Infanterie-Division* and dashed off a hurried note to his wife in the last few minutes of peace:

> The world is holding its breath ... Greater Germany is leading a free and independent Europe. These are really exciting hours that we're going through. In 1940 on June 22 at 7 o'clock in the morning there was an armistice (author: following the victory over France) ... Exactly a year later, almost to the hour, we will be the first to cross the border. This time there is no Maginot Line ahead of us, victorious campaigns under the most difficult conditions have strengthened the self-confidence of the troops so much that even the vastness of the East cannot shake them ... Perhaps history will one day say that the *Führer* was Machiavelli's greatest student, in a good sense.

Hans-Joachim *Hajo* Herrmann – a *Luftwaffe* pilot – was hundreds of miles away on a staff assignment in France that fateful night and was quite sanguine at the prospect of the invasion: "I was on duty during the night of 21/22 June 1941. The duty signals operator passed me a teleprinter message. It read 'War with Russia with effect from 0300hrs.' That, I thought, was all we needed."[21]

Amidst the woods on the frontier, as the sky began to lighten, extra rations were handed out. *Obergefreiter* Alfred Opitz in *18. Panzerdivision* remembered that "chocolate and cigarettes were distributed to troops, some of whom were fortunate enough to receive an allotment of Schnapps, one bottle for every four men". *Feldwebel* Fritz Ebert was another beneficiary. "Extra comforts issued, thirty cigarettes per head and a bottle of brandy for every four men."

Less than a mile away, Soviet border guards reported to their superiors that the barbed wire on the German side had suddenly disappeared – there was now nothing between them and their erstwhile allies.

4

Invasion Day

> The night before the war broke out, large numbers of telephone lines were laid to the gun, and in the morning lots of high-ranking officers arrived ... including several generals. We were told our gun would provide the signal to open fire. It was controlled by stopwatch ... when we fired, lots of other guns, both left and right of us, would open fire too, and then the war would start.
>
> Heinrich Eikmeier, gun crew member on the River Bug –
> *Heeresgruppe Mitte*[1]

As Heinrich Eikmeier and the rest of his crew prepared to fire the first shot of the new campaign in its central zone, another gun was being prepared in the same manner to the north, and yet another several hundred kilometres to the south. So big would the new front line be, that the invasion would start at staggered intervals to take account of the different timing of sunrise in each sector. So, *Heeresgruppe Nord* – Army Group North – would begin their campaign at 0305hrs, along with *Heeresgruppe Mitte*'s left wing, while Eikmeier and Bock's right wing would commence firing at 0315hrs. This would also be *Heeresgruppe Süd*'s – Army Group South's – start time. This wasn't a decision that found favour with everyone in German high command. Insisted upon by Leeb, Bock strongly disagreed, greatly concerned about the loss of surprise for the right wing of his army group. He was overruled by the OKH, much to his annoyance: "So, I'm the one who has to suffer and has to attack with my right wing at Rundstedt's time, and with my left wing at Leeb's time."

Eikmeier and his comrades might be firing the first shot, but they weren't the first Germans into the attack that Sunday morning. That distinction would go to two wildly different cohorts of the Barbarossa invasion force. The first would be small groups of Sepp de Giampietro's Brandenburger brethren, who would use the few hours of darkness to infiltrate behind Soviet lines and head for their designated targets: command and control centres, road and rail bridges and so on, there to sow confusion and panic by attacking while the Red Army was groping around in the dark as to what was happening. Alongside de Giampietro was another South Tyrolean special forces trooper, Eduard Steinberger, who explained what made his unit different: "The Brandenburgers originally consisted of mostly non-Reich Germans; Sudeten Germans who spoke Czech, a few Palestinian Germans, and volunteer Ukrainians. There were people from all over who mostly spoke other languages ... we always operated in decoy uniforms. We wore all kinds – Russian ones for example – over our *Wehrmacht* uniforms. We had to be able to swiftly get rid of our cover uniforms."[2]

While de Giampietro, Steinberger and their fellow Brandenburgers would use their covert tactics to cause chaos, they would be joined in the attack by a much more conventional force, the *Luftwaffe*, specifically the first wave of bombers, fighters and ground-attack aircraft selected to attempt the impossible – to destroy in a single day the greater part of the largest air force in the world before it even took off.

Much has been written about the *Luftwaffe* delivering day-one knock-out blows to enemy air forces in the run-up campaigns to Barbarossa, but they had been far from universally successful. The *Luftwaffe*'s maiden attempt, back in September 1939, had been a wash-out, with not a single aircraft of Poland's 800-strong *Lotnictwo Wojskowe* – Polish Air Force – caught on the ground, as the German first strike punched at thin air. Lessons were learned, and the 1940 western operation had gone better, with the *Aéronautique Militaire Belge* (AéMI) – Belgian Air Force – and Dutch *Militaire Luchtvaartafdeling* (ML) suffering heavy casualties; in fact, the Dutch lost almost half their aircraft on the first day of combat. More was to follow, with the *Luftwaffe*'s best performance yet against the Yugoslav *Vazduhoplovstvo Vojske Kraljevine Jugoslavije* (VVKJ) in spring 1941. But these were all minnows. The Dutch could muster just 155 aircraft, the Yugoslavs only 400, and while the Belgians had twenty fewer than that, and only a third of them fit to fly when they were attacked.

Targeting was easier in the West too, with the Germans able to focus on a handful of airfields at any one time; this would not be the case for Barbarossa. The *Luftwaffe* would have to simultaneously hit dozens of airfields across the whole length of front, against a force that outnumbered it by over three to one. To increase the challenge, the Army was adamant that H-hour must be at dawn to give them as much night cover as possible, but with the VVS's forward bases some thirty to forty minutes' flying time away from their German counterparts, how would the *Luftwaffe* achieve the surprise it desperately needed? As Albert Kesselring – *Luftwaffe* commander for *Heeresgruppe Mitte* – said, "It will be a whole hour before we are over the enemy's airfields, and by then the birds will have flown." Bock retorted, "The enemy will be put on his guard the moment your aircraft are heard crossing the frontier. From then on the whole element of surprise will be lost."

Hans Jeschonnek, the youthful Chief of Staff in *Luftwaffe* High Command (*Oberkommando der Luftwaffe*, or OKL), thought he had the answer. At the suggestion of his subordinate – *II. Fliegerkorps*'s lazy and dissolute commander Bruno Loerzer – Jeschonnek would commit some of his most experienced men to take off and enter Soviet airspace *before* H-hour, so they would arrive over their targets just as the Army was launching its attack. The risks were huge. Get it right, and the assault squadrons could wreak havoc among the VVS – get it wrong, and many of the *Luftwaffe*'s finest could be destroyed in enemy air space before a shot had been fired on the ground.

To help accomplish Jeschonnek's plan, a select number of bomber crews from *KG*s (*Kampfgeschwader* – Bomber Wing) 2, 3 and 53 – those with the highest number of night-flying hours – were picked out as pathfinders. Their instructions were to lead their comrades to high altitude as quickly as possible after take-off to minimise their engine noise on the ground. They would then fly to the sixty-six airfields designated as their primary objectives, rapidly descend to attack height and commence their bombing runs. Each airfield would be attacked by a mixed force of bombers, fighters and ground-attack aircraft, although only three bombers could be assigned to each flight due to an overall lack of numbers. *Oberfeldwebel* Josef Kronschnabel was a fighter pilot with Wolf-Dietrich Wilcke's *JG. 53* based alongside Heinz Knoke at the much-expanded Suwalki air base: "On the evening of 21 June, *Hauptmann* Wilcke called the pilots of *III Gruppe* together and explained to us that the *Führer* had ordered war against Russia to forestall an attack by the Russians on us ... Wilcke showed us photos of Russian aircraft types and told us the approximate numbers of them available. At the same time, he showed us an aerial photograph of a Russian airfield that we were to attack at low-level the next morning."[3]

With darkness that night barely lasting a few hours, hardly anyone – pilots, flight crews or ground staff – managed any sleep before they began preparations for take-off. It was still warm, the air humid, as the crews donned their bulky flight gear, and the *black men* – as the ground staff were called – finished last minute checks on aircraft and manoeuvred them out from under their camouflage netting and away from their splinter bays. Men coughed in the gloom, though with so much high-octane aviation fuel around no one dared light a cigarette. Johannes Kaufmann was readying himself some 190 miles to the south of Suwalki at Radzyn air base:

> None of us got a lot of sleep, there was too much uncertainty in the air to allow us to relax ... At about midnight we all re-assembled in a clearing close to the accommodation area. We were given yet another 'prior warning' of imminent action and started to get our things together for the mission. Flying gear and equipment were laid out ready. Emergency rations were issued. We still hadn't been told our intended target or targets; all we were given was large-scale maps covering the entire central sector of the front.[4]

Helmut Mahlke was readying his Stuka crews for action at Dubovo-South: "While the ground crews were out on the field in blackness, working by the light of shaded torches to get the aircraft ready, the pilots pored over maps and aerial photographs, each imprinting his own particular target firmly in his mind. We were scheduled to cross the border and carry out our attacks at first light." Already a veteran of the fighting in France, the Battle of Britain and the Mediterranean campaigns – and flying himself in that first wave – Mahlke found time to reflect on what was about to happen. "It was a peculiar sensation; another new and unknown theatre of war, another new and unknown enemy. Once again, we would have to get used to an opponent, his methods of fighting and the strength of his defences. There shouldn't be any particularly nasty shocks in store if the information we had been given was correct ... but we were always on the alert for surprises."

Mahlke was looking forward to the challenges of the new campaign. Having helped wreak havoc in the conquest of France, he had seen his beloved Stukas shot out of the sky over England, and was now hoping for happier times in the East. Fairly short in stature – like so many of his fellow pilots – he'd been shot down over Dunkirk the previous summer and now he walked, somewhat stiff-legged, towards his waiting aircraft. Climbing aboard and settling himself into his cramped seat, he ran through his pre-flight checks, touched his lucky charm and switched on his engine. "Exhaust flames began to flicker and splutter in the dispersal points around the edge of the field. The noise of engines shattered the stillness of the night. Red, green and white navigation lights emerged slowly from the camouflaged dispersals and seemed to be wandering around almost haphazardly in the pitch darkness as the pilots taxied out and formed into their respective *Ketten* (a 'chain' of three aircraft that flew together)." Then, finally, they were off. "At exactly 0203hrs on 22 June 1941 the three machines of my *Stabskette* (staff/leadership flight) lifted from the ground as one. We left a thick cloud of dust in our wake, which must have reduced visibility for those behind us to almost nil. Despite this, their lights could be seen emerging from the clouds at short, regular intervals as each Kette took off hard on the heels of the last. Like trios of tiny glow-worms they scurried across the unseen woods and fields below as they quickly closed up on us."[5]

Hundreds of aircraft were soon in the skies, climbing higher and higher as they headed east to their targets.

Like Helmut Mahlke, Günther Scholz and his *staffel* (squadron) were flying in the northern sector of the new front: "On 22 June 1941 at 0300hrs in the early morning we undertook our first mission over the Soviet border; our target was the airbases near Kovno. I will never forget flying over the border. As far as you could see … in the emerging dawn, to the north and south, white and red Very lights were climbing into the sky, as we fliers in the air crossed the border."[6]

In the dim light of cockpit and navigator lamps, maps were checked and re-checked, and eyes strained nervously for any sign of fighter or anti-aircraft activity from their new enemy – there was none. The crews peered through the gloom, searching for their targets, and then, suddenly, there they were below them. For most of the *Luftwaffe* strike force the sight that met their eyes was a total shock. The commander of *I./Jagdgeschwader 3*, *Hauptmann* Hans *Assi* von Hahn – attacking airfields near L'viv in western Ukraine – remembered it vividly: "We could hardly believe our eyes. Every airfield was chock full of row after row of reconnaissance aircraft, bombers and fighters, all lined up as if on parade. The number of landing strips and aircraft the Russians had concentrated along our borders was staggering." Günther Scholz saw the same to the north: "The aircraft weren't camouflaged but parked close to each other in neat rows. The Soviets seemed to be expecting an attack as all the airfields close to the border were full of bombers and fighters … Perhaps they hadn't expected to be attacked quite yet." Not quite believing their luck, Scholz and his men wreaked havoc. "We destroyed the majority of them with bombs and low-level strafing."[7]

In the central sector, Arnold Döring was a navigator in a Heinkel He 111 medium-bomber. Crossing the River Bug, he and his crew started their run. Then it was bombs gone, the aircraft immediately lifting as their 5,500lb payload smashed into a Soviet airfield. "Smoke clouds, flames, fountains of earth, mixed with all sorts of rubble shoot into the air … our bombers miss the ammunition bunkers on the right. But the lines of bombs continue the length of the airfield and tear up the runway. We'd scored two hits on the runway. No fighters would be able to take off from there for a long time."[8]

Surprise was total. Josef Kronschnabel – just like Günther Scholz – could scarcely believe his luck: "Close to dawn on 22 June 1941 our *staffel* took off – the front was already marked by fires. We attacked the Russian airbase with our guns – there was no reaction from enemy flak. During the flight we also saw no sign of any enemy aircraft in the air."

Down on the ground all was chaos. Ivan Konovalov, a Soviet fighter pilot, witnessed the unfolding disaster: "All of a sudden there was an incredible roaring sound. Enemy planes were overhead. Someone yelled 'Take cover!' and I dived under the wing of my plane. Everything was burning, a terrible, raging fire. At the end of it all only one of our planes was left intact." His compatriot, Vitaly Klimenko of the 10th Fighter Regiment based at Shaulai in Lithuania, was in his tent when the attack came in: "I flipped open my tent and saw planes with German crosses firing their machine-guns at us 'Guys the war has started!' – 'Fuck you, what war?' – 'It's a German air raid!' We jumped out of our tent, some of our neighbours had already been killed or wounded."

Particularly effective against the VVS aircrews and their machines were the *SD 2* and *SD 10* sub-munitions (*Sprengbombe Dickwandig)* fitted to some twenty to thirty German bombers. Nicknamed 'Devil's Eggs' and carried in racks under the aircraft's belly, these bomblets were released en masse over the target and allowed to spiral down to the ground whereupon they exploded, with hundreds of fragments causing mayhem out to fifty metres or more. Using them was a dangerous job though. Problems with the release mechanism meant that some of the bomber crews believed they'd dropped all their payload when in fact one or more were still stuck in the racks. Turning for home, the fuses were disturbed and the resulting blasts tore several of the bombers to pieces. As many as fifteen German aircraft were thought to have fallen victim to problems with the *SD 2* in particular, and Kesselring subsequently banned their use within his command until the problems were rectified.

The *Luftwaffe* wasn't just making its presence felt on the ground either. Obsessed with the cult of the air ace – the *Experten* as they were known – German pilots were already determined to claim kills in the air and reap the rewards in medals and promotions that came with them.

It is a matter of some debate as to which German pilot scored the first kill of Barbarossa – not that it really matters. Robert Olejnik is often credited with it. As the *Staffel* commander of *I/JG. 3 Udet*, he recalled: "Everybody knew I was an early riser and liked to fly the dawn missions. So, shortly before 0330hrs, I took off with my wingman to recce the Russian airfields along our stretch of the border. Everything seemed quiet in the semi-darkness below. It was not until we were returning to base and flying back over the first airfield we'd visited some twenty minutes earlier, that I spotted signs of activity. Two Russian fighters were preparing to scramble. As we circled 7-800 metres (2,300-2,600 feet) overhead, I saw the Russians start their engines and begin to taxi out. They took off immediately and climbed towards us, obviously looking for a fight. They were still some 300-400 metres below us when we dived to the attack. I caught the leader with a short burst on my first pass and he went down in flames. His wingman disappeared."

A possible rival to Olejnik's 'title' was Josef Kronschnabel's boss, Wolf-Dietrich Wilcke. Wilcke was in many ways the ideal *Experte* of Nazi propaganda; tall and blond haired, the twenty-eight-year-old Prussian was a bit of a clothes horse, even affecting a trademark tailored leather coat, which led to him being nicknamed '*der Fürst*' (the Prince) by his men. A veteran of the Condor Legion and the Battle of Britain, he already had 13 kills to his name when he went up for his first mission of the Barbarossa campaign. He proceeded to shoot down a Soviet fighter, swiftly followed by a further four, making him the first 'Russian Front ace'.

Johannes Kaufmann wasn't involved in the initial wave of attacks: "It wasn't until close on 0600hrs that we finally got our operational orders, were given a briefing, and began to prepare in earnest for our first mission against the Russians ... The operation was to be a maximum-effort raid on the Soviet airfield at Pinsk (in western Belarus), over 150km inside enemy territory." Having waited through the night, Kaufmann was surprised at the lack of detail he and his fellow crews were given: "When the briefing eventually came it was a very hurried and sketchy affair ... we weren't assigned specific objectives, we were simply told to find a suitable target ourselves, which wasn't a great deal of help under the circumstances." The situation didn't get any better once Kaufmann got into the air: "Having crossed the front lines we were nervously searching the sky around us as we fully expected to be engaged by Soviet flak and fighters at any moment. We hadn't been given any information as to the location and disposition of enemy forces in the area." The lack of detail caused chaos over the target zone. "Theory quickly turned into confusion the moment we arrived over Pinsk. Pilots immediately began to jostle for position and get in each other's way as we sought suitable targets on the airfield below." Eventually, some sort of order took hold, and the attack became a massacre. "After releasing our bombs we flattened out and circled the field at low-level before making several high-speed strafing runs along the lines of enemy aircraft standing unprotected around its perimeter. As there were no pens or blast walls between the parked machines, we were able to attack at a very shallow angle ... we could line up individual aircraft in our sights, hold them steady, and then let fly with a devastating barrage from our 20mm nose cannon and machine-guns."

On returning to base, Kaufmann was "both relieved and excited that I had my first operational mission as a Bf110 pilot safely behind me".

Like all the other pilots who'd made it back, he then followed protocol and reported what he'd hit: "Comparing notes with other pilots, we were fairly sure that the enemy aircraft based at Pinsk – the majority being twin-engine types – had been almost completely destroyed. We couldn't be certain of the exact numbers though ... the reports and claims of the various crews involved differed widely."

The same was true across all the *Luftwaffe* attack groups. When the claims were collated by higher headquarters, they amounted to a staggering 1,489 Soviet aircraft reportedly destroyed on the ground. No one could believe that number, it was utterly preposterous. When Goering was told, he flatly refused to accept it and ordered an immediate investigation – he was well aware that his pilots were notorious for over-claiming. Reconnaissance planes were sent over the target airfields to take photos, and *Luftwaffe* officials were dispatched to accompany the advancing spearheads as they overran them so that accurate reports could be made. Amazingly, the conclusion was that, if anything, the pilots' claims were an *understatement*.

Ivan Ivanovich Kopets – head of the VVS's Western District – took off to view his airfields and see for himself the casualties his command had suffered on the ground. Profoundly shocked and dismayed by what he saw, he landed back at base, went to his quarters, and shot himself. The Soviets, meanwhile, officially admitted to losing just 864 aircraft on the ground.

Some Soviet fliers did – somehow – manage to get into the air, but were hopelessly outmatched by their *Luftwaffe* opponents, as one German commander on the ground saw for himself: "The troops only saw flights of three or four reconnaissance planes, individual bomber squadrons and maybe a few fighters ... they all quickly became victims of German fighters."[9] Leopold Höglinger, a radio operator with *137. Infanterie-Division*, saw the same. "Squadrons of our planes flew overhead. There was no resistance from the enemy. A few hours later, as our troops began moving forward, some Russian bombers did appear – but they were immediately shot down." Wolfram von Richthofen, *VIII. Fliegerkorps*'s commander and cousin to the famed Red Baron, wrote in his diary: "The Russians that managed to get up in the air flew poorly, and we were able to bring most of them down." Josef Kronschnabel was back in the air after his first operation against a VVS air base: "On our second sortie, still early in the day ... we met several I-16 Ratas (a single-engine Soviet fighter) and there was a dogfight ... a Rata came straight at me, head-on, and fired at me. I could do nothing else except shoot back, after which we flashed past each other. As I turned sharply, I saw that the Rata was diving down, burning, towards the ground."

Kronschnabel wasn't the only pilot with the invasion force making kills that day. A Romanian flyer, Ioan Maga, found himself in a dogfight with several Soviet fighters down in the southern area of operations: "One started to attack me from the front but I opened fire first. Then he pulled his aircraft up, exposing his belly. I continued to fire at him while flying at a height of only 150-200m until he crashed into a cornfield." This was Maga's second victory of the day. He didn't escape unscathed though and was forced to belly land his damaged aircraft before hitching a lift back to his base. Maga's fellow Romanian Ioan Radulescu was sent to raid a Soviet naval base on the Black Sea coast: "Diving towards my target I focused my sights on three seaplanes anchored close to the shoreline. I opened fire from 400 metres and expended 1,400 incendiary and armour-piercing rounds ... I saw one of the seaplanes catch fire, and the other two were hit as well."

The slaughter among the VVS regiments was immense. Biala Polaska airfield – on the German side of the border near the fortress city of Brest-Litovsk – was the base for several squadrons of marauding Stuka dive-bombers. As the Stukas themselves were away blasting Soviet air bases, six VVS fighters appeared over the airfield and prepared to attack, but before they could start their strafing runs a trio of patrolling Bf 109s dived out of nowhere and shot them all down. Then another dozen came in and were shot down too. Then another flight, and another. It was suicide, yet still they kept coming.

Herbert Pabst, a Stuka pilot, had just touched down back at base after flying his first sortie of the day when the airfield came under attack from Soviet bombers. Before the bombers had time to drop their payloads on Pabst and his comrades, a flight of German fighters appeared and attacked: "As the first one fired, thin threads of smoke seemed to join it to the bomber. Turning ponderously to one side the big bird flashed silver, then plunged vertically downwards with its engines screaming. As it crashed a huge sheet of flame shot upwards." The other Soviet bombers were equally unlucky: "The second bomber became a glare of red, exploded as it dived, and only bits came floating down like great autumnal leaves. The third turned over backwards on fire ... A similar fate befell the rest, the last falling in a village and burning for an hour. Six columns of smoke rose from the horizon. All six had been shot down ... They kept on coming all afternoon, from our airfield alone we saw twenty-one crash, and not one got away."[10]

Attack after attack was shot to pieces, but still the Soviets came on. Albert Kesselring was baffled: "(The Soviets) seem to have a wholly different concept of the value of human life." Günther Rall – a young German pilot who would become a legend within the *Luftwaffe* and go on to be acclaimed as the third-highest-scoring air ace of all time – agreed with that sentiment whole-heartedly. Assigned to fly air cover over the Romanian naval port of Constanza on the Black Sea, he witnessed a constant stream of Soviet bombers sent to attack the port and its installations. The Soviets came in threes and fours, and sometimes even alone, to be met by Rall and his comrades. The twenty-three-year-old shot down an incredible eighteen bombers in the first days of the campaign. But still they flew. Hans Strelow – another fighter pilot who would go on to achieve almost legendary status – claimed a bomber as his very first kill:

Suddenly, north of Lake Wygonowski, we saw the dust clouds from exploding bombs, and soon after that, below us, fifteen Russian bombers ... I went straight into a steep spiral downwards but overshot due to excessive speed. To have pulled up and away would have achieved nothing, so I flew a 360-degree turn behind them. Then I shot at a DB-3 [two-engine bomber] from behind at a range of about 80 metres, so that pieces flew off ... suddenly another Messerschmitt shot at my victim and it immediately caught fire. At that, I found myself another machine that I shot at directly from astern ... the left engine caught fire ... the DB-3 rolled to the left and plunged vertically into the forest and burned. That was my first *Abschuss* [score/kill].

Strelow, Rall, and their fellow *jagdflieger* utterly decimated the Soviet bomber fleet. As one VVS pilot put it, "Yes, that was a hard time, but our task was clear. We knew that our Motherland depended on us, and we could endure anything." One *Luftwaffe* officer observed: "Soviet pilots were fatalists, fighting without any hope of success or confidence in their own abilities." On the first day of Barbarossa those words were apt indeed. Alongside the planes caught on the ground, the Soviets lost another 332 shot out of the sky. Almost 2,000 Soviet aircraft – a quarter of the VVS's entire strength in the western Soviet Union – were lost on day one of the invasion. It was a bloodletting like no other in aviation history.

As for the *Luftwaffe*, it lost seventy-eight aircraft destroyed and another eighty-nine damaged, mostly in combat, but by no means all. After his earlier successes, Josef Kronschnabel was hit, not by the Soviets, but by technical failure: "On my third mission that first day I flew a *freie Jagd* (free hunt) sortie with my wingman ... my engine suddenly stopped without any warning. I made a belly landing but didn't know if I was in enemy territory or not; I just heard artillery fire and rifle shots, and so I hid myself in the forest. Soon afterwards a German soldier on a motorbike and sidecar appeared – it was as if a stone had fallen from my heart ... a lorry carrying wounded men took me back to my airfield."[11]

Jeschonnek's gamble had paid off, and more handsomely than anyone could have predicted. In the most successful operation of its kind in the war, the *Luftwaffe* had effectively established air supremacy in a day. Wilhelm Lübbecke described how the simple German soldier saw it: "Then, as dawn broke, a ceaseless droning echoed in the sky above us. Wave after wave of aircraft were appearing; Heinkels, Junkers, Stukas and Messerschmitts, all flying east."

With the VVS decimated, the *Luftwaffe* swiftly shifted its sights onto secondary targets, as Heinz Knoke wrote in his diary; "We are to carry out a low-level attack on one of the Russian headquarters, situated in the woods to the east of Druskieniki ... the *staffel* takes off and goes into action ... four aircraft, including mine, have been equipped with a bomb-release mechanism ... now there is a rack slung under the belly of my good 'Emil' (Bf 109 E – for Emil), carrying one hundred five-pound fragmentation bombs. It will be a pleasure for me to drop them on Ivan's dirty feet." The young *jagdflieger* was enjoying his work:

> Great masses of dirt fountain up into the air ... one of the huts is blazing fiercely, vehicles have been stripped of their camouflage and overturned by the blast. The Ivans come to life at last. The scene below is like an ant-heap as they scurry about in confusion. Stepsons of Stalin flee for cover in the woods in their underwear. Light flak guns fire at us. I set my sights on one of them and open up with machine-guns and both cannon. An Ivan at the gun falls to the ground, still in his underwear.

Knoke's squadron would return twice more to the same headquarters complex over the next few hours, blasting it to ruins. "Every target we spot in the surrounding woodland is thoroughly strafed. I fire at every target I see until my magazines are empty. I place my bombs on the last building still standing ... The camp is totally destroyed."[12]

Like Knoke, Helmut Mahlke's Stuka squadron had been assigned a Soviet headquarters to attack as part of the German plan to disrupt Red Army command and control. "We dived almost vertically ... the bombs went screaming down and did their work in a matter of seconds. Pillars of flame shot up from the ground, multiplying and merging into one great inferno of smoke and fire . The ruins of the staff headquarters disappeared beneath a pall of dust, billowing smoke and leaping flames."

The *Luftwaffe* didn't have it all their own way though. This would be a campaign like no other the cocky young pilots had ever known, and just how different it was going to be was demonstrated on day one. Franz Schiess, a handsome young *leutnant* from the Austrian town of St Pölten, was on the staff flight of Günther von Maltzahn's *JG. 53* when he flew his first combat sortie on Sunday morning. Spotting a lone VVS fighter, he pounced, blasting the I-153 *Chaika* (Seagull) biplane to smithereens. Jubilant, he headed back to base before flying a second sortie that afternoon, claiming a twin-engine Ilyushin DB-3 bomber to take his tally to two victories for the day. Schiess, however, had pause for thought about this new enemy, whose aircraft were so much slower than his, but were far more manoeuvrable and whose pilots seemed willing to risk all in a deadly game of aerial chicken: "They would let us get almost into an aiming position, then they would bring their machines around a full 180 degrees, until both aircraft were firing at each other from head-on." This sort of near-suicidal behaviour was new to the German fliers. No British, French or other Western pilot would think of doing such a thing. However, Schiess's experience was child's play compared to what befell *Major* Wolfgang Schellmann, the dashing and rakish commander of *JG. 27.*

A graduate of the Lipetsk fighter school, Condor Legion veteran and Knight's Cross holder, Schellmann already had twenty-four kills to his credit prior to the invasion. Patrolling over the western Belarus town of Grodno that first day, he had already shot down one Soviet fighter when confronted by Lieutenant Georgi Kuzmin in his outdated I-153 biplane. Schellmann knew the Russian plane was more manoeuvrable than his Bf 109, but he was faster and supremely confident in his own abilities. Turning and twisting to try and get on the *Chaika*'s tail, the thirty-year-old Hessian couldn't believe his own eyes when Kuzmin turned and flew his aircraft directly at Schellmann's. He flung his Bf 109 into a savage dive to try and avoid the Russian, but too late. The impact rocked the German fighter, and Schellmann knew his aircraft had had it. Desperately unbuckling his harness, he reached up and drew back the canopy before standing on his seat and throwing himself out into the void. As soon as he was clear of the wreckage he yanked hard at the ripcord on his parachute, and relief swept through him when he heard the crack as it opened above him. Floating down to earth he saw both his Bf 109 and the *Chaika* spiral headlong into the ground and explode. Of Kuzmin there was no sign. Schellmann's wingman – his *katschmarek* – saw his boss land safely, discard his parachute, wave at him, and then head off west on foot towards the advancing *Wehrmacht* spearheads. He was never seen again.

Schellmann was the first *Luftwaffe* pilot brought down by a deliberate ramming – a tactic the Soviets dubbed *taran* – but he wasn't the only one. Eight other VVS pilots reportedly rammed *Luftwaffe* aircraft on 22 June, including Sub-Lieutenant Dimitri Kokorev who flew his I-16 fighter into a Messerschmitt Bf 110 over Kobrin after his guns jammed, and a Lieutenant Ivanov who flew his I-16 into the tail of an He 111; Kokorev survived, Ivanov did not.[13]

Incredibly, it wasn't just the Soviets who were using potential suicide as a tactic. The Romanian Undersecretary of State at the Ministry of

National Defence for the Airforce and Navy, General Georghe Jienescu, issued a proclamation to the Romanian air contingent involved in Barbarossa on the morning of 22 June: "Airmen! The order of the day is that aircrew who have fired all their ammunition but have not achieved a victory during the combat, are to dive on the enemy aircraft. Young airmen! The country expects great sacrifices from you ... Young airmen, let the trumpets sound, let the forests render their echo, let the skies tremble from the roar of your engines."[14] One young Romanian pilot, Ioan Florea, took Jienescu's exhortations to heart and, after running out of ammunition shooting down two Soviet fighters, proceeded to ram another with his Polish-made PZL P.11 fighter, before bailing out and safely parachuting down to tell the tale.[15]

Back on the ground, it was now the Army's turn to join in. In his observation tower south of Bohukaly, Heinz Guderian waited for Heinrich Eikmeier's stop-watch controlled gun to fire and officially begin Barbarossa in its central sector. "At 0315hrs our artillery opened up. At 0340hrs the first dive-bomber attack went in."

The irascible Prussian general's rather deadpan description of the invasion's opening bombardment wasn't echoed by others who watched it. Fritz Hübner was a junior NCO on the invasion start line and marvelled at the bombardment: "It roared and thundered as if the world was going under." Erich Hager, a radio operator in 17. *Panzerdivision*, thought much the same. "Our artillery fire begins. A mighty display of firepower. We are standing ready for attack." Helmut Pabst remembered: "The first salvo! At the same moment everything sprang to life. Firing along the whole front – infantry guns, mortars. The Russian watch towers vanished in a flash. Shells crashed down on all the enemy batteries ... in file and in line the infantry swarmed forward." Heinz Döll, a panzer crewman like Hager, watched in awe: "Somewhat restively I followed the minute and second hands of my watch until the firing order came. At 0315 a lightning bolt of gigantic dimensions tore through the night. Thousands of artillery pieces shattered the silence. I will never forget those seconds. But just what they signified for the world, for Germany — that was beyond comprehension."[16]

The artillery barrage that Eikmeier's first shot presaged was the heaviest of the war so far. A gunnery officer in *SS-Reich* remembered that "at 0315am German time, thousands of guns opened up a mighty barrage. Our battery commander and his headquarters group crossed the river with the infantry and set up the first OP (Observation Post) on the far bank. Resistance was weak. It was clear the attack had caught the enemy by surprise ... a good beginning, but as we advanced we saw why the Russian defences didn't need to be strong on this sector – before us lay a huge marsh."[17] Gerhard Frey was in the same central sector as Guderian and the nameless SS officer: "Punctually, at 0315hrs, the first shot ripped through the stillness, and all hell broke loose! It was a barrage unlike anything we had heard before. Left and right of us flashed the muzzles of countless cannon, and soon the flickering flames of the first fires on the other side of the Bug became apparent."

The 299. *Infanterie-Division*'s Hans Roth was somewhat taken aback by the ferocity of the barrage: "All of a sudden, at exactly 0315hrs, and apparently out of the blue, an opening salvo emerges from the barrels of hundreds of guns of all calibres. The howling and staccato of Stalin's arsenal fills the air as if Armageddon had begun. It is impossible to comprehend one's world in such an inferno." Heinrich Haape found himself caught up in the spectacle:

> We wait, faces rigid, our pulses racing. The whole world seems to be waiting ... A mighty clap of thunder as thousands of guns roar forth at one stroke. Their flashes turn dawn into daylight. In a split second ... Hell is let loose and history is made. Guns of every calibre fire point-blank at the Russian lines. With a heavy, droning hum, mortar shells arc over our heads toward the enemy. Machine-guns and automatics rattle out their urgent salvoes. The Russians return the fire. We hear the whine as heavy shells rend the night above us. But the German fire intensifies into an overwhelming crescendo as our forward assault troops and infantry battalions pour into the enemy's frontier defences. And the panzers, we know, are crushing their way forward, spitting fire. The East is aflame.

Haape's battalion commander – *Major* Peter Neuhoff – seemed to struggle to comprehend what he was seeing, as he whispered almost to himself, "Now we are at war with Russia. We're at war with Russia."

The Brandenburger, Sepp de Giampietro, was to the north of Haape and Neuhoff in what was now *Heeresgruppe Nord*'s sector. "We checked our weapons and ammunition, one last warm meal was being dished out – I'll never know how our cooks found us with it being pitch dark. We ate it without really tasting it, our throats were so tight, every bite seemed to get stuck halfway down – we could literally hear our hearts beating ... then came the order '*Fertigmachen*' ('make ready') ... then all of a sudden fire erupted everywhere ... within an instant the forest had come alive ... the wood was filled with the rumble of engines, gunfire and explosions. The clock read 0305hrs."[18]

In the northern sector the bombardment was purposefully short as relatively few targets had been positively identified beforehand. Wilhelm Lübbecke witnessed it for himself: "A cascade of explosions reverberated around us. Our artillery unleashed a short but devastating bombardment on the enemy's positions, and the flashes of light from the explosions lit the entire eastern horizon."[19]

Heeresgruppe Mitte's Richard von Rosen was nervously waiting in his assembly area at the time.

> I had a light doze. By 0300hrs with all the tension and excitement nobody was still asleep. We got up and talked. Then, at precisely 0315hrs, the first shots were fired. Our artillery batteries opened a massively heavy fire on the Russian positions from all sides … the morning sky had turned red, everywhere was on fire. The Soviets made no reply. After half an hour the firing ebbed somewhat, got heavier again, and then almost ceased altogether. We could hear the rat-a-tat-tat of machine-gun fire in the distance.

Underneath the shell storm a Soviet border patrol sent a panicked signal back to their headquarters: "We are being fired upon, what shall we do?" The reply was comical and tragic at the same time: "You must be insane, and why is your signal not in code?"

Hubert Hegele and his comrades were crouched on the border watching two Soviet border guards chat and smoke as they stood on their observation platform, totally unaware of what was about to happen. "0315 hours. Finally! A hand is raised up and gives the signal. As if drawn by a magnet, all eyes are on the hand of the assault troop leader. And with the raising of his hand, two shots from our sharpshooters resound through the night. The two Russian sentries collapse. The campaign against the Soviet Union has begun."

At 0445 Moscow time – an hour ahead of German time – the Red Army's Chief of the General Staff, General Georgy Zhukov, telephoned Stalin at his dacha, waking him up. Zhukov informed his boss that the Navy's enormous base at Sevastopol on the Black Sea had been bombed, and that reports were coming in of German attacks all along the frontier. Stalin – unwilling to believe that Hitler had sanctioned an invasion – asked Zhukov if it was possible that this was a provocation launched by dissident German generals. Stalin ordered the Politburo to meet in the Kremlin an hour later.

The German ambassador to Moscow, the capable Friedrich-Werner Graf von der Schulenberg, was summoned to give an explanation to the Soviet Foreign Minister, Vyacheslav Molotov. Von der Schulenberg – no friend to the Nazis – had dropped hints of what was being planned to several senior Soviet diplomats over the preceding few weeks, including Molotov, but none had been acted on. It was now von der Schulenberg's job to inform Molotov that due to the Soviet Union's *numerous hostile acts against his country*, Nazi Germany had been forced to act and was now at war with the communist State. Molotov was profoundly shocked.

At the new front, Hans Roth was in the first wave across the border:

> We crouch in our holes with pallid but resolved faces, counting the minutes until we storm the Bug fortifications ... a reassuring touch of our ID tags, the arming of hand grenades, the securing of our submachine-guns ... a whistle sounds, we quickly jump out from our cover and at an insane speed cross the twenty metres to the inflatable boats. In no time we are on the other side of the river where rattling machine-gun fire awaits us. We have our first casualties. With the help of a few *sturmpionieren* we slowly – much too slowly – cut through the barbed wire barriers. Meanwhile, shells fire into the bunkers at Molnikow [western Ukraine].[20]

Gefreiter Joachim Kredel of *23. Infanterie-Division* was also in the first wave. Cradling the twenty-six pounds of his MG34 machine-gun, he sprinted forward faster than he'd ever run before, almost as if trying to out-run the Soviet fire. Red Army defenders were shooting from observation towers they were manning on their side of the border. This was Kredel's first taste of combat and he was petrified. He watched with horrid fascination as an explosive shell from an infantry cannon hit one of the towers and turned it into match sticks. "Pieces of wood and Russians whirled through the air and fell to the ground like toys." *Oberleutnant* Siegfried Knappe was no novice, nevertheless the assault made quite an impression on him: "The crack of rifle shots, the short bursts of machine-guns and the shattering crashes of hand grenades. The rifle fire sounded like the clattering of metal-wheeled carts moving fast over cobblestones."[21] As Heinrich Haape's unit began their advance he noted, "The frontier customs post is already a blazing torch. The Russian frontier defences have been pulverized by fire and taken by storm. Only a few concrete bunkers are bravely and desperately fighting back, but they will soon be surrounded and overrun."

The village of Molnikow was *299. Infanterie-Division*'s first objective after crossing the Bug. Hans Roth remembered it as a hard fight.

> We're able to advance to the first bunker, reaching its blind spot. The Reds fire like mad but can't hit us. The moment arrives. An explosives specialist approached the bunker from behind and shoved a charge on a short fuse into the bunker's firing slit. The bunker shook, black smoke poured from its openings, signalling its doom. We move on. By 1000hrs Molnikow is completely in our hands ... our panzers are delayed

crossing the river, so we are ordered to clear out any remaining enemy combatants ... we comb the village house by house.

As Roth and his comrades worked their way through the village they came across scenes of horror: "Close to the Red's custom house lies a large mound of fallen Russians, most of them torn to shreds by the shelling. Slaughtered civilians lie in the neighbouring house. The horridly disfigured bodies of a young woman and her two small children lie among their shattered personal belongings in another small, cleared house." Roth was no stranger to the indiscriminate nature of war, but this gave him pause for thought. "I am compelled to think of you Rosel, and Erika, when I witness such horrible images."

Rudolf Kurth was a private soldier in the same regiment as Joachim Kredel and the aristocratic Axel von dem Bussche-Streithorst. Writing home, he described the assault that morning: "We came under fire straightaway. But then we came face to face with the Russians. We captured the first sub machine-guns from them, they look like real gangster weapons. We also got to know their trickery right away. They raised their hands, but when we went to take them prisoner, they shot at us. Then they hide in the cornfields, wait until we've passed by and shoot at us from behind. The *Wehrmacht* report will show how we react to this." That last sentence is coded – but not much. Hans Roth was a little more candid in his diary: "We have taken our first prisoners – snipers and deserters receive their deserved reward ... How wonderful it is that we are able to exterminate these murderous beasts." Both men were describing the shooting of prisoners – a war crime. The racial and ideological poison that Nazism had liberally poured into Germany's drinking water was bearing fruit in the very first moments of Barbarossa and would quickly become one of the campaign's defining features. As Heinrich Einsiedel acknowledged, "They'd told us for years before the campaign that 'the enemy isn't human, they're *untermenschen* – Slavs and Jews are *untermenschen*. They must be exterminated.'"

Erich Hager was in the rear of his division as it surged forward, and he managed to scribble a few notes in his diary: "At midday we come to the Bug, stand for an hour at the bridge which has been built. See my first air battle. Eight bombers were shot down by our aircraft. Awful to watch. Crossed the Bug. We come to the first of our dead. Snipers were the culprits? Wounded Russians are still lying here." Hager's army commander was actually a few hours in front of him, as Guderian pointed out in his own commentary: "At 0650hrs I crossed the Bug in an assault boat ... I followed the panzer tracks of *18. Panzerdivision* and soon reached the bridge over the Lesna (the Leśna Prawa river). There I found nobody except some Russian pickets who took to their heels when they saw my vehicles. Two of my orderly officers set off after them against my wishes, unfortunately they were both killed as a result."[22]

Also a member of *Heeresgruppe Mitte* – albeit a far less exalted one – was Helmut Pabst. Advancing with the rest of his signals team to help provide artillery support for the infantry, he and his comrades had already been fired upon by Red Army stragglers as they scrambled forward: "We moved fast, sometimes flat on the ground ... Ditches, water, sand, sun. Always changing position. By ten o'clock we were already old soldiers and had seen a great deal; abandoned positions, knocked-out armoured cars, the first prisoners, the first dead Russians."[23]

While Roth, von dem Bussche and Kredel were firing the first shots of the campaign on the ground, Arnold Döring, directly above them, was already several hours into his war in the air. With his first sorties against the VVS's forward airfields a success, he and his Heinkel crew were switched to support the Army's advance by hitting the roads choked with a confused Red Army: "We dropped the bombs at the side of the road to leave it intact for our own advance ... our bombs fell by the side of the tanks, guns, and between vehicles and panic-stricken Russians running in all directions. It was total chaos down there – no-one could even think about firing back. The effect of the incendiary and splinter bombs was awesome. With such a target you just couldn't miss."[24]

Heinz Knoke was on much the same mission in his converted Bf 109: "New operation orders have arrived. Russian transport columns have been seen by our reconnaissance aircraft along the Grodno highway with our panzers in hot pursuit. We are to support them by bombing and strafing the Russians as they retreat."

Helmut Mahlke and his Stukas were given the same orders: hit the enemy hard *but don't* slow the advance. "*Oberstleutnant* Hagen, as ever the quiet eye in the centre of the storm that was raging all about him, calmly acknowledged my report ... before handing me the orders. 'Attack the River Neman crossings at Grodno!' The *Kommodore* spelled out the operation in detail: 'The Neman crossing points are to be blocked, but only the approach roads – the bridges themselves are not to be damaged, they will be needed by our own troops.'" Mahlke drove back from headquarters to his air strip and prepared for the mission: "While the crews were being briefed, the mechanics had been giving their machines a final once over, checking the engines and making sure that everything in the cockpit was securely stowed and fastened down. The last thing any pilot needed during a steep dive was to have some loose item of equipment flying around his ears." Then it was time to go. "The crews climbed aboard their aircraft. They were strapped in, the engines sprang into life, and for the second time on this first morning of the war against Russia our Stukas taxied out to the take-off line." Knoke and Mahlke had been given the same target area. "We take off, accompanied by the Stukas ... The roads are clogged with Russian troops."

With much of the VVS lying wrecked on its own airfields, the *Luftwaffe* pilots had a clear run to their targets, as Knoke appreciated: "There has been no sign of the Russian air force the entire day and we are able to do our work without encountering opposition." With no air cover, the Red Army units on the roads below were easy pickings for the eager young flyer. "Thousands of Ivans are in full retreat, which becomes an utter rout when we open up on them, stumbling and bleeding as they flee from the highway in an attempt to take cover in the woods. Vehicles lie burning by the roadside after we pass. I drop my bombs on a column of horse-drawn heavy artillery – I am thankful not to be down there!"

It went just as well for Helmut Mahlke and his Stukas. "The mission went off exactly as briefed. The enemy's flak was a little heavier this time, but still not heavy enough to pose any serious threat. Our bombs blew deep craters in the approach roads to the bridges. Several houses collapsed, spilling their debris into the streets and creating additional barriers. The bridges would still be useable ... Mission accomplished as ordered." On returning to base Mahlke was told that the mission had gotten an unexpected bonus: "Signals intelligence picked up a plain language radio message from Grodno calling for help – 'Army staff wiped out!'"

Not everything was going quite so well for the invaders. To the south, Gerd von Rundstedt's *Heeresgruppe Süd* was facing the strongest grouping the Red Army had in the west. Rundstedt's force – the only one of the three German army groups to contain large contingents of allied troops – was destined for a tough fight. Just how tough, Helmut Paulus, a callow nineteen-year-old from the city of Pforzheim in Baden-Württemberg and eldest son to Erna and Ernst, was about to find out. Known as the 'gateway to the Black Forest', Pforzheim was a scenic and peaceful place to grow up, but perhaps a little quiet for a young man keen for adventure. After being called up for his compulsory military service, young Helmut was undergoing basic training during the *Wehrmacht*'s summer conquest of France, and fretted that the war would be over by the time he was ready to join in. He need not have worried. Sent to serve as an infantry private in *Infanterie-Regiment 305 (IR. 305)* under the command of the bespectacled *Oberst* Albert Buck, Helmut clambered into an inflatable dinghy in the early hours of 22 June on the River Prut, then part of the southern border between the Nazi and Soviet empires. Waved off by Buck, the mini armada began to nervously paddle across until one of Helmut's jittery comrades accidentally pressed the trigger of his sub-machine gun, sending a burst of hot lead into the side of the dinghy next to his. The shot-up inflatable immediately began to sink, and in the ensuing panic a neighbouring undamaged dinghy flipped upside down and capsized, its occupants flailing around in the river. Carefully stowed equipment, ammunition and weapons all disappeared beneath the threshing water. Nevertheless, Helmut and his comrades – quite a few of them now drenched and shaken – managed to make the eastern bank, and push on to reach their first objectives. This was new ground for all of them, and not just territorially.

Their division, *General der Infanterie* Otto Röttig's *198. Infanterie-Division (198. ID)*, was brand new and hadn't fired a single shot in anger – the dinghy debacle notwithstanding. The majority of the men were like Helmut, just-trained recruits, but almost one-third were older men, reservists aged between thirty-five and forty-five who would much rather have been at home with their wives and children and not digging in on an exposed hilltop near the village of Skuleni in modern-day Moldova. Their task was to establish a bridgehead that could then be used by follow-on units; only those follow-on units weren't due to cross the Prut for at least a week. Until then, Helmut *et al.* were more or less on their own. Just how alone they soon discovered when Soviet fighters – survivors of the slaughter on their home bases – appeared overhead and proceeded to plaster Helmut and his comrades with heavy machine-gun fire. Repeated attacks chewed up the ground, and there was little the men of *198. ID* could do except dig themselves deeper into the protective earth. Helmut survived until help finally came. Two-and-a-half years later he returned to Russia after a spell of home leave, only to be immediately posted as Missing in Action on 1 November 1943. Erna and Ernst did everything they could to try and find out what happened to their eldest – always hoping he had been captured and would be repatriated at some point. He never was. Thirty years later the *Deutsches Rotes Kreuz Suchdienst* (German Red Cross Tracing Service) found enough evidence to confirm that Helmut Paulus had been killed in Russia back in late 1943.

The teenaged *Luftwaffe* flak auxiliary Sigmund Heinz Landau was also part of the assault that morning, about 80 miles north from Paulus's crossing, but seemingly a world away, as the left – northern – wing of Rundstedt's army group went straight onto the offensive: "At 0500hrs on 22 June 1941 we crossed the River Prut at a place called Stalinesti. We met no resistance … soon we were deep in enemy territory without a shot being fired and received a friendly – almost frenzied welcome – from the Ukrainian population."

The phenomenon that Landau described – of being hailed as long-awaited liberators rather than vicious invaders – would become a major feature of the campaign. These two faces to Barbarossa – on the one hand the potential to leverage the goodwill of millions, versus an almost visceral urge to destroy and butcher on the other – would co-exist throughout the campaign.

Liberators or killers, neither label seemed to matter overly much to the front-line troops that first day, as most members of the *Wehrmacht*'s invasion divisions concentrated on just staying alive, as Ulrich Gunzert – a young *leutnant* – admitted: "In combat anything which isn't absolutely vital loses all importance. What the enemy is doing, how to deal with him, how to outmanoeuvre him, how to survive – these are the only things that occupy your mind. You can't think of anything else." The fighting that Gunzert described was some of the hardest the *Wehrmacht* had ever encountered, as a mountaineer from *1. Gebirgs-Division* experienced first hand: "That day we fought from dawn to dusk and then fell exhausted into shallow slit trenches. That first night the officers and NCOs kept watch while we slept."[25] The unnamed *gebirgsjäger* wasn't exaggerating about what they'd been through. He and his comrades had managed to reach their first major objective – the River Lubaczówka, some sixteen kilometres from their start line – as planned, but the division's war diary, its *Kriegstagebuch*, described the day as the bloodiest in the unit's history.

Heeresgruppe Süd was embroiled in fierce fighting in that first twenty-four hours, but some units fared better than others. Gustav Böker, a former commercial clerk from Oberg in Lower Saxony, was, like Hans Roth, a *panzerjäger*, but in Otto Stapf's *111. Infanterie-Division* to the south. The day after the invasion he wrote to his parents:

You must have been amazed on Sunday morning when you heard about the beginning of hostilities against Russia. Perhaps you can now understand why I didn't tell you where we were based before ... On Saturday evening I had to take my bike into position. I had to push the bike about two kilometres, you can imagine I was swearing a lot. Driving was forbidden so the Russians didn't notice or hear anything. We already knew what was going to happen, and on Sunday morning at 0315hrs the attack started. So, our first mission came. Now we are tens of kilometres inside Russia. Hopefully, everything will go on like this, then it won't take too long. The roads, or dirt tracks I should say, are pretty bad here. And then there's the dust, we all look pretty dirty, even now. But that's better than rain, because if it rained I think our vehicles would find it very difficult indeed.

Perhaps Böker was shielding his parents by not telling them anything frightening, but even so the picture he paints is one of steady advance rather than vicious combat. Ernst Preuss's experience chimed with Böker's: "On 22 June 1941 we marched into Russia. It was the longest day of my life. It started at 0500hrs, we'd been told that the Russians had attacked us, so off we marched to teach them a lesson. We had no contact with the enemy, we just advanced and advanced, with the panzers, and that continued into the night with hardly a pause, and it wasn't until the next day that we first met some light resistance."[26]

In contrast, some of the hardest fighting that first day was on the shores of the Baltic, as *Heeresgruppe Nord* launched its attack into Soviet-occupied Lithuania. North of the city of Memel (Lithuanian *Klaipeda* and *Libau* in German) the terrain was such that the German invaders were faced with taking an enormous risk from the very first. Leeb's chief of staff – Chales de Beaulieu – put it succinctly: "The obstacle was the Western Dvina river. We would have to overcome any enemy units in the border areas as quickly as possible and race the 300 kilometres to the river." The first leg of that race was bad enough. A deep and narrow river valley was the only possible axis of advance, and at its head was the big road viaduct across the River Dubysa at Ariogala. If the Germans didn't seize the viaduct intact on the first day they would be bottled up in the valley, unable to manoeuvre and sitting ducks for a Soviet counterattack. But Ariogala was 50 miles from the German start line.

The man tasked with the mission of reaching it as quickly as possible was the originator of the hugely successful Ardennes offensive the previous summer, Erich von Manstein.

I knew the Dubysa sector from the First World War. What we would find there was a deep, ravined valley whose slopes no panzer could negotiate. In the First War our railway engineers had laboured there for months on end to span the gap with a masterly construction of timber. If the enemy now succeeded in blowing up the big road viaduct at Ariogala our panzers would be hopelessly stuck and the enemy would have time on the steep far bank of the river to organise a defence that would in any case be extremely difficult to penetrate ... The Ariogala crossing was indispensable to us as a springboard.

Manstein now commanded *LVI. Armeekorps* and its component divisions: *SS-Obergruppenführer* Theodor Eicke's *SS-Totenkopf*, *General der Artillerie* Kurt Jahn's *3. Infanterie-Division (mot.)*, *Generalleutnant* Theodor Freiherr von Wrede's *290. Infanterie-Division* and *General der Panzertruppe* Erich Brandenberger's *8. Panzerdivision*.

To reach Ariogala, Manstein knew he would need Brandenberger's panzers to lead the way, but his sole armoured division was far from being the ideal weapon for such a bold operation. Only established in the winter of 1939–40, it was equipped with fewer than a hundred

German-manufactured panzers – many of which were under-gunned Panzer IIs – the other 118 being light Czech *Pz. 38(t) beutepanzers*.[27] With both of these panzer models discontinued there was a dearth of spare parts, which meant that if one broke down it would probably have to be abandoned. The division would need to rely on speed to cause panic in the Soviet ranks.

It did, however, have two aces up its sleeve. The first was its commander, Erich Brandenberger, and the second was Sepp de Giampietro and his Brandenburger compatriots. Erich Brandenberger was an under-rated officer, considered lucky by his peers to be given such a prestigious command as *8. Panzerdivision*. A former artilleryman, Brandenberger had fought in the First World War and thereafter undertaken various staff roles. A Bavarian and a Catholic, rather than a Protestant Prussian like so many of his fellow senior officers, his paunchy, bespectacled appearance was more akin to a village schoolmaster than a hard-charging panzer man, but beneath the unassuming exterior was a true convert to the discipline of blitzkrieg. Manstein for one had no doubts as to the capability of his only armoured formation leader. As for de Giampietro and his fellow commandos, they would prove crucial to the whole endeavour.

The first task, however, was to breach the Soviets' front-line defences, and that was the job of the infantry. Wrede's troopers led the way, splashing across a stream on the border and assaulting a line of pillboxes. In the very first minutes of the attack *Leutnant* Weinrowski became *Heeresgruppe Nord*'s first fatality of the campaign when he was mown down by a machine-gun nest camouflaged as a farm cart. The Soviets couldn't hold though, and with the defence line taken it was time for the panzers to move into the lead and charge for Ariogala.

Elsewhere in *Heeresgruppe Nord*'s sector, Wilhelm Lübbecke and his comrades in *58. Infanterie-Division* began their war: "Our artillery started, planes came over in waves – hundreds of planes – and we went into Russia. Ahead of us was a panzer division and we couldn't keep up, we just kept on marching." For *Leutnant* Hubert Becker it was his first time in combat, and an unnerving baptism:

It was a hot, early summer's day and I had no idea what to expect. We were crossing a meadow and came under artillery fire – a very strange feeling … standing next to me was my commanding officer and you had to play the hero – you couldn't just lie down, which would have been safer. Then, over there, was a German soldier. His hand was raised in the air which made his wedding ring shine in the sun, and his head – a little reddish and puffed up – had a mouth full of flies. He was the first dead man I had ever seen.

In *Heeresgruppe Mitte*'s sector, Heinrich Haape soon treated his first casualty of the new war: "He has a bullet wound in the arm. I remove the rubber tourniquet and emergency bandage applied by a stretcher-bearer. There is little bleeding as the bullet has passed right through the arm, only grazing the bone slightly ... 'How are things going up ahead?' I asked. 'Unteroffizier Schäfer has fallen, and one officer – I don't know who he is. Otherwise no casualties, but I'm not sure what's happening – it's all been so quick.'" Going forward on his beloved horse – Lump – Haape found the body of the dead officer. "It was young *Leutnant* Stock. Killed by a Russian sniper's bullet, his body lay in a trampled cornfield."

Heinz-Georg Lemm was an experienced company commander and remembered his unit's first actions on invasion day: "At the beginning of the attack the resistance of the Russians was weak and consisted of individuals with rifles, light machine-guns and the irregular fire of a light artillery battery. My *kompanie* advanced well, but the very great physical effort required to get through the roadless, sometimes sandy, sometimes marshy, terrain, and then wading through several swampy brooks with all our weapons and ammunition boxes under a hot sun, exhausted many soldiers. All were very thirsty." Tired and thirsty they may have been, but Lemm's Mecklenburgers were all veterans of the Polish and Western campaigns and kept on advancing. "The village of Debiliniai, in Lithuania, was captured at 0450. The first Russian prisoners appeared happy that for them the war, although hardly begun, was over. From the population nobody was to be seen and the cattle were gone as well. At the village well I had my men fill their canteens. Soon enemy resistance with artillery and machine-gun fire became stronger."

Helmut Ritgen, a junior officer in the *beutepanzer*-equipped 6. *Panzerdivision* in *Heeresgruppe Nord*, was surprised at the Red Army's reaction that first day:

> Enemy resistance in our sector was much stronger than excepted. Up to six anti-tank ditches had been dug in a series and these were stubbornly held by riflemen supported by snipers in trees. Fortunately, no enemy anti-tank guns or mines were in position. Since nobody surrendered, almost no prisoners were taken. Our panzers, however, were soon out of ammunition, something which had never happened before in either Poland or France.

It wasn't all close combat though. Max Kuhnert and his unit were bivouacked in a forest a few kilometres back from the border when the opening barrage began around them: "All hell was let loose ... the noise and sight were indescribable, the earth seemed to tremble, all the batteries came alive out of the darkness of the pine trees. Flames shot towards the border followed by the explosion of the shells on the other side. All around us were what appeared to be great sheets of lightning, torn through by flames while thunder crashed and boomed." Amidst all this tremendous show of firepower, Kuhnert was told to get himself, his horse Siegfried, and his colonel's mount, Albert, across the river by swimming through the fast-flowing water. On reaching the far bank, "I just sat down and let the horses graze. What next I thought?" He caught up with the rest of his unit that evening and was finally given his first mission of the new war: "Go back along the main route and find the field kitchen, the cook, his two helpers and their driver. We need the food." A glory-winning task it was not.

Back on the Ariogala axis, Sepp de Giampietro and his fellow Brandenburgers were up with the vanguard of *8. Panzerdivision*. "The forest at the border had soon been crossed, and before us lay large cornfields, criss-crossed by woody patches and deep, marshy hollows. The enemy's positions had been seized quickly, albeit having caused *290. ID* heavy losses. We hadn't been deployed yet." The Finns had sent the Germans stocks of Red Army uniforms they had captured in the Winter War, and the Brandenburgers had been liberally supplied with them, but de Giampietro and his brethren weren't keen: "The first prisoners passed our convoy, we took off their steel helmets and berets as well as their tunics, and we chucked away the Russian uniforms that had been sent to us by the OKH; they were all brand-new, clean and neatly pressed. Had we worn them we would have drawn attention to ourselves straightaway as no actual Russian soldier dressed like that. What we needed were dirty, sweaty uniforms, the ones that an Ivan would wear in battle ... we also got hold of two trucks, really old and rickety Ford models, with no benches in the back, low side-panels and a discoloured licence plate at the rear."

Despite having fought in the Balkans, de Giampietro soon realised that this campaign wouldn't be like any other: "Right from the start it was obvious that the Russians were going to be a totally different sort of enemy from the British ... the Russians allowed the vanguard panzers to roll past them while they hid in the woods and cornfields waiting for the unarmoured vehicles to come along, and only then would they attack, so our first casualties weren't among the leading panzers but to soldiers in the rear, in the field kitchens and so on."

He also noted the novel, but suicidal, way the Red Army soldier fought:

The Russians would dig holes, with just enough room for one man to stand upright in, but not connected to one another. They offered excellent shelter against artillery fire and shrapnel ... to kill him a panzer would have to turn round precisely above the hole, crushing him and grinding him down into the ground – this was done by both sides all the time ... while it gave the Russian excellent cover, he couldn't get out easily and if he did he wasn't covered by anyone else, so his death was certain – generally the Russians knew that and tended to remain in their holes until their last breath – we had to wipe out every single one of their nests.

Heinrich Haape, so excited on the eve of the attack, found his earlier ardour was cooling: "The first day in the campaign against Russia. We have a hard day behind us! The Russians fought like devils and never surrendered, so we engaged in close combat on several occasions; just now, half an hour ago, another four Russians were beaten to death with the butts of our rifles."

The infantry advance in the north was a success – particularly given the heat and the often-swampy terrain – but it was the panzers that were the key, and more especially those of 8. *Panzerdivision*. From the moment they were given the order to advance, Brandenberger's crews raced ahead, and at 1900hrs that evening the general received the signal from his vanguard he had been anxiously awaiting: "Ariogala viaduct taken." 8. *Panzerdivision* had charged 50 miles in a single day. It was a staggering achievement. Passing the information back to Manstein, the reply was "Keep going." De Giampietro was right up there. "By evening of the first day we reached Ariogala, some eighty kilometres inside enemy territory."

News of the invasion swept through the Reich like wildfire. Walter Stoll, an Army private not involved in the attack, recalled his sense of disbelief at hearing the news. "Preparations in the previous few weeks had suggested an attack against the Soviet Union might be imminent, but we could still hardly believe it when it happened." Stoll's reaction was mirrored across the country, as an official *Sicherheitsdienst* (SD – SS security and intelligence service) report on public opinion made clear: "The overwhelming response has been one of complete surprise." A sense of the invasion's inevitability was another reaction, as the student Lore Walb expressed in her diary: "Great apprehension and depression at the same time, but also, somehow, we breathed a sigh of relief." The Army reserve officer and journalist Jochen Klepper was of the same mind: "The first thought we all have is about the length of the war, but then the conviction that a reckoning with Russia was necessary sooner or later."[28]

Some, like Fritz Muehlebach and Franz Wertheim, chose to believe Goebbels' propaganda about an impending Soviet attack: "Suddenly, we were at war with Russia. This was the last thing anybody had expected, and I didn't like it at all. It wasn't until we realised the Russians had been double crossing us all the time that the reason for this new war became clear. It was the same old story of the *Führer* being one jump ahead – as usual." Muehlebach was an out-of-work sailor, making ends meet by working as a member of the *Reichsluftschutzbund* (RLB – National Air Raid Protection League), handling air raid precautions in residential areas,[29] whereas Wertheim was a doctor and an educated professional and should have, perhaps, been able to discern he was being lied to: "The *Führer* had crossed the Russian border ... this clash between National Socialism and communism was inevitable, necessary and right. The *Führer*, with his usual genius, had foreseen the menace from the east and now met it in good time."[30]

Hildegard Trutz – the baker's daughter now married to an SS man – was another who allowed Nazi propaganda to soothe her fears. "When war broke out against Russia, Ernst (her husband) was worried at first, but when the *Führer* announced that the greater part of the Red Army had been wiped out ... everyone felt much happier and I was sure that the war would soon be over."

Others were less sanguine. The businessman Hermann Voss was among them: "It came as a heavy blow to me and all other thinking people when we heard of the invasion of Russia. This should have been prevented at all costs. I couldn't believe it would end well."

Werner Baumbach was preparing to lead an anti-convoy patrol from Norway's Stavanger-Sola airfield when he was handed the announcement, along with an order to read it out to his crews. "I tear open the innocent-looking envelope in front of the men, none of us know its contents ... As I slowly read out the note it's some time before the full meaning and consequences of this declaration of war upon Russia dawn upon us, and we're still puzzling it out as lorries take us out to our aircraft ... so much for no two-front war."[31]

Hajo Herrmann, having already flown well over fifty operational sorties in the Western campaign as a Junkers Ju-88 bomber pilot, had no doubts about the invasion and was probably more representative of the ranks of the *Luftwaffe* than Baumbach: "I heard no criticism of Barbarossa; on the contrary the general hope was that it would be successful. I shared those hopes without being able to form my own independent assessment ... our Russian campaign seemed to me to be a daring enterprise, but fully justified."[32]

Melita Maschmann was walking on the shores of Lake Constance in Bavaria when the radio in a nearby beer garden announced the invasion. "The people round me had troubled faces. We avoided one another's eyes and looked out across the lake ... before the broadcast was over it had started to rain. I walked along the shore in a fit of depression ... There was one thing the invasion of Russia would certainly mean – the war would be prolonged for many years, and there would, perhaps, be immeasurably greater sacrifices."[33] For Baroness Mausi von Westerode – holidaying on the Baltic coast in the opulent Zoppot Casino Hotel at the time – the invasion seemed a world away: "When the Russian campaign began we were all startled but not worried, and everyone carried on; drinking the best wines, eating crayfish, lobster and caviar, and playing tennis, sailing and riding ... as gay as ever."

Intriguingly, reaction to the news amidst the ranks of the *Waffen-SS* was mixed. Richard Fuchs, an NCO in the *SS-Wiking Division*, spoke for the majority: "The bolsheviks were seen by me, and by the *Waffen-SS*, as the principal enemy against whom I wanted to fight as a member of an élite force." This view was felt outside the Reich as well, as the Belgian Fleming Remy Schrijnen, made clear: "On the very day that war with the Soviet Union broke out I reported to the *Waffen-SS* to offer myself as a Germanic volunteer. Unfortunately, as I was only 1.64m (5ft 5in) tall and the minimum height required was 1.78m (5ft 10in), I was rejected." Schrijnen would persist and end up winning the Knight's Cross for bravery on the Russian front in the summer of 1944.[34] On the flip side of the coin was none other than Kurt Meyer – an officer in the *SS-Leibstandarte*, Hitler's very own bodyguard – and already a legend in the SS: "The news of the attack against the Soviet Union struck us like a bolt of lightning ... with a gloomy foreboding that we might suffer the same fate as our fathers who fell victim to a war on several fronts in 1914–18."[35]

In a war that to many Germans had seemed as good as over, another chapter had just begun. In a café in Dresden, the diarist Victor Klemperer (born German-Jewish, he had converted to Protestantism) was sitting at a table with his wife when the invasion was announced over the radio. The Klemperers' waiter had been a prisoner of war in Russia back in the First World War and gave the couple his view that "the war will come to an end quickly now".

In Berlin, Joseph Goebbels held a soirée that afternoon to celebrate the news. Among the guests was one of his favourite actresses, Olga Chekhova, a niece of the famous writer Anton Chekhov, and herself of mixed Russo-German heritage. Fondly described by the Minister of Propaganda as "*eine charmante Frau*" (a charming lady), the diminutive demagogue asked her in front of the entire salon: "We have a Russian expert here. Will we be in Moscow by Christmas?" Annoyed at Goebbels' arrogance, Chekhova replied: "You know Russia, the endless land. Even Napoleon had to retreat." This was not what anyone in the room expected or wanted to hear. Ten minutes later a uniformed aide appeared at Chekhova's side and informed her, "I imagine madame, that you are ready to leave. The car is outside."[36]

Across the city from Goebbels' reception, Biddy MacNaghten, an Irishwoman married to a German, met her neighbour *Frau* Schroder in their apartment block garden. *Frau* Schroder was in tears: "Now the war will never end."[37] Nearby, the teenaged Werner Harz considered that "for Germany the war was already lost".

Back on the new front, a young NCO in the *SS-Reich* wrote in his diary that first night: "My conviction is that the destruction of Russia will take no longer than that of France, and then my assumption of having leave in August will be correct."[38]

5

Germany on the March!

Early on the morning of 23 June, *Leutnant* Hans-Joachim S., a company commander in *Armee-Nachrichten-Regiment 511* (Army Signals Regiment 511) with *Heeresgruppe Nord*, wrote a letter to his wife:

> This will now be my first real war letter. Garrison life is over – the war is here! The war – which we all couldn't and didn't want to believe would happen until the last moment – peace and homecoming have now moved into the distance with this new theatre of battle. Just twenty-four hours of war so far, we haven't experienced much, yet we were witness to the start of the mightiest war machine that was probably ever put into operation ... German aircraft; bombers, Stukas, fighters, were overhead. Russian pilots appear and seem to have no idea that they will fall victim to our fighters or flak minutes later. A plume of smoke announces the end of man and machine. After twenty-four hours we think we've advanced about ninety kilometres, and we're beginning to try and calculate when we'll arrive in Moscow. I could still write a lot, but I hope to be able to give this letter to a soldier going back to headquarters to post.[1]

Hans-Joachim S. was thirty-six, a businessman in civilian life who had been called back to the colours, like Hans Roth, and found himself leading a company of signallers deep into the Baltic states. He had already served in the Netherlands and France, and now he and his men were part of the smallest of the three German army groups in Barbarossa. *Heeresgruppe Nord* was the runt of the *Ostheer* litter, but it still boasted an impressive three armies, comprising twenty-three front-line divisions, including seventeen infantry, two motorised infantry, three panzer and an SS formation – the *SS-Totenkopf*. In reserve it had an additional four divisions, and three security divisions to help police the regions it was set to conquer.

With the Red Army's main strength lying to the south, *Nord* wasn't tasked with taking part in destroying the bulk of the Russian Army stationed in western Russia by daring operations led by deeply penetrating armoured spearheads – to paraphrase the original Barbarossa directive – rather its objective was the capture of the city of Leningrad. The former capital, Leningrad (St Petersburg as was and now) was still Russia's second city in 1941 and a major centre for industry, but that wasn't why Hitler set *Nord* to take it. For the Nazi dictator the city was the cradle – the very birthplace – of the Bolshevik credo he detested so vehemently. Its capture and subsequent destruction was more about symbolism than military logic. So, in accordance with his wishes, well over half a million men and hundreds of panzers and assault guns were sent on an advance that was of secondary importance at best.

Not that this mattered to the men caught up in it – soldiers like Gustav Klinter – as he and his comrades approached a burning Latvian town: "The air had that putrefying and pervasive burnt smell reminiscent of the battle zone and all nerves and senses began to detect the breath of war. Suddenly, all heads switched to the right. The first dead of the Russian campaign lay before our eyes like a spectre – a Mongolian skull smashed in combat, a torn uniform and bare abdomen split by shell splinters. The column drew up and then accelerated ahead – the picture fell behind us. I sank back thoughtfully into my seat."[2] The chances of the dead soldier actually being Mongolian were slim, given the relatively small number of Mongols serving in the Red Army. Far more likely was that he was a member of a related Turkic minority, a Kazakh, Uzbek, Tajik and so on, but in the propaganda world Klinter had been brought up in over the last few years the Soviet Union was full to the brim with Mongolian Asiatic hordes.

Klinter wasn't alone in commenting on the ethnicity of the new enemy. Even his army commander – Erich Hoepner – did so when writing home on 23 June: "Yesterday didn't go exactly as I had hoped ... the Russians fought back tenaciously. They were from the Caucasus, and as prisoners they made for an uncivilized impression – yellowish-brown, narrow-eyed; wide, coarse heads, closely shaved; powerful, wiry physiques. Many of them were asleep when our artillery fire began and were so startled that they only had on a single piece of clothing – a shirt, underwear, or a coat."

Hoepner's boss – and the man chosen to take Leningrad for his *Führer* – was a sixty-four-year-old devoutly Catholic Bavarian from a military family, with a distinguished service career in the First World War. He had commanded *12. Armee* as it annexed the Czech Sudetenland in 1938, and then led the army group that broke through France's Maginot Line in the 1940 campaign. His reward was promotion to *generalfeldmarschall* in the famous Kroll Opera House Field Marshal Ceremony of 19 July that same year. The same height as Hitler, shaven-headed, and second only in age among the *Wehrmacht*'s senior officers to the venerable Gerd von Rundstedt, Wilhelm Ritter von Leeb was a steady hand rather than a firebrand. The author of a celebrated text on military operations, he was viewed as more of an expert on defence[3] than the newer concepts of blitzkrieg and manoeuvre warfare, but was still respected by his officers and soldiers alike. Now commanding the smallest invasion force, and just a day into the operation, he would be tested as never before.

On 23 June the advance seemed almost unstoppable. *Generalleutnant* Philipp Kleffel was pushing the East Prussians of his beloved *1. Infanterie-Division* as hard as he could. Formed back in 1935 and built around the famous *1.(Preussisches) Infanterie-Regiment*, the division retained its traditional unit symbol of the Hohenzollern coat of arms, and was, perhaps, only rivalled by *23. Infanterie-Division* as the most aristocratic of Germany's field units. Now, advancing at pace, it encountered Soviet tanks for the first time. "Between twelve and fifteen Russian tanks drove down the road ... at the same moment *Gefreiter* Hasse from *14. Kompanie, Infanterie-Regiment 22*, had brought his gun into position at the fork one kilometre north of the Butkaicai estate. The gunners shot up six of the rapidly advancing tanks at close range, even though their gun was almost overrun."

This was the vanguard of not one but two Soviet mechanized corps committed to battle to try and halt the headlong charge of the panzers, as the bulk of the Red Army's armour in the northern sector was sent crashing into Franz Landgraf's *6. Panzerdivision* near the Lithuanian city of Raseiniai. The ensuing fight was a very rude shock for the panzer men. An entire regimental *kampfgruppe* (battle group) from the division was overrun and scattered, almost entirely owing to the presence among the Soviet force of tanks the like of which the Germans had never seen, as one eyewitness bitterly recalled:

The monster tanks' 70cm tracks literally ground everything in their path into the earth – guns, motorcycles and men. There wasn't a single weapon in the bridgehead that could stop them. After the massacre, the tanks waded through the Dubysa, easily crawling up the 45-degree banks. They were met by fire from the entire divisional artillery and enfilade fire from every anti-tank gun the division could bring to bear ... in instances of near panic the soldiers began to realise that their weapons were useless against the big tanks.[4]

These weren't the playground T-60s and T-37s that *Gefreiter* Hasse had blown to oblivion, but forty-three- and fifty-two-ton super-heavy

KV-1s and 2s with ninety millimetres of slab armour. In less than twenty minutes the German bridgehead on the eastern bank of the Dubysa was shattered.

In shock, the corps commander – Georg-Hans Reinhardt – ordered Friedrich Kirchner and his *1. Panzerdivision* to rush to *6. Panzerdivision*'s aid. Kirchner's Thuringians fared no better, as one of their number described:

> Our *kompanien* opened fire from about seven hundred metres, but it had no effect – we got closer and closer to the enemy but it didn't seem to worry them. Soon we were only fifty to one hundred metres from each other. A fantastic exchange of fire took place without any visible success for us. The Russian tanks continued to advance, and our armour piercing shells simply bounced off them. The Russians withstood point-blank hits from both our 5cm and 7.5cm guns ... the Russian tanks drove through our Panzer-Regiment 1 towards our infantry. We about turned and rumbled back, roughly in line with the Russians ... we succeeded in immobilising some of them with special purpose shells at very close range; thirty to sixty metres.[5]

The battle was touch and go for the Germans when, seemingly for no reason, the Soviet tanks halted at the outskirts of Raseiniai. Helmut Ritgen was in no doubt as to the significance of that day's fighting:

> That day changed the character of tank warfare. The KV represented a wholly new level of armament, armour protection and mobility ... no weapon in the Division was able to penetrate their armour. Rounds simply bounced off the Soviet tanks. In the face of the assault some infantry panicked ... German panzers had hitherto been intended mainly to fight enemy infantry and their supporting arms. From now on the main threat was the enemy tank itself, and the need to kill it at as great a range as possible led to the design of longer-barrelled guns of larger calibres.

At the time, the two German panzer divisions showed their mettle by reacting quickly and improvising. They surrounded the immobile Soviets and counterattacked. The Germans did everything they could to destroy the Soviet behemoths, including blasting their tracks to ensure they couldn't move, and then sending in *pioniere* on foot to finish them off with satchel charges.

In two days of fierce fighting the bulk of Soviet armour in the north was destroyed. Over 200 tanks, 150 guns, and hundreds of vehicles littered the battlefield in its aftermath. The Soviets also suffered several thousand dead, among them their commander, Major-General Yegor Solyankin. On inspection, the Germans discovered to their dismay that lack of fuel and ammunition had halted the Soviets, and not German action. In horror, they also found that one of the giant KV-2s had been hit more than seventy times by anti-tank and panzer rounds without a single one having penetrated its armour. Alarm bells began to ring in the ranks of the *panzerwaffe*.

Adolf Dick, a serious-minded and bespectacled *panzerjäger*, very quickly realised he and his comrades were facing something wholly new, calling their standard 3.7cm cannons "small guns" and describing the Soviet tanks as "real monsters and heavily armoured". Dick, however, was pleased at the outcome of his very first action against Soviet armour: "We survived our first fight well. We shot up several tanks and badly damaged one so that it could be destroyed by the infantry. Unfortunately, we lost one man killed and another wounded. The first battle was very tough and heavy because our attack collided with that of the Russians. The artillery fire was terrible. We took cover a lot."[6]

Heeresgruppe Nord had now defeated the Red Army's major mobile formations in its sector and could plunge on ever deeper into the Baltic states towards the old Soviet border. Manstein's corps – having not been caught up at Raseiniai – was surging forward, and by the morning of 26 June was nearing Daugavpils (known to the Germans as Dünaburg), Latvia's second city on the Western Dvina (also called the River Daugava).

Sepp de Giampietro and the Brandenburgers were up front with the men of 8. *Panzerdivision*, having already undertaken a number of missions, including the seizure of the bridge at Josvainiai on 23 June by *coup de main*: "The second day of the war was hot and humid, a merciless sun beating down on us, the panzers whirling up huge clouds of dust that settled on us, burning our skin and eyes. We heard the order, '*Oberleutnant* Knaak to the front' – we knew what that meant, it was our turn now." They changed into Russian tunics and helmets and hid their German weapons and field caps under tarpaulins. Glancing at his commander, Wolfram Knaak, de Giampietro said: "'Herr *Oberleutnant*, do Russians wear monocles?' 'Damn!' He took it out. We descended into a dip in the road as Germans, but moments later we emerged as Russians."[7]

Rolling into the town in their busted old Ford trucks, they headed straight for the bridge. "Tension was high, barely tolerable – we weren't allowed to stop, we had to keep going. We swung to our left and drove the three hundred metres down to the bridge. The last vehicle remained at the junction ... They pretended it had broken down, and some Russians approached them. Our Baltic comrade (a Russian-speaking Baltic German Brandenburger) got out and spoke to them. I had no idea what story he was dishing up, but all he had to do was gain enough time for us to reach the other end of the bridge." With tensions high, de Giampietro and his crew reached the far side: "Then, a sudden burst of fire erupted ... we drew our weapons and loosed off several bursts. Frozen with fear, the Russians stared at us incredulously, not able to grasp why they had been attacked by their own comrades. Their surprise only lasted an instant before they slumped in a heap, dead." Rushing to the bridge supports, the young Tyrolean and his comrades scrambled to find the demolition wires and cut them – only to find that "the bridge wasn't rigged. I was furious. There they were, committing us Brandenburgers to a mission on an unrigged bridge!"

Holding their prize until the lead panzers arrived cost them five men killed. They then moved out, and early the next morning went through the same routine to take the bridge at Kedainiai, which again turned out not to be prepared for demolition. Staying put, they were relieved some two-and-a-half hours later. "Finally, two German panzers appeared from between the houses on the other side. We immediately sent some white flares into the sky, then motorbikes thundered over the bridge followed by infantry ... in the space of ten hours we had carried out two operations and secured two bridges." Now would come the special forces' biggest test – the road and rail bridges at Daugavpils.

Fifty Brandenburgers were concentrated for the attack, but there were problems from the start. "We didn't have enough Russian uniforms for the whole team. Some of us quickly threw tarpaulins into the trucks and hid a bunch of our comrades in German uniforms underneath them." Seeing the size of the two objectives and the defences arrayed against them, the troopers were petrified. "Fear made me break out in a cold sweat ... my heart was beating like crazy. I looked over to my comrades for reassurance, but their faces were white as sheets too, their hands trembling and their eyes flicking around nervously."

Some of the Brandenburgers drove off to take the railway bridge, while de Giampietro and the majority of the tiny force headed for the road bridge, crowded with retreating Red Army units and civilians, desperate to escape. "We were hardly making any headway and were practically wedged in the throng of people pouring down to the river." The South Tyrolean realised the difficulties they were now in. "For our attack to be successful it relied entirely on the element of surprise ... the first volley of fire had to come from us, and it had to be as powerful as possible ... the enemy mustn't notice how few we were." In the midst of all the chaos, "Russian soldiers jumped onto our vehicles, asking us things we didn't understand, so we just pointed behind us and shouted 'Germansky, Germansky'." Finally reaching the bridge, the Brandenburgers sprang into action before their ruse was discovered. "We threw some hand grenades into the crowd, then jumped down and sprayed bullets wildly around us." Unlike the bridges at Josvainiai and Kedainiai, the huge Daugavpils structure was rigged for demolition, as de Giampietro found: "I sped off to the bridge with my two men, we pulled the wire cutters out from our belts and cut through every single wire in sight."

The Soviets reacted quickly, and soon the Brandenburgers were in danger of being overrun.

A comrade next to me got hit. He stood there for a second, dazed by the shot, and then collapsed in a heap on the ground. I heard yelling that sounded like 'Urrah!' ... there they were, storming the bridge, arms linked together as if they were one solid block ... even women were among them ... how many were there? One hundred, two hundred, five hundred? The entire road along the river was full of them ... we deployed our machine-guns and simply mowed them down. Each bullet must have hit at least one of them.

Somehow the German special forces held the Soviets off until the advance detachment of panzers arrived, to their immense relief. "The German panzers came rolling in, alongside them came the infantry and with that our mission was complete." The price had been high: "Out of fifty men, fifteen had survived. Five had died there and then another thirty had been wounded, some of them seriously, and many of them died in the field hospital." *Oberleutnant* Wolfram Knaak was among the dead on the bridge itself. 8. *Panzerdivision*'s War Diary described the battle and Knaak's death in action: "The second group was deployed against the road bridge with *Oberleutnant* Knaak in the lead vehicle. The Russian guards on the western side of the bridge were taken completely by surprise and gunned down ... an anti-tank gun fired on the lead vehicle, knocking it out and mortally wounding *Oberleutnant* Knaak ... the panzers motored across the road bridge without pausing, destroying the troops on the far bank." *Major* Gerhard Wendenburg rushed his entire panzer battalion across the river and established a bridgehead on the other side. The road to Leningrad was open.

In the aftermath of the battle, de Giampietro was witness to an astounding act by a Red Army survivor:

One of the supposed corpses jumped up, swung itself over the railing, and plummeted down into the river ... What kind of human beings were these? Why would someone pretend to be dead for hours, have panzers and soldiers pass them by, and then try to escape by jumping into the river? This act of desperation filled us all with respect and admiration, but also demonstrated what these enemies of ours were truly made of – no British soldier would ever have done something like that!

Helmut Ritgen was witness to a similar episode: "Beyond the forest we were waiting for resupply near a cornfield for at least two hours. Suddenly two Russians jumped out of the field with their hands raised. A sergeant waved to them to come forward. At that moment they both dodged; one threw a hand grenade and the other fired a pistol at the sergeant – wounding him. Those two Russians must have hidden themselves motionless in that field for three or more hours before we showed up."[8] Such acts weren't restricted to the north. Up and down the new eastern front, Soviet soldiers and airmen were displaying quite extraordinary determination and self-sacrifice in the face of the invader. One German anti-tank gunner, Helmut Pole, saw it for himself: "We came up against a light T-26 tank which we could easily knock out … There was a Russian hanging in the turret who continued to shoot at us with a pistol as we approached. He was dangling inside without any legs, having lost them when the tank was hit."[9]

In *Heeresgruppe Mitte*'s sector, *Major* Peter Neuhoff was riding alongside Heinrich Haape, when his 800-strong battalion was attacked by just five Red Army soldiers. Hiding in the middle of a cornfield, the five waited until Neuhoff's men had almost passed them before springing their ambush. Outnumbered 160 to 1, the Soviets refused to surrender, as Haape recalled: "Neuhoff and I strode into the corn. A commissar and four Russian soldiers were lying on the trampled earth. Their skulls battered into the soil, which had been freshly dug and thrown up into a mound for their suicidal ambush. Our casualties were negligible – one man with a bayonet wound in the arm, another man with a grazed calf." As Neuhoff noted, half in wonder and half in dread; "I didn't expect that. Sheer suicide to attack a battalion at close quarters with just five men."[10]

Rudolf Kurth – like Haape in the front's central zone – wrote a letter home describing the phenomenon as he saw it: "Saturday afternoon, I experienced the most violent fire. The bullets flew over my head, a grenade landed about two to three metres away from me, but I didn't get hit. My Unteroffizier was hit on his helmet, which was damaged but wasn't broken. The German steel helmet is better than any I have ever known. Then we combed through the fields, where seriously injured Russians shot at us. Some of them were in one-man trenches which they couldn't escape from without help – but they still shot at us."[11] Elmar Gustav Lieb, a volunteer in *Pionier Bataillon. 45* – the renowned Ulm Pioneers – told his parents in a letter home that "Russian soldiers, officers and the like are very determined – far more than all previous opponents – and often fight fanatically, even in a seemingly hopeless struggle, preferring death to an honourable surrender".[12] Fritz Hübner recalled: "With what doggedness did these Russian soldiers fight! Of course we had the bad luck on this first day to encounter Stalin cadets. They were aspiring officers and political officers who refused to surrender. Instead, they fought to the last man and had to be beaten or shot to death in their rifle pits."

The same was true down south. One German soldier recalled how "When the position was completely hopeless the Russians would take the pin out a hand grenade and hold it to their stomachs."[13] Intriguingly, he didn't see it as a sign of determination but as blind fanaticism and indifference to death. An NCO in Erich-Heinrich Clössner's *25. Infanterie-Division (mot.)* – Wilhelm Prüller – wrote in his diary: "We have to creep up to each and every hole and then finish off the Russians with pistols or rifles. There are no calls of surrender."[14] Gustav Böker, the anti-tank gunner from Oberg, was beginning to feel less optimistic about his prediction that the campaign would all be over in a month:

I was talking to infantry comrades who were in France and they told me: 'France was nothing like Russia!' Number One; here the roads are terrible, Number Two; Russia is a huge country in terms of area, Number Three; you can't live off the land here because the people themselves have nothing, and Number Four; the Russian does not run away like the Frenchman. The Russian is very tough ... They all believe that if they're captured they will be shot. A few days ago, for example, a few Russian planes were shot down. The crews jumped out with parachutes, but on landing they all shot themselves immediately.[15]

It seemed to many of the invaders that the Soviet was wholly different to any enemy they'd faced before; something strange and unnatural, something to be detested, but also feared. The cavalry officer Hans-Günther Stark said, "The British were adversaries. The French were adversaries too. We didn't regard either as the enemy. But the Soviets were the enemy, a bitter, bitter enemy." A *gebirgsjäger* (mountain infantryman) described how he and his comrades fought off a number of counter-attacks down in *Heeresgruppe Süd*'s sector:

It would be true to say that the Russian soldiers attacked across a carpet of their own dead, and not just once but repeatedly. The failure of earlier attacks, and the losses they incurred, didn't seem to deter them. They came forward in long lines and persisted in making frontal charges against machine-gun fire until only a few were left standing. Only when those few survivors realised their own isolation did they waver and begin to retreat, sometimes not even running away but walking. It was as if they no longer cared about being killed.[16]

The *Wehrmacht* was used to an enemy that understood when it was beaten – that wasn't Barbarossa. Fritz Hübner spoke for many when he said, "The nature of the war had fundamentally changed, and it was alien to us." Another German soldier wrote: "In the West, war was the same honourable old game; nobody went out of their way to be vicious, and fighting often stopped by five in the afternoon. But in the East, the Russians were trying to kill you – all the time."[17] An SS trooper who came across a badly wounded Soviet soldier realised much the same: "He'd been shot in the stomach which meant a certain and painful death ... he was still conscious and looked at us like he wanted to kill us ... all the hate in his face, we were the enemy and he wanted us dead."

No battle demonstrated the different character of Barbarossa better than Brest-Litovsk. Situated right on the border, the city itself was swiftly taken in the first few hours of the invasion, but the fortress and citadel held out, frustrating the attackers. The Austrians of Fritz Schlieper's *45. Infanterie-Division* found themselves in the fight of their lives with an enemy that was outnumbered, outgunned and without hope of relief. In the end, it took no fewer than nine horrific days to subdue the main redoubts, using air strikes, heavy artillery, flamethrowers and then eventually flushing out the remaining defenders by flooding the cellars. Even then a few survivors held out, and it wasn't until a month after the first shots were fired that the very last hold-out succumbed. Taking the fortress, and winning a battle that was over before it had begun, cost *45. ID* forty officers and 442 men killed, and over a thousand wounded.

This ferocious will to resist, coupled with a seemingly fatalistic attitude towards their own mortality, was mirrored in the skies above as the pilots and crews of the VVS sacrificed themselves against a *Luftwaffe* that was qualitatively in a different league. It wasn't just in utilising the *taran* tactic that the Soviet fliers demonstrated their resolve, it was also their willingness to go up again and again and attack the Germans, even when shot out of the sky in droves. Hans-Joachim S. saw it in the north: "Constant air raids by Russians. They're shot down immediately and are lying in heaps in the fields ... The day before yesterday one of the cheeky dogs shot at Helmuth's car – he came down to fifty metres off the ground ... Anyway, I'm happy to be part of the biggest campaign in world history." Franz Siebeler – the former bank apprentice – explained that "the last time we saw Red planes our fighters shot down all nine of the attackers before a bomb was dropped". Heinrich Haape witnessed the same:

A flight of eight Russian bombers came towards us from the east. But this time they had to reckon with the Messerschmitt. The Bf 109s swooped like hawks into a flight of pigeons. They attacked from the sun, firing as they dived ... One by one the bombers were picked off. One Russian burst into flames, a second followed, and like two torches they sank toward the ground. It surprised me to see how slowly they fell. A wing broke off another bomber and the plane spun earthward ... Our fighters continued the attacks until every bomber had been shot down. The action had taken ten minutes at most.

Albert Kesselring's reaction was one of awe mixed with horror. "It seemed to me almost a crime to allow these floundering aircraft to attack us in tactically impossible formations ... one flight after another came in innocently at regular intervals – easy prey for our fighters – it was sheer *kindermord* (usually translated as 'slaughter of the innocents')."

A slaughter of the innocents it certainly was. On just one day, Werner Mölders shot down five attacking bombers himself, with his *geschwader* destroying an almost unbelievable 114 in total, while his friend and comrade Johannes 'Hannes' Trautloft and his *JG. 54 Grünherz* (Green Heart) shot down sixty-five out of seventy-three bombers trying to attack the *Heeresgruppe Nord* spearheads. Their fellow fighter leader Günther Lützow, down south with *JG. 3*, found himself caught on the ground by a VVS bomber attack. Lützow and his men managed to get airborne and shoot down all twenty-seven attacking aircraft in the space of a few minutes.

Hans Roth and his comrades cheered from the ground as they saw their *Luftwaffe* brethren above them: "Our *Luftwaffe* comrades deliver a bit of entertainment. Dogfight after dogfight is fought over our heads." Hans-Joachim S. was dumbfounded by the Soviet tactics. "What damage the Russian air force could do to us if it was in order? Their bombers are a total disaster. Completely unable to manoeuvre, they stubbornly just fly straight ahead and our fighters just shoot them from behind – then they crash."

By the end of Monday 23 June, the *Luftwaffe* was claiming to have destroyed 2,582 Soviet aircraft, and 4,990 six days later. The VVS's bomber arm was almost wiped out. But still the Soviets kept on coming.

For many Germans this behaviour was proof that the Russian wasn't a human being like them, but was indeed the subhuman – the *untermensch* – of Nazi propaganda. Max Simon, a regimental commander in *SS-Totenkopf*, viewed them as such, his description sounding like an observation on a different species: "The native frugality of the Russian and Asiatic allows the restriction of the supply train of their combat troops to the minimum, and also makes it possible to exploit the strength of the individual in a measure that seems unbelievable to the European." *Major* Johann von Kielmansegg, as an officer on the divisional staff of *6. Panzerdivision*, was an educated member of the German officer class and no Nazi fanatic, but even he wasn't immune to seeing the Russians as a breed apart, as he recalled how the Red Army cleared a path through German defensive minefields: "First they would herd cows through the minefields, and when they ran out of cows they used men linked arm in arm, with machine-guns behind them, forcing them over our mines."

For years the Nazis had sought to induce a collective sense of racial superiority among Germans, and now those seeds would bear a harvest of rotten fruit in the East. Alois Breilmann was a simple soldier who described what he saw as he marched into the Soviet Union. For him it was a primitive world lacking in the basic trappings of civilisation: "There are hordes of children, if one is sickly it dies ... The women are no better than the men, they are pitiful cripples." The poverty and human suffering he witnessed elicited no sympathy in the young infantryman; years of vile propaganda had conditioned him to look at them without pity. "We are too good to these people, it's such a shame."[17]

The atrocities such views engendered would be met by fanatical resistance and counter-atrocities, and an already brutal conflict would descend into almost primeval savagery, as Kielmansegg saw for himself on the Dubysa after the Raseiniai battle when the Germans re-crossed to the eastern bank and found their vanguard – or what remained of them: "We found all the men shot, that is murdered, and atrociously mutilated. Eyes had been gouged out, genitals cut off and other cruelties inflicted. Only two of the men had obviously fallen in battle. This was our first such experience, but not the last. I said to my general 'Sir, this will be a very different war from the one in Poland and France.'" All too often the German reaction was to try and outmatch such brutality. In the heat of combat, soldiers took the law into their own hands: "It was incredible the way the Russian fought, they would let us approach to within three metres and then mow us down. Can you imagine them letting us walk right on top of them? When we capture them we make an end to them at once, we hit them on the head with rifle butts."[18] Henk Kistemaker tried to explain why prisoners were sometimes shot out of hand: "When you'd just lost a couple of your own comrades, and the enemy then raises their hands to surrender, you're so full of anger and rage that you just shot them." While at other times, "we just didn't know what to do with all the prisoners".

While individual or 'localised' acts of murder are bad enough, a culture of atrocity, often sanctioned by commanders, is of an altogether different order of magnitude. The war diary of Hans Roth's 299. *Infanterie-Division* stated in the first days of the invasion: "Prisoners were not taken because troops were bitter about the dishonest fighting style of the enemy." 299. *ID* wasn't unique by any means. The actions of Axel von dem Bussche's division – the proud Prussians of the venerable 23. *ID* –

were typical of what was widespread behaviour. On 25 June during a skirmish with retreating Red Army men near Bialystok, the Soviets raised a white flag. Looking to take them captive, a number of Germans went forward, only to be shot down. Six Germans were killed. Retaliation was immediate and disproportionate. The divisional commander, Heinz Hellmich, ordered that no prisoners would be taken for the next twenty-four hours. Hundreds of Soviets were killed as a result, prompting complaints even from some of the unit's own officers, one of whom was Charlotte von der Schulenberg's husband, Fritz-Dietlof. "The Russians must only be shot in battle or upon the order of an officer. Anything else removes all constraints of conduct and allows baser instincts to run riot."

Disappointingly, Schulenberg was more concerned about the maintenance of discipline among the men, rather than the basic criminality of shooting prisoners: "Obviously there is a threat to discipline if our people start to bump off the enemy on their own initiative." Wilhelm Schröder, a radio operator in *10. Panzerdivision* of *Heeresgruppe Mitte*, was more forthcoming in his diary: "A tough fight with the Russians today. At the end of it, all the prisoners were herded together and shot by a machine-gun. This wasn't done in front of us, but in a clearing behind us. However, we all heard the firing and knew what was going on."[19]

Officially, members of the *Wehrmacht* were explicitly banned from committing murder, as was made abundantly clear in the one document every soldier carried with them at all times: their *Soldbuch*. This small document served as their personal military ID, but much more besides. It listed where they had served, any specialist qualifications or courses they had taken, combat days achieved, awards granted and so on, and on the inside cover were the 10 Commandments Governing the Conduct in War of the German Soldier. Several dealt directly with the subject of war crimes:

Number 1 – The German soldier fights fairly to win victory for his people. Acts of cruelty and unnecessary destruction are unworthy of him.
Number 3 – Prisoners of war may not be mistreated or abused.
Number 7 – The civil population is inviolable. A soldier is not permitted to plunder or deliberately to destroy.

Robert Rupp, a junior officer in one of the Army's motorised infantry divisions, saw for himself how often these supposedly iron rules were disregarded: "Many Red Army soldiers whom I saw lying around were without weapons and had been shot with their hands raised ... I saw at least a hundred like this. They say that even an emissary who came with a white flag was shot down. They also shot the wounded."[20] A miner in civilian life, Jakob Geimer was a Saarlander. Drafted into the Army as an infantryman, Geimer wrote to his wife describing how he and his comrades dealt with Soviet soldiers: "The Russian who fights honestly and fairly is respected as an opponent, with the others we know only one word, 'kill'. But don't worry about it … we'll talk about it more when I'm home." Which begs the question, in the heat of battle, how could he accurately distinguish between the two?

It wasn't just enemy soldiers either, the civilian population were often on the receiving end of maltreatment, not least the theft of the few goods or little food they had, as Richard von Rosen remembered: "I came across soldiers breaking into a shop, and I left with a giant sack filled with cigarettes and soap … our panzer ended up with thirty bars of toilet soap." One German soldier back home on leave from Russia told his friends on a drink-fuelled night out: "Do you know how we behaved to Russian civilians? We behaved like devils from hell, we left them to starve to death behind us, thousands and thousands of them … if the Russians should ever come knocking at our door and pay us back just one half of what we've done to them, then you wouldn't ever smile or sing again!"

Ever since the war, such acts have been portrayed by defenders of the *Wehrmacht* as isolated incidents carried out by rogue elements, but there is simply too much evidence to the contrary for this to be believed. While there was no Army-wide order either sanctioning or encouraging this type of behaviour – as there infamously was regarding the treatment of captured political commissars and other Communist Party functionaries – it is clear that the murder of prisoners and abuse of civilians was too widespread to be written off as a few aberrations.

Was it Lucan's famed *furor Teutonicus* (Teutonic fury) – an innate Germanic savagery – or was it something different entirely? One clue can be found in the language used by the invaders themselves. Again and again, in letters, diaries, journals and memoirs, the Soviets – both soldiers and civilians alike – are described by German soldiery as more akin to animal than human; they are not just *the other*, they are a race apart, one with no feelings and no humanity. This was a direct result of a Nazi philosophy that had spewed its venom across Germany for almost a decade, tainting the minds of millions. In this light, tenacious resistance wasn't viewed as brave and honourable, but as senseless and dishonourable, and the primitive conditions people lived in weren't due to poverty and deprivation but a lack of civilisation and culture. In such an atmosphere, whatever the Germans did was justified. It was true that on many occasions the behaviour of Red Army soldiers was dreadful – as the Dutch SS volunteer Henk Kistemaker said, "they shot at our Red Cross vehicles, they killed wounded German soldiers in hospitals and shot many more on the spot after surrendering" – but the German response was to then label every Soviet soldier and civilian as abominable and give the green light to indiscriminate atrocities. Max Simon – the senior *SS-Totenkopf* commander – sent a report to his superiors detailing an incident where he claimed his men were approached by upwards of two hundred Red Army men ostensibly surrendering, when several of them opened fire on the unsuspecting SS men. His men reacted by shooting all two hundred dead. Simon displayed no regret at the slaughter, rather he was incandescent with rage and railed against the now-dead Soviets as "bandits, whipped into a frenzy by bolshevik commissars and fanatical Red Army officers".

In such a febrile atmosphere, Red Army soldiers who "fight fanatically to the point of self-sacrifice, even in a seemingly hopeless fight, and prefer death to an honourable surrender" weren't seen by the Germans as a legitimate enemy, but as brutish vermin who deserved extermination. Heinrich Haape – trying to find his battalion after staying behind to treat some badly wounded artillerymen – was shot at as he went forward. Taking cover with a *hauptmann* and his men, the young doctor was told by the young officer: "We've been playing this game with them since early morning. My job's to comb these woods and cornfields and get rid of these partisans. I've already shot God knows how many." It is telling that he describes the Soviets as partisans and not soldiers. In his mind their resistance was futile, so if they were soldiers they would surrender, but by fighting on they put themselves outside the normal laws of war, and so any atrocity was justified, and even more so given their racial make-up, which plainly horrified him. "What a mixture they are! I've got Mongolians, Tartars and Kalmucks. It's a queer business fighting these slit-eyed bastards, like being in China."

Albert Neuhaus wrote to his wife on 27 June, explaining what this attitude led to in practical terms, and detailing one particular incident:

> We are only taking very few prisoners now, and you can imagine what that means … In a village that we passed through this afternoon, our soldiers hanged a woman from a tree because she had been stirring up the people against German troops – we are making short shrift of these people … The war is being cruelly fought on both sides.

The last line feels like a half-hearted deflection. He had taken a photograph of the hanged woman to show his wife and included it with the letter.

A host of the *Ostheer*'s most senior officers knew what was going on and condoned it, including Erich Hoepner, commander of *Panzergruppe 4*, who issued a directive to his troops before the campaign explicitly framing the upcoming fight as one of all-out annihilation:

The war against Russia is an important chapter in the struggle for the existence of the German nation. It is the old battle of Germanic against Slav peoples, of the defence of European culture against Muscovite-Asiatic inundation, and the repulse of Jewish-Bolshevism. The objective of this battle must be the destruction of present-day Russia and it must therefore be conducted with unprecedented severity. Every military action must be guided in planning and execution by an iron will to exterminate the enemy mercilessly and totally. In particular, no adherents of the present Russian-Bolshevik system are to be spared.

That it was Hoepner who issued this Nazi diatribe was somewhat incongruous. A confidant of such prominent anti-Nazis as Ludwig Beck and Erwin von Witzleben, he believed that Hitler's foreign adventures could destroy Germany, but just as with so many other senior officers at the time, he was prepared to co-operate with the dictator, especially if that meant the destruction of Soviet communism.

Such exhortations confirmed to many members of the *Ostheer* what Nazi propaganda had always told them; that all Soviets were uncivilised brutes who deserved everything they got. A member of a construction unit repairing bridges in the wake of the advance, Fritz Pabst's views were typical: "With these people, stealing and cheating is the order of the day. We guard the vehicle park at night … Last night several locals crawled through the fence trying to steal whatever they could find. Challenged by our guards, they fired at us with pistols, of course we shot back. One of them was seriously wounded and six were arrested. This morning we handed them over to the field police, where they will face the most severe punishment. This is not an isolated case, almost every night we arrest a few."

Very quickly, the atrocities multiplied, and some senior officers began to become concerned. One such officer was Joachim Lemelsen, a full general and corps commander in Guderian's *Panzergruppe 2:* "I am repeatedly finding out about the shooting of prisoners, defectors or deserters, carried out in an irresponsible, senseless and criminal manner." Lemelsen was clear about what he thought of it. "This is murder." Although, as with his young compatriot, Fritz-Dietlof von der Schulenberg, he seemed less concerned with the grotesqueness of the acts themselves, and more worried about the impact on the enemy's will to resist: "Soon the Russians will get to hear about the countless corpses lying along the routes taken by our soldiers, without weapons and with hands raised, dispatched at close range by shots to the head. The result will be that the enemy will hide in the woods and fields and continue to fight, and we shall lose countless comrades." The truth in Lemelsen's words was witnessed by one German soldier behind the front: "The shout went up, 'Alarm!' The Russians were outside regimental headquarters.

They had surrounded it, and with fixed bayonets broke into the officers' quarters. They shot the adjutant, orderly officer and the medical officer in the doorway of their forest hut. NCOs and headquarters staff were killed before they could grab their weapons. The regimental commander, *Oberstleutnant* Brehmer, barricaded himself behind a woodpile and held the Russians off for two hours with his submachine-gun."

The truth was that the *Wehrmacht* had come across an enemy unlike any other they had fought. The Red Army and the VVS weren't like the Royal Yugoslav or French Armies, the *Armée de l'Air* or even the Royal Air Force; their history, their outlook and the very geography of the land they sprang from made them willing and able to resist the invader with utter ferocity. It was something the Germans had not spent any time or effort in trying to understand before Barbarossa was launched, as Max Simon himself acknowledged: "At the beginning of the campaign, we German soldiers, generally speaking, knew little about our enemy."

As early as day two of the war, soldiers like Hans Roth were beginning to see what this lack of forethought meant on the ground: "The Russian tank attack commences at noon ... never have we experienced anything like this – one hundred Russian tanks are fighting against us ... Encirclement of the enemy has been achieved by dawn despite the desperate attempts by the Reds to break out ... Our own casualties are also high – we are so exhausted we could pass out." Those Red Army men flinging themselves against the guns of Roth and his comrades were responding to the calls of young officers like Captain Ivan Krylov, who summarised the spirit of defiance in blood-curdling language: "The men have been ordered not to die before taking at least one German with them ... kill them with your rifle, with your bayonet, with your knife, tear their throats out with your teeth. Don't die without leaving a dead German behind you."[21] Men like Krylov were, as the young Elmar Gustav Lieb put it, "the implacable, hateful soul of the resistance". For the young *landsers* facing such unstinting resistance it was incredibly frightening, as Henk Kistemaker described so vividly: "We heard them coming. It started with a loud 'Urrah!' like a thousand throats yelling, and they ran at our line." German machine-guns opened up and "like being struck by a giant hand the first wave and then the second just fell, but they kept on coming. They pushed on, climbing over their own dead and wounded and getting closer and closer to us ... we had no time to think, we just fell back on our training; shoot, load, shoot, load, change the barrel, shoot, load. It went on and on. The Russians were falling within 10 metres of our trenches ... if they didn't give up pretty soon we'd be in big trouble." Then, just before calamity struck, "the attack stopped and the enemy retreated, or rather what was left of them did. We finally allowed ourselves to breathe deeply – in, out, in, out. Oh my God that was a close call."

In the skies above the invasion front the first few days also offered worrying glimpses of what was to come for the Germans. For Johannes Kaufmann, the Soviet airfields at Pinsk and Volkovysk were still the target and were remorselessly hit. "These missions proved far more effective than our previous efforts. We had already gained sufficient experience to know exactly what was expected of us." But it wasn't all plain sailing, despite the dreadful losses the Soviets had suffered: "The Russians were clearly starting to recover from the shock of our initial assault. The missions of 23 and 24 June saw the *Gruppe* (usually two or more *staffeln*) suffer its first combat fatalities. The unfortunate 2. *Staffel* lost an aircraft on 23 June to ground fire, with both crew members being killed. The following day it was the turn of 1. *Staffel* when one of their machines was brought down by Soviet fighters, again with both crew members losing their lives." Kaufmann himself was on the receiving end of unwelcome enemy attention: "My own aircraft was hit in the radiator and I had to limp back from Pinsk to Radzyn on one engine. It was not a pleasant experience."

Helmut Mahlke had a worse trial in his Stuka: "24 June; for the third time today, at 1414hrs, we took off from Dubovo to attack the enemy. Our mission was to disrupt Soviet supply lines by destroying the northern exit routes out of Minsk." Approaching the city all seemed well until "Achtung! Enemy fighters!" Diving down through cloud, Mahlke and his fellow dive-bomber crews managed to evade the Soviet fighters, only to come up against

> … a quadruple flak cannon mounted on a truck chassis. It was already spitting fire from all four barrels … I let fly at him with my two MG17 wing machine-guns. My aim was good, but the Russian was still firing too – straight back at me and with twice as many barrels … Suddenly a deafening bang! The engine had collected a nasty packet, a very nasty packet! Cordite smoke filled the cockpit … A thick stream of oil started to gush out of the tank in front of me. Within seconds rivulets of hot oil from the punctured tanks and pipes had covered everything.

Realising the stricken plane couldn't make it back to base some 120 kilometres away, Mahlke searched for a flat piece of ground. Espying one, he went for it, only to see a ditch running through the middle at the last second. "I deliberately slammed the machine down into the ground … sure enough it bounced into the air again, cleared the ditch and came back down in the tiny field on the other side." Mahlke and his rear gunner clambered from the burning aircraft and managed to hide out in a nearby wood. Evading Soviet patrols, the two airmen set off westwards, and after a couple of days – and with the help of some friendly local ethnic

Poles – finally reached the onrushing German spearheads. Hitching a ride on a motorcycle and sidecar, the two fliers managed to get back to Dubovo on the evening of 27 June, to the surprise and delight of their commander: "'God in heaven Mahlke – you've managed to make it back, and so quickly, I can scarcely believe it!' Then came the first bit of official paperwork – removing our names from the 'Missing in Action' list." The twenty-seven-year-old pilot realised how lucky he had been: "Another crew had also failed to return from the 24 June mission. But *Leutnant* Friedrich Bornemann and *Gefreiter* Franz Jordas hadn't been as lucky as us. They had been attacked by enemy fighters and had gone down in flames ... neither had managed to escape from their burning machine before it hit the ground and exploded."

The Soviets had taken a hammer blow in the first days of the campaign, but they were already beginning to fight back on land and in the air.

For Leeb's *Heeresgruppe Nord*, this fightback manifested itself in Soviet determination to smash Manstein's bridgehead over the Daugava and throw the Germans back over the river. Ferocious counterattacks were launched by elements of two Soviet armies against the erstwhile attackers now turned defenders, and one group of Soviet tanks almost managed to reach the road bridge before being smashed into scrap by a newly arrived anti-tank battery. For three days the Red Army flung itself at Manstein's men, Dmitry Lelyushenko's 21st Mechanized Corps losing seventy-nine of its 107 BT-7 and T-26 tanks in action. One *landser* described the fighting; "German panzers ... flew in the air like toys. Many, many German graves. Worse than France. Non-one's seen anything like this before." To try and salvage the situation, Reinhardt was ordered to reinforce Manstein, but his men were still fighting at Raseiniai. By the time Reinhardt crossed the Daugava to the north and joined up with Manstein's men, the Soviets had already bled themselves white. The offensive could push on once more.

Erich Brandenberger was straining at the leash to press on – after all, his division had advanced an astonishing 200 miles in just 100 hours to reach the Daugava; truly one of the great feats of the war so far. With Lelyushenko's corps burnt-out, the way was open for Brandenberger's panzers, only for the Bavarian to then receive an astonishing instruction from Hoepner as his Army commander: "The Commander-in-Chief of the Army Group (Leeb) is strongly of the view that ... the *Panzergruppe* alone cannot break enemy resistance between the Daugava and Leningrad and is taking measures to bring up the infantry armies."

That was it. In a single paragraph, Leeb had abandoned the blitzkrieg upon which the *Wehrmacht* was relying for the success of Barbarossa. Since invasion day, the watchwords of the offensive had been tempo, tempo, tempo; von Reichenau had made it obligatory for every officer in 6. *Armee* with a map-board to write the legend "Pursuit without rest" at its top, and Manstein had issued a standing order to his men – "Keep going, keep going. Never mind about your flanks. Never mind about cover." Leeb himself – just one week earlier – had been emphatic: "Forward! Don't stop for anything. Once the enemy has been thrown back don't let him consolidate." Now, that was cast asunder as the hatchet-faced *feldmarschall* ordered the advance in the north be reduced to the speed of a marching man – just as in 1812. The brittle consensus among the Barbarossa leadership that speed was the key to the invasion's success now faced its first major test.

Leeb's decision would have huge ramifications, but its significance was drowned out by events elsewhere, in particular almost 200 miles south in a lozenge-shaped slice of the Polish-Belarussian plain. There, with the Polish city of Bialystok at its western end, and Minsk, the capital of Belarus, over 100 miles away at its eastern end, the first great encirclement battle of the campaign was being fought. In a pre-planned operation, *Heeresgruppe Mitte* surged forward, two claws outstretched in a giant pincer to surround and then crush Dmitry Pavlov's entire Western Front (a Red Army Front was roughly equivalent in size to a German *Heeresgruppe*).

The northern pincer was Hermann Hoth's *Panzergruppe 3*, a concentrated mass of four panzer and three motorised infantry divisions, while to the south was Heinz Guderian's more amorphous *Panzergruppe 2*, already large at five panzer, one cavalry, one *Waffen-SS* and no fewer than five infantry divisions (two of them motorised), and now increased by the addition of the three infantry divisions of Walter Schroth's *XII. Korps*. Both panzer armies were told not to stop for anything.

In the midst of *Panzergruppe 3* was 7. *Panzerdivision* and Hans von Luck. Much to his chagrin, the young von Luck had been ordered to leave his battalion to become his divisional commander's adjutant right at the start of the invasion, and within a day or two he was champing at the bit to get into the action. Unsurprisingly, he jumped at the chance for some excitement when sent on a mission to try and find the 'missing' divisional motorcycle battalion. Driving off into a wilderness of forest in his beloved Mercedes, accompanied only by his ever-present orderly Erich Beck, he soon found himself on "roads that we wouldn't even designate as country lanes". Having found the battalion, he was returning to headquarters when he came to a clearing "where both sides of the track were full of Russians. They recognised us at once and I saw them bring their guns up ... bullets were already whistling past us, inaccurately since Beck had forced them into cover by firing bursts from his machine-pistol. Our Mercedes, which definitely hadn't been designed for Russian roads, jolted and bounced over the undulating ground.

One shot struck the car but didn't cause much damage." Escaping the Soviets, Luck reached headquarters and the headlong advance continued. "Our aerial reconnaissance reported large concentrations of troops west of Minsk and around it. our Division was to thrust past the city to the north and cut off the Russians retreat to the east. Another panzer corps was to thrust past the city to the south."

In that southern panzer corps was *4. Panzerdivision* and Richard von Rosen. "At 0230hrs we got underway again ... that night the *kompanie* had advanced sixty kilometres, a remarkable achievement bearing in mind the early heavy going and interruptions. To our annoyance *3. Panzerdivision* had got to Kobryn before us and was already continuing on the *Rollbahn* (German-designated main advance and supply road)." Advancing behind Walter Model's *3. Panzerdivision*, Rosen and his comrades witnessed the destruction left in its wake: "An indescribable sight met our eyes, one burnt-out Russian tank after another, some with great shell holes in them, some destroyed by our aircraft in low-level attacks. On that morning alone we saw the wreck of at least a full armoured division. In addition, there were guns of every calibre, field kitchens and a host of other military equipment. It was really difficult to take it all in ... We kept going flat out."

Those low-level air attacks were being carried out by the likes of Helmut Mahlke and his fellow Stuka pilots:

> The Army's fast armoured spearheads had driven deep into enemy territory ... shattered enemy units were trying desperately to form a new line of defence ... our task now was to cut off their retreat and prevent them escaping from the armoured pincers that were inexorably closing in around them. Our attacks therefore were aimed at stopping them streaming eastwards; complete stretches of railway track were torn up by our bombs, bridges were destroyed, numerous temporary crossing points were knocked down almost as quickly as they were erected ... at many places on the river banks were large untidy collections of abandoned vehicles of every kind. Our bombs rained down on the thousands of enemy troops trapped by these bottlenecks, sowing death and destruction and adding yet more confusion to the already panic-stricken masses.

Exalted by the success of mission after mission, Mahlke also pitied his enemy. "The altitude at which we operated spared us most of the grisly details, but nevertheless the scenes of carnage were terrible to behold." Heinz Knoke had no such reservations, his concerns were centred on the fact that bombing missions were denying him the opportunity to score his first aerial kill: "The business of bombing is becoming increasingly distasteful to me. We who are engaged in bombing operations miss the airborne fighting. It is high time for me to bag my 'first'."

The Bialystok-Minsk battle was pure blitzkrieg; the *Luftwaffe* overhead acting as airborne artillery, and massed panzers on the ground seeking out weak spots and smashing through, driving ever deeper into the enemy's rear, sowing confusion and chaos. Co-ordination between land and air was spot on, with Rosen and Mahlke almost meeting when Rosen was ordered to "make a feint ... and then operate against the nearby town of Baranovichi", even as Mahlke was told, "We were to move forward to Baranovichi, southwest of Minsk." The two never met, but the outcome of this hand-in-glove approach was dramatic, as Rosen discovered: "By radio came the report that *18. Panzerdivision (Panzergruppe 3)* was already in our vicinity, which meant the encirclement of Bialystok was completed." Von Luck was there too. "Minsk was enveloped in a pincer movement, the pocket was closed and a large number of prisoners were taken."

Just how many prisoners soon became clear. The Red Army's Western Front was wiped off Moscow's Order of Battle: four armies, comprising twenty divisions, were destroyed. The Soviets lost some 4,800 tanks and over 9,000 guns and mortars – more than the entire *Wehrmacht* invasion force possessed at the beginning of Barbarossa. The human cost to the Red Army was astounding, with some 417,729 men lost, the majority becoming POWs. As for the Germans, they lost 101 panzers, over 250 aircraft to the VVS's eleven hundred, and just 12,157 men, the majority from *Panzergruppe 2*. Heinz Knoke was full of admiration for the victory: "The Army has been able to achieve success beyond the most optimistic expectations."

By Wednesday 9 July, when the pocket was declared destroyed, Bock's panzers had advanced 200 miles into the central Soviet Union, and were already a third of the way to Moscow. Bialystok-Minsk was a huge victory, but it could have been even larger.

The panzers actually shut the Bialystok-Minsk pocket twelve days earlier on Friday 27 June, but only had enough men to position a wafer-thin picket line around it, through which trapped Red Army soldiers poured like water through a sieve. Tens of thousands of Soviet soldiers escaped to be reformed into new units and sent back into battle. What was needed to hold a pocket closed and crush it wasn't Bock's precious panzers but the infantry of *Heeresgruppe Mitte*'s *4.* and *9. Armees*. The problem was that the infantry lacked motorised transport and were having to slog forward on foot and horse.

Gotthard Heinrici – a corps commander in *4. Armee* – described what it was like to his wife: "It means running, running until our tongues hang out, always running, running, running ... you wade ankle-deep in dust.

Every step, every moving vehicle, raises up impenetrable clouds of it. The march routes are characterized by yellow-brown clouds that hang in the sky like long veils."[22] One of Heinrici's soldiers complained that "even after a short while, the dust is lying finger-thick on my face and uniform". The Saxons of Alexander von Hartmann's *71. ID* felt the same. "A miserable fight against the dust. You can't describe it. How often do you have to stop because you just can't see two metres because of thick brown-yellow dust … Excessive heat, dreadful roads and the barely tolerable dust."[23] Hans von Luck sympathised with his footsore brethren: "Our infantry, whose inhuman hardships made us feel sorry for them, followed up on foot." Helmut Pabst recalled how even nightfall didn't bring any rest: "We marched with the moon behind us into a dark, threatening sky. It was like marching into a black hole; the ghostly landscape was pale and bare."

Snatching some desperately needed rest, Pabst and his comrades were soon ordered to push on. "We slept like the dead for an hour and got up unsteadily. You wake up slowly, and at each stop you sleep. At any time during the advance you can see troops sleeping by the roadside, exactly where they had thrown themselves down. Sometimes they're doubled up like they're dead." Fit and well-trained as they were, the *landsers* were feeling the strain. "The thought of having to get up penetrates your drugged sleep with difficulty. When I woke the man next to me he kept falling back with a completely blank face … Another man had started to write a letter to his girl and had fallen asleep. I took the sheet away quietly; he hadn't quite managed three lines."[24]

Trudging ever onwards to help seal the Bialystok-Minsk pocket were Rudolf Kurth and RB – the latter a *pionier* in *31. Infanterie-Division*: "My mosquito net is always over my head and neck, because even in the sun the mosquitoes annoy us poor soldiers. Tonight, during my guard duty, the beasts were almost unbearable. Our scheduled march day goes something like this; wake up between 02.00 and 05.00 … As the advance regiment of the division we build bridges here and there where necessary. You can imagine it isn't an easy task to withstand the attempts of the Russians to break out. Now, as we march, we are constantly having to deal with scattered parts of the Russian army that are in the great forests." Kurth's experience was no better.

> You also get wet feet, the water runs in from above, and that quickly makes your feet sore, which is the most unpleasant thing. I have weathered the hardships as best as I can so far. On a muddy forest path my left boot got stuck and in freeing it I tore off the sole … but now my boot is repaired again. We are in the most beautiful landscape, but today there is little sense in it, the hardships … Such marching is shit.

To the north Wilhelm Lübbecke described much the same experience as he and his comrades in *Heeresgruppe Nord* marched towards Manstein and his panzers on the Daugava: "We plodded countless miles through stifling heat and thick clouds of dust ... we could hear the perpetual din of gunfire and explosions in the distance. In drainage ditches, and out in the fields that lined the road, hundreds of still-warm, contorted bodies lay where they had fallen. The enemy tanks we passed were wrecked hulks, often still belching an oily black smoke ... our planes swept along roads crowded with Russian men and vehicles ... they destroyed everything in their path."[25]

That march across a land seemingly without end, plagued by dust, heat and innumerable insects was an experience that would be endured by hundreds of thousands of ordinary German soldiers that summer. It was these men, the *Wehrmacht*'s *landsers*, who would bear the brunt of Hitler's war in the Soviet Union. The term *landser* itself comes from *landsmann*, a title adopted by the soldiers of the kingdom of Saxony in the late nineteenth century to differentiate themselves from the soldiery of other German mini-states. Over the years it gained national currency and became a catch-all nickname for Germany's soldiers as a whole, akin to Britain's tommy, but slightly different; a *landser* was a common soldier but also a veteran, an old sweat so to speak, whose life was "basic; eat the food, evacuate the food, sleep, guard and fight". In Russia they led a wretched existence: "Many were glad they were constipated, even though it brought headaches and stomach cramps ... those with dysentery suffered the most ... together with all the odours from unwashed bodies, feet and clothing, you can imagine we didn't smell very sweet."[26]

The panzer crews were far better off than the foot-sloggers, but also suffered, as Rosen recalled: "In our filthy uniforms we were a seedy looking crowd, not a clean spot anywhere, our skin grey with dust, the pores black ... everything was dirty, sticky and we stank. The dust made us suffer terribly, our throats were dry, our eyes smarted. Even the protective goggles weren't totally effective as dust found its way through every tiny crack." Franz Siebeler remembered the same. "You wash yourself at every opportunity, but after five minutes of driving you look dirty again. Your eyes smart from the dust. But I can't drive with goggles, they fog up immediately and then you can't see anything at all ... The going is so slow and you swallow a lot of dust. Yesterday the march continued until midnight. This night driving is the worst of all."

As it was it took Rudolf Kurth and his fellow infantrymen over a week to arrive and take over responsibility for the Minsk pocket – a whole, precious week when, as Luck said, "The Russians lacked any organised opposition, our advance had been too rapid for our opponents to have had time to construct effective lines of defence. It looked very like another blitzkrieg." Now, once more, they were free to advance east again. Dog-tired, stinking of oil and sweat, Rosen, Siebeler and their fellow panzer crews set off through the forest "along wretched roads".

The encirclement and annihilation of the Western Front was a disaster for the Red Army. Its destruction cost the Front commander his life. Recalled to Moscow in disgrace, Dmitry Pavlov and almost his entire staff were executed on Stalin's orders for incompetence.

The German hope now was that Moscow would have nothing left to fill the massive hole torn in their front line, and that *Heeresgruppe Mitte* could march more or less unmolested to victory. They were to be sorely disappointed. Losing over 400,000 men might have been a fatal blow for the Red Army had it not been for the fact that even before the Bialystok-Minsk battle was over, Moscow had called another 5,000,000 men to the colours. The State couldn't hope to clothe, train and arm such a host any time soon – and it didn't attempt to – as the young SS trooper Andreas Fleischer knew: "The Russians had some excellent units, but many of the rest were rubbish, we called them 'second-line units' – they weren't trained and just had rope holding up their trousers. A lot of them didn't even have weapons. They were told before they went into an attack, 'take the weapons from the dead', they were still soldiers though."

Benefiting from a post-Civil War baby boom, almost half the Soviet population in 1941 was under twenty years old. The 1923 Soviet age-class would produce 3,000,000 eighteen-year-old males in 1941, and roughly the same in the succeeding years. This gave Moscow a huge well of eligible manpower to drink from, and drink it did, sacrificing them in their hundreds of thousands. The real question was whether the Germans could wipe out Soviet formations quicker than Moscow could create them. What Moscow needed to win that race more than anything else was time, and that time was being bought by Pavlov's Western Front, even as it was being annihilated, and by its brethren in the VVS who were paying their own blood price as Kesselring's *kindermord* in the skies wiped out whole classes of Soviet aviators.

To keep the fight in the air going, Moscow cut pilot training in the academies to the bare minimum, focusing the youngsters on mastering take-off and landing and little else. With as few as eight to ten hours flying time, they were then sent forward to their regiments and given I-153 biplanes which had been destined for the scrapyard before being pressed back into front-line service. As one of the more experienced fliers said of his new comrades, "The hardest thing was to get the novice pilots to maintain their position in combat formation. As soon as the Messers (German Bf109 fighters) appeared they would close up tighter on the formation leader. Instead of concentrating on the target you had to watch out not to collide with one of them." Luck remembered these benighted young men and their machines: "It soon became clear that the Russian air force only had obsolete machines at its disposal, but that, above all, their pilots weren't as good as ours. This was naturally a great relief to us, and when Russian aircraft appeared we hardly bothered to take cover. We often had to smile in fact, when, for want of bombs, thousands of nails rained down on us from their bomb bays." Henk Kistemaker didn't think much of the Soviet pilots either: "In the beginning there wasn't much Russian fighter activity, but once in a while some appeared and attacked us ... but when they attacked us they always shot at the flank of the convoy, and that only caused minor damage and casualties. Our planes always attacked the length of a convoy because it caused more enemy casualties ... I never understood the Russian tactics."

If Moscow had the men, it also needed the weapons to arm them, and, while Erich Marcks had based his original plan for Barbarossa on his belief the Red Army would have to defend its supply and industrial centres in the west, Moscow took an altogether different approach – the one alluded to by Werner Baumbach as he toured the country; the Soviets would build an industrial megalith in the east from the ground up.

Just two days after the opening of Barbarossa, Stalin ordered the establishment of an Evacuation Soviet under the auspices of Gosplan – the State Planning Commission. Its president was Nikolai Schvernik, but its driving force was the pragmatic, 'glacial' Leningrader and administrative genius, Alexei Kosygin. Working at an almost maniacal pace, Kosygin managed to assemble some one and a half million railway wagons and use them to transfer no fewer than 2,593 industrial enterprises eastwards, of which 1,523 were classed as 'major'. One such factory was Aircraft Production Plant No. 295 in the southwestern Russian city of Voronezh. Dismantled and packed onto waiting freight wagons, it was shipped 3,000 kilometres east to Kuybyshev in Siberia. Just over 30 per cent of its workforce went with it, with the remainder to be recruited locally and trained-up. Unloaded and reassembled, one month later the very first Il-2 ground-attack aircraft rolled off the new production line from parts made earlier in Voronezh, and one month after that the new plant – now renamed No. 18 – was producing seven complete *Shturmoviks* per day.

German aerial reconnaissance quickly detected the evacuation, overhead flights reporting the huge build-up at rail heads and the constant stream east, but there was very little the *Luftwaffe* could do about it. A pre-war focus on providing the Army with its airborne artillery had led the *Luftwaffe* to focus on building a tactical bomber fleet rather than a strategic one. So its frontline *geschwader* boasted hundreds of twin-engine, short-range Heinkel He 111s, Dornier Do 17s and Junkers Ju 88s, but not a single long-range, four-engine, heavy bomber. The situation suited the Army very well, with troops usually having to wait no longer than twenty to thirty minutes for a called-in airstrike to arrive overhead – and now it suited Moscow too, which was able to carry out its industrial relocation programme in peace. As the renowned historian Norman Davies points out, this helped the Soviet Union produce no fewer than 15,735 aircraft, 6,590 tanks and a staggering 67,800 artillery guns in 1941 alone. Little wonder the exercise was later described as an 'economic Stalingrad'.

With the German advance in the northern and central sectors stopped in its tracks waiting for the infantry to catch-up, what of the south, what of the thrust into the agricultural and industrial riches of Ukraine and the Donets? Responsibility for conquering this vast, almost sub-continent, lay with *Heeresgruppe Süd* – Army Group South – in many ways the odd one out of the three *Ostheer* strike forces. It was a powerful grouping, considerably larger than Leeb's *Nord*, but smaller than Bock's *Mitte*. It was infantry-heavy, with twenty-nine foot-slogger formations of various stripes, including one mountain and three light divisions, and only one panzer army – Ewald von Kleist's *Panzergruppe 1*. But what really set it apart from its two siblings was its diversity.

Except for the Finns, all the Reich's allied troops were with *Heeresgruppe Süd*: the Italian *CSIR*, Budapest's *Carpathian Group*, the Slovaks Corps, and the daddy of them all – the Romanian 3rd and 4th Armies. In all, the allied contribution constituted some twenty divisions and thirteen separate brigades. Poorly equipped, lacking in training and transport, and often indifferently led, they were nonetheless a major force and one to be handled with care by whoever Hitler felt best suited to command such a disparate conglomeration. His choice was Gerd von Rundstedt.

Sixty-five years old in the summer of 1941, the straight-backed Prussian was a scion of one of his country's oldest noble families, and a living legend in the German Army. Having retired in 1938 after a distinguished career, he was brought back at Hitler's express wish for the invasion of Poland and held commands in all the subsequent Hitlerian operations. Celebrated throughout the *Wehrmacht* as the epitome of the military professional, he was in poor health – not helped by his cognac and cigar consumption – and wasn't noted for his diplomacy or tact with peers and subordinates. Given a role where he would need both in spades, he struggled to adapt, tending to treat his charges simply as inferior Germans.

The other defining aspect of *Heeresgruppe Süd* was the way it was positioned. Right in the middle of its frontage towered the Carpathian mountains, effectively dividing the sector into two. This necessitated a split in the army group with three of Rundstedt's four German formations, Walter von Reichenau's *6. Armee*, Carl-Heinrich von Stülpnagel's *17. Armee* and Kleist's *Panzergruppe 1*, to the north abutting *Heeresgruppe Mitte*, and with the 65,000 square kilometres of the Pripet marshes as their boundary. Everything else would be to the south, along the River Prut all the way to the Black Sea – including his last remaining German force, Eugen von Schobert's *11. Armee* – and the Romanians. Invasion day was also different for Rundstedt's men. His northern – German – grouping went into action straightaway, but not his southern wing. There, apart from a few actions to secure bridgeheads – such as Helmut Paulus's at Skuleni – the Germans and their allies held firm and waited.

For the northern grouping, the fighting was fierce, as Hans Roth testified: "Our rapid advance has created a terrible situation for us; only the road and its borders are cleared of enemy troops, there's no time to comb the forests on either side, and that's precisely where the enemy are assembling. Time and again there are small battles to the rear of the frontline. Supply convoys are being attacked and obliterated ... Red aircraft are hanging over us like flies. It's a miracle their relentless attacks have only caused a few casualties ... the enemy fires unceasingly at our bridgehead." It was hard going precisely because this was where the main strength of the Red Army was positioned – nearly a million men and almost 5,000 tanks, deeply echeloned in prepared defences. There would be no quick breakthrough here, no dashing charge *à la* Manstein, and not enough armour to repeat Bock's Bialystok-Minsk success.

Losses were heavy as the German spearhead ground forward through the Soviet bunkers and trenches. "A sad day for me. Four dear comrades have fallen; Walter Wolff, Horas, Muegge the ever good humoured, and Schielke. Many more have been badly wounded. I myself am totally exhausted; spiritually and physically. We have just had another attack from a Red bomber. Gruber was killed." This was Hans Roth after just three days of combat. Franz Siebeler wrote to his parents about the bunker battles: "The enemy has suffered heavy losses ... According to the assault troops, enemy soldiers had left the bunkers as a result of our artillery bombardment, but political commissars forced them back into them at gunpoint."

Fighting alongside Roth, Siebeler and their comrades were the troopers of Felix Steiner's *SS-Wiking* and Sepp Dietrich's *Leibstandarte-SS Adolf Hitler.* The former had Scandinavian, Dutch and Flemish volunteers in its ranks, and the latter were the dictator's own bodyguard, fresh from glory in Greece. One of Dietrich's battalion commanders was Kurt Meyer, soon to earn the nickname *Panzermeyer*, and the man who in 1944 would become the youngest divisional commander in the *Wehrmacht* as he and his men battled the western Allies in Normandy. That was for the future; now, here in southern Russia, he was in a wholly different type of war. "The situation was completely new to us. Confused, I looked at my maps to brief my men on the situation, but the old criteria no longer applied. Where was friend and where was foe? Far ahead of us were the panzers, infantry were fighting a few kilometres in front of us, Russians were to the north and south of us ... I summed up the situation thus: 'As of today the enemy is everywhere.'" Ordered to advance sixty kilometres in a single bound and capture Rovno, Meyer had no choice but to use speed as a weapon. "At first slowly, then more swiftly, we drove towards the dark forests. Destroyed Russian tanks were on both sides of the road. Trucks and horse-drawn vehicles were abandoned beneath the trees. At one place we found twelve camouflaged Russian T-26s. Out of fuel, they had been left behind."

Meyer was full of admiration for his foe – "The Russians fought tenaciously and obstinately for every inch of ground" – but was also witness to the flip side of the coin. "The naked bodies of a brutally butchered *kompanie* of German soldiers lay before us. Their hands had been fastened with wire. Widely staring eyes gazed at us. The officers had met an even crueller fate ... we found their bodies torn to pieces and trampled underfoot."

It would later be claimed that after finding the mutilated bodies of half a dozen of his own men, Sepp Dietrich gave the same 'no prisoners' order to the *Leibstandarte* as Heinz Hellmich had to his own *23.ID*, but there is little credible evidence to back this up. Not that the invaders behaved with restraint, they didn't, as Roth wrote after he and his unit captured Lutsk: "A few comrades have pulled the remaining Red Army soldiers and Jews from their hiding places. A solo gun performance echoed across the square, and with that the mob ascended to the heavens." Operating alongside some German armour, Roth and his team left a lone panzer to re-position a cannon. "When we returned, we found it in flames. A civilian, who was in hiding, had set it on fire. He was captured and also set on fire."

As the fighting raged on, *Heeresgruppe Süd* received the same shock that their northern cousins had had at Raseiniai when confronted by KV-series behemoths, only this time it was at the hands of arguably the finest tank of the war – the Soviet T-34. Armed with two machine-guns and a powerful 76.2mm main gun, it boasted frontal armour over 40mm thick – the *Panzer III*'s was 15-30mm – and the Soviet tank benefited from that armour being sloped to a precise degree to maximise the chances of a shot simply bouncing off it. It also had very wide tracks and a Christie suspension system that allowed it to perform extremely well off-road, and its diesel engine made it less likely to catch fire if hit. This masterpiece of armoured engineering was the closest thing yet to the perfect balance between the three central tenets of firepower, protection and mobility, and it knocked the vast majority of the *panzerwaffe*'s vehicles into a cocked hat.

Heeresgruppe Süd's opponent – the Red Army's Southwestern Front – had several hundred T-34s, and their appearance in battle had much the same effect in the south as the KVs had had in the north. One of their first encounters was with the men of Hans-Valentin Hube's *16. Panzerdivision.* A single T-34 drove towards the oncoming Germans and was engaged by the unit's anti-tank gunners. At a range of 100 yards the first shot rang out, hit, and then, nothing, the tank kept on coming. Another shot, another hit, and then more and more – twenty-three in all from several guns, and still the tank was moving. Eventually the troop commander ordered his men, "Aim at the turret ring!" At last, the fire had an effect, and with its turret jammed, the lone Soviet tank turned and headed back the way it had come, damaged but still undefeated.

Time and again T-34s would appear and be deluged with fire from the Germans' standard 37mm *PaK36* anti-tank gun, only for the gunners to see their shells bounce harmlessly off the Soviet machines. One soldier in Hans von Tettau's *24. Infanterie-Division* wrote in his diary:

> Indescribable chaos. Motorised columns and infantry in hasty retreat. Now we had seen with our own eyes what headlong flight, what turmoil and horror are called forth by that one word: tanks! ... Their tracks crush everything, make mincemeat of motorcyclists and their machines, ride over guns, gun-carriages, gun-crews and horses. It's been said that two battalions were ground completely into the dust.[27]

Having seen them bash his own panzers around, Kleist described them as "the finest tanks in the world". In a matter of days the troops began to deride the *PaK36* as the *Panzeranklopfgerät* (tank door knocker). It is hard to express just what a terrible shock this was for the *landsers* on the frontline. A nation they had believed primitive and backward had somehow produced a tank that was apparently unstoppable. The widespread belief in the superiority of all things German took a major knock.

Von Rundstedt himself expressed surprise at the existence of the T-34 and its KV stablemates, echoing officers like Johann von Kielmansegg: "It was a complete surprise, nobody in Germany knew about these tanks, or even that they were under construction."[28] That their existence was a total secret seems difficult to believe. Earlier that same year, no less a figure than Heinz Guderian hosted a Soviet delegation on a tour of Germany's panzer factories and training schools. On being shown the latest *Panzer IV* model, the Red Army officers complained that the Germans must be holding out on them, as the brand-new panzer couldn't possibly be the heaviest tank they had. "It seems that the Russians must already possess better and heavier tanks than we do." Having reached that conclusion it is inconceivable that Guderian would have kept such a revelation to himself. After all, the majority of the panzers earmarked for

Barbarossa were outdated by invasion day, even by German standards, with Kielmansegg's own division almost entirely outfitted with the obsolescent Czech-built *PzKpfw 35(t)* model. However, it was probably easier for German high command to gloss over that awkward truth rather than face it. Admitting to Soviet superiority in any way would puncture the balloon of racial supremacy that was the foundation stone of Nazism.

It wasn't only the new tank models that were challenging the shibboleth of Aryan superiority, as one *landser* in Reichenau's 6. *Armee* acknowledged: "The Russians proved their mastery in forest fighting ... they moved among the impenetrable undergrowth easily, their positions were superbly camouflaged, their dugouts and foxholes impossible to see and only providing a field of fire to the rear, so from the front and above they were invisible and could pick us off from behind as we passed."

Fighting such an enemy put an enormous strain on the troops, as Hans-Joachim S. wrote: "The efforts are enormous. It is indescribable what demands are placed on the troops with such a gigantic advance ... we only see Russian bombers very rarely, but we have daily skirmishes with snipers, who are hidden in the vast forests. From early to late, we are always moving, our nerves always tense, rifles always at hand."

For Rundstedt's army group the shock of meeting the T-34 was matched by the nature of the fighting as they found themselves having to grind their way through line after line of Soviet defences. Arthur Grimm, a war correspondent and photographer with the Nazis *Signal* magazine, was in the spearhead with *11. Panzerdivision* and described a typical action; "Hand-to-hand fighting took place in the weak light of dawn. The fields were infested with enemy riflemen. Every metre of ground was fought over. The Soviets didn't give up. Even hand-grenades didn't bring them out of their hiding places."

As the northern wing of the army group doggedly fought its way forward, the southern wing was finally given its orders and just over a week after Barbarossa was launched it crossed the Prut in strength and smashed into the Soviets. One young soldier who was mightily relieved at this turn of events was Helmut Paulus, who had spent the intervening nine days under constant fire, as he and his comrades lay dug in defending their hastily established bridgehead. By the time the rest of the division crossed the river, about forty of the original two hundred men of Helmut's *kompanie* were dead, wounded or missing.

Rundstedt's assault went on, only now the attack by his right wing into Kirponos's southern flank proved a game-changer. For the Soviets, withdrawal was the only option available and their strong defensive front began to break apart under Axis pressure. The key for the Germans was to turn that fracturing into a rout, and Kurt Meyer was at the forefront.

The enemy was suffering severe losses, our own were minimal. I wanted to carry out a motorised attack to advance into the depths of the Russian defences and take advantage of surprise ... The *kompanie* commander was my old and trusted comrade Gerd Bremer. I had forbidden the *kompanie* to engage the enemy or reduce speed. It was supposed to thunder at full steam through the enemy and leave everything else to the following *bataillon* ... At exactly 1730hrs the guns started roaring and smashed the forest on both sides of the road. My comrades rushed down from the rise and raced towards the detonation of the rounds ... we rushed after the *kompanie*. Not a round was fired at us. Escaping Russians ran north ... But then what happened? The *kompanie* came to a halt and began to fight with the fleeing Russians. This couldn't be allowed to happen! We had to reach the crossroads and deny the Russians an orderly retreat.

Frustrated as the young *Waffen-SS* officer was, the reality was a general Soviet withdrawal across the whole southern sector. The Germans then found themselves marching eastwards, foot-sore and exhausted, trying to catch up with their enemy. One of Hubert Lanz's *gebirgsjäger* described what it was like: "We were woken up just after 3am ... and were on the march by dawn. The regimental commander had been told to keep on the enemy's tails. The roads – such as they were – were so bad and so congested with vehicles that we preferred to go cross country. The weather was blindingly hot and when we marched on the roads we were shrouded in dust with the sand ankle deep in a fine yellow dust which clung to our sweating faces ... the enemy seemed to have vanished except when a small group formed a rear-guard and opened fire – that was a suicide mission."

Arthur Grimm marvelled at the land into which the Germans were advancing: "The landscape stretches flat ahead with wave-like undulations. There are few trees and little woodland. Trees are covered in dust, their leaves a dull colour in the brilliant sunlight ... Over everything hangs a brown-grey pall of smoke, rising from knocked-out tanks and burning villages ... scattered trees and wide cornfields aren't pleasing as they mean danger ... gun reports crack out from beneath every tree and from within every cornfield."[29]

Drilled to react in a certain way when fired upon, the Germans soon adopted different tactics: "For the first few days we deployed as we had been taught but we soon stopped such timewasting tactics, and instead sent a small group – usually a section of the lead *kompanie* – to locate where the enemy was firing from and then the infantry cannons would be brought into action. Four to five rounds were usually enough and then Ivan would come stumbling out, arms raised. It wasn't always that easy;

sometimes he fought with tanks and artillery, and sometimes he fought to the last man ... once the enemy was beaten the march resumed and, sometimes, we carried on marching well into the night." Not that the few hours of darkness brought much relief. "At the end of the day it was a matter of digging in and standing guard until the march started again. We soon became accustomed to the weather; blazing hot by day and then in the evening, about eight or nine, torrential rain which lasted for hours and soaked us to the skin. We dried out during the next day's march and then got soaked again the following night."[30]

Rundstedt's panzers were advancing, just as Leeb and Bock's were stalled, but it was no rapier-like thrust. Their Soviet opponents were battered and had suffered heavy losses, but the mass of their forces were still intact. If the *Ostheer* was going to destroy the Red Army's Southern and Southwestern Fronts and seize Ukraine and the Donets, something had to change. The question was, what?

Back at OKH, Halder had a lot on his mind, not least the growing casualty lists. Helmut Paulus's *kompanie* was far from the only German unit to suffer heavy losses in the opening days of the campaign. In under two weeks the Germans lost 25,000 men killed. They would lose two and a half times that number the following month. For a nation without the Soviet Union's manpower reserves, this was troubling indeed. The field hospital nurse Ingeborg Ochsenknecht saw the horror herself: "The patients all had fresh wounds and were brought directly from the battlefield with only a simple field dressing. Some were so bad that we feared they would bleed to death – and that did indeed happen a lot ... It was about life and death. None of us had a moment's rest. The doctors operated day and night."[31]

6

Murderers & Liberators

"The Germans are possessed by the demon of destruction."
Diary of Count Galeazzo Ciano, Mussolini's Foreign Minister

"It struck us like a clap of thunder – WAR! What joy! People met and congratulated each other with tears in their eyes. Everyone felt that the hour of liberation was at hand."[1] The anonymous Lithuanian who penned those words on the opening day of the invasion wasn't a lone voice among his countrymen and women, as *Gefreiter* Gerhard Bopp of Walther Fischer von Weikersthal's *35. Infanterie-Division* saw for himself: "The populace (Lithuanians) greets us joyfully, some with tears in their eyes. The girls and children throw flowers at us and all the vehicles are decked out with lilac blossoms, like on manoeuvres." Up and down the new front line the reception for the invaders was the same.

We are often warmly welcomed by the population. Some put flowers on the vehicles, others give us buttermilk or white bread. Yes, the Ukrainians are actually German-friendly, I certainly wasn't expecting this ... I expect that this war against Russia will not last too long – four weeks? It can happen differently I suppose but who knows? ... We received a friendly, almost frenzied, welcome from the Ukrainian population. We marched or drove over a veritable carpet of flowers, we were hugged and kissed by the girls, and we, in turn, handed out fistfuls of sweets and chocolate to the girls and children.[2]

Sigmund Landau was far from the only German soldier to be amazed by the reception he and his comrades received as they swept into the Soviet Union. A land they had been told was filled with hateful bolshevik fanatics turned out to be filled with human beings, many of whom seemed delighted at their arrival – it was a profound shock, and a joyful one for most. One soldier in *Heeresgruppe Nord* – advancing through the Baltic states – remembered that "the attitude of the population was striking, some stood with flowers on the roadside to greet us, it is of course possible that they were volksdeutsche. Even the prisoners of war who ran along the path without supervision sometimes greeted us with the Hitler salute!"

In *Heeresgruppe Mitte*'s zone the picture was the same, as Siegfried Knappe recalled as he and his men entered the ethnically Polish city of Bialystok: "Polish civilians in a church service applauded us, they were very happy because they hadn't been permitted to conduct church services under the Russians, and now they felt liberated."[3] The Germans would soon disabuse the applauding Poles about their liberation, but in the meantime the authorities in Berlin estimated that up to three-quarters of the population of the Baltic states and Ukraine welcomed the arrival of German troops as an opportunity to throw off Moscow's murderous rule.[4]

That rule had been bloody indeed. For the three Baltic states of Lithuania, Latvia and Estonia, the backdrop to Barbarossa was their ever-so brief independence of the 1920s and 1930s. Tiny as they were, all three had managed to break away from Tsarist rule during the chaos of the Russian Civil War, only to see their freedom ruthlessly crushed by Moscow in the summer of 1940, when – with German connivance – they were effectively ceded to the Soviet Union under a secret protocol of the Nazi–Soviet Non-Aggression Pact. From day one of the occupation they were subjected to the brutal excesses of Stalinism, with mass arrests and the execution of former army officers, politicians, civil servants, business leaders and church elders – in fact anyone whom Moscow considered a potential threat.

From August 1940 up to June 1941 the Balts suffered four successive waves of repression, the last just four days before Barbarossa. Under the so-called Serov Instructions,[5] those individuals designated as anti-bolshevik elements were rounded up along with their families, herded to train stations, crammed into filthy cattle trucks and deported without trial to the east. The adult men were then imprisoned in gulags, while the women and children were forcibly resettled in remote areas of Siberia. Conditions were dreadful, disease rampant, and mortality rates were as high as 60 per cent. Figures vary, but the final wave of 17 June alone included over 17,000 Latvians, between 16,000 and 17,000 Lithuanians, and around 10,000 Estonians.

Little wonder, then, that as the Germans advanced Red Army formations filled with Balts had major desertion problems, with whole battalions simply melting away. Thousands of young conscripts sought shelter in the region's almost trackless forests, as the Estonian Juhan Jaik described: "The forests and bogs have got more people in them than the fields and farms, they are our territory while the fields and farms are occupied by the enemy." As far as he and most of his countrymen were concerned it wasn't the Germans who were *the enemy*. Adolf Dick saw it for himself: "Our leaflets (propaganda leaflets dropped to Red Army units calling on them to shoot their commissars and desert to the Germans) work, and in various places Red Army soldiers come over to us after they've beaten their commissars to death with clubs. They weren't worth a bullet, said a prisoner yesterday evening who knew something of the German language. First there were three of them, then during the night they brought another fourteen in from the forest."[6]

The horrors visited by Moscow on the Baltic nations were multiplied a hundred times and more for that most afflicted of peoples: the Ukrainians. Cursed to be born into an indefensible land of immense natural riches, the Ukrainians suffered a genocide in the early 1930s that left well over three million of them dead – almost all from starvation. In an orchestrated campaign of state-run brutality, Stalin devastated the country with a forced collectivisation programme that combined the mass confiscation of foodstuffs with restrictions on movement and a spurning of outside help. In one of the most agriculturally productive regions on Earth, whole communities went hungry unto death or were forced to turn to cannibalism to survive. The American socialist writer Arthur Koestler, travelling in the Soviet Union at the time, wrote of peasant women holding up to his train carriage windows "horrible infants with enormous wobbling heads, sticklike limbs, and swollen, pointed bellies ... like embryos out of alcohol bottles".

Unsurprisingly, Stalin's mass murder fed the flames of anti-Soviet agitation and Ukraine in 1941 was ripe for revolt, as one SS trooper noted: "More than once, Ukrainians, especially young people, requested weapons from us."[7] Perhaps even more than their Baltic counterparts, the Ukrainians felt the breath of possible freedom as the panzers swept forward. Kurt Marlow, from the small Baltic German island of Usedom, told his wife: "The situation here was indescribable ... the Ukrainian men were forced into military service, which is why many hid. People told me such things; that a lot of women were simply dragged away, that children were stabbed with bayonets, and all out of anger because the men refused to serve and hid in the huge forests so as not to become Russian soldiers. They told me that they prayed day and night that the Germans might appear very soon."

As Kurt Marlow and his fellow invaders advanced, Moscow's deportation trains still rattled east, but the prisons and gaols of the Soviets' western republics remained stubbornly full of enemies of the people, as the NKVD secret police struggled to transport their captives away. The result was an order from Moscow to kill the detainees by whatever means possible rather than leave them behind. The result was the murder of up to 100,000 prisoners, the majority of them never having been charged with any crime, let alone convicted of one.

In the aftermath, as the German spearheads captured cities and towns alike, they came across scenes of utter horror. In L'viv in western Ukraine, a German military investigation team comprising two judges and a doctor arrived in the city on 30 June, immediately after its capture, to look into reports of atrocities committed against German POWs by Soviet forces. They found no evidence of any such incidents, but in the three main prisons of Brigidky, Yaniwska and Lontsky they discovered carnage. In Lontsky alone more than 2,000 corpses were found, piled up in the cellars and courtyard like firewood. Grief-stricken relatives surrounded the gaols. "The air was full of the stench of decomposing bodies."[8]

Leutnant Wolfgang Schöler saw it for himself: "The Russians had thrown grenades into the cellars, then they'd fired machine-guns into them. Finally, they'd bricked up the windows so that any survivors suffocated." Manfred von Plotho – an aristocratic officer in *Heeresgruppe Süd*'s *71. Infanterie-Division* – wrote to his wife expressing his shock at what he saw: "Here we really have come as liberators from an unbearable yoke. I have seen images in the NKVD cellars which I cannot, and will not, describe to you ... three to five thousand bodies lie in the prisons, butchered in the most bestial fashion. Mostly Ukrainians, a lot of Poles. I have sometimes thought the depictions of bolshevik Russia were exaggerated, a primitive appeal to sensationalism – today I know better."[9] Schöler felt much the same: "At that point I felt the war wasn't now without reason, and that we must stop these people from doing these things ever again." Martin Meier, a soldier in Friedrich Kühn's *14. Panzer-Division*, wrote to his wife Gerda in lurid detail about the scenes he witnessed in the city:

> The actions of the bolsheviks were so monstrous it can hardly be described ... civilians horribly mutilated; men, women and children nailed to doors, people wrapped up in barbed wire, shot, some had gasoline poured on them and then been set on fire. People had been thrown alive into tanks of boiling water. These are just the least horrible things, I cannot describe the rest. I never wanted to believe that such things happened, but this time it's not propaganda, it's the real truth.

Little wonder then at how von Plotho and his men were treated by the local population. "In the bright morning sun our brave soldiers moved into Lemberg (German name for L'viv) in long columns. Every soldier was decorated with flowers by the people who lined the streets in dense rows. Every vehicle, every horse, was covered with flowers. Many a woman wept for joy."

Time and again the advancing Germans found the NKVD had left slaughter in their wake, as Hans Roth saw in Lutsk: "The local prison is a gruesome sight. Prior to their retreat the bolsheviks staged a terrible bloodbath. More than a hundred men, women and children were slaughtered like cattle. Never will I forget such appalling images."[10] Three days later he saw much the same in Dubno. "We reach Dubno in the evening following a rapid march. The town is free of enemy troops ... the Russians were forced to give the place up after putting up a desperate fight. They didn't leave before half-destroying the town like a bunch of *Schweine* (pigs), everything has been smashed to pieces. We find a large pile of mutilated corpses in the town prison."

The result of such atrocities was a civilian population only too willing to welcome the invaders, as Hans Albring, a twenty-three-year-old from Gelsenkirchen, saw as he and his fellow *landsers* marched into Ukraine: "An extraordinarily large number of peasant women in brightly coloured lilacs and white headscarves stand at the entrance to the villages and everyone has a bouquet of meadow flowers in their hands. When we march in some of the young girls come forward and put some of the flowers in our hands and cheerfully encourage us to come in." As a devoutly religious man, Albring was deeply affected when he saw the locals' Orthodox devotion – something that had been suppressed under bolshevik rule – and wrote to his friend and fellow Catholic youth league member Eugen Altrogge about it: "Here everyone knew what this simple holy communion meant to each Russian after twenty-four years of suffering."

Hans von Luck – unused to cheering locals in his previous campaigns in Poland and France – was genuinely taken aback by the welcome he and his men received. "I was astonished to detect no hatred for us among the Russians. Women came out of their houses with icons held before their breasts saying: 'We are still Christians, free us from Stalin who destroyed our churches.' Many of them offered an egg and a piece of dry bread as welcome. We gradually had the feeling that we were being regarded as liberators."

The sheer weight of evidence, in letters, diaries, journals and reports, is so great it is clear that the liberation phenomenon was real and not a construct of Nazi propaganda. "In the Ukraine the locals saw the German forces as their liberators from their hated Russian oppressors."[11]

"The people were so intimidated by the Communists and Jews and commissars that they are happy to be rid of the scoundrels and really do see us as their liberators."[12]

"The people suffered so much under Soviet and Jewish rule. And now the Germans are here and the people can see for themselves that the Germans are nice decent chaps."[13]

Hans-Joachim S. wrote that "the population is happy that we are here and want to see Stalin on the gallows". Wilhelm Lübbecke – the farmer's son from Püggen – remembered that "crowds along the streets greeted us with shouts of 'Befreier! Befreier!' ('Liberator! Liberator!') and presented us with flowers or chocolate in gratitude for their rescue from Russian occupation".

In truth, despite Moscow's protestations to the contrary, large sections of the Soviet populace had had enough of communist rule and fervently hoped that Barbarossa would bring them freedom. Helmut Nick, in *Heeresgruppe Mitte*, believed it signified a desire on behalf of local people simply to be left alone: "I am getting to know the country and its people. Most are happy to be liberated from bolshevik rule and ask no more than to be able to live their lives in peace … Hopefully we will finish quickly here in the east."

The goodwill generated at the advent of Barbarossa was genuine and widespread – and completely squandered. German soldiers – welcomed as liberators – proceeded to steal anything and everything that caught their eye. For a civilian population with almost nothing to start with, this was bad enough, but what really poisoned the well of amity was the theft of that most precious commodity: food. Rudolf Kurth described how he and his comrades acted: "I eat fruit from the gardens as often as I can, I've often had diarrhoea from it. Everything grows wild in the gardens; tomatoes, potatoes, pumpkins, all in between cucumbers and melons, we just help ourselves." Kurt Marlow was even more explicit. "Here in the most beautiful and deepest south, the fruit is ripe, you cannot imagine what a perfect harvesting technique we use to pick the trees clean, swarms of locusts couldn't do a better job." Martin Meier explained why the *landsers* turned to looting. Recognising the locals' own poverty gave him no pause for thought:

> The hunger. I only remember fat or butter by name now. We get just three slices of bread a day, mostly mouldy. We sneak around in the fields and dig potatoes that aren't ripe yet … Then we keep eating green, unripe apples to try and satisfy our hunger. The result is very clear: diarrhoea. In addition, the water is undrinkable. I think I have to eat a green apple again because my stomach keeps growling … we search around for something to eat but there isn't anything … I never imagined Russia to be so poor. It's even worse than we've been told over and over.

Theft was so accepted that even the likes of Hans von Luck thought it normal practice and wrote of his disappointment on entering villages where there was nothing to 'requisition', "in order to improve the diet of the troops". His fellow panzer man Richard von Rosen was just as guilty: "My loader, Walter Aschlimann, went off on a hunt for poultry and came back after a while with a chicken he'd shot. We cooked it in our wash bucket." He noted how upset he was on arriving in a small town and finding that the lone shop had already been thoroughly plundered.

Soldiers looting from civilians is nothing new, and it's also long been recognised to stir up resentment and anger. In the Napoleonic Peninsular War, the Spanish people found themselves caught between the French and British. The French policy of living off the land by stealing food from the populace was a major driver in creating the guerrilla movement that plagued the French throughout the war and, recognising this, Wellington himself banned the forced requisitioning of food by his army, and insisted instead on buying it from the people – transgressors were hanged. In the western Soviet Union, where the inhabitants had so few material goods, and where the stealing of food by soldiers had such a recent and tragic history, German looting had huge negative repercussions, as *Major* Hans Meier-Welcker – chief of staff in Hans Kratzert's *251. Infanterie-Division* – realised: "If only our people were just a bit more decent and sensible! They are taking everything that suits them from the farmers." Meier-Welcker should perhaps have pointed out the truth to the likes of Erich von Manstein, who boldly claimed, "Naturally, there was no question of our pillaging the area. That was something the German Army did not tolerate." Gotthard Heinrici would also have been surprised at his fellow general's statement: "Everywhere our troops are looking for harnesses and taking horses away from farmers. There is great wailing and lamentation in the villages – thus is the population 'liberated!' ... soon the land will likely be sucked dry."[14]

It wasn't just the Germans either. In the south, the Hungarian soldiery was so rapacious that they soon earned the nickname the Austrian Huns, for "stealing everything that wasn't nailed down".

The issue for the invaders was that this behaviour wasn't due to individual soldiers taking the law into their own hands – or even the odd unit – this was the way Nazi Germany fought its wars. Unlike in the United States Army for instance, the logistics branch of the German armed forces was the poor relation of the fighting arms. Looked down on by infantry, panzer and artillery men alike, the officers and soldiers manning the German supply system were the runts of the litter; often older men with no combat experience and little aptitude, they consistently failed to deliver efficient, timely, support. Viewed with contempt by their fellow soldiers, they were derided as *etappenhengsten* – rear-area stallions. Hans von Luck recalled how he and his orderly – fresh from the front – came upon a canteen full of supply staff: "We thought we were dreaming. Officers of the base units were sitting at the tables with women, apparently leading la dolce vita ... No-one wanted to know about the war. We bolted our food in disgust, handed in the voucher provided by headquarters and disappeared." The result of being at the end of an inefficient supply line was that it was understood soldiers would take matters into their own hands and take whatever they needed from the local populace instead. What made a bad situation worse in the Barbarossa campaign was that living off the land was not only standard *Wehrmacht* practice but an integral part of the invasion plan.

Since a major reason for the invasion in the first place had been to seize and secure an abundant source of food for the homeland, it made no sense to the Nazi agronomists in Berlin to press the *Wehrmacht* into stockpiling huge amounts of already scarce food for the invasion; in fact, the opposite made sense to them – most of the food required should be seized before it reached useless Slav mouths.

Having persuaded Hitler that Ukraine was the solution to Germany's calorie deficiency, Herbert Backe and his sidekick at the Ministry for Food and Agriculture, Hans-Joachim Riecke, were given the responsibility of drawing up a blueprint for delivery that would be the basis of Nazi occupation policy in the East. This was the origin of Nazi Germany's genocidal Hunger Plan. At a weekend house party just before Barbarossa was launched, the head of the SS, the bespectacled pedant Heinrich Himmler, breezily told his companions, "The purpose of any future Russian campaign will be to decimate the Slavic population by thirty millions." Himmler wasn't exaggerating – he rarely did when it came to mass murder. He was simply spelling out the objective of Backe and Riecke's plan. The starvation duo understood that although Ukraine produced a massive surplus of food, that same surplus was then shipped straight to hungry Russian cities, leaving little for export. Their plan, therefore, envisaged that captured Soviet cities would be cut off from those food supplies, with a proportion of that same food going to the German occupation troops and the remainder shipped back to the Reich. Backe's boss, Georg Thomas, went so far as to declare at a meeting on 2 May 1941 that "the war can only be continued if the entire *Wehrmacht* is fed from Russia in the third year of the war (i.e. 1941) ... If we take what we need out of the country, there can be no doubt that many millions of people will die of starvation."

The logic of the Hunger Plan was that as those many millions of Soviet city-dwellers starved, they would be forced to abandon their homes and head out into the countryside to try and find food. This would lead to Soviet society and civilisation more or less breaking down, and the whole country would then revert to a sort of medieval, peasant state, where the Germans would find it relatively easy to establish and maintain control.

As the cities became ghost towns, Hitler foresaw Leningrad bulldozed back into the marshland from whence it sprang, and as for Moscow, "I'll raze it to the ground and build a reservoir there. The name Moscow must be expunged."

Simultaneous to this policy of mass murder, the Reich would annex vast tracts of land, extending Germany's border a thousand kilometres to the east. This huge new territory would then become the breadbasket that would feed Germany. Some twenty million Aryan Germanic settlers – one-third of whom would be former SS men given land grants by a grateful nation for war service – would live in and farm this new National Socialist Eden. Hitler postulated:

> The German colonist ought to live on handsome, spacious farms, German services will be lodged in marvellous buildings, the governors in palaces ... around the cities, to a depth of thirty to forty kilometres we shall have a belt of handsome villages connected by the best roads. What exists beyond that will be another world, in which we will let the Russians live as they like. It is merely necessary that we rule them.

The new German settlements would be connected to the homeland by autobahns that would stretch as far as the Crimea and the Black Sea – for holiday travel. Heinrich Einsiedel heard his peers excitedly discuss their futures after victory had been achieved: "There were men who I admired as pilots and as soldiers who believed that after the war they'd all have estates on the Black Sea near Odessa filled with Russian serfs."

As for the poor unfortunates already living in the Nazis' new empire, the planners estimated that 80 per cent of Poles, three-quarters of Belarussians and 60 per cent of Ukrainians would either starve to death or be deported further east. In total, Backe's Plan called for the murder of some 30,000,000 men, women and children – not including Jews. In Hitler's words, "It's inconceivable that a superior race should exist on land that is too small for it, whilst amorphous masses, which contribute nothing to civilisation, occupy infinite tracts of a soil that is one of the richest in the world." This would be the ultimate conclusion of Germany's historic *Drang nach Osten* – the drive to the East. Officials even costed the whole monstrosity, estimating a price to the Reich's treasury of half a million *Reichsmarks* per square kilometre, some 67 billion *Reichsmarks* in total.

The Hunger Plan suited the *Wehrmacht* and its policy of supplying its men with fresh food. German soldiers were used to the issued bread bag and its *Kommissbrot* (a dark bread made from rye and wheat and noted for its long shelf life) and hot meals of meat and vegetables cooked up in the eponymous *Gulaschkanone*. With a single infantry division getting through 200,000lbs of food and fodder a day for its men and horses, the German approach put a huge strain on their supply system and meant that local requisitioning (or purchase) were key to feeding the troops. American and British troops, in particular, may have envied their enemy his tasty fare, but their reliance on tinned and packaged rations meant their dietary needs could be easily transported, stored and stockpiled. Not so for the *landser*.

For Barbarossa, the German emphasis was on *requisition* – that is *theft* – rather than *purchase*. The Belarussian city of Vitebsk experienced what that meant in practice. On arrival, the German spearhead proceeded to strip it of food. One collective farm in the area – a *kolkhoz* – had a dairy herd of two hundred head. Delighted at their find, the Germans left the inhabitants eight for their own use, and took away the remaining 192, having paid for just a dozen. At a stroke, the locals' already meagre supply of milk, cheese and beef disappeared.

Things were made even worse for the civilian population by their own authorities carrying out a scorched earth policy that called for nothing less than the wholesale destruction of anything and everything that could be used by the invader; buildings for shelter, food supplies, water, industrial and agricultural equipment and so on. Hans-Joachim S. described what that policy meant on the ground for the city of Vitebsk:

> A sea of flames. The Russians burn everything, thinking it will harm us. They only kill themselves as a result ... All wells contaminated or empty. Water pipes, bridges, everything destroyed ... Imagine a city of 160,000 people with everything destroyed, no house undamaged. It's like this everywhere!" [The signals officer soon changed his tune.] We are all fed up. Above all because the Russian burns everything that could be of any use to us ... As a result, the advance is becoming increasingly difficult.

Desperate for a scapegoat, he found one in the communist bogeyman: "As a murderer, he now races across the country and plunges the remaining population into dire need." But one scapegoat wasn't enough, and he soon added another. "This morning 1,500 Jews were shot here in retaliation for the destruction of the city."

Policy was one thing, but what the Hunger Plan really relied on was the willingness of ordinary German soldiers to thieve, loot and plunder from people who had very little to start with, and who often welcomed them as would-be liberators. Compassion would normally mitigate against such a policy working, but the men who were marching and fighting across the western Soviet Union had been subjected to years of virulent Nazi propaganda which portrayed the peoples of the East as uncivilised sub-humans, unworthy of life, limb and property. In so doing the Nazis were simply building on the fear and hatred of the barbarian from the East that had already existed among the Germans for centuries. Wilhelm Lübbecke encapsulated that view: "I was fighting out of a belief that Soviet communism posed a great threat to all of Europe and Western civilisation ... if we didn't destroy the communist menace it would destroy us. For us the Slavs were simply the ignorant inhabitants of an uncivilised and backward country."

Klaus Becker was thirty-eight years old with a middling education, married with children of his own, and an artilleryman serving in Russia – he was also a Nazi Party member – and his behaviour towards the local people was typical of so many ordinary members of the *Ostheer*: "We get potatoes from the cellar of the house we're quartered in. We don't ask whether they want to give up these things, we just take it if they don't give it to us voluntarily. You slowly get rid of humanitarian fuss here. The most important thing is that we eat, drink and get a roof over our heads, and only then do you think about the civilian population. Of course, there is no other way if you want to wage war. At first it is a bit difficult, but you get used to it pretty quickly." He went on to describe the arrangements made between occupier and occupied, excusing their behaviour by insisting it provided an element of protection to the very people they were stealing from. "As long as we are in the house, no other soldiers come to take away the pigs and sheep that she has in the stable." The result was the same though. "Better the population starve than the troops ... the Russians are like children anyway ... If the German soldier needs something, he just takes it. What should the German soldier do after all? His safety and health must take priority over those of the population."

Alois Breilmann confided much the same thinking in a letter to his sister:

> I am writing to you from a Russian collective farm. I got a woman here to darn my sweater this afternoon after she did my laundry – I don't see why I should do it. Dear Lisbeth, you asked me in one of your letters about furs ... but I haven't found any beautiful furs here, although I've looked everywhere. In Polotsk [a Belarussian city on the Dvina River], pistol in hand, I went into almost every house, and there were fur coats lying there, but heavy as lead and totally bug-infested like everything here ... The farmers are very poor. Their houses are generally just one room. Their furniture consists of a table and bench, possibly a chair, a few trestles with boards, and the family sleeps on the stove ... Often ten people live in one room, the windows are boarded up and cannot be opened. Only soldiers have boots ... everyone else wears rags.[15]

This abject poverty neither stopped his attempts to loot a fur coat for his sister or elicited any compassion from the young soldier.

In no time at all, the entire invasion resembled a giant *chevauchée*, reminiscent of the Hundred Years War, as the advancing *landsers* stripped the countryside of everything they could find: "In the evening, after reaching the day's destination, we set up our usual gypsy camp. Between the tents simmering in many pots and pans – chickens, eggs, potatoes and ham – everything 'organised' (stolen). That's how you get by."[16]

In briefing after briefing the men of the invasion force had been told they would be entering a backward land filled with sub-humans, and so, by implication, any and all behaviour was permissible. Panzer gunner Richard von Rosen remembered the speech given on the eve of the campaign to his regiment by its commander, Heinrich Eberbach: "You are going into a country in which the people live so primitively that you won't believe it. They don't even have proper toilets!" Martin Meier thought much the same as Eberbach:

> This is where the glorious Soviet paradise really shows itself for what it is. Aside from the ravages of war you can see what kind of culture the Reds had. The living conditions here are catastrophic. The houses are dilapidated, lousy and full of bugs. So, we sleep in tents. I asked an old man who speaks German about these things, and he said that if the communists in Europe spent just one month in Russia they would give up their bolshevism. He now lives on green, unripe apples that he cooks for himself and his family. He hasn't eaten bread for four years. And you hear that everywhere.

Meier's opinions didn't get any more positive during the advance – in fact, they worsened: "The further we get into Russia, the more neglected the land becomes. This is bolshevik culture. People look like criminals. The women take out their breasts and suckle their children while walking on the street. Otherwise, everyone is lolling around in the dirt."[17]

At first, the troops advanced through what had been eastern Poland, the republic of Belarus, or the old Baltic states, but they noticed a marked difference as they plunged deeper to the east. Erika Ohr – a twenty-year-old shepherd's daughter turned nurse – found the change striking: "Everything looked totally different; the countryside, the houses, the train stations, even the script on the signs." Almost universally the *landsers* found the change for the worse and were appalled at what they saw: "Before the war we were grouped in eastern Poland, and the conditions we encountered there were abysmal. But here, in the real east the villages – although you can't really describe the collection of hovels as a village – are wooden, verminous and in a rotten state. There is no sanitation, no electric light and the so-called roads are rutted tracks in the sandy soil."[18] 8. *Panzerdivision*'s Gustav Klinter agreed: "The country totally altered after we crossed the Reich border. Lithuania gave us a taste of what we were to find in Russia proper; unkept sandy roads, intermittent settlements and ugly houses, which were more like huts ... heat, filth and clouds of dust were the characteristic snapshot of those days."[19] Henk Kistemaker – from a working-class neighbourhood and no stranger to poverty – was dumbfounded by what he saw; "I'd never been out of Amsterdam before, so everything I saw was an eye-opener for me and it left me astounded. How could the Russians live like this? They were so very poor and lived in tiny houses – if you could call it a house, to most of us the houses looked like nothing more than sheds."

One young soldier from Wilhelm Stemmermann's 296. *Infanterie-Division* said: "At first we travelled on beautiful roads through German country, lots of forest and the villages were well-kept. Little changed beyond the 1918 border. Only when we crossed the old border did it suddenly change. The tar road gave way to gravel, the villages were made up of untidy wooden houses, all very primitive." Another *landser* thought that "things here are even worse than in Poland. Nothing but dirt and tremendous poverty rule the roost, and you simply can't understand how people can live in such circumstances."

For many, this meant that if what they had been told about the conditions was true, then surely what Nazi propaganda had told them about the people was true too – they were *inferior*. Hans-Albert Giese wrote to his mother early on in the campaign: "If I hadn't seen with my own eyes the primitive nature of the Russians I wouldn't believe that such things still existed ... our cowstalls back home are luxurious compared to the best rooms of the houses in which the Russians choose to live. They are a worse rabble than the gypsies." Johannes Hamm went further in a letter to his wife Kathe: "We can thank God that he (Hitler) saved Germany, that he saved you and everyone else at home from the horrors of the war and from these bolshevik sub-humans. Everything beautiful died in Russia."

In many cases this link between the poverty of ordinary Soviet civilians and their supposed racial inferiority took some time to become embedded in the psyche of the invaders and lead to violence. Kurt Marlow's personal journey along this road was typical. After an unremarkable childhood on the northern German coast, he left school and trained as a dental technician. It obviously wasn't what he'd hoped it to be, as he soon gave it up, moved to Berlin and became an apprentice gardener. Preferring daffodils to dentures, on completing his studies he moved back home and opened a flower shop with his mother. Like all young German men of his generation, he did his labour service and then his military service, finishing his time in uniform in 1936. As a second-wave reservist, Marlow was recalled in the summer of 1939 and became a medic – a *Sani* in Army slang – in Georg Braun's newly established 68. *Infanterie-Division*. He served in Poland and France, before his division was transferred east to join *Heeresgruppe Süd*. He was an avid letter writer, firstly to his mother back home in Usedom, and then – after his wedding – to his new wife. Most of his early letters focused on the personal: sadness at being away from home, talk of food, family and friends, and a certain optimism about the campaign. "Our pilots make hay here, the Russian aviator is no good at all, otherwise we would be in a lot more trouble because Russia has an enormous number of aircraft. It is the same with tanks. According to the radio report, their aircraft losses are said to be 11,000, we all believe that number is too low, because of what we see lying around us."

Like many of his brethren he marvelled at the courage of the ordinary Soviet soldier but was troubled by their attitude to the loss of human life. "The Russian actually fights like a lion, they run into our fire in long lines and are annihilated. A human life is nothing to them. This war must have cost them millions of lives already." As the advance continued, the conditions of the march began to wear Marlow and his unit down: "At the moment we all suffer from a terrible bowel problem, no-one can explain where this evil came from ... I think it is from the many flies here, they are everywhere and settle on our food. You simply cannot protect yourself from this plague ... you can't get rid of these beasts at all."

Before long, a combination of physical and mental stress and prolonged exposure to the extreme violence of the fighting wrought a marked change in Marlow's letters: "The Mongols live the wildest here, when I see this slit-eyed race ... I can't tell you how it feels ... you only have to see how this sub-humanity lives to understand. The meanest thing is when they fire on our people, yesterday a twenty-year-old comrade fell. We don't care anymore ... we Germans are way too humane with these guys." All too soon, Marlow's descent into brutality was complete. "Our good nature, which borders on stupidity, is used by our enemies, while they flout the rules of war and do all kinds of things against us ... The penny has finally dropped for me. You will be amazed at how I have changed, all compassion has ceased to exist ... there is nothing left ... selfishness can never be wrong." Sadly, Marlow even seems to have understood what was happening to him: "In a war like this, people change fundamentally."

Karl Fuchs was a panzer gunner in Erwin Rommel's old 'Ghost Division', 7. *Panzer*, and felt much the same when he wrote home to his wife: "Believe me dearest, when you see me again, you will face quite a different person ... you can't afford to be soft in war, or you'll die."

The fighter pilot and fervent Nazi Heinz Knoke wrote the following entry in his diary just before he was posted back to the West in early July: "Our feeling towards the enemy is not exactly one of hatred, so much as utter contempt. It is a genuine satisfaction for us to be able to trample the bolsheviks into the mud where they belong."[20]

It wasn't just the rank and file and Party fanatics whose thinking began to change. Manfred von Plotho was a well-connected member of the Prussian nobility, and like many of his social class he found Hitler and his cronies vulgar and uncouth, but Barbarossa changed him too: "There is no longer any compromise here, here we are the hard soldiers of Adolf Hitler, who are either leading European culture to a new blooming or pulling it down with us into the abyss of complete annihilation."

What this meant, in practical terms, was described by a young soldier in Kurt Kalmuekoff's *Lion Division*, who told his brother Friedrich about his own part in the horror:

It's been raining cats and dogs since the early hours of the morning. The purest hangman's weather. While all the other sections are building roads like they do every day, we're resting after some unusual work. We were given the task of hanging three civilian bandits who'd attacked an ambulance from our *bataillon* several days ago. That was taken care of this morning and now they are dangling at the village entrance. A warning for the locals. A commissar was also shot dead. This is how one comes to the cruellest acts in this war, which seem downright medieval.[21]

Even an otherwise mild-mannered ex-bank clerk and devoted husband like Martin Meier soon echoed the brutality and racism that was fast becoming a hallmark of the campaign:

The beasts [the Soviets] get their just punishment. Perhaps it has already been noticed that so few prisoners have been taken in the fighting. Everything that is done to us by the enemy will be repaid ... The Russians set everything on fire; villages, cities, fields, forests. But they only harm themselves. We can get by on our diet. Let them starve, these beasts. They have no right to live. We make sure that there are fewer and fewer of them left.

Incidents that Meier would have found horrific scant weeks previously were now run of the mill: "In Berdichev (in Ukraine) we found a severed human tongue." But even now he half-heartedly tried to claim this was a defensive war: "You can't imagine what they would have done if they'd invaded Germany."

If it was the *bolsheviks* who were to blame for it all, then who were the bolsheviks? Were they just Red Army commissars, Communist Party functionaries and members, or was the definition wider still? In Nazi propaganda, *bolshevism* was irrevocably intertwined with being *Jewish* – the term *jüdisch-bolschewistische* (Judeo-Bolshevism) was constantly used on radio, in film and in print, so for the German soldiers marching into the Soviet Union, the two were inseparable – to be Jewish was to be a bolshevik, and vice versa.

The Jewish issue was also brought to the forefront of the invaders' minds by the sheer number of Jews they came across. For most *landsers*, seeing large numbers of discrete Soviet Jewish communities was something of a shock, especially given that most of the Jews they had seen in Germany and the rest of western Europe were thoroughly assimilated and indistinguishable from everyone else, while in the east, the *shtetl* – that small-town unit of Ashkenazi Judaism – was commonplace across the old Pale of Settlement and nearby regions.

The *landsers*' reaction to the *shtetl* and the prevalence of Soviet Jewry was almost universally hostile. In the north, Hans-Joachim S. wrote that "Jewish scum populate town and country here. The primitiveness regarding the standard of living is indescribable … Only the Jews have nothing to laugh about here. For the first time they have to work. Again, this only affects the poor Jew, the rich Jew has long disappeared over the mountains." Rudolf Kurth thought that "the number of Jews living in the cities is terrifying". Helmut Nick, in *Heeresgruppe Mitte*, even half-jokingly compared the Jews he saw to vampires: "As we advance, the women in lots of villages throw flowers at the soldiers, although I believe that some of them are Jewish. If so, it would have been better for us to take garlic!"

This is not a book about the Holocaust, this is a book about Barbarossa, but the two are inextricably linked. Barbarossa was the point where the murder of an entire people began to become a reality. Hitler did not invade the Soviet Union to destroy bolshevism only, he invaded to destroy Judaism too. His intention wasn't some dirty secret, hidden away in a memo in a safe in the Reich Chancellery, it was as plain as day in the turgid prose of *Mein Kampf*, and in speech after speech the dictator made throughout the 1920s and 1930s. After ascending to power, he made no attempt to hide it either, in fact he had the platform to publicise it even more widely – and he did. Most may not have believed the rhetoric, but the dictator and his senior circle made plain their objective in numerous documented conferences and meetings – often attended by hundreds of guests – many of whom subsequently issued instructions of their own, parroting their master's decrees.

Walther von Brauchitsch was one such individual. No ordinary officer, he was the Commander-in-Chief of the German Army from 1938 up to and including the launch of Barbarossa. As with so many of Germany's senior officer corps, he was from a distinguished Prussian military family, and had served with distinction during the First World War. Rising to the very top of his profession, he was close to Hitler, and privy to his plans. He was present on 30 March 1941 when the *Führer* held a briefing with some two hundred of his most senior officers and told them plainly that Barbarossa would be "a war of extermination ... commanders must be prepared to sacrifice their personal scruples".

Three days before that particular conference, Brauchitsch issued his own instruction to the Army stating that troops "must be clear that the conflict is being fought between one race and another and proceed with the necessary vigour". Then, on 6 June, he issued twelve copies of what became known as the *Kommissarbefehl* (Commissar Order) to the most senior commanders involved in the invasion, who were specifically instructed not to distribute it in writing but rather to inform their subordinates of its contents verbally. The *Kommissarbefehl*'s official name was *Richtlinien für die Behandlung politischer Kommissare* (Guidelines for the Treatment of Political Commissars), and it stated:

> In the battle against bolshevism, the adherence of the enemy to the principles of humanity or international law is not to be counted upon ... In this battle mercy or considerations of international law are false ... The originators of barbaric, Asiatic methods of warfare are the political commissars. So, immediate and unhesitatingly severe measures must be undertaken against them. They are, therefore, when captured in battle, as a matter of routine, to be dispatched by firearms.

Given what we now know about the Nazis, the idea of an order to shoot captured communist functionaries doesn't seem too outlandish – murderous yes, but not surprising for the creators of the death camps. But at the time it was profoundly shocking. Here was the army of a supposedly civilised European state decreeing that the execution of unarmed prisoners was officially to be the norm.

Heinrich Haape was present when his commander Peter Neuhoff received the Commissar instruction: "'All Russian commissars are to be shot on capture.' Neuhoff's face was serious and a little bewildered as he told us the news. He then impressed on us that we were not to communicate the order to the troops – it was information for officers only." *Unteroffizier* Robert Rupp saw what this meant, after he and his men captured a village and rounded up some fifty or so prisoners. "One of them had had his cheek torn open by a hand-grenade. He asked me for water and greedily slurped down some tea I gave him." A short time later Rupp saw four prisoners dig a shallow hole, whereupon the tea-drinker was ordered forward and told to lie down in it. He was a commissar. Rupp shot him.[22] This, no doubt, would have been news to the ears of Rupp's army commander, Heinz Guderian: "The so-called Commissar Order never even reached my *Panzergruppe*. No doubt *Heeresgruppe Mitte* had already decided not to forward it ... the Commissar Order was never carried out by my troops either."

This was the context in which commanders such as *Panzergruppe 4*'s Erich Hoepner issued his own instruction for the "defence of European culture against Muscovite-Asiatic inundation, and the repulse of Jewish-Bolshevism", and 6. *Armee*'s Walther Reichenau his directive that "the most important objective of this campaign against the Jewish-Bolshevik system is the complete ... extermination of the Asiatic influence in European civilization ... For this reason the soldier must learn fully to appreciate the necessity for the severe but just retribution that must be meted out to the sub-human species of Jewry."

Reichenau, for one, practised what he preached. As his men advanced into Ukraine he sanctioned the massacre of the Jewish population of Bila Tserkva by a *Sonderkommando* of SS killers. Franz Kohler was a radio operator in Karl Gümbel's *295. ID* and was resting nearby when he heard shooting and went to investigate. "Rows of people were all doing somersaults. I wondered what was going on, and it was only when I got closer that I realised they were being shot and were then falling into a pit." Kohler carried on watching until "there were just three left, an older man with two women – they must have been his daughters – anyway, he took them in his arms and an SS man shot both women in the neck. The old man carried on holding them so they didn't fall – then it was his turn." Noticing a large group of children standing off to one side, Kohler asked one of the killers, "What about the children?" To which he replied, "We shoot everyone from fourteen years old up to grandpas ... we don't have anything to do with children." Those children – some ninety in all – were confined inside a former school on the edge of town to await their fate. News of the massacre spread through Kohler's division like wildfire, and two of its chaplains, Ernst Tewes and Gerhard Wilczek – the former a Catholic priest and the latter a Lutheran pastor – went to see for themselves what was going on. Reinhold Emmer – a young *landser* – went with them: "The two chaplains and an *Oberleutnant* saw the children and walked round the building. They had tears in their eyes, just like us." Tewes and Wilczek wrote to Reichenau and implored him to save the children. Their monocled Army commander was incensed: "The conclusion of the report in question contains the following sentence, 'In the case in question, measures against women and children were undertaken which in no way differ from atrocities carried out by the enemy about which the troops are continually being informed.' I have to describe this assessment as incorrect, inappropriate and impertinent in the extreme." While dismissing the plea out of hand, he was also keen to try and keep such actions secret: "This comment was written in an open communication which passes through many hands. It would have been far better if the report had not been written at all."

SS-Obersturmführer August Häfner witnessed the result. "The *Wehrmacht* had already dug a grave. The children were brought along in a tractor. The Ukrainian militiamen were standing around trembling. The children were taken down from the tractor. They were lined up along the top of the grave and shot so that they fell into it. The Ukrainians did not aim at any particular part of the body ... The wailing was indescribable." All ninety were murdered. Reinhold Emmer recalled his reaction on hearing of the slaughter; "What could you do? You can't just turn around and say 'you must be against what's going on here', it wasn't possible. It just wasn't possible."

So, even as crowds of Balts and Ukrainians in particular cheered the advancing Germans, their Jewish fellow countrymen and women did not feel the same elation. A farmer in the western Lithuanian town of Plungė declared that "the Germans only have to cross the border and on that same day we will wade in the blood of the Jews of Plungė".[23] The anonymous Lithuanian anti-Semite wasn't exaggerating. When the Germans captured the town on 25 June, they immediately shot sixty young Jewish men accused by their fellow citizens of being Red Army soldiers in civilian clothes. Those same accusers then formed a provisional administration and police force headed up by a well-known local nationalist, Jonas Noreika. Under his leadership, the remaining 1,700 or so Jews in the town were used as forced labour for a couple of weeks before being marched to the nearby village of Kausenai, where they were shot. Little wonder that a Lithuanian Jew wrote, "Crowds of Lithuanians greeted the Germans with flowers, but ... we closed our shutters, lowered our curtains and locked ourselves into our houses."

The wholesale slaughter of Jews began as soon as the invasion was launched. The historic city of Kaunas (also called Kovno) fell to *Heeresgruppe Nord* on 23 June. A day or so later the 562. *Feldbäckereien Kompanie* (562 Field Bakery Company) arrived. A *feldwebel* in the *kompanie* recalled:

We were quartered in an old Russian barracks and immediately started to bake bread for the troops. I think it must have been a day after we arrived that I was told by a driver in the unit that Jews were being beaten to death in a nearby square. Upon hearing this I went to the square with other members of the unit ... I saw civilians, some in shirtsleeves ... beating other civilians to death with iron bars ... there were about 15 to 20 bodies lying there. These were then cleared away by the Lithuanians and the pools of blood were washed away with a hose ... then another group of offenders was herded and pushed into the square and without further ado simply beaten to death by the civilians armed with iron bars. I watched as a group of offenders were beaten to death and then had to look away because I couldn't watch any longer. These actions seemed extremely cruel and brutal ... the Lithuanian civilians could be heard shouting out their approval and goading the men on.

Local people were in the majority, but there were numerous German soldiers in the crowd, and the baker asked one the reason for the slaughter. The answer was that "they were Jews who had swindled Lithuanians before the Germans had arrived". Another watcher was told that the victims "were all Jews who had been rounded up by Lithuanians and then brought to the square. The killings are being carried out by recently released Lithuanian convicts." The Lithuanians involved in the round-up were "wearing armbands and carrying carbines ... identifying them as members of the Lithuanian Freikorps (the Lithuanian Activist Front, or LAF)".[24]

The following day, having helped set up the headquarters for *Generaloberst* Ernst Busch's *16. Armee* in the city centre, a senior staff officer heard loud cheering nearby and walked 200 yards down the road to where a crowd had gathered:

There were a large number of women in the crowd and they lifted up their children or stood them on chairs or boxes so they could see better. At first, I thought this must be a victory celebration or some sort of sporting event because of the cheering, clapping and laughter that kept breaking out. However, when I enquired what was happening I was told that the 'death-dealer of Kovno' was at work, and that this was where collaborators and traitors were finally getting their just punishment. [Moving closer he saw] probably the most frightful event I had ever seen during the course of two world wars ... On the concrete forecourt of the petrol station a blond man of medium height, aged about twenty-five, stood, resting on a wooden club. The club was as thick as his arm and came up to his chest. At his feet lay about 15 to 20 dead or dying people. Water flowed continuously from a hose washing away blood into the drainage gully. Just a few steps behind him some 20 men – guarded by armed civilians – stood waiting for their turn in silent submission. In response to a cursory wave, the next man stepped forward silently and was then beaten to death with the wooden club in the most bestial manner, each blow accompanied by enthusiastic shouts from the audience.

Another eyewitness to what became known as the Lietukis Garage killings was the German Army photographer Wilhelm Gunsilius, who was horrified and fascinated at the same time: "Heave ho with the club. Heave ho, down on their skulls, they fell to the ground. If necessary he hit them when they were down on the ground too." Asked at interview why he didn't try to stop it, his reply is illuminating: "I certainly wasn't going to intervene on my own with that crowd there. Besides, we had orders not to interfere in anything where the Lithuanians were concerned." Gunsilius stayed to the end. "Within three-quarters of an hour he had beaten to death the entire group of 45 to 50 people ... after which the young man put the club to one side, fetched an accordion, went and stood on the mountain of corpses and played the Lithuanian national anthem." Gunsilius almost had his camera confiscated by an attendant SS officer who didn't want the scene documented. Striking up a conversation with the would-be censor, Gunsilius asked why the man was killing the victims, only to be told that his parents "had been taken from their beds two days earlier and shot because they were suspected of being nationalists, and so this was the young man's revenge".[25] Almost all the victims were Jews.

There were 30,000 Jews in Kaunas, and pogroms like this – horrific though they were – weren't going to diminish that total by very much, so a different approach was called for if the Germans wanted to exterminate the entire Jewish population. Franz Stahlecker, commanding officer of the *Einsatzgruppe* A murder squad, explained why he was using local Lithuanians to do his dirty work: "Our security force was determined to solve the Jewish question with all means at our disposal, and as quickly as possible ... at the beginning it was preferable that our force kept in the background, since the harsh measures we were planning might upset some circles of German opinion."[26] Under Stahlecker's guidance the locals switched tactics, and the same staff officer who witnessed the Garage murders then reported seeing "long columns consisting of some forty to fifty men, women and children, driven out of their homes, herded through the streets by armed civilians ... I was told that these people were being taken to the city prison, but I assume that they were led directly to their place of execution." He was right. In a matter of days just under 4,000 Jews were marched out of the city to the Seventh Fort – one of ten built in Tsarist times to protect Kaunas from attack – and shot.

Sixty miles southeast of Kaunas is Lithuania's capital, Vilnius. Renowned as the Jerusalem of Lithuania owing to its famous Jewish museum and religious schools, the city was an obvious target for Nazi barbarity. Taken by the Germans on 24 June, it didn't suffer the same sort of homegrown pogroms that struck Kaunas and other Lithuanian towns and cities, mainly because the number of Jews in the city was simply too large; roughly half the population of 150,000. That difficulty was overcome on 2 July with the arrival in the city of *Einsatzkommando 9*, a sub-unit of Stahlecker's *Einsatzgruppe A*. Aided by a locally recruited *Ypatingasis būrys* (Special Squad) of some fifty to sixty militiamen, the Germans got busy.

Two German Army truck drivers and a filing clerk saw columns of Jewish men marched out of the city, guarded by civilians wearing white armbands and armed with discarded Red Army rifles. Out of curiosity and boredom, they followed them. "They were all men, aged between about twenty to fifty. There were no women or children. The prisoners were quite well-dressed and most of them were carrying hand luggage such as small suitcases, parcels and bundles." Told they were being relocated to work as forced labour, the men were marched about 6 miles west to a place called Ponary. The site had been selected as a fuel depot by the Red Army and was under construction when the Germans invaded. Abandoned, the Germans thought its half-dozen partially excavated pits were perfect as a killing site. Once there, the Jews were sorted into batches of ten, given hoods to put on, and marched to the edge of a pit, where a Lithuanian killing squad awaited. The German clerk went on: "We stayed there for about an hour, and during this time some four to five groups of ten men each were executed, so I myself watched the killing of about forty to fifty Jews."

Several surviving members of collaborationist death squads were interviewed for television programmes in the 2000s, including *The Nazis: A Warning from History* and *Hitler's Holocaust*. Their testimony is harrowing. Twenty-four-year-old Lithuanian Petras Zelionka was one such murderer.

You could shoot or you could not shoot, but you just pressed the trigger and shot, and that was it, it wasn't a big ceremony ... you just pull the trigger, the shot is fired and that is it ... they were only Jews, none of them were our countrymen. The Germans would give us ammunition, schnapps and vodka – you could drink as much as you wanted to – and when it started to take effect the men became bolder and we'd start the *Aktion* [official Nazi title for a massacre]. After we'd finished one shooting (killing eight hundred people in Vilkija) we had lunch at a restaurant in Krakės.[27]

Juozas Aleksynas was another Lithuanian executioner: "I don't remember the first place where I shot Jews, it was a small place, but I forget the name. The Jewish men were off at war, so it was only old folk, women and children left." When asked if he'd shot children, he replied, "Yes, we shot children in the pit, or they'd have died of suffocation. Since they had to die anyway it was more merciful, to kill them quickly that is. First, we shot the parents, so they didn't have to see their children die, then we shot the children ... the smaller ones would try and crawl to their dead parents on all fours. The Germans kept the pit surrounded during executions, it was the Lithuanians who did the killing ... during the shootings German soldiers would take photographs."[28] Aleksynas's namesake – Juozas Maleksanas – also took part in the killings: "I always tried to hit the heart where the yellow star used to be so they'd die quicker." Maleksanas was matter of fact about what he did. "The job was always the same, you couldn't escape it, it was like going to the forest to collect wood ... only now you had to kill people."

The same events occurred across all the Baltic states in the wake of *Heeresgruppe Nord*'s advance. Hermann Gieschen – a Bremen shopkeeper turned reserve policeman – wrote to his wife Hanna about an *Aktion* that he and his unit carried out in Latvia – "One hundred and fifty Jews from this place were shot; men, women and children, all bumped off ... Please don't think about it, that's how it has to be."

Ukraine and Belarus were not spared. In L'viv in western Ukraine, after the NKVD massacred the remaining prisoners in the local gaols and abandoned the city, families entered the prisons to try and find their missing relatives. One, a medical student, described what he found:

> From the courtyard, doors led to a large space, filled from top to bottom with corpses. The bottom ones were still warm. The victims were between fifteen and sixty years old, but most were twenty to thirty-five years old ... Among them were many women. On the left wall, three men were crucified ... with severed male organs. Underneath them, on the floor in half-sitting, leaning positions – two nuns with those organs in their mouths. The victims of the NKVD's sadism were killed with a shot in the mouth or the back of the head. But most were stabbed in the stomach with a bayonet. Some were naked or almost naked, others in decent street clothes. One man was wearing a tie, most likely just arrested.[29]

Maria Seniva was a L'viv resident whose husband had been rounded up by the NKVD in their last sweep. "There was a message on the radio from the Germans, it said: 'Wives, mothers, brothers, sisters, come down to the prison.' I got to the entrance, I can't remember which one ... I could see the bodies ... I walked up and down the rows and I stopped to look at one ... it was covered by a blanket. I lifted the blanket and there he was, I'd found him. I don't know what had happened to him, but his face was all black. He had no eyes, nothing there, and no nose." Local Ukrainian nationalists – including the German-sponsored *Nachtigall* (Nightingale)

Battalion – blamed the city's 200,000 Jews for aiding and abetting the killers, and distributed flyers reading: 'Don't throw away your weapons yet. Take them up. Destroy the enemy ... Moscow, the Jews – these are your enemies. Destroy them.'

Many Ukrainians heeded the words. An eyewitness – Joachim Schoenfeld – described what happened: "Jews were arrested in the streets or dragged out of their houses and marched to Brigidky prison where they were brutally tortured, shot, hanged and beaten to death. Six thousand Jews; young, old, lawyers, workers, doctors, merchants, professors ... among them L'viv's chief rabbi – they all died in the pogrom. After the pogrom the building with the murdered Jews' bodies in was burned down ... with inmates still in their cells."[30] David Kahane, a rabbi in the city at the time, wrote in his diary that "the Germans seized Jews in their homes ... the Polish and Ukrainian populace rendered wholehearted assistance to the Germans".[31]

This first pogrom was only the start of the horror. A few days later, in early July, Otto Rasch's *Einsatzgruppe* C arrived in L'viv. Among their ranks was a thirty-one-year-old Viennese, Felix Landau. An early convert to Nazism, Landau had served time for his part in the murder of the Austrian Chancellor, Engelbert Dollfuss. Released from prison in 1937, he had been repaid for his loyalty to the Party by being appointed a security police official in Radom, in occupied Poland. Although married and with a young family, his eye fell upon a secretary working in the same office – Gertrude Segel. Dark-haired, with a round face, prominent jutting jaw, fleshy lips, and a truncated education, Landau wasn't anyone's idea of a great catch, but then neither was Segel. Gertrude – *Trude*, or *Hasi* ('Bunny') as Landau affectionately called her – had been described on her job application by the SS doctor who'd examined her as being of short stature and 'Dinaric descent' i.e. south-eastern European, with brown eyes, and thick, curly brown hair, although after damning her racial heritage with faint praise he had commented favourably upon her "open and honest character". Ten years Landau's junior – and already engaged to a serving soldier – Gertrude was flattered by the older man's attentions, and within weeks the two became lovers.

Unceremoniously dumping her soldier beau, Segel tied her wagon to Landau, who in the meantime had volunteered for the killing squads to further his career. Transferred east to Ukraine, Landau found himself entering L'viv under Rasch's command. In his diary entry for 2 July, he stated: "Shortly after our arrival we shot our first Jews. As usual a few of the new officers became megalomaniacs and really go for it wholeheartedly." The next day he wrote a letter to Segel after returning from another execution. "We have just come back. Five hundred Jews were lined-up ready to be shot ... I have little inclination to shoot defenceless people – even if they are only Jews. I would far rather be in good, honest, open combat. Now, good night, my dear Hasi." Two days and another mass killing later, he wrote, "One of them simply would not die. The first layer of sand had already been thrown on the first group when a hand emerged out of the sand, waved and pointed to a place – presumably his heart. A couple more shots rang out ... we'd all been given ten *Reichsmarks* to buy ourselves a few necessities. I bought myself a whip costing two *Reichsmarks* ... Twenty-three people had to be shot ... the death candidates are organised into three shifts as there aren't many shovels. Strange, I am completely unmoved, no pity, nothing. That's the way it is and then it's all over."[32]

Trude would later join Felix in his new posting at Drohobych, 40 miles south of L'viv, where the two would set up home in a country house and terrorise the local Jewish population. Known and feared as the 'Jew-General', Landau and his lover would spend their afternoons drinking and playing cards on their summer balcony, and in scenes reminiscent of Ralph Fiennes's portrayal of the sadistic Amon Goeth in the film *Schindler's List*, they would take turns to shoot their Jewish gardeners as they hurried about their work amidst the flower beds below.

Heinrich von Einsiedel was clear as to what was driving the butchery: "You heard it said that the Jews must be eradicated, and by then the idea was basically accepted. The Jews, the Jewish bolsheviks, Jewish international communism, that was our enemy, and anything was justified to destroy it."

The Ukrainian city of Ternopil was next on the Nazis' list. *Oberst* Otto Dorfes, the commanding officer of *Infanterie-Regiment 518*, wrote in his diary about the killings he and his men witnessed there on 3 July. "We saw trenches five metres deep and twenty wide – they were filled with men, women and children, mostly Jews. Every trench contained sixty to eighty people. We could hear their moans and shrieks as grenades exploded among them. On both sides of the trenches some dozen men dressed in civilian clothes were hurling grenades down into the trenches ... later, officers of the Gestapo told us that these men were Banderists (Ukrainian nationalist followers of Stepan Bandera)."

Across Ukraine the killing snowballed. Annette Schücking, a Red Cross nurse, found herself riding shotgun for an Army truck driver near the town of Koziatyn, south-east of Kiev. The young soldier was in a bit of a state: agitated, sweating, almost babbling. Seeing he needed to unburden himself, Schücking asked what was wrong. The story came pouring out. Just a few days previously he and his unit were tasked with marching several hundred Jews to a large barn where they were locked up. They then kept them there for two days, denying them food and water, despite their pleas for help. With them severely weakened, an execution commando arrived; the exhausted and thirst-wracked Jews docilely accepted their fate and submitted quietly to their executioners' guns. The young nurse was horrified. A short while later she found herself once more talking to a soldier about the killings, this time a *feldwebel* who told her he had volunteered to take part in an *Aktion* to help him get promoted – she pleaded with him not to do it, telling him "it would give him nightmares". She later met the NCO again, who confirmed he had indeed gone through with it. Writing to her mother back home, Schücking said, "What Papa says is true; people with no moral inhibitions exude a strange odour. I can now pick out these people, and many of them really do smell like blood. Oh Mama, what an enormous slaughterhouse the world is."[33]

Jews and bolsheviks were the main victims of German brutality, but they weren't the only ones. A culture of impunity gripped the *Ostheer*, and murder became commonplace. "A small German detachment was sent to a village on some job or other, was ambushed and every soldier was killed ... there were fifty men in the village; forty-nine of them were shot as a result and the fiftieth was hounded through the area so that he could spread the word about what happens when a German soldier is attacked."[34] Another *landser* was ordered to torch a village in reprisal for the killing of four German soldiers.

"The whole village?" he asked. "Why? Is it large?"

"Yes," came the reply.

"Then at least it's worth the effort."

The invaders adopted a coded language to talk about the killings, so the victims were usually referred to as bandits, partisans or saboteurs. In letters, diaries and journals these would be the words invariably used as cover for atrocity after atrocity. The same holds true for conversations with veterans, where a *landser* might very well speak in glowing terms of the matronly *babushka* who fed and looked after him and his comrades in his *izba* billet (traditional Russian rural house), but would then switch to the harshest of tones when discussing the wholesale destruction of nearby villages and his self-justified mass murder of their inhabitants as 'terrorists'.

A report from *Polizeibataillon 314* dated Friday 22 August detailed the shooting of three 'partisan women' and nineteen 'bandits' in one *Aktion*, for instance. But as one German policeman candidly admitted, "The expression 'combat the partisans' is strictly speaking a complete misnomer. We didn't have a single battle with partisans after we left Mogilev. The fact of the matter [was] that being found without an identity card sufficed for arrest and execution."[35]

The word partisan in particular was used in so many ways that it was often hard to know who was being referred to. Franz Kneipp described an incident where "a group of partisans attacked a transport of wounded soldiers and killed them all. We caught them half an hour later ... They were thrown in a sand-pit and it started from all sides – machine-guns and pistols." These partisans could well have been uniformed Red Army men cut off by the German advance and determined to carry on the fight – in which case they were POWs. Or they could have been locals in civilian clothes with nothing visible to mark them out as combatants, in which case they wouldn't be covered by the rules of warfare. Equally, they could have just been innocent villagers who were in the wrong place at the wrong time and ended up paying the price.

The green-uniformed *Ordnungspolizei* (Order Police, or Orpo) played a major role in the killings, often either assisting the SS death squads with guard or support functions, or carrying out the slaughter themselves. Boris von Drachenfels was one such policeman: "I was on sentry duty one day when I heard an endless wailing when the wind blew towards me. At first I didn't know what it was until I realised it was Jews being shot." Drachenfels recalled the aftermath of one *Aktion*: "Before, we'd associated mass killings with communism, but now it was the cultured German race that was doing it – it changed us."

The killings weren't confined to the Army and police either. A downed *Luftwaffe* pilot, captured by the NKVD and interrogated, reported that he "participated in the execution of a group of Jews in one of the villages near Berdichev at the beginning of the war. They were executed as punishment for handing over a German pilot to the Red Army." Even the *Kriegsmarine* were involved. A naval mechanic called Kammeyer was in Liepaja in Latvia that summer and witnessed an execution by his own. "The commander of the execution belonged to the naval artillery. A lorry arrived, stopped, and nearby there was a trench about twenty metres long. The prisoners all had to get into it, and they were hurried up by blows from rifle butts and lined up. The *feldwebel* had a machine-pistol and he shot them one after the other. Most of them fell like that with their eyeballs turned up. There was a woman among them."[36] Another naval marine in Liepaja – Karl-Heinz Mangelsen – recalled seeing "Jews walking some 20 to 30 metres to a trench where the firing squad stood ready. There was a commotion every time a new batch had to go down into the pit."

Despite oft-repeated denials from surviving veterans, and constant refrains that they saw nothing of these atrocities themselves, there is simply too much evidence for this view to be credible. Many people back in the Reich couldn't claim ignorance either. Boris von Drachenfels "told my uncle back in Germany when I was on leave. He was so horrified he didn't reply." Marie-Luise Müller – a young girl living in Weimar at the time – explained how she reacted when she heard about the killings from a neighbour on leave from the front: "I repressed it, as we all did. We'd have gone under if we'd had to face up to everything that was being done."

Soldiers were officially banned from taking photos of executions in a bid to try and keep the killings under wraps, but a multitude of photographs show ordinary members of the *Wehrmacht* watching executions and taking pictures. Official acknowledgement of this policy can be found in one of the few surviving *Ordnungspolizei* reports of the time. In it, Max Montua – a career police officer and commander of *Polizei-Regiment Mitte* in 1941 – issued an order to his men on 11 July regarding the shooting of 'Jewish plunderers', as he called them, stating, "I forbid photography and the permitting of spectators at the executions. Executions and grave sites are not to be made known." In the same document Montua also showed concern not only for the secrecy of the various *Aktionen*, but for the well-being of his men. "Commanders are especially to provide for the spiritual care of the men who participate in the *Aktionen*. The impressions of the day are to be blotted out through the holding of social events in the evenings."[37] In short, this meant supplying the men who pulled the triggers with plenty of alcohol and female company to help grease the wheels of butchery. The Germans even came up with a nickname for it – *Ostrausch* – literally East rush, a heady mix of adrenalin and freedom of action for members of a western society more or less defined by a moral code and the rule of law, both of which could now be discarded in a welter of violence and sexual licence.

Another tactic used to try and avert guilt away from the ordinary German soldier was to blame all atrocities on the SS, and its armed wing, the *Waffen-SS*. After all, they were meant to represent the ideological tip of the Nazi Party spear, so it would be natural for them to be in the forefront of the slaughter. This was a very successful ploy, partly because there was more than an element of truth in it. When *Standartenführer* Hilmar Wäckerle, a senior *Waffen-SS* officer, stopped his command car to inspect the wreckage of a smashed-up Soviet tank near L'viv on 2 July, he felt curious enough to want to look it over – perhaps to see if there were any souvenirs to be had. Unbeknown to him, a surviving crew member was hiding out in the hulk. On seeing the German officer, he shot him dead, before being killed himself by a member of Wäckerle's staff. Enraged at the death, members of his division – the *SS-Wiking* – took the law into their own hands, as described by twenty-one-year-old SS trooper-cum-butcher, Günther Otto: "The members of the meat train and bakery *kompanie* rounded up all Jews who could be found based on their facial characteristics and their speech, as most of them spoke Yiddish. *Obersturmführer* Braunnagel of the bakery *kompanie* and *Untersturmführer* Kochalty were in charge. Then a gauntlet was formed by two rows of soldiers, most of whom were from the meat train and bakery *kompanie*, but some were from *1. Gebirgs-Division*. The Jews were then forced to run the gauntlet while being beaten with rifle butts and bayonets. At the end of the gauntlet were a number of SS and Army officers with machine-pistols, who shot the Jews dead as they entered the pit at the end ... about fifty to sixty Jews were killed."[38]

One of the *Waffen-SS* units most heavily involved in atrocities was its one and only mounted formation at the time, Hermann Fegelein's *SS-Kavallerie-Brigade*. Tasked with clearing the vast Pripet marshes of Jews, Red Army stragglers and would-be partisans, the SS cavalrymen were given clear instructions: "If the population is generally hostile, racially inferior, or ... made up of escaped POWs, then all those suspected of aiding the partisans are to be shot." Villages were either to be designated as German-friendly or "they should cease to exist". Those in the former category were reported as "setting out a table with a white tablecloth, on which there would be bread and salt, which was offered to the unit. In one case there was even a band waiting to welcome the troops." Regarding everyone else, the SS riders went on a murder spree.

Ordered to drown civilians in the swamps, the commander of one of the brigades' two regiments, *Sturmbannführer* Franz Magill, complained that "driving women and children into the swamp wasn't successful because it wasn't deep enough for them to be submerged. Below a depth of one metre, for the most part it was solid ground (probably sand) so that drowning wasn't possible."[39] Those who survived were shot instead. Heinrich Wulfes was one of the SS cavalrymen:

> I was inducted into the SS cavalry in Warsaw in September 1940, our training was tough, and mostly on foot ... We went right into Russia and advanced to Minsk. On the way we often had to deal with snipers, who were usually ex-Red Army soldiers hiding out in the forests ... It was early July 1941, we were told we had to comb the swamps for Jews ... panzer units were no good there because of the terrain, and they assigned us rather than regular Army troops, but they used Army soldiers later. We went into the swamps and stayed there for six weeks. We came to a town of about 3-4,000 people and were told to round up the Jews – local militia pointed them out, there were a few hundred – and then we took them to a quarry, surrounded by big cliffs so they couldn't escape. Then the *Einsatzgruppe* turned up, there weren't many of them, maybe 40 to 50, so they were too small to do that sort of thing on their own.[40]

In less than a month Fegelein reported that his men had shot 13,788 partisans and saboteurs. His own losses were "just two men, killed by a mine".

Heinz Rahe was a twenty-nine-year-old Protestant pastor in Wolfsburg in 1939. Having completed his obligatory military service back in 1935 he was somewhat surprised to be pressed back into uniform in the newly formed *13. Panzerdivision*. As a preacher, Rahe was deeply religious and disliked the aggressive atheism of the Nazis, but regardless of his own personal views he reported for duty and took part in the French campaign, earning promotion to *feldwebel*. He was too old to have been in the Hitler Youth, and in his letters home to his beloved wife Ursula, he never espoused loyalty to either the Nazis or Hitler – indeed, when he did mention politics he actually questioned the reasons for the invasion: "Is it worth sacrificing German blood for this? How does the east concern us! ... we needed fertile Ukraine as a source of food. That made sense to me: take precautions so that the homeland can eat. But this struggle with Russia seems pointless. In addition, the vastness of Russia is a great concern. We are now 500 kilometres into the country. Is it the beginning or the end?" His letters are full of questions about his wife, family and friends, and oft-repeated pleas for Ursula to look after herself and keep safe. He was also something of an amateur poet, jotting down his love for her in little vignettes and pleading with her not to laugh at his scribblings. However, on the same pages as his clumsy verse, he felt no compunction in describing a scene from a village he and his unit had just taken: "The rubble of some houses was still burning ... Many soldiers stood in a small square and eagerly abused a Jew who was in fear of his life. He was pleading on the floor. He was said to have been complicit in the mutilation of two German airmen who had had to make an emergency landing. Shortly afterwards I heard some gunshots. I slept very well in the truck that night." He also detailed how houses were routinely set on fire to try and crush any lingering resistance: "The homesteads went up in flames, there were quite a few of them." But it was the subject of Soviet Jews that he kept on coming back to, and most vividly when "our quarters were in need of cleaning, so I asked our orderly to get a prisoner ... no prisoner came, but a Jew instead. She wears her Jewish star on her arm and has a hideously Jewish face, one of the unpleasant kind that could easily be used as a photo in *Der Stürmer* (*The Striker*, a viciously anti-Semitic weekly Nazi tabloid). Our Sarah, as I call her, was happy to be allowed to do housework. For that she gets something to eat at lunchtime, for which she is very grateful. She speaks broken German like all the Jews of the East. As I said, she has a typical Jewish face and is therefore quite disgusting to me, but she does a good job." This was Heinz Rahe, the pastor, loving husband and part-time poet.

7

Uncharted Territory

Franz Halder was not a man given to making lurid statements or flamboyant gestures. At 5 ft 9 in – the same height as his political master – with his pince-nez and severe haircut, he appeared to be pretty much what he was, the professional Army staff officer. He kept a diary during much of his time as Chief of the OKH General Staff, and his writings were published after the war in both German and English. From a purely military standpoint they are interesting documents, but what makes them fascinating is the picture they paint of a man at the very pinnacle of Nazi Germany's *Wehrmacht* who oscillated wildly between jubilation and despair. The most celebrated instance of the former is an entry from 3 July 1941: "The campaign against Russia has been won in fourteen days." As an example of historical hubris this statement has few rivals and has often been quoted to highlight misplaced German arrogance in the face of an opponent who was far from beaten. However, the context of the entry paints a markedly different picture. "On the whole, one can already say that the task of destroying the mass of the Russian Army in front of the Dvina and Dnieper rivers has been fulfilled. It's really not saying too much if I claim that the campaign against Russia has been won in fourteen days ... The extent of the theatre, and the tenacity of resistance that will be conducted with every means, will still claim many weeks." That final sentence not only partially qualifies Halder's claim of victory, but demonstrates at least some understanding of what still awaited the *Ostheer*.

Having said that, it is clear that Halder felt the campaign was going to plan and that victory was within the Reich's grasp. The crew-cutted Bavarian wasn't alone in his belief. Ulrich de Maizière, a staff officer of French Huguenot descent serving in OKH's planning centre, said, "Our initial victories were utterly exhilarating. I'd wondered how we would supply our troops once we penetrated deep into Russia, but now I put those concerns aside. Our advance was rapid, and the speed we were moving made everybody feel supremely confident. I was convinced that the campaign would be over by the autumn. As I wrote to my mother, 'By the end of September the Russian army will be crushed.'"[1] Given what was happening at the front, this seemed a reasonable position to hold, and chimed with Halder's forecast that the Germans would defeat the Soviet Union in eight to ten weeks. Hitler himself was slightly more pessimistic, telling his generals that he thought it wouldn't be over until mid-October.

Why was the second most senior officer in the German Army so optimistic so early in the campaign? Halder would, no doubt, point to what had been achieved thus far. Firstly – and just two weeks into Barbarossa – the three German and allied army groups had beaten their Red Army opponents in the border battles. Bock's *Heeresgruppe Mitte* had achieved huge success in encircling and crushing much of the Soviet Western Front in the Bialystok-Minsk pocket, and Leeb's *Heeresgruppe Nord* had leaped forward to Daugavpils, destroying the majority of the Red Army's armoured forces in the Baltic states on the way. Rundstedt's *Heeresgruppe Süd* had had the toughest time, but was finally making headway and driving into western Ukraine. The Soviets had suffered massive casualties, with some 590,000 men killed, missing or captured and were losing well over 40,000 men a day.[2] Furthermore, the *Ostheer* was already more than halfway to Moscow, and the threat posed by the VVS had been neutralised by the *Luftwaffe*.

In essence, the German plan to destroy the mass of the Red Army in the west, before it could retreat into the interior, was working – all that was needed was to push on, and the final collapse would come. As Halder also noted in his diary with great satisfaction, "The Russians can no longer offer a continuous front, even using the best defensive positions."

For Moscow, things were about to get even worse. Almost 1,200 miles north of the Soviet capital was the Finnish city of Petsamo (now Russian Pechenga). An important nickel mining centre, it lay almost on the Soviet-Finnish border. Some 80 miles east was the Soviets' only year-round ice-free port in the north, Murmansk, the destination for British aid convoys. The first of those convoys wouldn't arrive until September, but nevertheless it was vital the port city remained in Moscow's hands. It was equally important for the Germans to capture it, or at least cut the Kirov railway line that it sat on.

On 29 June, *Unternehmen Silberfuchs* (Operation Arctic fox) was launched to do just that, with Eduard Dietl leading his joint German/Finnish force east across the tundra. Valerian Frolov's 14th Army opposed them, however it soon became crystal clear that the terrain and environment were just as big an enemy as the Red Army, as Dietl knew only too well: "There has never been a war fought in the high north. The region is unsuited to military operations and there are no roads." The Finns appreciated this, and during the winter their policy had been to withdraw all their forces south until the few pale months of summer returned. The Germans were soon to find out why.

Oberjäger Lamm recalled what it was like: "We had nothing with which to overcome the conditions we encountered. On active service, and especially in a combat zone, the soldiers first task is to dig in, but we couldn't. The ground was either solid rock or else the topsoil was spongy, and we met groundwater ... digging-in was impossible, so we made blockhouses of logs built on top of the swamp ... damp was everywhere, our uniforms were always wet and our leather equipment was soon covered in mould. The worst things were the mosquitoes and other flying pests which bred in the water and now had human blood to suck on. They moved in clouds and made our lives a misery ... in the early days the insects were a worse nuisance than the enemy." So dreadful were the mosquitoes that they soon earned the nickname 'Stukas' from the tormented *landsers*. One of Lamm's officers simply wrote, "If there is a hell for soldiers, then this is it."

With motorised transport of limited use due to the non-existent roads, the advance was a crawl. Lamm described how the invaders coped: "Up in the Arctic we used, among other things, sledges, just like explorers, each of which was drawn by twelve dogs. They were quite savage animals, more like wolves than the domestic dogs with which we were familiar."[3]

As part of the offensive, a secondary force some 200 miles south – based on the troopers of *SS-Kampfgruppe Nord* – were all set to launch themselves against the Soviet defenders of Salla, and then cut the Kirov railway at Kantalahti. Relatively well-equipped, but poorly trained, the SS men moved forward to their jump-off points on 1 July with a sense of foreboding. "The whole area was a forest growing on a marsh, through which we could only move along tree-trunk roads." Beginning their assault, the former policemen and concentration camp guards who constituted much of *Nord*'s ranks came up against fierce resistance, and were unable to make any headway. Their new commander, Karl-Maria Demelhuber, went forward to see for himself what was happening: "I found some 30 to 40 men from Nr.'s 1, 2 and 4 *Kompanien*, together with the commander of Nr. *1. Kompanie*. The men were physically and mentally at the end of their tether. It was clear that the demands made on them had been too great to be borne by men who were aged between thirty and forty. Many were showing signs of battle exhaustion."[4]

The Germans' problems multiplied when the Soviets counter-attacked, leading to some SS troopers fleeing in panic. With 300 dead and another 400 wounded, the SS were withdrawn, and the Germans forced to rethink.

Dietl's offensive did however make it impossible for Moscow to re-direct troops from the far north to the south where they were desperately needed. This problem increased dramatically on 10 July when the Finns themselves finally launched their own attack on the Soviet Union to try and regain the territory they had lost in the Winter War – the Karelian Isthmus. They also laid siege to the naval base at Hanko, trapping its 30,000-strong garrison, and laid minefields in the Baltic to impede Soviet shipping. The main Finnish offensive was a fairly turgid affair, grinding forward as the Finns attempted to reach their old border. By Christmas the Finns would lose 25,000 dead and twice that number wounded, while inflicting almost a quarter of a million casualties on the Soviets.

The Germans were keen that the Finns did their bit in the air too, requesting that the 235 aircraft of the Finnish Air Force – the *Ilmavoimat* – put pressure on the 700 or so VVS planes in the region to stop them being sent south to face the *Luftwaffe*. The Finnish fighter pilot Jorma 'Joppe' Karhunen flew antiquated US-made Brewster B-239E Buffalos in the fighting. "The Brewster was good against the older Russian fighters, the I-153 Chaikas and the I-16, so the first period of the war in 1941 was good for us." Karhunen – who had been the first Finnish pilot to test fly the dumpy little fighter – was referring to the astonishing kill/loss ratio at the time of 33/1 in the Finns' favour. Waldemar Erfurth, attached to Helsinki high command by Berlin, was impressed: "The Finnish fighters can successfully hold their own against a very superior enemy. Numerous aerial combats such as at Lahdenpohja on 9 July show proof of the great flying skills and splendid fighting morale of the Finnish fighters."[5] At Lahdenpohja a dozen Finnish fighters – including Karhunen's – shot down eight out of fifteen Soviet bombers and fighters in a ferocious ten-minute combat.

The *Ilmavoimat*'s 'happy time' wasn't to last. The Buffalo (known as the Brewster to the Finns, or more colloquially as the *Lentävä kaljapullo* – flying beer-bottle) was all too soon outclassed by newer Soviet models and as one pilot acknowledged "later, it became a fight to the death." However, Helsinki's main influence on Barbarossa was to tie down Soviet forces needed elsewhere, rather than deal the Red Army a mortal blow.

In direct support of their allies were some sixty aircraft from the *Luftwaffe*'s *Luftflotte V*, one of which was piloted by *Oberleutnant* Karl-Friedrich Schlossstein: "We moved to Kirkenes and from there flew missions against Murmansk – airfields, the harbour, ships – and supported the mountain army in the far north – low-level attacks against troop concentrations, artillery and so on."

The Finns also received limited help from Alfred Keller's *Luftflotte 1* as it flew over the heads of *Heeresgruppe Nord*. Keller was an energetic commander, but not particularly imaginative, owing his position more to his dedication to the Party and his personal friendship with Hermann Goering than to his ability. His 380-aircraft-strong command was much the smallest of all the *Luftwaffe* groupings for Barbarossa, although he was truly blessed in being allocated Hannes Trautloft's *JG. 54 Grünherz*. Filled with some extraordinarily talented pilots, *JG. 54* would go on to become the second-highest-scoring fighter wing in the *Luftwaffe*. They would show that skill early on, when, on 30 June, they flew in support of Manstein and his panzer crews at Daugavpils, shooting down no fewer than sixty-five VVS aircraft, mainly unescorted bombers trying to smash the bridges over which the Germans were driving headlong.

As *Heeresgruppe Nord* advanced up the Baltic coast, and the Finns began to push south on either side of Lake Ladoga, the Soviet Red Banner Baltic Fleet found itself being squeezed from both sides. Despite hugely outnumbering its German and Finnish rivals, the Soviet armada – which contained two battleships, two cruisers and no fewer than seventeen destroyers – fared poorly. Its main opponent, Günther Guse's *Der Kommandierende General der Marinestation der Ostsee* (Commander Naval Forces Baltic Sea), headquartered at Kiel, was a mixed bag of *Schnellboote* (S-boats), minelayers and minesweepers, converted trawlers, transports, tugs, and five U-boats. As Karl Dönitz commented ruefully on the *Kriegsmarine*'s preparedness for Barbarossa: "Seldom has any branch of the armed forces of any country gone to war so poorly equipped." This notwithstanding, the Reich's sailors did well, acting in concert with Keller's *Luftflotte 1* to lay several thousand mines, which took a heavy toll of Soviet shipping right from the start. Leeb's men played their part too, capturing port after port and robbing the Soviets of their bases: Ventspils and Liepaja were lost on 27 June, Riga by the end of the month, and Pärnu in Estonia was evacuated on 3 July. The Soviet fleet was now confined to Tallinn and the huge naval base at Kronstadt near Leningrad, and was effectively neutralised.

Having now advanced some 300 miles or so into the Soviet Union, the *Wehrmacht* had reached about the greatest distance it had had to cover in any campaign of the war so far. The Germans were now in uncharted territory militarily, and the major deficiencies in their planning were beginning to make themselves felt. For the troops themselves, many were beginning to realise they had entered a whole other world. Erhard Raus – who would go on to command 6. *Panzerdivision* – described it thus: "He who steps for the first time on Russian soil is immediately conscious of the new, the strange, the primitive. The German soldier who crossed into Russian territory felt that he entered a different world, where he was opposed, not only by the forces of the enemy, but by the forces of nature itself."[6] Johann von Kielmansegg, who would serve under Raus as a staff officer, was a little more prosaic. "The terrain was awful, a thick green jungle. We could only see a short distance ahead, and the lack of roads was appalling."

For the *landsers*, the sheer scale of the landscape was daunting, and somehow frightening. Eugen Altrogge wrote to his friend Hans Albring with envy: "What a tremendous adventure now lies ahead of you, you who enter old, mysterious Russia." It wasn't a feeling reciprocated by the young Catholic signaller, who wrote back of the "vast pine forests stretching into the distance, here and there a few huts – endless nature". For the men of *Heeresgruppen Nord* and *Mitte*, the huge forests of northern and central Russia were numbing, as the former Bremen shopkeeper Hermann Gieschen observed: "Primeval forests, undergrowth, thickets, disordered, untended and terrifying."

Down in the south, the prevailing terrain was the farmland of Ukraine and its seemingly never-ending fields of sunflowers and wheat. A replacement paratrooper destined for *Oberst* Albert Sturm's regiment noted the vastness:

> The train journey seemed endless … we were held up for long periods while other units were rushed through. That journey made me realize for the first time the enormous vastness of Russia. We went via the Generalgouvernement [part of occupied Poland] and into Belorussia. Once through that region, which was more or less westernised, we entered the Russia of our imagination, of fields so vast they stretched to all horizons – imagine a field of sunflowers 30 kilometres long. Truthfully, the terrain was a sort of prairie, a land sea on which the occasional little village far away was the only sign of human life. It was at the same time a depressing and exciting country; depressing in its monotonous vastness, and exciting because it was so obviously fertile.[7]

A mountain trooper described it almost wistfully: "Fields which extended from horizon to horizon in all directions … sunflowers which in the early morning dipped their heads so that the colour of the field was a monotonous shade of brown, but when the flower heads stood upright as they did at midday, they pointed to the sun and changed the field to the colour of bright yellow … an unforgettable picture of fruitfulness."[8] One of the anonymous *gebirgsjäger*'s comrades recalled those days with a little less sentimentality:

The days passed without us knowing if it was Monday or Friday, we were just a column of men, trudging endlessly and aimlessly, as if in a void. We could have been any of the armies that had invaded Russia in the past. We had horses – as those other armies had – and the only sign that this was the twentieth century were the Stukas that flew over our heads ... how the ration parties found us was a mystery, but usually within an hour or two of arriving at some map reference the ration parties would appear with hot food, fresh water, mail, and sometimes, even canteen goods. We went without alcohol, there wasn't any anyway. The only time we had spirits was when we had a day's rest and the spirit ration came up with the announcement that we had a difficult task to achieve – we had to smash through a set of defences called the Stalin Line.

As the advance continued, the lack of mechanization in the invasion force acknowledged by the unknown mountaineer became ever more acute. Well-trained and fit though the majority of *landsers* were, the physical strain they were under was immense. The heady pace of forty to fifty kilometres a day didn't slacken and even the fittest began to struggle, with the average man taking a daunting 80,000 steps to cover fifty kilometres. Wilhelm Lübbecke recalled it with antipathy: "Battling both stifling heat and thick clouds of dust, we plodded countless miles. There were few breaks from our march ... after a while a kind of hypnosis would set in as you watched the steady rhythm of the man's boots in front of you. Utterly exhausted, I sometimes fell into a quasi-sleepwalk. Placing one foot in front of the other. I somehow managed to keep pace, waking only briefly whenever I stumbled into the body ahead of me."[9] Helmut Pabst, in Bock's *Heeresgruppe Mitte*, remembered, "We marched till our knees were shaking ... our thirst was awful." Another *landser* recalled how "our feet sank into the sand and dirt, puffing dust into the air so that it rose up and clung to us ... The men marched in silence, coated with dust, with dry throats and lips."

While carrying on like this was possible for short periods, inevitably it began to grind down the men, particularly as they weren't equipped to deal with the prevailing conditions. A report later written by a number of senior officers who served in Russia concluded that "the clothing worn by the *landser* proved too heavy for summer ... men sweated too easily, became very thirsty and were soon caked with dirt. Hard-packed dirt roads cut like glass into boot leather, and boot soles quickly went to pieces ... Flies torment men and animals in hot weather. Many of the wooden huts in the northern and central regions were infested with vermin such as bed bugs, head lice and body lice. The mud huts of the south are cleaner, but the dust storms there cause inflammation of the eyes and respiratory organs. Diarrhoea was frequent ... many soldiers contracted jaundice diseases which lasted two to three weeks."

Fritz Pabst, building bridges for Walther Reichenau's 6. *Armee*, found the flies a particular problem: "Rather four weeks in action than another day here with all these flies. There are thousands in our quarters. I'm sitting here in my swimming trunks and hundreds of them are trying to eat me up." One of Guderian's cycle-mounted infantrymen in *Panzergruppe 2* spelt out his routine on the march: "Our average march day runs approximately as follows; wake up between two and five in the morning. Get on our bicycles and off we go ... The mosquito net is always thrown over my head and neck, because even in the sun the mosquitoes bother us. Tonight, during my guard duty, it was almost unbearable with the beasts."

Although a fully qualified doctor called up from his post at the Kaiser-Wilhelm Hospital in Duisburg – and at thirty-one years old the oldest officer in the unit – Heinrich Haape suffered the endless marching with the men of his battalion, as he and his fellow officers struggled to keep them going with minimal rest:

> The hour and a half's sleep had done more harm than good. It hadn't been easy to awaken the dog-tired men. Our bones were cold, muscles stiff and painful, and our feet were swollen. We only managed to pull on our boots with great difficulty. Each man's war at this stage was circumscribed by the next few steps he would take, the hardness of the road, the soreness of his feet, the dryness of his tongue and the weight of his equipment.

Sleep wasn't the only thing the endlessly marching soldiery was short of, as Wilhelm Lübbecke bemoaned: "The only information we received came in twice weekly news sheets issued by the division's headquarters. Excerpts of speeches filled most of the space, but there would also be brief reports about battles and advances on the Eastern Front ... these newspapers offered us at least a general sense of what was happening elsewhere."

Lübbecke and his comrades plodded on, hunger beginning to gnaw at them as the logistics system struggled to cope with the huge distances, terrible roads and large numbers of Red Army stragglers only too ready to pounce on poorly protected supply wagons. One unit was reported to have survived for three days on nothing but a supply of tinned tomatoes they were carrying, although more often than not hungry soldiers responded by stealing food from the local populace: "We take onions and small yellow turnips from the gardens of the villagers, and milk from their churns. Most of them part with it amiably." It's difficult to believe that the villagers had any real say in the matter, especially as the same *landser* described how "The peasants take off their caps when you look at them sharply." Given the German propensity for brutality towards the civil population, the villagers probably considered themselves lucky if they only lost some of their meagre food supply.

Not all German units behaved in that way though, Wilhelm Lübbecke's for one had a more benevolent approach. "Our division was able to put a Soviet flour mill back into operation, which helped to feed both German troops and the local civilian population." The only drawback was that the retreating Soviet forces had poured oil into the grain store to spoil it, so that "the bread possessed an unpleasant taste that was barely hidden by the salt we mixed into it".

Max Kuhnert was also a victim of the Red Army's policy to deny any and all comfort to the advancing invaders, as he and his thirsty troop alighted on a village well in the middle of another baking hot day: "Full of anticipation we rushed to the well and lowered the bucket, thinking already of a lovely drink and a cool wash-down. But what a disappointment. When we got the water up it was useless to us because the Russians had put chlorine into the well and it was undrinkable. Our disappointment bordered on despair."

Back in the Reich, the newsreels were full of smiling, bronzed *landsers* cheerfully marching onwards, rifles slung, sleeves rolled up on brawny forearms, their steely gaze fixed on a far horizon. Heinrich Haape detailed the reality: "There was no singing, no joking, no talking of any kind that wasn't strictly necessary." A *landser* in *Heeresgruppe Mitte* described the misery of it all: "We only ever had a little sleep. Once, when we finally managed to secure accommodation in a barn, our section was assigned to sentry duty, and we spent yet another night in a rain-soaked meadow."[10]

It wasn't only humans that were affected by the exhausting toll of it all. A German campaign study reflected on the *Wehrmacht*'s reliance on draught horses: "Heavier horse breeds were less hardy and needed excessive amounts of forage. It would have been better not to have used them in Russia." The right conclusion perhaps, but impossible in a military that relied so completely on the horse for most of its transportation.

The bald fact was that the Barbarossa invasion force was woefully under-equipped for the campaign it had to fight. In 1940 the Army could only muster 120,000 vehicles and just 10 per cent of it was motorised. Victory in the West was a boon in providing access to the French Army's 300,000 trucks, cars and prime movers, and, like locusts, the Germans stripped the Belgians, Dutch, Danes, Norwegians, Greeks and Yugoslavs of everything with wheels and an engine – even the British Expeditionary Force kindly donated its transport fleet left behind at

Dunkirk. This large-scale pillage was typified by the action of a slightly portly forty-four-year-old mechanical engineer with thinning hair and a ready smile – *Major* Alfred Becker. An artillery officer by training, Becker marched into Amersfoort in the Netherlands during the western campaign, where he discovered the well-stocked and abandoned vehicle park of a Dutch artillery regiment. Swapping his 126 draught horses for large-wheeled lorries, he motorised almost every gun in his regiment. The biggest problem he then faced was ensuring he had enough qualified drivers for his new vehicle fleet; in 1939 the ratio of motor vehicles to people in Britain was 1:14, and in the United States – the most motorised country in the world at the time – it was 1:3. In Germany it was 1:47 – relatively few Germans knew how to drive. By the launch of Barbarossa those figures hadn't changed, and with only a small percentage of the *Wehrmacht* motorised, the *Ostheer* was relying on its infantry divisions to keep on marching, day after punishing day.

Desperate for a few hours' sleep after yet another day choking on dust, and seeming never to reach the far-off horizon, the *landsers* were denied even that: "We were witness to another form of Soviet aerial warfare; night harassment. One night, as we were just about to go to sleep, we heard the sound of a ratchety aircraft engine from somewhere overhead. This was the distinctive noise made by a Russian U-2. These antiquated biplanes – nicknamed Nähmaschinen (sewing machines) for obvious reasons – were armed with small two-kilogram bombs and were used by the Soviets to attack our lines and rear areas during the hours of darkness. Although indiscriminate and causing little material damage, these nuisance raids were part of the Soviets' nocturnal war of nerves." Hans-Joachim S. wrote to his wife about them. "Bombing raids at night, some bombs landed just twenty metres away from us – thank goodness they were only little baby bombs, but two comrades had to be evacuated injured."

Erwin Bartmann remembered the *Nähmaschinen* well: "When I first heard them they brought to mind an image of my mother working the treadle of her sewing machine … we came to dread them, they were tough little birds that could take rifle or machine-gun fire with apparent impunity." He was clear about their effect on him and his comrades. "These attacks drained our strength, not only by causing us casualties, but by denying us precious sleep."

Lieutenant Georgiy Pavlov was one of the Soviet pilots who flew this sort of mission, in his case in an old UT-1b trainer: "The aircraft was only armed with two ShKAS machine-guns and four RS-82 rocket projectiles. Our task was simply to deprive the Germans of their sleep. We flew at night and made our attacks randomly, such as against the headlights of a car, or against a searchlight on the ground." The tactic was remarkably effective, as one German infantryman grudgingly admitted: "We lie exhausted in our holes, waiting for them." An official *Wehrmacht* report detailed the impact. "The Russians' unchallenged air superiority at night has reached an unbearable level, the troops get no rest, and their strength will soon be dissipated." What was becoming clear to the Germans was that what had begun as a headlong charge littered with brilliant victories, was now descending into a slog.

The key to maintaining the momentum of the invasion was obvious – the *panzerwaffe*. The *Ostheer*'s panzer divisions, and their linked motorised infantry formations, were still largely intact and had already proven themselves against their Soviet opponents. Now was the time to throw them once again at an enemy still reeling from the border battles.

For *Heeresgruppe Nord* that meant re-starting their advance from the Jekabpils/Daugavpils bridgehead, and charging forward the hundred-odd miles to the major railway junction at Ostrov, breaking through the pre-war Stalin Line border fortifications on the way. Following Leeb's hold order, the panzers had been forced to sit idle for six whole days while the infantry caught up – time that the Soviets had used to bring up reinforcements and steady their panicky troops. Nevertheless, Reinhardt and Manstein gave the go-ahead on 2 July, and once more their panzers surged forward, soon leaving their accompanying infantry and support services behind them once more, as Hans-Joachim S. wrote: "I am currently limping behind the troops. The Panhard was not built for Russia ... You will have already seen in the newsreel the roads peppered with Soviet tanks. We drive those roads too. Endless dust. In the evening we stop at a farm, guards are set up, we eat, and then someone starts playing on a Russian guitar and comrades sing songs about home."

Two days after starting their engines, Reinhardt's spearhead had broken the Stalin Line and captured Ostrov. The Soviets had no choice but to fall back to the last defensive line in front of Leningrad – the River Luga. Reinhardt and Manstein gave chase, determined not to give the Soviets a moment's breathing space. For Hans-Joachim S. the advance was interminable. "We live a completely timeless existence. We only focus on the sun, get up when it gets light, spend up to thirty hours at the wheel – other comrades up to fifty hours – then stretch out our tired limbs when the moon is shining. We are exposed to glowing sun and dust for eighteen hours a day." Exhausting though it was, he was still excited by it all: "Sometimes you think you will be the eternal soldier. Of course, I am happy that I am part of it and can take part in this most incredible war. These experiences will give me memories for life ... here, far from culture and the slightest distraction." He had no doubt about the way the invasion was going: "It won't be long before the first panzers roll through Moscow."

A week after taking Ostrov, Reinhardt's lead panzers crossed the Narva at the Estonian border, and his entire corps were in Russia proper. The Soviets fought back hard. The *SS-Totenkopf* senior NCO – *SS-Oberscharführer* Wieninger – was in the thick of it: "You simply can't describe the situation here, you have to see it with your own eyes to understand it ... not that we're afraid of dying, we've gotten used to that idea." Used to it he may have been, but it was also taking its toll on him. "All the dirt and dust, the loneliness, all the confusion and everything else, overtime is making me both physically and emotionally ill." Wilhelm Lübbecke – now a *Vorgeschobener Beobachter* (VB – Forward Observer) – was in the forefront of the advance as he directed artillery fire missions to support the lead infantry. He was also on the receiving end of Soviet shelling: "The air around us suddenly filled with the shriek of incoming artillery fire." Diving into nearby cover,

> There was nothing to do but to press myself into the bottom of the foxhole. When shelling is that heavy and that close, you simply hope the enemy gunners don't manage to land a direct hit that will turn your refuge into a grave ... If there was one thing I learned fast, it was that you couldn't avoid being scared for the first five or ten minutes of combat. It is an instinctual animal reflex to danger ... Combat might be described as controlled chaos, but you have to maintain a sense of calm so you can focus on your mission. My composure would return as my mind and training took over. There was a job to do and I was going to do it.

Using hastily brought-up infantry units to shield his precious armour, Hoepner abandoned Leeb's plan for a frontal attack on the fortified town of Luga and, instead, sent Friedrich Kirchner's 1. *Panzerdivision* and Franz Landgraf's 6. *Panzerdivision* to cross the river nearer the coast at Porechye. Once again, the Brandenburgers came into their own, surprising the guards in the darkness and capturing the town's twin bridges intact. At 2200hrs that night the lead panzers sent a message to Reinhardt: "Bridgehead established – the gates to Leningrad are open!" VVS aircraft in the area were so disbelieving that the Germans could have advanced so far and so fast that they flew low and dropped leaflets asking for identification – only to be met by a hail of anti-aircraft fire. In another hugely daring operation, *Panzergruppe 4* had advanced a further 200-plus miles in twelve days and was now fewer than 90 miles from Leningrad itself. It was like the first few days of the invasion all over again. Philipp von Boeselager, a staff officer with *Heeresgruppe Nord*, spoke for many: "We were going forward so quickly. A heady optimism swept through the ranks. We genuinely thought Russia's fate would be decided in six weeks."[11]

To the south, Fedor von Bock's *Heeresgruppe Mitte* was also on the move again. Having finally sealed the Bialystok-Minsk pocket, Hoth and Guderian were raring to go, now that the leading infantry units had caught up with them. This was easier said than done. The infantry might have moved up, but the ever-creaking German logistics system was still lagging behind. *Feldwebel* Willi Born of *17. Panzerdivision* was holed up in a wood near Minsk one evening, waiting for the fuel tankers to arrive so he and his fellow crews could fill their thirsty panzers. Finally, a solitary tanker pulled up, driven by a *Gefreiter* Piontek. Born went up to him.

"Let me have thirty jerrycans of fuel."

Piontek replied that he could let him have a dozen: "That's all, twelve jerrycans and no more."

"That's not enough to fill my lighter!" retorted Born angrily.

Piontek explained. "Russian fighters got us. Five lorries burned out, all the drivers killed, and the Russians further back have broken through and cut the road; supplies are all messed up."[12]

Gefreiter Piontek could also have told his fellow NCO that the staff planners back in Berlin hadn't helped the situation by hugely underestimating the campaign's fuel consumption. The figures they used – the *Verbrauchssätze* – was an allotment of 60,000 litres per day per panzer regiment, but the appalling state of the roads meant that the actual requirement was twice that, and in bad weather that amount would increase again to a draining 180,000 litres per day. The result was that the divisional supply systems didn't have enough fuel to supply their panzers and were forced to call for more from the depots set up prior to the invasion. These fuel dumps were hundreds of miles to the west of the advancing spearheads, and the Army was struggling to get the gasoline eastwards with too few trucks, through enemy ambushes, and on a shambolic road network.

It was that self-same road network – or rather the lack of one – that was fast becoming the biggest obstacle facing the German armour. Advancing across eastern Poland, the Baltic states and Belarus, the Germans noted how swiftly the road system deteriorated the further east they went, and now they were in old Russia proper they really began to struggle. Guderian's *Panzergruppe 2* was a case in point. *Fast Heinz* had been allocated two main roads for his advance east – that's two roads for the 27,000 vehicles under his command. Albert Neuhaus saw the motorised mass and wrote to his wife in awe: "Columns of vehicles roll through here day after day, hour after hour. I can tell you that such a thing happens only once in the whole world. You grasp your head again and again and ask where all these endless millions of vehicles come from." Richard von Rosen, on the other hand, told of the frustration as the different German units within those columns jostled for position: "Not until the afternoon did we get onto the Rollbahn, but irritatingly we often found the highway blocked – sometimes three convoys would all be heading in the same direction alongside each other ... It was very depressing always to be following 3. *Panzerdivision*."

Ordered to drive for Bobruisk and cross the Berezina River, Rosen described the less than auspicious start to the renewed offensive: "We set off very early on the morning of 3 July 1941. The going was extremely poor as a result of the continual rain, and we made hardly any progress. Our drivers had to call on all their know-how, and we had to tow wheeled vehicles through the morass, since they couldn't move otherwise." A few hours later he couldn't hide his elation when 3. *Panzerdivision* branched off to the south, "leaving the *Rollbahn* free for us!"

Rosen may have been over the moon but the state of the roads in general was something to behold. In such circumstances the Army's engineers came into their own; repairing roadways, building new bridges, clearing obstacles and keeping the panzers going. *Major* Hans Hinrichs's engineer unit was in the thick of it. "Russia was completely different from France of course ... France had a very dense road network, there were only a few woods and the population were indifferent and didn't ambush us – it was really rather civilised. In Russia, there were very few roads and you had to stay on them because of the huge forests, and we had to cross lots of rivers and streams without bridges – myself and my engineer *kompanie* built more than a hundred bridges on our advance."[13]

The traffic congestion Rosen witnessed became so bad that Guderian introduced a priority system in his zone: Priority 1 meant that every other vehicle had to clear the road for you; Priority 2 meant every vehicle had to get out of the way except for those who were Priority 1; and Priority 3 was everyone else. A *Luftwaffe* signals unit erecting telegraph poles behind the advance was most put out when allotted Priority 3 status. The commander complained to Hermann Goering personally, whereupon the *Reichsmarschall* made clear his displeasure to Guderian's staff and demanded a Priority 1 pass instead. Guderian's riposte was blunt: "Can telegraph poles shoot?"

The problem for Guderian – and Hoth's *Panzergruppe 3* – was that the state of the roads was causing terrible attrition among their precious motor vehicles, much more even than the Red Army. Erhard Raus described the effects. "We experienced the havoc dust can wreak on motor vehicles. Even panzers sustained severe damage from the dust they stirred up while crossing vast sandy regions. Many panzers had no dust filters, and those with them were soon clogged up. Quartz dust was sucked into engines which became so ground out that many panzers were rendered unserviceable. The dust also reduced engine efficiency and increased fuel consumption.[14] As the noted historian Charles Luttichau commented, "The roads were abominable, leading through sand, bog, swamp, forest and dense undergrowth ... the tracks the Germans had to use had never seen a motor vehicle before."

Richard von Rosen's panzer was one of many that broke down as a result. "Our panzer had engine trouble and was running too hot. If you opened the radiator cap all the water gushed out, so we had to keep refilling it. The problem was the right-hand fan, which had stuck and couldn't be got going again."[15] The fan was repaired a day or so later, only for the problem to recur again and again, until eventually the engine caught fire. The answer was clearly replacement vehicles, but yet again, high command in Berlin had failed to accurately predict, or indeed plan for, anything but the best-case scenario. Halder himself calculated that only 431 new panzers would be needed by the end of July, about 12 per cent of the invasion force total. The actual number was more than twice that, as a report from Walter Model's 3. *Panzerdivision* made clear:

> *PzRgt* 6 entered combat with 208 tanks ... As of July 1941, we have lost 54 tanks due to enemy action and two by a shortage of spare parts. At the moment there are some 40 tanks in the workshop with engine problems which cannot be repaired because of a shortage of cylinder-block liners and a shortage of rubber-banded running wheels. We expect a larger number of damaged tracks in the near future, especially on the *PzKpfw IV* ... the large amount of dust generated in Russia has caused disproportionately more engine damage. Almost all engine wear can be attributed to dust accumulation.

Halder's parsimonious forecast was a curse for the *panzerwaffe*. Reassured by his chief of staff, Hitler had decreed that all panzers rolling off the production lines from late June onwards were to be held back in Germany to fill the rosters of a raft of new panzer divisions he planned to create. Only when the hue and cry from the likes of Guderian, Hoth and Hoepner became a cacophony did the dictator relent and agree to send east all the remaining Czech-made panzers, and some eighty German ones, including fifteen new *PzKpfw IV*s. It wasn't nearly enough, and in desperation 350 brand-new Panzer III engines were loaded onto trains and shipped east to replace those already worn-out in the campaign.

Of course, the real story was Germany's lack of preparedness for anything other than a short war: the type of war it had fought so far under Hitler's leadership. Poland, Scandinavia, France and the Low Countries, Yugoslavia and Greece – none of these campaigns had lasted more than two months or required advances of over 300 miles. Now, the *Wehrmacht* was going beyond those boundaries and into uncharted territory – and since the maps they were using were hopelessly out of date and a massive 1:300,000 in scale, it was almost literally *uncharted*.

The lack of preparedness touched almost every facet of the German military. Panzer production – a key measure – was just 212 vehicles per month leading up to Barbarossa, while Guderian himself noted that "as far back as 1933 I had visited a single Russian tank factory which was producing twenty-two tanks of the Christie-Russki type per day! Our annual production of all types at the time amounted to no more than one thousand."

The problems in the *panzerwaffe* were mirrored in that other vital arm of blitzkrieg, the *Luftwaffe*. When the air force's Chief of Staff, Hans Jeschonnek, heard of the decision to launch Barbarossa, he exclaimed delightedly to his Head of Intelligence, "At last, a proper war!" Perhaps he didn't realize at the time how monumentally unprepared he and his service branch were for the campaign. As Goering himself pointed out to Hitler before Directive 21 was signed, the *Luftwaffe* was the only service not to have had a significant break to rest, recover and rebuild its strength since the war had begun. For the air force, campaign had followed campaign, with its men and machines in constant demand. All the while, significant increases in the numbers of aircraft, and the pilots to fly them, failed to materialise. Little investment was made in repair facilities and in stockpiling spare parts, the assumption being that each campaign would be over before they were necessary. Apart from the defeat over the skies of England in 1940, it was a strategy that had worked well so far. Even now, Hans von Luck was able to comment favourably on the *Luftwaffe*'s performance, as he and the rest of 7. *Panzerdivision* streamed forward once more: "Our superiority in the air was quite clear, both in quantity and quality ... Russia had waged war mostly on land and her cumbersome military bureaucracy had obviously never given much thought to building up a modern air force."

Hans Strelow was one of the pilots in the skies above Luck as the advance resumed: "We saw a DB-3 bomber, that I attacked first, but without any result. Jochen (*Leutnant* Jochen Steffens) then shot it down, so that it belly-landed. Then he shot it up on the ground until it burned. Soon after that we happened on two more DB-3s. I took the front one, Jochen the rear one. I attacked several times but could soon only fire with machine-guns as my cannon jammed. However, I was missing by a wide margin ... Jochen had already shot his down and now guided my next attack. I hit him many times, but also missed with many shots." The appearance of several Soviet fighters forced the two German fliers to break off their attack and head home without the exasperated nineteen-year-old Strelow claiming a victory.

Both pilots were part of the *Luftwaffe*'s most powerful grouping in the East, Albert Kesselring's *Luftflotte 2*. Over 1,200 aircraft strong,

Luftflotte 2 also had the best close support unit in the *Luftwaffe* in its ranks, Wolfram von Richthofen's *VIII. Fliegerkorps*. Tasked with blasting a way forward for the panzers, Kesselring's command was a potent force, but the demands placed on the pilots and their machines were huge. For example, in the first month of the campaign, one of *Major* Walter Storp's thirty to forty-strong *Gruppen* of Messerschmitt Bf 110s flew over 1,000 sorties, claiming 165 tanks, over 2,000 vehicles and sixty locomotives destroyed, plus dozens of Soviet aircraft smashed on the ground and in the air. The reward for their handsome East Prussian commander was a coveted Knight's Cross. However, amidst the success the cracks were already beginning to show.

Johannes Kaufmann was one of Storp's pilots, and soon noted the difference in the East from earlier campaigns: "Even this early it was becoming all too clear that – unlike most other troops who very sensibly took cover when attacked from the air – the rank and file of the Red Army had the annoying habit of standing their ground and firing back with every weapon they could lay their hands on. So a pilot ... would be faced with a veritable curtain of lead as the enemy troops let loose with everything they had at their disposal, from pistols to heavy machineguns." Kaufmann and his comrades were far from invulnerable: "We knew only too well what our fate was likely to be if we had to force-land or bail out behind enemy lines and fall into Soviet hands ... we all pictured the *leutnant* who had been one of the first members of our *Gruppe* to be brought down over enemy territory. Our rapidly advancing ground troops had found him shortly afterwards, his hideously mutilated body lying stretched out beside his neatly belly-landed Bf 110."[16] Casualties weren't the only issue either.

As the advance went on the *Luftwaffe staffeln* had to leave their purpose-built bases and move forward in the wake of the troops. Often, this meant setting up home on nothing more sophisticated than an open field, with ground crews digging slit trenches for cover and erecting tents for sleeping and camp tables for eating. Kaufmann recalled the conditions: "On 7 July 1941 we transferred forward to a field just outside Minsk, and so began our nomadic existence under canvas. From now on there would be no permanent quarters for us. Barrack blocks and wooden huts had been replaced by tents. Day-to-day living became much more basic ... The Ops room and all the other necessary admin offices were also under canvas, as were the sick quarters." It is, perhaps, easy to imagine this as some sort of romantic idyll, but of course it wasn't. The pace of operations was relentless; fighter pilots averaged five to eight sorties a day, while their bomber colleagues chalked up between four to six. The prize went to the Stuka crews, who seemed to spend more time in the air than on the ground as they were constantly called upon to support the Army with precision dive bombing of anything from pillboxes and strongpoints to bridges, roads and even armoured trains. As Kaufmann recalled, "Our working day began at sunrise and ended at sunset," and with the short summer nights that meant first take-offs were usually at 0300hrs and final landings at 2200hrs. Stuka pilot Hans-Ulrich Rudel said, "Every spare minute we stretch out underneath an aeroplane and instantly fall asleep." Even that couldn't be guaranteed as the forward airstrips were subjected to the same nightly nuisance raids as the marching infantry. "There was one Russian aircraft we came to know very well ... it was an ancient biplane which always came at night and hurled all sorts of stuff down at us; stones, bits of iron, everything, it was all very primitive." *Feldwebel* Heinrich Rosenberg – a Bf 109 fighter pilot – remembered it too: "On the ground we lived rather primitively in tents, mostly in swampy ground next to our airfields, and at night we were often disturbed by flying biplanes, known as 'sewing machines', that threw small bombs overboard by hand."[17]

The ground crews were little better off, struggling to keep aircraft flying in dreadfully difficult conditions, with a lack of spare parts and facilities. Overall serviceability rates – how many of the available aircraft were airworthy on any given day – were at 70 per cent on invasion day itself, but thereafter quickly began to deteriorate. This put huge pressure on pilots and crews as each serviceable aircraft had miles of front to cover even at the outset of the attack. The *Luftwaffe*'s logistics system – just like the Army's – couldn't keep up with demand. By 5 July, only two days into Bock's renewed drive, Richthofen warned the ground commanders that the number of sorties his men were flying had to reduce, mainly due to lack of fuel. The idea was mooted to ferry fuel and supplies forward over the congested roads, but the German air-transport arm had been gutted during the invasion of Crete, losing almost 300 aircraft destroyed or damaged, leaving just 150 available for Barbarossa – hardly an armada. The idea was shelved, and Richthofen left to fume. "For us, supply is the greatest difficulty in this war."

The practicalities of trying to carry out a very high pace of operations, requiring constant repair and maintenance of machinery, coupled with the basic necessities of living, meant that – just as with the *landsers* – a high tempo could only be kept up for a relatively short time, and that time was fast running out. In human terms, the strain of the fighting was becoming all too apparent, as two *Luftwaffe* pilots from different *staffeln* discussed: "We've got an old observer in the *staffel* who's still flying, he's been in over seventy-five operations ... and he's completely finished."

"How old is he?"

"I believe he's only twenty-three or twenty-five, but he's lost his hair. He's practically bald, like an old man. He's hollow-cheeked and looks terrible. He once showed me a picture of himself as a recruit, when he first joined up – he had a face full of character and looked so fresh. When you talk to him now he is so nervous, he stutters and can't get a word out."

"Why does he still fly operations?"

"He has to."

On the ground, as Rosen and the men of *4. Panzerdivision* began their advance, so did Walther Nehring and the Saxons of his *18. Panzerdivision*. One of Hitler's *new* panzer formations, Nehring's men had already made quite an impression by swimming across the Bug on invasion day using several battalions of submersible panzers originally intended for the attack on Great Britain – *Unternehmen Seelöwe* (Operation Sealion). After the invasion was cancelled, the specially adapted panzers had lain almost forgotten in a reserve depot, until the doubling of the *panzerwaffe* had brought them out of retirement and into Barbarossa.

Now, the division sat in the Borisov bridgehead on the eastern bank of the Berezina. Cranking up their engines, the panzer crews prepared to move out, some of them rigged with loudspeakers that broadcasted Tchaikovsky as they rolled forward. Then came a signal from *Luftwaffe* reconnaissance warning of "Strong enemy armoured columns, with at least 100 tanks, advancing along both sides of the Borisov-Orsha-Smolensk road ... Among them very heavy, hitherto unobserved models." *Heeresgruppe Mitte* was about to make the acquaintance of the T-34 and KV-series. Nehring was heard to ask, "Where do they come from? These Russians seem to have nine lives."

Nine lives or not, the Germans met the Soviets in an engagement near the village of Lipki, where they had much the same experience as their northern cousins at Raseiniai. Panzer and anti-tank gun shells bounced off the heavy Soviet tanks, while their bigger guns brewed up panzer after panzer. Nevertheless, Nehring's men won out. The great majority of the attacking armour were light T-26 and BT models, and were easy prey for the panzers: "All we had to do was spit at the Russian tanks and they blew up." The panzer gunner Karl Fuchs was enjoying himself. "I knocked off a Red Army tank, as I did two days earlier ... the Russians are fleeing everywhere."[18]

The few T-34s and KVs, however, were a different matter altogether, and even when three short-barrelled Mark IVs – nicknamed 'the stubs' for the length of their guns – arrived, their larger 7.5cm cannon did no real damage. Just as at Raseiniai, it came down to the men on the ground improvising, with panzer and gunner crews blasting away at their tracks and turret rings to immobilise them and stop them rotating their guns. It worked. To help them complete the job, Helmut Mahlke and his Stukas were in the sky above them: "Our task was to mount non-stop attacks against the oncoming Soviet armour. A job after our own hearts! Whenever our troops on the ground were in a jam, it was always a pleasure to help them out." Flying through some fairly heavy but inaccurate flak, the Stukas saw their target: "There it was! Hordes of Soviet tanks and trucks all bearing down on the thinly held bridgehead. More tanks could be seen massing in the many small woods and thickets on either side of the main road. A wealth of very juicy and worthwhile targets." Mahlke led his men into the attack; "'Preparing to dive.' I said. *Feldwebel* Wüstner who was in the back seat calmly replied: 'All clear behind.' ... I pointed the nose downwards. Our chosen victim, a medium tank, slid slowly into the centre of my sights. I let go the first bomb – recovered – watched for the result – missed! Ten metres away from the target – oh, sh... me!" Climbing for a second run, Mahlke tried again: "The same target – and this time a direct hit! The Soviet tank slewed sideways and began to brew up ... on to the next ... our second bomb detonated close alongside another tank, which first spewed a brief ball of flame before commencing to burn fiercely." With all their bombs dropped, the Stukas turned to the soft-skinned vehicles. "We each made several strafing runs until the road was littered with burning wreckage ... we flew at low-level, machine-gunning everything we came across on the way; troop positions, gun emplacements and vehicles." Unfortunately for Helmut Mahlke he was shot down by ground fire for the second time in the campaign, and after crash-landing, he and *Feldwebel* Wüstner had a hard slog to return to base a day later.

The combination of panzers and Stukas smashed the Soviet attack, and in its wake Nehring and Guderian took the time to inspect their new enemy. Nehring climbed over a KV, marvelling at the eleven hits it had received without one penetrating its hull, while Guderian checked out three T-34s which had fallen into German hands undamaged, stuck, as they were, in swampy ground. In reference to the Soviet delegates tour the previous year, he exclaimed, "With the appearance at the front of the T-34 the riddle of the new Russian models was solved."

With the Soviet counterattack destroyed, Bock's two *panzergruppen* surged forward once more. In the north, Hoth targeted the important rail and road hub of Vitebsk, while in the south, Guderian went all-out to reach the mighty River Dnieper. The aim was to complete an even bigger encirclement than Bialystok-Minsk, with the two armoured pincers meeting at Smolensk and surrounding a mass of Soviet forces in and around the Dnieper bend.

Richard von Rosen was in the forefront of Guderian's southern drive. "The commander called us together and told us our assignment: 'Stary-Bychow (modern-day Bykhaw) and the Dnieper bridge. We leave in fifteen minutes.' No time for washing or breakfast, and no coffee either

... our engines were warmed up, the spearhead vehicle moved off, the advance was rolling." At first, Rosen's company made good time, until "suddenly, enemy fire was raining down on our panzers. Never in training had I got inside and closed the hatch so fast." Two Soviet anti-tank guns and infantry were blocking the road "Our spearhead was shooting ... the guns were quickly silenced, though the Russian infantry kept firing, but they had nothing which could penetrate our armour. We pressed on, leaving the rear-guard to mop up the resistance. For us, the race to the Dnieper bridge was the important thing."

Hans von Luck – now commanding the reconnaissance battalion in 7. *Panzerdivision* – recalled Hoth's advance in the north: "My battalion was to form the spearhead ... we came upon Russian stragglers, who were usually quick to surrender. Word had gotten out it seemed that we didn't shoot prisoners. We made good progress and struck a wide trail that wasn't shown on our maps. We soon discovered that the Russians had laid out the trail as a future highway, and it had already been paved with asphalt." Just like Rosen, when Luck met opposition the important thing was to keep on going: "Before long we met with fairly strong resistance, so we veered away to the northeast. The encirclement of Smolensk was literally there on offer."

Luck was right. Once again, the speed of the panzer advance had proven the Soviets' undoing. Rosen's lead group charged ahead, crossing a small stream via a rickety old wooden bridge, until the sixth panzer in the column proved too much for it and the bridge gave way. "Our only chance of success lay in taking the enemy by surprise. *Oberleutnant* von Cossel decided to press on with just our five panzers to try and reach the objective." Arriving some hours later at the outskirts of the town, the Germans found a half-finished anti-tank ditch, which they picked their way through, and then they were in the streets of the town itself. "Now the Russians responded. They let us get within range and then opened up with heavy anti-tank guns from prepared positions ... we replied with round after round of HE (high-explosive). People ran, took cover, fled. We forced our way through and got to the town centre, a marketplace crammed with horse drawn carts, military vehicles, lorries and crowds of people all intent on getting to the bridge over the Dnieper." Without stopping, Rosen and his comrades sped across the bridge. "Whatever got in our way was simply run down. Right and left of us Russians jumped over the railings into the river – chaos reigned."

Reaching the far side unscathed, Cossel's five panzers were dismayed to see another bridge some two kilometres or so away that wasn't marked on their maps but was over a tributary – it too had to be secured for the bridgehead to be properly established. Leaving one panzer to hold their main prize, the four remaining crews prepared to move off. At that point, "all hell was let loose. Anti-tank guns to the left of us, anti-tank guns to the right of us." What followed was the hardest fight Rosen had been in since enlisting. Taking hit after hit, disaster was moments away. "Suddenly the rear of the panzer was burning fiercely." Abandoning the stricken vehicle, Rosen and his crew found themselves under fire from Soviet infantry as they were joined by survivors from the other panzers, all of which were now burning.

Somehow they found a hideaway, and nervously waited for nightfall. Red Army search parties combed the area but didn't find them, although they came very close. "They advanced in a chain, as if beating for game … next came harsh shouts of '*Rucki verkh*!' (Hands up!)." Two other survivors crawled out of their bolt hole and gave themselves up; Rosen and the others didn't move a muscle. Keeping under cover until dark, Rosen and his fellow survivors worked their way down to the river and got across to the German side, most by boat, but a couple ended up swimming – only one made it. Twelve of the original twenty-five crewmen had been lost.

Despite Rosen's calamity, the Germans had reached the Dnieper in the south. Hoth's northern pincer was making good ground too, with Horst Stumpff's 20. *Panzerdivision* crossing the western Dvina river on July 7 and moving north of Vitebsk the following day.

One of Stumpff's men was nineteen-year-old Otto Carius. Twice rejected by the Army for being seriously underweight, he had finally been accepted for training and now found himself in a Czech-made *PzKpfw 38(t)*.

It happened like greased lightning. A hit against our tank, a metallic crack, the scream of a comrade, and that was all there was! A large piece of armour plating had been penetrated next to the radio operator's seat. No-one had to tell us to get out. Not until I had run my hand across my face while crawling in the ditch next to the road did I discover that they had also got me. Our radio operator had lost his left arm. We cursed the brittle and inelastic Czech steel that gave the Russian 47mm anti-tank gun so little trouble. The pieces of our own armour plating and assembly bolts caused considerably more damage than the shrapnel of the round itself.

Carius would go on to become one of Germany's most celebrated panzer aces, with 150 tank kills to his credit.

20. *Panzerdivision* may have lost Carius's panzer, but the rest pushed on in concert with Luck and 7. *Panzer* and were soon northeast of Smolensk and poised to swing south to form the northern jaw of the trap. In the south, Guderian was preparing to cross the Dnieper in

force and complete the encirclement, when, just as with Hoepner a fortnight previously, he was ordered to halt. The situation was an exact replica of the Daugavpils stand-off. Guderian had far outstripped the bulk of Bock's infantry, who were strung out miles to the west, and high command fretted that its precious armour might be cut-off and destroyed before its shielding foot soldiers could reach it. Army group also considered a major river crossing solely by armour to be highly unorthodox and risky in the extreme. The Germans lack of motorised transport for the infantry was once again proving a crippling handicap. The *landsers* – footsore and exhausted – were hurrying east as fast as they could, but the strain was immense. Harald Henry was with *Heeresgruppe Mitte* and wrote home about the misery of the march: "Think of the most brutal exhaustion you have ever experienced, direct burning sunlight, weeping sores on your feet – and you have my condition ... It takes hours before your feet become insensitive to the painful wounds at each step, on these roads which are either gravel or sand at the edges."[19]

On top of that, the bypassed Soviets didn't seem to know when they were beaten. Gotthard Heinrici's frustration was palpable: "The Russians are very strong and fight with desperation. They appear suddenly all over the place, shooting, falling upon columns, individual vehicles, messengers etc ... our losses are considerable." Some of his *landsers*' comments were more succinct:

"They fight to the very last, by God the Russians can fight."

"You wouldn't believe how fanatically the devils fought."[20]

Guderian understood the situation with the infantry, but nevertheless wanted to press on and cross the Dnieper as he knew that Barbarossa's best hope for success was for the panzers to keep on moving, no matter what. He raged at his superiors, "You're throwing away our victory!" The stage was set for the next bust-up within the *Ostheer*'s senior ranks, one that would be between *Fast Heinz* and his new boss.

Back in Berlin a week earlier, Brauchitsch had made a momentous decision. To simplify command and control, Hoth and Guderian's forces would be combined, and their new commander would be the current leader of *4. Armee*, Hans Günther von Kluge. His nickname, *der kluge Hans*, which literally means *clever Hans*, can be translated several ways, and in his case was never intended as a compliment, being akin to the English *tricky dicky*. The man himself was an experienced professional, but he was no blitzkrieg commander, rather he was a conservative Prussian artillery officer fighting a campaign that strict military logic said he could never win. He was, however, a *generalfeldmarschall*, honoured by Hitler himself at the famous Kroll Opera House ceremony in July the previous year. Now, almost exactly one year on, he turned up at

Guderian's headquarters in Tolochino, determined to put his recalcitrant subordinate in his place.

Guderian was up for the fight. In a heated debate, he refused to waver from his demand to cross the Dnieper – even going so far as to lie about the disposition of his forces – and Kluge finally relented: "Your operations invariably hang by a silken thread." The crossing was on. It was Wednesday 9 July.

Richard von Rosen, barely recovered from his close shave a few days earlier, was in the vanguard once more. On 10 July the division began its attack across the Dnieper. Crossing the river over the same bridge he had driven over previously, he found his comrades' bodies: "Krompert, Lindenberger and Stössel ... still seated in their panzer, where a direct hit had taken off Lindenberger's head. Further on lay Gerlsberger, and finally Hans Ebersberg, who had covered the way back for us, and while doing so had received a fatal wound in the stomach."

As usual, Guderian's men were provided with close-air support by Helmut Mahlke and his Stukas. "Soviet tanks, nose to tail in one long column, and all heading towards a village occupied by our troops ... we lost no time in diving to the attack. Our first bombs went down along the road among the enemy tanks. One or two exploded violently. Smoke poured from several others as they began to brew up." Panicking, the remaining tanks drove off the road and straight into a swamp, where they sank in the morass. "There must have been twenty at least. They wouldn't be doing our boys any harm." Mahlke and his crews returned to base, to a message from the *17. Panzerdivision* – "Bravo the Stukas!"

Mahlke's dive-bombers weren't the only *Luftwaffe* aircraft involved in the battle – Hans Vowinckel was a member of a bomber crew: "Smolensk is burning – it was a monstrous spectacle ... we didn't need to look for our objective, the blazing torch lit our way through the night from far away." The city fell to Walter von Boltenstern's Thuringians on 16 July – the trap was closed.

Hans von Luck was in the thick of it. "With the help of our air force we enveloped Smolensk from north and south and formed a huge pocket, in which there were said to be over 100,000 Russians ... with my reinforced battalion I held and closed the Smolensk-Moscow trail." For once, the precise Prussian was wrong – there were more than a hundred thousand Soviets trapped in the pocket, a lot more – in fact there were around four times that number. *Heeresgruppe Mitte* had won a tremendous victory. Three Soviet armies were encircled and facing destruction.

Hoth and Guderian didn't rest on their laurels. Instead, *Fast Heinz* sent Ferdinand Schaal's *10. Panzerdivision*, Erich Straube's Bavarian *268. Infanterie-Division*, and Paul Hausser's *SS-Reich* 50 miles southeast to form another bridgehead; this time across the River Desna at the town of

Yel'nya. This would be the launching pad for the final drive on the Soviet capital. As Luck jubilantly exclaimed back at Smolensk, they were "only 400 kilometres from Moscow!"

Moscow. Every *landser* knew what that city meant. Philipp von Boeselager summed it all up. "Moscow was the spider in the web – the transport, commercial and political hub of Russia. We understood that once you took Moscow you would control the whole country." Yel'nya was even closer to the capital than Smolensk – only 300 kilometres. All the Germans had to do was send their panzers once more into the attack and the city would be reached, as one anonymous soldier wrote: "I predict that the swastika will be flying over the Kremlin in four to five weeks ... we aim to reach Moscow in a month with our invincible Army. We only need to wage another blitzkrieg."[21] Morale was sky high, as the tired but expectant soldiery saw the end in sight. Gerhard Dengler, a junior officer at the time, said: "The conductor of our divisional orchestra had already composed a special march for our entry into Moscow. It was rehearsed for the expected victory parade in the Russian capital."[22]

There would be no parade. The panzers weren't unleashed for another blitzkrieg, and they weren't unleashed because the Germans faced exactly the same problem they had at Bialystok-Minsk and on the Daugava – where were their infantry? One of them – thirty-two-year-old *Gefreiter* Alois Scheuer of *197. ID* – gave the answer: "In the last few days we have marched a lot, always towards the enemy. Sometimes we march during the night and rest during the day, sometimes the other way around. But it is always over dusty and seemingly endless country roads ... We have now marched some 400 kilometres eastwards over dusty dirt roads, through forest, swamp and moorland, past places where bitter battles have taken place, scattered with war debris of all kinds and innumerable dead ... I think we are marching ourselves to death, almost every day we advance 45 kilometres."[23]

To hold the Smolensk pocket closed and allow *4. Panzerarmee* to surge forward to Moscow, *clever Hans* needed infantry, and he needed them now. But all he had were the nine or so motorised and semi-motorised infantry divisions that had managed to keep up with the advance, the rest were strung out over almost 200 miles back west, with some of them only just now finishing at Minsk. This meant Guderian and Hoth's precious mechanised troops having to act as pickets to try and keep their prize in the bag. One of the pickets was a young *leutnant* in the *Grossdeutschland Regiment:* "The battalion had taken up a so-called security line spread improbably far apart ... we had never practised it. There was no defence, only security, what if the enemy launched a strong attack?" His question was apposite, as a senior staff officer admitted: "The conduct of the Russian troops was in striking contrast to the behaviour of the Poles and the Western allies ... when encircled, the Russians stood their ground and fought."

In fact, they didn't just stand and fight, they hit back, and hit hard. Eduard Kister, an *Unteroffizier* in Hans-Jürgen von Arnim's *17. Panzerdivision*, was another of those trying to hold the line:

> They came in thick crowds, without fire support and with officers in front. They bellowed from high-pitched throats and the ground reverberated with the sound of their running boots. We let them get to within 50 metres and then started firing. They collapsed in rows and covered the ground with mounds of bodies ... Fresh attack waves stormed forward behind the dead and pressed up against the wall of bodies.

Kister's unit saw off no fewer than seventeen such attacks in a single day.

Helmut Pabst and his signals unit were also guarding a section of the pocket perimeter when they came under attack: "Four Russian tanks appeared, of which three were quickly knocked out ... From the left came the Russian infantry – 'Urrah!'" Beating them off, Pabst and his comrades had little respite. "That night brought two more attacks, which cost us two dead and one man badly wounded. Now I know the meaning of the word 'frightful'." Richard von Rosen and his fellow crewmen had been promised some rest after their part in the encirclement but instead, "the order came for battle readiness. No information was forthcoming as to why ... later we discovered that the Russians had recaptured the Rollbahn in our rear and surrounded the panzer *pionieren* who had camped on it."

The conditions in the pocket were dreadful, as Hubert Goralla, a medic in Eduard Kister's unit, recalled: "The Russian wounded lay left and right of the Rollbahn and the severely injured were howling so dreadfully it made my blood run cold." Two of his fellow medics went to treat them, only to be shot by the very men they were attempting to help. "I saw the Russians crawling and hobbling towards us. They began to throw hand-grenades in our direction." With calls to surrender ignored, the Germans were left with no option but to kill the wounded Soviets. "Every single wounded man had to be fought to a standstill. One Soviet sergeant, unarmed and with a severely injured shoulder, struck out with a trench spade until he was shot. It was madness, total madness."[24]

In the face of such determination, the outnumbered Germans simply couldn't hold the ring. As von Bock himself said, "There is only one bag on the *Heeresgruppe*'s front, and it has a hole in it!" The result was inevitable, much of the Soviet 20th Army managed to break out east and escape the pocket. Nevertheless, the Germans still rounded up some 300,000 prisoners and masses of equipment.

Adolf Hitler delivers a speech to a hand-picked audience in Berlin's Sportpalast arena minutes after signing the Barbarossa invasion order. The *Luftwaffe* fighter pilot Heinz Knoke (arrow points to him) sits enraptured among the crowd. (Author's collection)

Young draftees are drilled in the *Reichsarbeitsdienst* (RAD) as part of their preparation for the military. (Author's collection)

Above: A *Wehrmacht* infantry section, their NCO on the left, present the very image of the purposeful German fighting man. (Author's collection)

Left: Happier times. Heinz Guderian (centre) jokes with a Red Army officer as both men review the joint German–Soviet victory parade in Brest after the conquest of Poland. (Author's collection)

Herbert Backe – the author of the genocidal Hunger Plan, and the epitome of the mass-murdering bureaucrat. (Courtesy of Bundesarchiv Bild 183-J02034)

Adolf von Schell. The German truck supremo repeatedly warned Berlin about the *Wehrmacht*'s lack of motorisation but was never heeded. (Courtesy of Bundesarchiv Bild 146-1994-031-08A)

German troops pass a border marker on invasion day – the die is cast. (Author's collection)

Soldiers of the *197. Infanterie-Division* advance into the Soviet Union. Newly captured Red Army POWs file past in the other direction. (Author's collection)

The commander of *8. Panzerdivision*, Erich Brandenberger (left), confers with his boss Erich von Manstein during the first heady days of the advance. (Courtesy of Bundesarchiv Bild 101I-209-0086-12)

Soldiers of *Heeresgruppe Nord* joyfully welcomed as liberators in the streets of Latvia's capital, Riga, in early July 1941. (Courtesy of Bundesarchiv Bild 183-L19397)

Political prisoners murdered by the departing NKVD secret police in L'viv, 30 June 1941. (Author's collection)

Years of brutal Stalinist rule encouraged many to view the invading Germans as liberators. (Author's collection)

Above: Two *Waffen-SS* machine-gunners move through a burning village. (Author's collection)

Opposite, top: Motorcyclists from *SS-Reich* – part of *Panzergruppe 2* – continue the advance. (Author's collection)

Opposite, middle: A German Mark III panzer passes a burning Soviet BT-7 tank. The Red Army had more tanks than the rest of the world combined on invasion day, but most were obsolete like the outgunned BT-7. (Author's collection)

Opposite, bottom: The Barbarossa invasion force was famously reliant on captured vehicles and equipment, such as the Czech Panzer *38t* in this photo. (Courtesy of Bundesarchiv Bild 101I-265-0037-10)

Above: Wilhelm Lübbecke, arrowed, marching towards Leningrad. (Author's collection)

Left: Contrary to the myth, the majority of the German invasion force was composed of marching men and horse-drawn wagons. (Author's collection)

German infantry pass a well in a Russian village. The retreating Red Army destroyed or poisoned most such wells, often dumping chlorine in the water. (Author's collection)

Three T-34 tanks lie abandoned in a swamp. The appearance of models such as the T-34 was a profound shock to the invaders. (Author's collection)

Red Army dead litter the battlefield. The Red Army's willingness to take enormous casualties and carry on fighting soon began to wear the Germans down. (Author's collection)

The Uman pocket. Forced to ward off repeated attempts by trapped Red Army units to escape, these German pickets cover their own dead with a tarpaulin. (Author's collection)

Above: An army marches on its stomach; a famed German *Gulaschkanone* field-kitchen prepares hot food for hungry soldiers. (Author's collection)

Right: Exhaustion took its toll on the invaders. These motorcycle riders are asleep on their machines. (Author's collection)

Opposite, top: The war in the Far North was the forgotten theatre of Barbarossa. Here an infantry cannon of *SS-Nord* prepares to fire. (Author's collection)

Opposite, middle: The Germans soon realised that the primitive nature of most roads in the Soviet Union was seriously slowing their advance. Here, a villager has been told to help push an SS motorcycle combination through the thick mud. (Author's collection)

Opposite, bottom: A German horse-drawn supply wagon fights its way through Russia's glutinous mud. (Author's collection)

Above: Soviet POWs wait to be moved to the rear after capture by *Waffen-SS* troopers. Many were not so lucky and were shot out of hand.

Below left: Behind the advance the horror begins. The infamous Death Dealer of Kovno inspects his work at the Lietukis Garage massacre. (Author's collection)

Below right: Ukrainian militia recruited by 6. *Armee* as it advanced. Many of these units would carry out horrific massacres, particularly of Soviet Jews. (Author's collection)

The Germans didn't only rely on local collaborators to carry out mass shootings. These victims executed by firing squad were supposedly partisans captured by *Heeresgruppe Nord*. (Courtesy of Bundesarchiv Bild 101I-212-0221-07)

This picture, taken near Orel in late 1941 by one of the *Wehrmacht*'s own photographers, exposes the falsehood that front-line German soldiers knew nothing of the mass killings behind the lines. Despite it being expressly forbidden, at least four of the assembled crowd are taking pictures of the hanging. (Courtesy of Bundesarchiv Bild 101I-287-0872-28A)

Ruins as far as the eye can see

Above left: Kiev – the greatest battle. A German 3.7cm anti-aircraft gun smashes Soviet aircraft and a field kitchen near the River Sluch. (Author's collection)

Above right: This is how the Nazi *Signal* magazine reported the victory at Kiev. (Author's collection)

Over 600,000 Soviet POWs were taken at Kiev. Most would not survive the year in a war crime of horrendous magnitude. (Author's collection)

Above: The jumping-off point for Moscow. SS troopers move forward in the Yel'nya salient. (Author's collection)

Right: Hans Albring, a former Catholic Youth League member and avid letter writer to his boyhood friend Eugen Altrogge. (Courtesy of Museumsstiftung Post und Telekommunikation Briefsammlung)

Below right: Eugen Altrogge would carry on writing to his friend Hans Albring until posted missing in action in early 1943. (Courtesy of Museumsstiftung Post und Telekommunikation Briefsammlung)

Above left: Kurt Marlow, medic and former flower shop owner from the Baltic island of Usedom. (Courtesy of Museumsstiftung Post und Telekommunikation Briefsammlung)

Above right: The German cavalryman and former upholsterer Max Kuhnert. He survived the war and wrote a memoir of his experiences. (Author's collection)

Panzers of *Heeresgruppe Süd* drive towards the horizon. After the Kiev victory ordinary German soldiers were asking themselves, how could they conquer the land ocean that was the Soviet Union? (Author's collection)

From a German perspective, this was a pyrrhic victory. Barbarossa's only hope of success lay in the *panzerwaffe*'s ability to run riot, fragmenting the Soviet leviathan and paralysing it. This was how the *Wehrmacht* would win against a far larger enemy. However, the troops who were trained and equipped to achieve that goal were a minority in the *Ostheer*. The mass of the German Army in the East was still composed of marching divisions of infantry, who – well-trained and motivated as they were – would never be able to force a successful conclusion to the campaign. The Smolensk battle proved the point. Ordered by Berlin to hold their positions and allow the infantry to catch up, *4. Panzerarmee* was stuck in a grim slog to crush the pocket. Helmut Pabst summed up much of what the *landsers* thought at the time: "It was war with intervals. No decisive moments. An anti-tank gun or a tank opens fire, we reply with mortars. Then after a few shells there's quiet. Our batteries plaster an enemy observation post, and the Russians drop a few packets on us, we just munch our bread and duck when the music starts."

As for Bock, he fumed at the halt: "They will have failed to exploit the bloodily-won success of the battle ... they are committing a major error if they give the Russians time to establish a defensive front ... In my opinion we have already waited too long."

He wasn't the only senior German officer to rage at the constant hold-ups. In the Luga River bridgehead to the north, Georg-Hans Reinhardt wrote in his diary: "More delays. It's terrible. The chance that we opened up has been missed for good." With Hoepner's men static, three of the *Ostheer*'s four *panzergruppen* were now stationary and fighting battles for which they were wholly unsuited. It may have seemed like madness to panzer generals like Reinhardt, but to the majority of the senior Barbarossa leadership it made perfect sense. Brauchitsch, Leeb – even Kluge – and, most importantly, Hitler himself fretted that the armoured forces would over-extend, become isolated, and then be annihilated in Russia's vastness. *Panzergruppen* were frighteningly powerful creations, but they were as vulnerable as any military formation if they didn't have ammunition to shoot, food to eat, and fuel to burn. Supplies needed to be brought up, and the Germans were struggling, especially with gasoline.

Given the logistics situation, the *Wehrmacht*'s senior command considered it sensible to call a temporary halt for re-supply. Reinforcements were needed too, with casualties in men and machines far higher than anything the *Wehrmacht* had experienced before. Even as Bock was reluctantly reining in his panzer commanders, the casualty figures for the *Ostheer* stood at 213,301 men killed, wounded or missing since the launch of the invasion some six weeks before – roughly the same as had been suffered in all the other campaigns the *Wehrmacht* had fought since the start of the war combined.[25] Kurt Schmidt, a veteran

NCO in the *SS-Leibstandarte*, said of it, "I was in France in 1940, but the battles there were nothing like as heavy as in Russia, nor were casualties anything like as bad."[26] Heinrich Haape was finding the ever-growing casualty lists hard to bear. After one failed VVS attack, a lone bomber "had crashed into an artillery column ... I galloped over and found fifteen gunners already dead." Beside the dead were "nine more soldiers with serious burns. Five were so badly burned I didn't think they'd last more than a day or two." Depressed beyond measure, the doctor filled in casualty cards for the wounded: "A schoolmaster from Duisburg, a locksmith from Essen, a miner from Hamborn, a tailor from Dinslaken, a forester from Lipperland, a tram driver from Osnabrück, and three students from Münster."

The losses themselves were bad enough, but were made worse by the fact that only 47,000 replacements had been sent east by the training depots to fill the gaps, and some of those new draftees weren't the most enthusiastic: "My apprenticeship ended in 1941, after two years, not because of anything I'd done but because in the factory where I worked someone had been listening to English radio programmes – he was sentenced to death, but when the Gestapo wanted me to make a statement against him I refused, and the next thing I knew the Gestapo told me I could sign up for the Russian Front or go to a concentration camp – and my parents would be shot – so I signed up for Russia."[27] Rudolf Oelkers was the son of a Social Democrat, so his family were under suspicion by the Nazi authorities: "My father was told 'keep quiet or you'll be put in a concentration camp' ... I wanted to join up – for my own safety really – I joined the panzers and was sent to Russia."

The shortfall in reinforcements meant the thin field-grey line of *landsers* was getting thinner. Walther Neuser, a twenty-six-year-old gunner from Brandenburg, wrote home from his picket post: "The fighting we're involved in is very dangerous. Of course, we are very careful. The Russians show white flags, you go up, then they shoot. Many soldiers have already lost their lives in this way. Mercy is hardly shown any more. Very few of the Russians look like soldiers, they are tattered and neglected. We caught one who still had two egg grenades in his pockets. His life was forfeit." Rudolf Kurth described how he spent his days "in a shallow hollow, a steel helmet pulled as low as possible over my face, a rifle at the ready, spare cartridges next to it, the inevitable cigarette in the mouth".

It wasn't just the men who were wearing out: *18. Panzerdivision* could only field a dozen functioning panzers. The division's commander, Walther Nehring, thought the Germans were in danger of "winning ourselves to death". It was the *Luftwaffe*, however, that was most in need of a break.

Despite its size, Germany's pilots had been pretty dismissive of the VVS since the launch of Barbarossa. Werner Baumbach's thoughts epitomised the general view: "The little I saw of the Russian air force gave me the impression that it was antiquated and couldn't be regarded as a military factor."[28] Karl Born was more forthright: "They were very bad. The Russian pilots were cowards. They used to turn away when we came on the scene. They never attacked us, except once when we were in a Fieseler Storch (a small, unarmed aircraft mainly used for liaison) ... the Russian shot past before he could pull the trigger." Regardless of what the likes of Born and Baumbach thought, the Soviets were still taking to the air, and still inflicting casualties. One of whom was Helmut Mahlke. While supporting *17. Panzerdivision* trying to hold the Smolensk pocket closed, three VVS fighters latched onto his Stuka: "They were so close they couldn't miss. We collected a full salvo from each. The left-wing fuel tank immediately burst into flames – and then the right tank was ablaze as well." Mahlke somehow managed to coax his stricken aircraft high enough to give him and his rear gunner a chance of parachuting, and then they jumped. "The fierce tongues of flame were already licking at my hands and face. I jumped – felt myself get caught up on something – and then fell free. But I was still surrounded by the unbearable heat of the flames from the burning fuel." Realising he was still in the slipstream from his plane, he knew he was in grave danger. "The parachute silk would catch fire and that would be the end. So, I forced myself to wait until I was out of the flames." Free-falling, he remembered an accident he'd witnessed back in Wertheim in 1939. "An aircraft had crashed in a ploughed field, and I could still see the medics using forceps to gather up bits of the crew." Then, "Whoa! A muffled crack above my head. The harness yanked me upwards. The parachute had opened!" Badly burned, Mahlke was picked up by German ground troops and hospitalized. He would never fly in combat again. His gunner, Walter Hartmann, died when his chute failed to open. By 19 July, the German air force in the East had reported losses of 550 aircraft destroyed and many more damaged, with their operational roster on that day standing at just 906 aircraft as serviceability rates continued to drop.

As far as Halder and the rest of Nazi high command was concerned, a period of re-configuration and re-supply was sorely needed. Many *landsers* agreed. Helmut Nick was one of them. "We have already made a good deal of progress. I think the biggest difficulties in this war will not be the enemy resistance but the beautiful roads. But there are no difficulties that cannot be overcome. Even if I don't believe in a blitzkrieg, I do believe in a quick end ... You should see us, I think you would hardly know me as we are so covered in dust and dirt ... Above all, you can see progress, that's the main thing." For the likes of Nick and Halder everything was going to plan. The Germans were inflicting casualties well in excess of a ratio of ten to one on the Soviets, and the much-feared Soviet air force had proven itself something of a paper tiger, losing almost 7,000 aircraft, over half on the ground. The Bialystok-Minsk and Smolensk pockets had shown that blitzkrieg worked in the Soviet Union, and huge parts of the Red Army had already been smashed. Plus, the invasion was on schedule to achieve the Army chief's pre-invasion timetable, having already reached Smolensk – two weeks quicker than Napoleon.

And yet despite their gargantuan losses both the Red Army and the VVS were still fighting. Nowhere was there a collapse, or any sign of one. Halder's response was an exercise in wishful thinking. Leafing through *Oberstleutnant* Eberhard Kinzel's[29] pre-invasion study, 'The Military Armed Forces of the Soviet Socialist Republics', he wrote: "Of the 164 infantry divisions which the Red Army mobilised, eighty-nine have been completely or partially destroyed. Forty-six are still fighting and in reasonable condition, eighteen are in other sectors (fourteen in Finland and four in the Caucasus) and a maximum of eleven are in reserve in the interior. Of the twenty-nine armoured divisions mobilised, twenty have been completely or partially destroyed and nine are still fully fit for combat." This was wilful delusion. If this really was the case, then how was the Red Army still able to hold the *Ostheer*? Anyone on the ground could see that the Soviets still had a plentiful supply of manpower and equipment. Equally bad for the Germans was the situation in the air.

Otto Hoffmann von Waldau, Chief of the *Luftwaffe*'s Operations department, wrote in his diary, "The military means of the Soviet Union are considerably stronger than studies before the start of the war indicated. We had regarded many Soviet statistics merely as propaganda. The material quality is better than expected ... we have scored great successes with relatively low losses, but a large number of Soviet aircraft remain to be destroyed. The will to resist and the toughness of the mass of the population has exceeded all expectations." Waldau went to see Halder to tell him the bad news in person. "The *Luftwaffe* has greatly underestimated the enemy's numerical strength. It is quite evident that the Russians initially had more than 8,000 aircraft. Half of this number has been destroyed, either on the ground or in the air, so numerically we are now equal with the Russians." Even this was too rosy a view. The truth was that the VVS still heavily outnumbered the *Luftwaffe*, even after the *kindermord* of the preceding weeks.

Halder had no wish to face the truth, clinging to the woefully inadequate pre-invasion estimates of Soviet strength. If he had doubts he allayed them with a belief that while Moscow could *possibly* mobilise millions of men, it would have neither the time nor armaments to train and equip them before the campaign was over. There was therefore no reason to risk losing Bock's panzers in an unsupported drive towards Moscow – or Leeb's in the north for that matter. Let the infantry catch up, and the *Luftwaffe* take a breath. In the meantime, an opportunity had finally arisen in the difficult southern operational area.

Since invasion day, *Heeresgruppe Süd* had been slogging its way forward through a well-organised and powerful Soviet defence. Rundstedt's sole armoured force – *Panzergruppe 1* – was led by Ewald von Kleist, a capable officer but no Manstein. Regardless, Kleist had handled his troops well at Dubno (also called the Battle of Brody) at the end of June, with Hans Roth in the thick of the fighting:

> The Russians are encircled, and since the encirclement is weak around Dubno they are trying to break out there ... the Russians have organised an entire tank division with infantry in the forest, they are going to attempt to break out. It is now 0330hrs, there, on the hill directly in front of us the Russians suddenly appear ... the first wave approaches, they have all the time in the world to floor us. Let these *Schweine* come closer; 100 metres, 90 metres, 80, now 70 metres, almost as one, ten shells from our ten anti-tank cannons strike the steel monsters.

Having destroyed the first wave, the second wave brought down fire on Roth and his comrades. "My comrade on the left throws his arms in the air – he's been hit. The cannon suddenly breaks apart – a direct hit. Another comrade lies motionless on the ground right in front of me, dead; and to my right a soldier is shouting for a medic." Desperately seeking cover, Roth came under fire. "The ground is ripped up right in front of me, I almost stumble over two comrades who have been torn apart by the shelling ... another impact, the shrapnel is howling around my ears, a fist sized chunk shreds my gas mask, and another piece severs the hand-grip from my machine-pistol. And then I make it! I am in a trench!" A third tank wave then appeared, only for Roth to be saved by none other than Kurt Meyer's comrades: "A miracle happens. SS troops in camouflage jackets appear to our rear. It's the Leibstandarte." Roth survived, though wounded through the upper arm. Dubno was no Bialystok-Minsk, but it still left some 800 Soviet tanks from three mechanized corps burning on the steppe, and now Kleist's men were driving deep into Ukraine.

In the vastness of the open steppe, air power was critical, and Rundstedt had the 630 aircraft of *Generaloberst* Alexander Löhr's *Luftflotte 4* for support, as well as the various assorted contingents from the Reich's allies. Löhr – the former commander of Austria's tiny air force before his country's annexation by Germany in the 1938 *Anschluss* – was nicknamed the *little emperor* on account of his slightly far eastern looks, and his aircraft had so far proven vital in supporting the advance. Determined to stop the German drive, the Soviets had thrown everything at them, including mounted Cossacks, in scenes more reminiscent of the nineteenth rather than the twentieth century. Horst Ramstetter was one of Löhr's pilots:

> I was immediately sent into action in our last open cockpit biplane, the Henschel 123, the forerunner of the Ju87 Stuka ... it was so manoeuvrable that we used to say 'you could turn it round a lamp post' and it was a robust aircraft – they shot at me from below and there was a hole through the lower and upper wings that I could almost crawl through and the thing still kept flying ... we flew missions against mounted units at the beginning ... imagine that, Cossacks! On horses! I was in my HS-123 when I saw some galloping horses and riders, one of them turned around and I looked into his eyes, so full of fear – I couldn't fire. He suddenly became a human being, why? In war it's either him or me, that's the rule for every soldier the world over, whoever is faster survives longer, but I couldn't fire, not that time.

Ramstetter's Romanian brethren weren't having a good time of it, however, with one of their commanders complaining, "We are inferior to the enemy's equipment both in quantity and quality." Radu Gherghe, the hatchet-faced commander of Romania's one and only panzer division, commented that "control of the air by the enemy air force is absolute" while a German observer with Romanian troops said that "the Russian air force has clear superiority" and the VVS "generally dominates the air ... the Romanian air force is obviously unprepared to face the enemy, as is being seen almost every day". The Romanian fliers themselves complained bitterly about it all, with fighter pilot Lieutenant-Colonel Mihail Romanescu, speaking for many in a letter home: "Because of the small number of fighter aircraft available to us we are always outnumbered by the enemy ... we have lost over 80 per cent of the aircraft we started the campaign with. We have scored 139 confirmed and thirty-one unconfirmed air victories and another forty-seven enemy aircraft destroyed on the ground, but my command will soon disappear." In some ways the Romanians were reaping what their German allies had themselves sown. Back in 1930 when the designer and aircraft manufacturer, Ernst Heinkel, lost out to his bitter rival Willy Messerschmitt in the competition to provide the *Luftwaffe* with its future single-engine fighter, the close to useless *Luftwaffe* chief of procurement, Ernst Udet, told Heinkel, "Sell off your birds dirt cheap to the Turks, Japanese or Romanians, they're all licking their lips for them." So, he had, and now those birds were coming home to roost.

On the ground, the Germans marched with Italians, Romanians, Hungarians, Croats and Slovaks. Accompanying the lead troops was Curzio Malaparte, an Italian war correspondent, author and film-maker:

> Dust and rain, dust and mud. Tomorrow the roads will be dry, the vast fields of sunflowers will crackle in the hot, parching wind. Then the mud will return ... This is the Russian war, the eternal Russian war, the Russian war of 1941. *Nichts zu machen, nichts zu machen* [German slang for 'can't do anything about it']. Corpses, gutted houses, hordes of ragged prisoners with the air of sick dogs, and everywhere the remains of horses and vehicles, the wreckage of tanks, of aeroplanes, trucks, guns, the corpses of officers, NCOs and men, women, children, old men and dogs, the remains of houses, villages, towns, rivers and forests – *nichts zu machen, nichts zu machen.*

Giovanni Messe, as commander of the Italian expeditionary force, was determined that he and his men would fight the war in as civilised a fashion as possible. For the Italians there would be no Commissar Order or casual murder of prisoners: "Right from the beginning I wanted to establish our relationship with these people who didn't know us, based on the principle of paying for anything we took. Nobody could ever stop any Italian soldier from showing his kindness, innate generosity, and sensitivity towards the Russian population, and to reassure prisoners captured by us of treatment and conditions worthy of civilised people, which was often in stark contrast to the Germans."

Arrigo Paladini, a twenty-year-old artilleryman serving under Messe, saw for himself what the Germans were capable of when he witnessed the massacre of 150 Jews by German soldiers on 31 July: "Until now we thought this would be an easy war, but today our eyes were opened ... They preach 'civilisation' but we are becoming soiled by their barbarism. I used to admire the German soldier, but from today he presents himself in a different light, that of a strong but profoundly barbaric warrior."

The Hungarians of the Carpathian Group marched into Ukraine under the leadership of Major-General Bela Miklos, a respected senior officer and personal confidant of the Hungarian dictator. Overhead flew their contribution of three fighter squadrons, two of obsolete Fiat biplanes and one of Hungarian-built *Hejjas* (a licensed version of the Italian *Reggiane Re2000* monoplane fighter). The Magyars reached Kamianets-Podilskyi on 11 July, leaving a trail of abandoned and broken-down vehicles behind them as the rutted dirt roads took their toll on the already meagre motor pool. Increasingly forced to resort to foot marches, the exhausted Hungarians staggered on towards the city of Nikolayev, some 300 miles southeast. Enmity between the Romanians and the Hungarians meant

Rundstedt had to keep the two contingents physically separate, or an outbreak of fighting between them was considered inevitable. As for the Slovaks, they had even less motorised transport than the ill-equipped Hungarians, and often lagged far behind their German comrades. Within a month, having lost some 300 men killed, wounded or missing, Bratislava had a re-think and decided to concentrate all their vehicles, the dozen remaining panzers and most of the heavy weapons, into a 10,000-strong Fast Division (*Schnelle Division* or *Rychla Divizia* in German and Slovak respectively), with a further 8,000 formed into a new Slovak Security Division to carry out rear area security duties. This latter unit would have no artillery or armour, and its only transport would be two-and-a-half thousand horses and six hundred wooden farm carts. The remaining four thousand men were sent home.

Rundstedt's right, or southern, wing was making good progress, his left, or northern, wing less so, hampered as it was in its ability to manoeuvre by the Pripet marshes on its left flank. Curt Emmerich – a middle-aged doctor serving with an infantry division in the south – wrote of the advance: "We marched from sunrise to sunset through the endless fields of the Ukraine ... the pace of the advance was murderous. The horses had grown so lean that they showed every rib. None of us had an ounce of superfluous fat."[30] The fighting was brutal, as Klaus, a young flak gunner with *Heeresgruppe Süd*, described to his parents in a letter home: "We imagined it would be a little easier. The French campaign, on the other hand, was a walkover in comparison, but we'll make it. This morning we were woken up by Russian planes ... Our battery has shot to pieces all kinds of tanks and the Russians are falling back now." Klaus was very candid about what he and his comrades did to captured commissars: "You wouldn't believe what the Russian commissars are like, they aren't human ... we were told that they murdered over five hundred Ukrainians near here – we shoot the commissars right away ... Look after yourselves."

Franz Siebeler of *14. Panzerdivision*, like Klaus, felt able to write to his parents about the savagery of the struggle he was involved in: "The war against the Soviets is tough and cruel, no quarter is given. The Reds are a fanatical opponent who are only gradually being worn down. They often prefer to be shot rather than surrender, and we are making slow progress as we face the Red Army's élite forces. There are also significant losses on our side. Many soldiers' graves line our advance." In Siebeler's sister division – Friedrich-Wilhelm von Rothkirch und Panthen's *13. Panzerdivision* – the former Protestant pastor Heinz Rahe also appreciated just how tough the Soviets were proving to be: "The Soviets fight with great determination. A prisoner opened his shirt and said: 'Go on then, shoot me!' Another, a pilot who'd jumped from his plane with a parachute, still resisted when we tried to capture him. He fired his pistol at us, killing one man and wounding another before being shot himself. You have to admit that these people are willing to die for their convictions."

Determined resistance sometimes spilled over into barbarity. "In Lutsk, the Reds murdered four comrades – if you hadn't seen it you wouldn't believe it – some of their eyes were cut out, legs and hands chopped off, and they had been burned with red-hot irons. Tears came to my eyes with anger." Franz Siebeler described the German reaction to such atrocities: "The civilian population has participated in these ambushes. Twenty people, including two women, were shot under civil law." The young *landser* was under an enormous amount of strain, but put a brave face on it for his parents back home.

On the whole, the war is bad. We sleep very little and have to dig trenches every day. The Russian artillery regularly shoots at us and their planes also attack us. Yesterday though, a German fighter shot down five enemy, three of them bombers, and the flak also brought some down. There are a lot of destroyed enemy tanks, some of them the heaviest types ... I send a prayer to God! Anyway, enough of the war!

Anton Böhrer, an older man at twenty-six, and hailing from the north Baden village of Höpfingen, was far more optimistic as he wrote to his sister: "We have had quite a few successes for a few days now ... the Reds are having a big slump and Russia will finally become Baden." Böhrer was an artillery *Spiess* in Otto Gabcke's *294. Infanterie-Division*, and a gardener by profession, so couldn't help but talk about his true passion: "If planting is no longer possible due to my military service, lease the plot back to the old owner or sow it with green manuring plants."

Rundstedt may have had only one *panzergruppe*, but alongside Romania's 1st Armoured Division he had five of the *panzerwaffe*'s best in Kleist's formation, and none better than the Westphalians of *16. Panzerdivision* under their superb commander, Hans-Valentin Hube. Originally established back in 1935 as *16. Infanterie-Division*, it had fought in France and was then converted into a panzer division in Hitler's doubling programme that autumn. Now, it was at the forefront of the first proper bid by the army group to fight an encirclement battle. The 300,000 men of the Soviet 6th and 12th Armies were massed around the city of Uman, south of Kiev, attempting to try and slow the invaders advance and counterattack if at all possible. However, the Dubno battle had seriously depleted their armoured strength, so now they could muster just 317 tanks, most of them light T-26s and BT models – easy prey for the panzers, who, for once, now heavily outnumbered their opponents.

From 15 July, in a series of lightning thrusts, *Panzergruppe 1* and *17. Armee* fought to entrap them.

Under the scorching summer sun, Karl Nünninghoff, a baker's son from Mühlheim on the River Ruhr, and now a gunner in *16. Panzerdivision*, told of his part in the battle: "We have been on the march again this morning since 0245hrs. The sun burns our heads with its heat. We are covered in an impenetrable dust." March, march and counter-march were the order of the day, as the Germans sought to exploit holes in the defence and get into the rear of their enemy in classic blitzkrieg fashion: "Everywhere on the horizon in front of us black clouds of smoke rise against the sky, a sign of burning oil, tanks and vehicles. This smoke is interrupted by huge explosions, which then cause scary flashes of flame. Our path mostly leads through the endless fields. Most of the grain has already been brought in here in the south-east, but the stubble fields were set on fire by the Russian on his 'victorious retreat' to slow down our advance, but we are still moving forward. We have met Hungarian soldiers several times who always give us a joyful greeting."

The Hungarians weren't the only ones pleased to see Nünninghoff and his comrades:

The people of Ukraine are always very friendly to us German soldiers, they are happy that we are here to help them. Wherever we stop we ask the people for malako (milk) and jeiski (eggs). Everyone is happy to give us something. Then, when we go to pay them, they wave and don't want anything for it. Today, in our current position, even the Ukrainian women and children came and brought us eggs, bread, cucumbers, milk, etc. You wouldn't believe how happy they are that they have German soldiers with them. These people would like to hand over everything to us if we can just turf out the Russians … If this continues, the matter with the Russians will soon be settled.

A mountain trooper taking part in the encirclement was a little more prosaic: "Whatever happens we must never get tired, but must keep marching."[31] The anonymous *landser* was correct, on 26 July his division somehow covered 43 miles in a single day.

Kurt Meyer and the *SS-Leibstandarte* were heavily involved in the action too: "The *bataillon* was given the mission of reaching Nowo Arkhangelsk and closing the Uman pocket. On reaching the first houses we came under lively artillery fire from the west … we then came under rifle fire and had to fight our way through to the bridge." The SS men captured the town by dusk, but then came under attack. "As darkness fell the Russians attacked our positions on the north-eastern outskirts of the town with strong infantry forces and eight tanks. Our 3.7cm anti-tank guns opened fire at point-blank range, but what was going on? The tanks weren't bothered in the least! Shells ricocheted all over the place. We could have done without this bullshit!" Meyer and his men were the latest in a long line to discover the joys of facing Soviet T-34s.

The Germans fell back, with Meyer praying that it "wouldn't turn into a rout". Some of his men did indeed start to run away. "I couldn't believe my eyes! A few words were enough to restore some sort of order to the situation." Eventually the Soviets were stopped by a German self-propelled tank-killer: "Four Russian tanks fell victim to the assault-gun." An additional attack was also bloodily repulsed. "At 0330hrs a hefty infantry attack collapsed under the weight of the *bataillon*'s fire ... At dawn the enemy troops that had gotten into the town were wiped out or captured."

Peter Neumann of the *SS-Wiking* was also involved in closing the pocket, and he and his comrades found it nerve-wracking: "You have to be very careful where you walk since the entire countryside is mined ... opening a door may set one of the infernal things off. In some places everything is a booby-trap." It seemed to Neumann that the Soviets were baiting items to tempt light-fingered Germans: "The magnificent pistol lying on the floor conceals a wire connected to an explosive charge. In the harmless interior of a samovar, pounds of cordite are hidden, waiting to blow up. Jam-jars, vodka bottles, even a well, the rope of which you're tempted to pull to get a drop of fresh water – they're all death traps to be steered clear of." There seemed only one way to be sure: "The simplest system is – from safe cover – to toss in three of four hand-grenades before entering any building. The explosions set off the booby-traps at the same time." Despite the efforts of Meyer, Neumann et al, the Germans themselves acknowledged they were only partially successful in keeping the encircled Soviets penned in: "Again and again elements of the Russian forces succeeded in breaking out eastwards, at points where the gaps in the net drawn around them were widest." One senior officer thought the conclusion was obvious. "The general view was that we would be unable to prevent the planned encirclement and elimination of the Soviet forces."

As the pocket closed, the trapped Soviets sought desperately to escape through what was a thin ring of German, Hungarian and Slovak troops. Wilhelm Moldenhauer, a *landser* in Wilhelm Stemmermann's 296. *Infanterie-Division*, was one of those on picket duty, and wrote to his wife Erika about it. "A great flood of Russian infantry swarmed forward and reached divisional headquarters ... we fought hard to fling back the Russians and succeeded." The Soviets kept on trying though. "We could see a dense and unbroken column of soft skinned vehicles ... on the road in our sector those columns that hadn't succeeded in smashing through stood six to eight abreast. Anti-tank gun fire brewed up the leading vehicles ... then the last truck was hit and began to burn, the fire spreading from truck to truck ... the main breakout attempt had failed." The surviving Soviets refused to just sit back and wait to go into captivity, throwing themselves at the German lines. The slaughter was dreadful, as Kurt Meyer witnessed: "The encircled Russian forces in the pocket were constricted ever more tightly, and the pressure on our positions became ever greater. More and more Soviets disappeared into a patch of woods five kilometres away. The slender trees now covered thousands of men; infantry, cavalry, artillery, didn't they realise we could see every movement? The Russian officers were leading their men to their deaths." Meyer knew there were too many of the enemy to wait for them to attack. "They would overrun us in the dark. The Uman pocket would have a hole in it. The moment had come ... the outline of the wood could only just be made out in the growing darkness ... Fire!"

Using cannons, *Nebelwerfer* multi-barrelled rocket-launchers, and every other weapon they had to hand, the SS poured fire into the woods. "The forest burst asunder like an anthill. Men and animals struggled for their lives, but still ran to their deaths. Galloping horses, wildly running away along with carts and guns, collapsed under the fire ... The butchery disgusted me." Hubert Lanz had a near panoramic view from a hill near Mogila Tokmak: "Disorganised groups of Russian infantry, their officers mounted on horses, marched to and fro without an objective. The enemy artillery was caught and shot to pieces by our guns. Horses without riders galloped about ... even the commissars were powerless, and soldiers began to surrender." A German War Diary described the aftermath: "Smashed armoured fighting vehicles and trucks littered the field; the remnants of the break-out attempt of the night of 6/7 August ... the incinerated and broken bodies of the crews lay amid the wreckage ... a frightful picture of destruction." Kurt Meyer watched as "thousands marched into captivity. The greater parts of the Russian 6th and 12th Armies were effectively destroyed – the fighting for Uman was over."

The young *Waffen-SS* officer was right. Two Soviet armies were annihilated, although a third of the trapped men had managed to break out, reducing the scale of Rundstedt's victory. As it was, the Germans took 103,000 prisoners. The Soviets lost a staggering 100,000 additional men killed in the fighting. German losses amounted to just 4,610, a ratio of almost twenty-five to one.

Karl Nünninghoff was relieved when it was all over – and he wasn't the only one: "Endless columns of Russian prisoners come towards us, greeting us with a cheerful smile and a German greeting, everyone is happy that the war is over for them. Then we passed another group that had been left behind. When they saw our panzers at dawn, they immediately surrendered – almost five hundred men."[32] A junior officer in Nünninghoff's regiment told his wife what he saw: "You can see the most diverse faces; from the European type we know to the Mongolian face with its small eyes and protruding cheekbones ... they look pretty shabby. We have already found many boys of fifteen and sixteen among the prisoners. Yes, there is one more thing about the war here: it is not only people against people, but also worldview against worldview ... the Russian must be forced to his knees."

With the Uman pocket smashed, a big salient had been created to the north, with Ukraine's capital – Kiev – at its centre. Having now achieved three successful encirclement battles, Berlin had acquired a taste for them – and was hungry for more.

Fedor von Bock, meanwhile, had announced to Berlin that with the Smolensk pocket immolated, *Heeresgruppe Mitte* would pause for breath, and then be ready to go again – destination Moscow. His *Panzergruppe 2* had already pushed on and seized the Yel'nya bridgehead and its adjoining heights, and from that launch pad his forces would once more sally forward with the goal of reaching the Soviet capital in one more lung-busting surge.

That moment couldn't come quickly enough for the men tasked with holding the Yel'nya position, one of whom was the *SS-Reich* artillery NCO, Heid Ruehl: "The battery fired a barrage into the woods where we thought the Russians would be concentrating. Through the scissors periscope we could see trainloads of their reinforcements being brought forward – obviously for an attack – but the railway line was beyond the range of our guns." The Soviets knew just how important the bridgehead was and threw in men and *matériel* to crush it. Out on a limb, the Germans at Yel'nya were relying on their artillery to keep the Red Army at bay, but poor logistics meant ammunition was in short supply, as a German War Diary made plain: "The Korps has absolutely no reserves available. Artillery munitions have been so depleted that no shells remain for counter-battery fire against the enemy artillery." Ruehl saw this for himself at the sharp end: "We were smothered in enemy fire ... soon the ammunition began to run out and we were only allowed to fire at certain, specific targets." The Germans' only armoured formation in the bridgehead was in no better shape. "*10. Panzerdivision* has been immobilised because oil and fuel supplies are lacking." The conclusion made for grim reading for men like Ruehl. "The *Korps* can perhaps manage to hold onto its positions, but only at the price of severe bloodletting."

With Bock's main force stalled and no relief in sight, Guderian thought the price for holding the bridgehead too high: "I proposed that the Yel'nya salient – which now had no purpose and was a continual cause of casualties, be abandoned." High command had a different view: "It is far more disadvantageous to the enemy than it is to us." The panzer leader's frustration was plain. "The whole point of my suggestion – that human lives be spared – was brushed aside."

As July ended, the situation worsened for the Germans at Yel'nya. Smelling blood, the Soviets hammered away at the isolated SS men.

Eight Russian tanks appeared, the NCO in charge of the anti-tank gun – *Unterscharführer* Rossner – used the tactic of killing the first vehicle, then the last, and then destroying the trapped remainder. The first Russian tank was hit and killed, but the second was a flame-throwing one that sent huge gouts of flames at the anti-tank gun. The Russian crew then leapt from their machine and charged the gunners, who grabbed entrenching tools and grenades to meet the charge. On that bright July morning a small knot of men – Russian and German – fought for their lives. When at last the Russian tankmen had been killed, the anti-tank gun crew went back to their gun and destroyed the rest of the tanks.

The *SS-Reich* was the only *Waffen-SS* formation involved in the Yel'nya fighting, with the majority of Germans in the bridgehead being regular Army – the Bavarians of the 268. *Infanterie-Division* and the Württembergers of the renowned 78. *Infanterie-Division* – but the battle reverberated through the ranks of the armed SS, as the men of *SS-Reich* were pushed to the very limits. Ruehl found himself dug in at the village of Ushakova. "We had been in position for two days, fighting off incessant Russian infantry attacks that eventually came so close to the OP (observation post) that Kindl ordered our guns to lay a curtain barrage." Having gone forward with a machine-gun crew to direct the artillery fire more accurately, Ruehl and his comrades had to retreat due to Russian pressure. "We pulled back through the burning village, holding off the pursuing Russians with bursts of machine-gun fire and grenades. Our officer was busy organising the evacuation of our wounded, but he was hit and lost a leg – he died on the way to the dressing station." There was no respite. "The gunners, working like fury, finally beat off the first Russian tank attacks, but these were then renewed in greater strength, and then our motorcycle battalion came under heavy pressure. We were smothered in drumfire (*trommelfeuer*) such as we had never before experienced."

Ruehl's fellow gunner Roman Geiger remembered the same battle: "We were firing in support of *Hauptsturmführer* Klingenberg's motorcycle battalion near Ushakova. We were told that because of the severity of the fighting and the losses in his battalion that every man had been put into the line. To cover our own losses our *Spiess*, *Hauptscharführer*

Bierleutgeb, went forward to replace the FOO (Forward Observation Officer) who had gone forward to Klingenberg's battalion." Medics, drivers, administrative staff; every man who could carry a weapon was pressed into the line, as Ruehl remembered: "One of our stretcher bearers won the Iron Cross by knocking out an enemy tank with a hand-grenade, he threw it into the open hatch – bang! Finished!"[33] Casualties were high. "Because of the severe losses it had sustained, the motorcycle battalion had to be taken out of the line and replaced by an East Prussian engineer battalion." Geiger: "After two days we were running short on ammunition. The OP was overrun and the Spiess wounded ... the battery commander called for volunteers to rescue him ... every man volunteered." Geiger was one of the men selected to go forward. "Two comrades were killed and *Obersturmführer* Schülke was carried off with a bullet through the jaw. *Oberscharführer* Dressler took over ... he took the machine-gun from me and rested it on my shoulder as he fired bursts into the enemy positions. We found our Spiess dead in a ditch, killed by a shot in the neck."

Johannes Kaufmann was well aware of what was at stake at Yel'nya: "The Soviets knew the threat it posed to their capital ... our hard-pressed ground troops were in urgent need of air support, and so, for the third time in little over a month we found ourselves moved closer to the front." By now an experienced front-line pilot, Kaufmann began a demanding series of missions over the salient.

> The importance the Soviets placed on maintaining a constant flow of supplies and reinforcements to the Yel'nya front was immediately apparent to us. Every single target we found and attacked was heavily defended. Never had we encountered such volumes of flak. The nature of our operations – low-level bombing and strafing runs through seemingly impenetrable curtains of ground fire – meant we were suffering damage on almost every sortie.

Despite the obvious dangers, Kaufmann believed what he and his fellow pilots were doing was of real value to the men on the ground. "It was undeniably true that the Army was bearing the brunt of the fighting at Yel'nya, but we felt that we were doing our bit too. Every Red Army troop convoy we prevented from reaching the front, every supply train that we destroyed, and every artillery emplacement that we knocked out helped to relieve the pressure on our comrades on the ground just a little bit more."

Heid Ruehl would doubtless have agreed had he not been preoccupied with the simple matter of staying alive. "Motorcycles loaded with our wounded ... all of them completely exhausted, dusty and sweaty. The

Russian advance had rolled over our thin infantry defensive lines and a lot of our lads didn't get out." An SS trooper in *Regiment Deutschland* observed, "Even the Russian wounded take up arms and carry on fighting, we have to be damned careful – it's another type of fighting to the one we knew in the West."[34] He wasn't kidding. An Order of the Day on 10 August 1941 read:

After a heavy defensive engagement on the north-eastern front of Yel'nya, *Unterscharführer* Förster's section of … SS Motorcycle Battalion, SS-Reich Division, whose task it was to cover the *kompanie*'s left flank were found as follows: *Unterscharführer* Förster, his hand on the pull-ring of his last grenade, shot in the head; *Rottenführer* Klaiber, his machine-gun still pressed into his shoulder … shot in the head; *Sturmmann* Buschner and *Schütze* Schyma dead in their foxholes; *Sturmmann* Oldeboershuis, still kneeling by his motor-cycle, killed at the moment when leaving with his last dispatch; *Sturmmann* Schwenk, dead in his foxhole. Of the enemy, only dead bodies were to be seen, lying in hand-grenade range in a semi-circle around the section's position. An example of what 'defence' means. We are in awe of such heroism!

Ferdinand Schaal of *10. Panzerdivision* explained the pressure his unit was under. "*10. Panzerdivision* lost the bulk of its heavy Mark IV panzers … The men of the maintenance units worked like Trojans, but they were short of spares, and the spares didn't arrive because the supply system no longer functioned. The distances from the supply centres had become too great. Every ammunition or supply convoy lost about one third of its vehicles, either through breakdown or enemy ambush … the men were overtaxed too. Parts of a column would fail to move off after a short rest because the drivers, officers and men had dropped off into a comatose sleep."

It wasn't just the ground troops who were feeling the pinch of an over-extended and creaking logistics system, as Johannes Kaufmann remembered: "Now that we were nearly 700 kilometres inside enemy territory, our own lines of communication were starting to show the strain. Deliveries of supplies and spare parts were becoming increasingly irregular, and this had an effect on morale." And not just on morale, there was a direct impact on his unit's fighting capability. "The *Gruppe*'s serviceability figures plummeted. Our ground crews worked tirelessly … improvisation, even cannibalization, was the order of the day. But some losses were beyond making good." In Kaufmann's case that meant any of the unit's Bf 110s that needed major work had to be flown – or more accurately nursed – all the way back to Warsaw where there were proper repair facilities.

Why was the fighting so fierce at Yel'nya? The reason lay in the number one hundred and eighty-five. It was 185 miles from the forward German positions at Yel'nya to the outskirts of Moscow – just 185 miles – a distance the panzers could cover in a matter of days. Except they weren't moving east, in fact they weren't moving at all, and they weren't moving because at the most senior levels of military and political leadership in the Third Reich there was a bitter struggle going on. This struggle pitched Hitler against the majority of his senior generals, including Halder, Bock, and his two panzer commanders, Hoth and Guderian. It was a fight for the very heart of Barbarossa, and its outcome would decide the fate of the campaign. It began on Saturday 19 July with the issuing of *Führerbefehl Nr. 33* (*Führer* Directive No. 33).

The *Führerbefehle* were the official instruments Hitler used to control and direct the war, and this one – entitled *Continuation Of The War In The East* – was one of the most important he would pen. It began by stating that "the second series of battles in the East has ended", acknowledged that the fighting at Smolensk would continue for some time to come, and then set out what Hitler saw as the aim of the next phase of operations, which was "to prevent any further sizeable enemy forces from withdrawing into the depths of Russia, and to wipe them out". It then dropped a proverbial bombshell.

> After the destruction of the many pockets of enemy troops which have been surrounded … *Heeresgruppe Mitte* forces, chiefly motorised … will advance south-eastwards in order to cut off the withdrawal of enemy forces which have crossed to the further bank of the Dnieper River, to prevent their withdrawal deeper into Russia, and to destroy them … while continuing to advance on Moscow with infantry formations, *Heeresgruppe Mitte* will use those motorised units which are not employed in the rear of the Dnieper River line to cut communications between Moscow and Leningrad, and so cover the right flank of the advance on Leningrad by Army Group North.

It concluded by ordering *Heeresgruppe Nord* to clear the rest of Estonia before it advanced further, and tasked the *Luftwaffe* with bombing Moscow "as reprisal for Russian attacks on Bucharest and Helsinki".

The implications of what the Directive proposed were huge. Bock's armour would be split and sent north and south to support the other two army groups, while the advance on Moscow would be left to his infantry alone, supported by an aerial bombing campaign. The shock caused by the Directive within German command was dramatic. Many felt that with the Red Army reeling, and the way to Moscow open, Hitler was gifting the Soviets what they wanted most: time – weeks and weeks of it.

Such was the consternation among senior officers that Wilhelm Keitel, forever his master's voice, brought out a supplement to *Führerbefehl Nr. 33* just four days later. It confirmed that Guderian's *Panzergruppe 2* would head some 300 miles south and, in conjunction with Kleist's *Panzergruppe 1*, destroy the Soviet forces centred on Kiev. Hoth, meanwhile, would lead *Panzergruppe 3* north and assist Hoepner in the capture of Leningrad. Keitel went on to confirm that capturing Moscow was to be left to Bock's footsore *landsers*. "*Heeresgruppe Mitte*, whose infantry formations are strong enough for the purpose, will defeat such enemy forces as remain between Smolensk and Moscow ... It will then capture Moscow."

The plan of operations described in the original order and the supplement lasted barely a week before the infantry advance on Moscow was postponed by yet another directive – this time Number 34 – which ordered that "*Heeresgruppe Mitte* will go over to the defensive, taking advantage of suitable terrain. Signed: Adolf Hitler." Moscow was let off the hook.

Opponents of the *Führerbefehl Nr. 33* strategy refused to give up. They hoped that Hitler would change his mind and abandon what they regarded as a criminal dispersal of effort. Guderian – cheerleader for a continued advance on Moscow – continued to hold the Yel'nya bridgehead and even sent some of his panzers forward to capture Roslavl as further preparation for an attack on the capital. The fall of Roslavl turned out to be the last action for Richard von Rosen for quite some time: "On 3 August Roslavl was taken. Other units were ahead of us and we detoured around the town to stay on the enemy's heels. I was in the spearhead panzer and we increased the pace to keep up the pressure on the retreating Russians. It was hot inside the panzer and we drove with the side hatches open. A wooden bridge on the town's outskirts failed to take our weight and collapsed. We plunged off it ... three fingers of my left hand were crushed by a falling beam." Evacuated to a main dressing station, he was sent home for treatment. He wouldn't return to the Eastern Front until 1943.

Almost a full month after *Führerbefehl Nr. 33* was circulated to senior commanders, Halder and Brauchitsch submitted a memorandum to the dictator on 18 August strongly recommending that Moscow be prioritised as the focus of attack. Five days later Guderian was called to a conference at Bock's headquarters in Borisov. Arriving in a Fieseler Storch liaison plane, he found all of Bock's senior commanders were already there; *4. Panzerarmee*'s Kluge, *9. Armee*'s Adolf Strauss and *2. Armee*'s Max Weichs. The guest of honour was none other than Franz Halder himself. Never one for visits to the front, the assembled officers knew this had to be important if it meant Halder leaving his headquarters desk. Around a conference table in Bock's spacious offices, coffee was served and then all eyes turned to the short-statured chief of the OKH. Looking distinctly pale and uncomfortable, Halder began by telling his audience that he and Brauchitsch had spent the past several weeks trying to persuade Hitler to abandon his plans to split Bock's armoured forces and instead head for Moscow. "Here is the reply." Clutching a single sheet of paper, he nervously read out the following:

> The Army's proposal for the continuation of operations in the East ... is not in line with my intentions ... The most important objective to be achieved before the onset of winter is not the capture of Moscow but the seizure of the Crimea and the industrial and coal-mining region of the Donets, and cutting off Russian oil supplies from the Caucasus.

There was a moment's silence and then Guderian exploded.

"This can't be true."

Halder replied, "It is true."

Everyone present understood the implications of the note. In a few short lines Hitler had admitted that the campaign as originally envisaged was dead. There would be no quick victory, no Soviet collapse – rather a winter in Russia and then a second year of campaigning for which the *Wehrmacht* was wholly unprepared. There followed a heated debate among the generals, with broad agreement that the decision had to be challenged once more. Even though von Bock and Kluge were clearly the most senior men present, it was Guderian who was nominated to accompany Halder to Hitler's East Prussian headquarters – the Wolf's Lair (*Wolfsschanze*) – and there put the case personally to the *Führer* for an attack on Moscow.

The two generals flew west in Halder's own Junkers Ju 88, mulling over the arguments they would use before the Nazi dictator. Guderian thought back to his last meeting with the *Führer* less than three weeks earlier when Hitler had visited *Heeresgruppe Mitte*. After being briefed by Bock and Guderian on the forces they were facing, he had murmured almost to himself, "Had I known they had as many tanks as that, I'd have thought twice before invading."

Landing at the nearby airfield, the two officers drove into the twilit forested world of Hitler's eastern headquarters, a depressing, insect-infested place, built back in the winter of 1940 and described by Jodl as "a cross between a cloister and a concentration camp". Arriving at the *Wolfsschanze*, they were left kicking their heels for two hours before Guderian was summoned to the *Führer Hut* – pointedly, Halder was not asked to accompany the panzer general.

Alone in the room except for a seated Jodl taking notes, and a stiffly silent Keitel, Guderian stood before Hitler and laid out his argument for an all-out, concerted assault on Moscow to finish the war in the East before winter. His case was persuasive and powerful, but the dictator breezily waved it away. The rebuttal he used has become part of German military folklore: "My generals have all read Clausewitz, but they understand nothing of the economic aspects of war." Hitler continued, exclaiming that Ukraine's grain and the Donets's minerals were far more important for the war effort than the capture of a single city. Guderian completely disagreed, yet – after railing against the abandonment of the offensive on Moscow – *Fast Heinz* did the kind of volte-face that his peers always mistrusted him for, as he accepted the decision and meekly resigned himself to carrying it out. He even wrote to his wife, "I left the meeting well satisfied, and with high hopes."

Reunited with Halder, the latter exclaimed angrily to him, "Why don't you fling your command in his face?"

Guderian replied, "Why don't you?"

Neither did, and neither would; regardless of all their protestations of honour, duty and service, the moral vacuum at the highest levels of German military command was cavernous.

For the men on the frontline the dropping of Moscow as the next goal came as a huge shock: "Everyone naturally assumed that *Heeresgruppe Mitte* would continue its drive eastwards to Moscow ... but Hitler's order came as a massive surprise." For Johannes Kaufmann and his comrades – and for hundreds of thousands of others – it would herald their involvement in one of the greatest battles in human history.

8

Kiev

"Quintilius Varus, give me back my legions!"
Roman Emperor Augustus after losing three entire legions at the
Battle of the Teutoburg Forest in Germania, 9 CE

Back on 3 July, Franz Halder had written in his diary that the campaign in the Soviet Union had effectively been won, and while there would still be some hard fighting to come – *cleaning up* as he called it – he was supremely confident as to the outcome.

Five weeks into that cleaning up, on Monday 11 August, he penned a new entry: "It is becoming clearer that we have underestimated the Russian colossus … this conclusion applies to its economic as well as its organisational forces, to its transport system and above all to its military capacity. At the outset of the war we reckoned on about 200 enemy divisions. Now we have already counted 360. These divisions are not armed and equipped in our sense of the words, and tactically they are often poorly led – but they are there." His exasperation at Soviet obstinacy was clear. "If we destroy a dozen, the Russians simply produce another dozen."

Halder may have found some comfort had he known that Soviet supreme command, the STAVKA (*Stavka Verkhovnogo Komandovaniya*),[1] had decided several weeks earlier to introduce sweeping changes to the organisation tables of the Red Army to help it produce that *other dozen*. Directive No. 1 set out that, henceforth, Soviet Armies were to be much smaller than previously authorised, with the key building block of all formations – the rifle division – reduced in strength from 14,500 to 11,000 men. It would also have just three-quarters of the artillery it deployed previously, and two-thirds fewer trucks. As casualties mounted, even this establishment was a struggle, so in reality several dozen front-line rifle divisions barely numbered 5,000 men each. It wasn't just the infantry that saw a diminution of their strength. Red Army tank divisions were downsized too, being cut to an ideal of 217 tanks in each – although as with their infantry brethren, casualties meant this figure was hardly ever reached. Nevertheless, this reorganisation, and mass mobilisation, enabled the STAVKA to create an astonishing 170 new rifle divisions, and several dozen tank divisions, between autumn 1941 and early 1942.

As for the VVS, the strength of an aviation regiment was slashed in half to thirty aircraft. The result was that Halder was confronted with a depressingly large rash of new ground and aerial units on the *Ostheer*'s situation maps.

However, regardless of Soviet reorganisations, what made Halder's diary entry so devastating was that it wasn't made by some anonymous soldier at the front, or a disbelieving junior officer, but by one of the two most senior commanders in the German Army. Gone was the Bavarian's previous triumphalism, replaced now by a creeping sense of dread. The easy victory over France had convinced many in Germany – Halder included – that the *Wehrmacht* truly was invincible, and yet here were the Slav *untermenschen* ripping up the Nazi script. Halder's foreboding was shared by many officers in the field, Gotthard Heinrici being one: "Their units are half-destroyed, but they just fill them with new people and attack again."

A few days after his despairing words of the 11th, Halder went further, and made this remarkable entry in his diary: "In view of the weakness of our forces and the endless space, we can never achieve success." In his view, Barbarossa had failed. Less than eight weeks into the invasion and yet the military brains behind the entire operation was flatly stating that ultimate victory was unobtainable. Halder did not communicate his doubts to his *Führer*, and if he did discuss them with Walther von Brauchitsch as his immediate superior, the conversation went nowhere – Brauchitsch was in any case far too indebted to Hitler; quite literally as he had used taxpayers' cash handed over by the dictator to pay off a hefty divorce settlement. By now Brauchitsch had become little more than a glorified errand-boy anyway. Instead, Halder, a man fixated on his self-image as the epitome of the duty-bound German officer, had flown east to tell Bock and the others that the attack on Moscow was off. As he did so he saw the latest casualty reports. By Wednesday 13 August – the fifty-third day of the campaign – German losses stood at 389,924, more than 10 per cent of the invasion force, and no fewer than 98,600 of those men were dead or missing.[2]

Now, with his reluctant generals towing the line, Hitler studied the situation maps spread out over the gargantuan oak conference table in his East Prussian headquarters and spied an opportunity in Ukraine.

What the Nazi dictator had seen was a huge and growing mass of the Red Army in a potentially fatal situation. Centred on Kiev were the STAVKA's Southern and Southwestern Fronts, well over one million men strong and commanded by one of Stalin's favourites, Semyon Budenny. The Soviet dictator was determined not to surrender the Ukrainian capital, and that determination was a gift to the Reich. If the *Ostheer* could get behind Budenny then the great bend in the Dnieper River could be turned from a Soviet defensive barrier into the net in which two whole Fronts could be caught. It would be twice the size of Bialystok-Minsk and would be nothing less than a *Vernichtungsgedanke* (literally, concept of annihilation), the stuff of every senior German officer's dreams.

Ever since the time of that most revered of Teutonic military heroes – Frederick the Great of Prussia – *Vernichtungsgedanke* had been the dominant theory in German military thinking. Taking the battle of Cannae in 216 BC as its inspiration, *Vernichtungsgedanke* aimed to achieve the total extermination of an enemy army, and it had been drilled into generations of general staff officers as the pinnacle of the military art. Kiev was just such an opportunity. Surely, if two entire Fronts were annihilated, this would be the elusive knock-out blow that would finally shatter the Red Army's capacity to resist. Rundstedt didn't have nearly enough mobile forces to make the attempt, so Bock was ordered to release *Panzergruppe 2*. The capture of Moscow was abandoned for the possibility of destroying the Red Army's entire southern wing and grabbing the region's resources – it made sense to Hitler and tempted his generals with the whiff of glory.

For the likes of Rudolf Kurth, such an attack couldn't come quick enough. "I am now lying in a cornfield, the sun is relentlessly burning down. My steel helmet glows. I was freezing last night even though I covered myself with corn sheaves and a tent sheet. The contrasts between day and night are just too great here. I don't know where I am in Russia either … We hear nothing of the outside world, our slogan is fighting and only moving forward. I have already seen huge stretches of this country. Russia is unimaginably large."

The die was now cast. Hitler had put his personal stamp on the final act of Barbarossa by turning away from Moscow and looking south, and the destiny of Kurth's *unimaginably large* Russia would be decided in eastern Ukraine and around its capital, Kiev – the city which would lend its name to the ensuing grand battle.

At the tail end of the ninth century, two Scandinavian Viking ship's captains, Askold and Dir, sailed down the Dnieper from Novgorod, on their way to try and sack Constantinople. On their journey they came across "a small city on a hill" held by the Khazar people. Capturing it, they garrisoned it and over time the outpost became the most important city – and capital – of the Kievan Rus state. By the summer of 1941, Kiev was still a capital, now of Ukraine, and one of the largest and most populous cities in the Soviet Union. It was also on the front line of the war, with Rundstedt's forces driving towards it – hard – as Hans Roth saw when he and his comrades entered another shattered village:

> An elderly couple are sat at the corner of a house. The old man is hunched over – dead. The babushka leans against her husband … their sons and grandsons lie inside the house in large, black pools of blood. A little further away a group of about twenty comrades lie, mown down by machine-gun fire. Two dead soldiers are locked in a deadly grip in the neighbouring garden. The Red is still grasping his bayonet in his rigid hand. Gauging from the wound, he stabbed the German in the neck. The Red's head is swollen; the Germans hands are still clamped around his throat like iron clamps … we're unable to separate the bodies.

Roth did not know it, but his division – Willi Moser's *299. ID* – would now become the chest of the bull, alongside the rest of Reichenau's *6. Armee*. Kleist's *Panzergruppe 1* would be the right, southern pincer, first pushing east and crossing the Dnieper at Kremenchug and Cherkassy, before hooking up north behind Kiev. Guderian's *Panzergruppe 2* was the key though; it would leave *Heeresgruppe Mitte* and drive south, getting across the Desna River – a northern tributary of the Dnieper – and then meeting Kleist in the area of Romny, some 140 miles east of Kiev. Unlike Kleist's panzer crews, Guderian's men wouldn't have the Dnieper covering their flank like a crash barrier, but would instead be vulnerable to thunderous Soviet counterattacks across a distance of several hundred miles, constantly threatening to cut them off in the middle of the Ukrainian steppe. When the armoured pincers met, the Germans would be looking to encircle as much of the Soviets' Southern and Southwestern Fronts as possible; four separate Armies up front with an additional two in reserve. The loss of so many men in a single, stunning blow would surely precipitate a general collapse, and the Germans could then advance all the way to Rostov as they had in the First World War in their triumphal eastern Railway Offensive. The plan was simple; its successful achievement was not. In total, the *Ostheer* was committing no fewer than thirty-five divisions to the operation – a force bigger than the entirety of *Heeresgruppe Nord* – in what would become the largest single battle it had fought up until now.

The first major task fell to *6. Armee* who were instructed *not* to try and take Kiev, but instead apply enough pressure to keep Soviet eyes fixed on them, and them alone. The fighting that followed was bitter and attritional, more reminiscent of the Western Front in the first war rather than the blitzkrieg of the second. Once again Hans Roth was at the forefront: "We are advancing to Kiev ... We are only able to make slow progress. The first line of bunkers lie in front of us – apparently there are a dozen more lines of defences beyond that – bunkers, minefields, swamps, automatic flamethrower traps and who knows what else." In what was fast becoming standard Soviet practice, the local civilian population were mobilised en masse to help build fortifications; in Kiev's case some 750 pillboxes strung out along an almost 30-mile front riven with anti-tank ditches, trenches and a hundred thousand mines. Fighting their way through each successive defence line, Roth survived a near miss: "A shower of glowing hot shrapnel rains down on us. Comrades to the left and right of me have been torn apart, my uniform is splattered with their blood. The blow throws me on my back, but I'm not hurt." The very next day he wrote to his wife, "It is our wedding anniversary dear Rosel!"

By 4 August Roth's unit was only 15 kilometres from the outskirts of the city. Reichenau's infantry was doing its job and keeping the Soviets busy, but the fighting was bleeding the Germans white. "In the past two days *Infanterie-Regimenter 529* and *528* have lost 380 and 304 men respectively. The replacements are coming too slowly." The front-line companies were in a terrible state, as Roth acknowledged: "We have almost reached the end of our fighting strength. The unbearable heat and brutal combat have battered us. We will only be able to hold the waves of Russian attacks for a little while longer – we need fresh troops!" By now the *Ostheer* was almost 200,000 men short of its establishment, and with precious few reinforcements coming forward Reichenau was left with little choice but to disband a raft of infantry regiments and distribute the survivors among the remainder to try and keep them up to strength.

This made little difference on the front line where Roth and his comrades found themselves almost entombed in their own trenches by massed Soviet artillery fire, and subject to constant Soviet attacks: "My hair is charred. A large chunk of earth flies against my helmet and knocks me out for a few moments, and then they come, the Red devils – Urrah! Urrah! The first ones close to within fifty metres of us. We clamber out of our trenches, our machine-guns staying behind to give us cover ... we end the fighting half an hour later." Even Roth was disturbed by the savagery of it all. "I don't remember the details of the butchery ... we ran forward like homicidal maniacs. We shot, slashed, and beat. My shirt is torn, my hands and knees are bleeding, and there is blood all over my uniform. On my left boot is a piece of pulverised brain. I vomit ... I feel dizzy and have cold chills."

Once again, the Soviets' determination to fight to the death was seen not as courage but as proof of their racial inferiority. "The battles during these last days remind me of the grim forest battles in France a year ago, but the Russian is a different opponent to the Belgians and French. At that time we fought against men who, as soldiers, applied intelligence, endurance and experience; the enemy here resembles a dull, indifferent, soulless machine of destruction and death ... the French would have learned from experience and attempted to avoid unnecessary casualties. These guys fight like mad until nothing moves. They never surrender!" Gustav Böker – in the same corps as Roth – also witnessed the slaughter: "The Russians ... almost come in marching order, like a parade. They are either without fear or believe that there won't be any resistance. They are just shot down with machine-guns."

Roth's frustration at his Soviet foe was exacerbated by his parlous physical state: "Most of us are suffering from serious intestinal issues – commonly known as shitting yourself uncontrollably – I am one of them." Bad though this was, Roth was in better health than some. "One comrade has nerve fever, during the attacks, he jumps up, shoots all over the place and tries to attack the Reds, even when there aren't any. The poor devil is being transported to the rear this afternoon."

About to be rotated out of the line for a brief rest, Roth and his comrades witnessed with horror a new Soviet tactic. "Before we retreated, we laid minefields. The Russians somehow found out, at which point they collected the sick and disabled from nearby mental homes. The infantry then herded them over the minefields in front of them. It was an extraordinary sight; naked as they were when they were taken from their beds. They ran in lines towards our positions. Hundreds were torn apart by the mines." The Nazis' own *T-4* euthanasia programme used gas and lethal injection to murder almost 300,000 mentally and physically disabled Germans by the war's end – so perhaps the only difference between these two unspeakable horrors is one of utility.

The time bought by the blood of Reichenau's infantry was invaluable for the *panzergruppen* who were designated as the great attack's pincers. Guderian – having completed his *volte face* on the operation as a whole – desperately needed it to refit his exhausted panzer formations. Looking down their rosters made for grim reading. Walther Nehring's *18. Panzerdivision* was in the best shape with just over half its complement of two hundred-odd panzers, while Hans-Jürgen von Arnim's *17. Panzer* had seventy-four runners. Walter Model's *3. Panzerdivision* could muster sixty of its original 198 panzers, but Willibald von Langermann und Erlencamp's *4. Panzer* only had forty-four still operational.

The men were also in poor shape. Losses in action had been high, and many more had been wounded or gotten sick; typhus, jaundice and dysentery were rampant. Erich Kern described the ravages of dysentery: "The hospitals were soon full and overcrowded. The first of my friends to get it was Paul (who then died). He complained of severe internal pain, and when I met him I saw for myself what that meant; he was terribly pale and thin ... many men were sent back to their units after just one day in hospital and came back with shocking stories; many of the sick only had straw to lie on, there were no bed pans and the men had to make do with shitting in old steel helmets."

Hunger was becoming a major problem. Despite stripping the populace of almost everything that was edible, the *landsers* were always complaining about the lack of food, and men found their summer uniforms were hanging off them. Replacements for the *panzergruppen* were arriving, but nowhere near quickly enough, with the gaps in specialist motorised infantry formations the most damaging. Nevertheless, the reinforcements that did arrive were quickly absorbed into their units, and all the available fuel and munitions were stockpiled ready for the launch of the attack.

All too soon for the tired troops that fateful day came, and on Monday, 25 August 1941, *Fast Heinz* launched his men southwards towards the River Desna. Designed to be a lightning thrust with his armoured and motorised formations smashing through the Soviet defences and breaking out into open country beyond, Guderian quickly had to acknowledge that instead it was a "bloody boxing match" – Soviet resistance was simply too great.

The much-awaited attack couldn't come soon enough for Hans Roth who, although wounded, refused to leave his unit, and instead stayed with his comrades: "After prepping us with heavy artillery fire the Russians attempt to storm our position. Wave after wave come towards us and break apart under our fire. Man oh man it's like target practice! What reserves they possess! It's sheer insanity to attack our position. Regardless, new masses of them still come forward ... our shells tear them apart and our machine-guns mow them down."

He witnessed an incident that helped explain why the Soviets soldiers carried on attacking when it was obviously hopeless: "Two Russian soldiers, the last of the wave, ran back to their blockhouses crazed with horror. Ten metres from the houses their own machine-guns rattle and hack them into mounds of flesh ... Can anyone understand these people?" Roth had seen one of the Red Army's infamous blocking detachments in action, tasked with shooting down those who were deemed to have run from the fight. As the Soviet marshal Georgy Zhukov was fond of saying, it took a brave man to be a coward in the Red Army.

With the northern pincer slowly slogging forward, what of Ewald von Kleist's *Panzergruppe 1* in the south? In truth, Rundstedt's main strike weapon was in much the same state as *Panzergruppe 2*. Barely half-strength, many of its best formations were still caught up in dogged fighting, even as they tried to regroup ready to head north and cross the Dnieper. Kurt Meyer and the *Leibstandarte*, for instance, were battling their way through the port city of Kherson: "*SS-Hauptschar* Erich was leading the attack. He knew he had to reach the harbour to prevent the Soviets setting up a proper defence ... we reached a small square, sailors were positioned among the ornamental bushes to try and stop our attack ... I suddenly saw Erich pitch onto the flagstones ... his hands sought something to grab onto and he was scratching in the dirt of the street. Some of his men dragged him over to the wall of a house and shouted for a medic. A round to the head had torn up his skull."

Curzio Malaparte, an Italian fascist and war correspondent for the *Corriere Della Sera* newspaper, was with his baby-sitter, *Leutnant* Weil, amidst the ranks of *Panzergruppe 1*: "The road, if this series of cattle-tracks may be so described, is covered with a thick layer of dust, which with every breath of wind rises in dense red clouds. But in places, where the clayey soil has failed to absorb the rainwater, where a stream crosses the track, the sticky, tenacious mud grips the wheels of the lorries and the tracks of the panzers." Malaparte observed the now-veteran *landsers* as they fought their way forward. "In this fluid type of warfare there is no time for meals – one eats when one can, with every soldier carrying with him his ration of black bread (*kommissbrot*) and marmalade and his thermos of tea. Periodically, even during battle, he will take a slice of bread from his haversack, spread the marmalade on it, raise it to his mouth with one hand while with the other he grips the steering wheel of his lorry or the butt of his machine-gun."

Pushing on towards the Dnieper, the Italian often found himself right at the forefront of the action:

> I hear distinctly the clatter of its tracks [a Soviet T-34] ... it seems to be sniffing the air, trying to locate an invisible rail leading through the corn ... the tank starts firing with its machine-guns, but half-heartedly, as if it wanted to test them ... some men emerge from the corn ... All told they must number about a hundred. Evidently this is some rear-guard detachment or perhaps a detachment that has been cut off ... the men seem to hesitate. They are seeking a way of escape ... some German soldiers appear over to our right, walking with their heads down, firing at the Russians. They advance in a line, blazing away with their sub-machine guns – an anti-tank gun fires a few rounds at the Russian tank. And now the outlines of two panzers appear on the brow of the hill behind it.

As Malaparte, Weil and Kurt Meyer moved up to the Dnieper, the *Luftwaffe* unceasingly flew overhead, playing their part in fixing

Budenny's vast forces in place and isolating them from the rest of the Red Army. Johannes Kaufmann was one of the *jagdflieger* involved: "I took off from Sechinskaya at 0952hrs on the morning of 30 August 1941 ... our targets were trains and railway installations in the area east of Konotop, a town about two hundred kilometres northeast of Kiev. The moment we crossed over into enemy territory medium flak opened up on us. It steadily grew in intensity until bursts seemed to fill the whole sky and we were forced to break formation in order not to make ourselves too closely bunched and an easy target for the Russian gunners ... The Red air force then decided to put in one of its rare appearances." Kaufmann wasn't too worried though. "This particular gaggle of enemy fighters didn't seem overly aggressive and even though we were still in loose formation we managed to fend them off without too much bother. One of the attackers selected our machine as a likely-looking victim, but my wireless operator/gunner held his nerve and his fire. Letting the Russian pilot get to within 150 metres of us before giving him two brief bursts from his machine-gun. This was more than enough for our assailant, who immediately veered away and disappeared in a steep dive earthwards. We didn't see what became of him." In all likelihood the VVS pilots were some of the barely trained novices rushed in to fill empty Soviet cockpits.

With the plan now in motion, the key for the Germans was for Kleist's and Guderian's panzers to meet up and shut the door behind the Soviets before they realised their predicament and made good their escape eastwards. This was easier said than done. Kleist's men could hide behind the Dnieper before making their final move, but Guderian's troops had no such luxury, they had no option but to grind their way forward, leaving their left flank exposed for over a hundred miles. One of them wrote: "It's going even slower, the difficulties are increasing, the land stands defiantly in our way." Theo Scharf's division was reduced to commandeering every wagon and cart they could find to try and keep going. "The division stretched out to a length of about sixty kilometres, with hardly anyone on foot."

Kurt Feldt's *1. Kavallerie-Division* had the unenviable task of shielding that horribly open left flank, using their horse-powered mobility to try and screen the advance across dozens of miles. Max Kuhnert remembered it all. At first, Kuhnert marvelled at the fertility of the farmland they were riding through, even though the tobacco fields in particular, were an obstacle in themselves: "A large encirclement was in progress around Kiev ... we were urged to move faster. Trying to ride through a tobacco field was murder in more ways than one ... as the horses ploughed through, crushing the leaves, the fumes and juices were released, which, despite the kerchief covering your face, intoxicated you and stained you brown from top to bottom. The nicotine was so strong it found its way right through our saddlebags."

It wasn't all nightmarish, especially when the young trooper noticed the friendly attitude of many Ukrainians: "Some offered bread and salt ... I did meet some of them and was able to try out my little red book of Russian phrases." Reaching yet another village on the way south, Kuhnert's small picket group soon discovered why so many of the local inhabitants were well-disposed towards them.

> I went straight into the nearest house. I saw nobody at first, but then I heard noises behind the enormous fireplace ... I shouted to whoever it was to come out. All women and children, no men at all, so I asked them where the head of the household was hiding ... they started to wail ... it eventually became clear that Russian soldiers had taken all the men, young and old. Apparently the soldiers had been a cavalry brigade and, in need of help to look after their horses ... just dragged them along. This had happened three days ago.

Kuhnert felt sorry for the villagers and deplored the behaviour of his Red Army counterparts, but that didn't stop him from stealing one of their few chickens. "Having chased the little fellow through gardens of mixed vegetables for almost half an hour. I was eagerly looking forward to roasting him."

It was now early September. *Panzergruppe 2* was still making progress – albeit at a crawl. Kleist was moving up to the Dnieper and was just about ready to go. The jaws of the trap now had to snap shut. From his headquarters, Semyon Budenny could see what was happening and asked Moscow for permission to withdraw east and escape the approaching disaster. Stalin refused. Budenny asked once more. Stalin refused again – the dictator ordered his Civil War comrade not to abandon Kiev and hold his ground. Given the example the Soviet dictator had set when he executed the Western Front commander, Dmitry Pavlov, back in July, Budenny could do little except comply. Rundstedt may have described Budenny as a man with an "enormous moustache – tiny brain", but the looming crisis was far more Stalin's blunder than the ex-cavalry NCO's. In any case, Germany's generals were hardly ones to throw stones given their own unwillingness to go against a dictator's orders, even when they went counter to military logic.

With Stalin forbidding his armies from taking their necks out of the noose, the biggest obstacle the Germans faced to success was their growing transport problem. As early as 28 August, Halder noted that the *Ostheer* had lost 38,000 trucks destroyed or damaged beyond repair since the beginning of Barbarossa, with half of those losses concentrated in the vital *panzergruppen*. The worst affected were the *beutefahrzeuge* (booty vehicles), particularly the French models, whose two-wheel drive systems, low ground clearance and weak suspension made them especially unsuited to Soviet road conditions. Forced to run the engines hard to keep them moving, drivers found they were using well over twice the engine oil the planners had bargained for, and spare parts – or rather the lack of them – was a major issue, with the mechanics having little option but to cannibalise vehicles to keep at least a portion of runners going. Gottlob Bidermann saw it for himself: "Due to this method of salvage and use, our Army appeared to consist of vehicles of every type and description from half of Europe, sometimes making it impossible to obtain even the simplest replacement parts. We found ourselves growing envious of the uncomplicated Russian supply system." The end result was an advance marked by huge numbers of immobile truck carcasses that littered the roadsides of eastern Ukraine. A 27 August report from Friedrich-Wilhelm's von Loeper's *10. Infanterie-Division (mot.)* with *Panzergruppe 2*, laid the problem bare: "Aside from earlier fallouts, 30 per cent of the remaining trucks are sitting with some form of damage on the road north of Surash. As a result of the catastrophic oil shortage … there will be even more trucks lost. Consequently, the battalions at the front sometimes consist of just five platoons and are often without heavy weapons. The Division will reach the Desna in some cases on foot and almost without heavy weapons."

Knowing just how poor many of their trucks were, the Germans were always on the lookout for Soviet models, which they much preferred. "The Russians possessed large numbers of robust Ford heavy trucks (from a Ford plant set up in the Soviet Union before the war) as well as those of Sis manufacture. Those two types seemed to make up the entire inventory of trucks possessed by the enemy, and we always chose the American-manufactured Fords wherever possible, as many replacement parts always seemed to be available."

Max Kuhnert was lucky not to have to rely on his division's trucks – even for food – as he and his fellow cavalrymen began to emulate the local Ukrainians who "practically all had a sunflower head in one hand and with the other were throwing the seeds one by one into their mouths, spitting out the inedible parts before tossing in another one. We also tried it when we had a chance … their teeth, lips and tongues were all blue." The unit's head vet told Kuhnert why. "Dr Pohl told us that sunflower seeds were indeed very nutritious, as long as we didn't overdo it, as the acid in the kernels was very strong, hence the blue mouths."

Released from the inferno at Yel'nya, Paul Hausser's *SS-Reich* were part of Guderian's spearhead as they marched south as fast as they were able. One young SS man wrote of the trek: "Russian shells sink into the swamp we're crossing and don't usually explode ... one shell which did go off fell between me and another man but didn't injure us, except my comrade has been affected by the blast. He won't go back for medical treatment, so I've taken over his machine-gun, and am using the sling to tie him to me as every time I let him go he walks around in circles." The pace of the advance may not have been stellar, but the SS men were already outstripping their supply system: "0615hrs, 7 September. The rations which came up during the night are distributed. Two and three-quarter loaves between twelve men; that's four slices of bread for a day's ration."[3]

By now, Rundstedt and Halder were growing increasingly frustrated. The plan had envisaged a swift, powerful drive from the north and south to trap as many Red Army divisions as possible before they could escape east, but the slowness of the advance, and the ferocity of the fighting, seemed destined to foil the Germans and let the flat-footed Soviets off the hook. Guderian's men in particular needed a slice of luck – and they got it.

A captured Red Army map revealed a gap between two Soviet formations, and Walter Model needed no further encouragement. He shoved his panzers forward and burst through. As the Soviets scrambled to react, their resistance began to fracture, and Model once more punched forward, covering 36 miles on Wednesday 10 September through the driving rain to reach the town of Romny on the River Sula. The lead panzers arrived to find the Soviets in chaos as they hastily abandoned the place and fled. The relief of the panzer crews at reaching their initial objective turned to joy on the discovery of large amounts of stockpiled food, munitions and, even more welcome, fuel, some 80,000 litres of it. On hearing of the fall of Romny, something akin to panic swept through Budenny's headquarters, and the marshal once more requested permission from Stalin to abandon Kiev and try and save his armies from the looming disaster. The dictator responded by sacking his one-time friend and appointing Semyon Timoshenko in his stead. It would make no difference.

The day after Budenny's sacking, Ewald von Kleist finally began the long-awaited attack out of his bridgeheads at Cherkassy and Kremenchug. Hans-Valentin Hube's *16. Panzerdivision* led the way, covering an astonishing 43 miles on the very first day. Behind Hube's chargers came *9. Panzerdivision* under its Austrian commander, Alfred von Hubicki, and the Soviets simply folded before the weight of armour being thrown at them.

Soviet high command now finally realised their mistake, but it was far, far too late. With Kleist's panzers roaring north, Model once more set off, leaving Romny on Saturday 13 September and dashing southwest to Lokhvitsa and its bridge over the Sula. The gap between the two *panzergruppen* was shrinking rapidly, and was further reduced as Hube drove his men relentlessly forward, ordering them to continue the attack until their tanks literally ran dry.

They took the town of Lubny on the Sunday. There were fewer than 30 miles between the two pincers now. With success tantalisingly close, Model decided to force the issue. He ordered the formation of a small *kampfgruppe* and tasked it with dashing south to meet up with Hube's leading panzers. An *Oberleutnant* Warthmann was given command of a solitary Mark III panzer, several half-tracks and a few soft-skinned vehicles, and a grand total of forty-five men for the job. Feeling their way forward, they tried to avoid any skirmishes, skirting round opposition and only fighting if they had to. By the end of the day, with dusk approaching, Warthmann's ad hoc unit reached a creek. While trying to find a ford to cross over, Warthmann noticed "Grey ghost-like figures leaped to their feet ... covered in clay, with stubble on their chins, and they waved and waved." They were members of 2./ *Pionier-Bataillon* 16 under *Oberleutnant* Rinschein – Warthmann had found 16. *Panzerdivision. 3. Panzerdivision*'s War Diary recorded "14 September 1941, 1820hrs: link-up of *1.* and *2. Panzergruppen*". The Kiev pocket had been formed. The pocket was actually a triangle, one of staggering proportions encompassing some 20,000 square kilometres of eastern Ukraine, a landmass as big as the entire country of Slovenia. Within it were four complete Soviet Armies – the 5th, 21st, 26th and 37th – and elements of two others, the 38th and 40th. In total more than forty-three divisions with all their equipment and weaponry. Those men were now cut off from resupply, their shortest escape route east blocked by the panzers.

That didn't mean their position was hopeless. As Bialystok-Minsk, Smolensk and Uman had shown, the *Ostheer*'s pockets were invariably riddled with holes through which huge numbers of men could escape if they acted quickly enough. The race was now on. For the Germans it was about bringing up infantry as fast as possible to man the picket lines around their prize, and for the Soviets it was a matter of breaking out before those same infantry arrived to seal their fate.

Max Kuhnert recalled the initial Soviet reaction to being encircled: "At first they tried to break through towards a town called Nizhyn, northeast of Kiev, and that meant exactly in our direction. First it was their planes, then their tanks – not only T-34s but also 60-tonners, huge green monsters." Kuhnert considered himself and his comrades lucky: "We were behind a panzer division, and only fragments of the Russian armour got through to us." In particular, he heaped praise on the anti-aircraft gun crews who switched to engage ground targets. "Most of the time they were shooting at Russian tanks with their powerful 88mm guns. The Russians were simply no match for them." The only real problem Kuhnert identified in his sector was the guns' lack of mobility. "The batteries weren't always in the right place, and our *14. Kompanie* (usually this was the regiment's anti-tank company) couldn't, with its smaller guns, always pierce the Soviet armour ... we were utterly helpless in those situations. Warfare against tanks we had hardly trained for because it wasn't our job on horseback. The best we could do was get out of the way, find cover in wooded areas, and hope for the best."[4]

Within twenty-four hours of the pocket forming, the situation for Kuhnert and his division changed dramatically as the ferocity of Soviet attacks went up a few notches: "A defensive position had to be established and so we gathered the horses from most units into the woods and left them with a skeleton staff so that the rest of us could find a good position from which to fight." Thousands of trapped men threw themselves at the German picket line in what Kuhnert described as "the desperate onslaught of Russian forces". For the lightly armed cavalrymen, the pressure was intense. "We were simply exhausted and had many casualties, not only men but horses too ... on the way to my horse I couldn't avoid seeing a truck full of our dead, it was just ghastly, and these were only a few from our immediate area. Blood was literally running down the side from the floorboards of the truck, and the driver – despite the heat – was white as a sheet." Outnumbered, the besiegers were in danger of becoming the besieged.

The German infantry were marching as fast as they could towards the sound of the guns. Günther von Scheven, an acclaimed sculptor in civilian life before being drafted in 1940, recalled the hellishness of that trek: "There is no rest ... always the same marching through woodless areas and along endless roads, column after column. Horses, riders and guns like spectres in thick clouds of dust." A trooper in *SS-Reich* remembered it, too:

> We march along a railway embankment. It's very tiring walking on the sleepers ... our feet are suffering from being continually wet from the rain and the swamp. A grenade explodes near our squad and shrapnel ignites the Very light pistol ammunition carried by the platoon runner. He is soon enveloped in flames and suffers not only burns but shrapnel wounds as well, from which he dies. [Later] The burning hot sun has dried the ground and our feet begin to hurt ... we come under fire ... everywhere there are calls for stretcher-bearers Our *kompanie* suffered fourteen killed and seventeen wounded ... our wounded comrade Gail died on the way back. His death depresses us all very much as only two days ago he received a telegram telling him he was now the father of a healthy boy.

Curzio Malaparte wrote of the strange juxtaposition between the endless advance during the day, and the utter stillness of the nightly halts.

> During the night all fighting ceases. Men, animals, weapons, rest. Not a rifle shot breaks the damp nocturnal silence. Even the voice of the cannon is hushed. As soon as the sun has set, and the first shadows of evening creep across the cornfield, the German columns prepare for their night's halt. Night falls, cold and heavy, on the men curling up in the ditches, in the small slit trenches which they have hastily dug amid the corn, alongside the light and medium assault batteries, the anti-tank cannon, the heavy anti-aircraft machine-guns, the mortars ... shielded from sudden attack by the sentries and patrols, the men abandon themselves in sleep.

Night may have brought some blessed relief, but long before dawn the men were on the move once more, fighting their way forward, as an anonymous SS man described: "On roads that have been washed away, in pouring rain, carrying all our weapons and equipment, we fight our way against enemy resistance. We are at the end of our strength, we've been marching for days with only poor rations. The supply trucks are stuck fast in the mud thirty or more kilometres away." Giving the lie to the oft-heard Army complaint that the *Waffen-SS* always received the best of everything, the *Reich* trooper detailed the sorry state of the men. "Many of my comrades have only socks to cover their feet. Their boots have fallen to pieces ... Others go barefoot, and their feet are torn from the marching ... we are told that we are taking part in a gigantic, destructive battle."

Over the next twelve days eastern Ukraine saw some of the heaviest fighting of the entire Barbarossa campaign. Just as in all the previous encirclement battles, the trapped Soviets didn't throw down their arms and wait placidly to be rounded up, instead they fought tooth and nail to break out. This part of the battle is often brushed over in the histories, the focus being on the advance of the German armoured pincers, and particularly the mad rush that ended with them joining up near Lubny. For many, this seemed to signal the finale of the fighting, when in fact it only signalled the start of almost a fortnight of blood and terror – both for the men trying to escape the pocket, and those trying to keep them in. *Leutnant* Kurt Meissner was commanding a unit of anti-tank guns, and he recalled the Soviets break-out attempts as something almost primal: "This great mass of singing humanity had been told to break out in our direction ... they came on in a shambling, shuffling gait, and all the time they were calling out in this low, moaning way, and every so often they would break out into this great mass cry of 'Urrah! Urrah!'"[5]

The slaughter was horrific. With no air support, and virtually no covering artillery fire, the Soviets would charge onto the German guns again and again, desperate to find a way out.

Whether they come in with tanks, or whether the infantry comes in without support, whether their Cossacks charge in on horses or whether they come rolling forward in motor lorries, the end is always the same. They are driven back with such losses that you wonder how they can find the courage and the men to keep on coming ... do they have any feeling of fear? ... Some of my comrades think the Bolsheviks must either be drugged or drunk to keep coming on like that ... the dead stretched for miles ... we lost men too, for this was no easy victory. But their dead, particularly where there had been a fierce fight, formed a carpet.[6]

Others were not so blasé, especially when they had to face the dreaded T-34s. Fritz Koehler was with a motorised infantry unit trying to reduce the pocket. Dug in and covered by anti-tank guns, he felt somewhat safe until some T-34s arrived and "the rounds ricocheted straight off". The Soviet tanks then simply drove over the guns, crushing them and their crews under their broad tracks. "The tanks then drove right up next to our position. We experienced some very uncomfortable minutes. One even crunched by about five metres from my foxhole ... I hunched up and tried to make myself as small as possible, hardly breathing. Finally, it drove on."

Walter Oqueka found himself in much the same position when he and his unit came face to face with a T-34. Oqueka was a crewman on a light anti-aircraft gun, a 2cm FLAK 38 mounted on a half-track chassis. "'T-34' – hissed the gun commander ... we had all heard about these tanks ... we weren't going to win any prizes with our 3.7cm *Panzeranklopfgerät* against these things, so how would our even smaller 2cms do?" With no choice but to stick it out, Oqueka's crew concentrated their fire on the tracks of the lead Soviet tank until, almost miraculously, it began to spin around uncontrollably. They then switched to its turret. After a few seconds the hatches opened, and the crew came out with their hands up. The German gunners then did the same to the next tank, however, that crew came out shooting and were killed. It turned out that the sound inside the hull of the multiple shell hits on the turret convinced the crewmen they were about to be destroyed so they abandoned their vehicles.

Max Kuhnert recalled the total horror of it all: "The punching of bullets into flesh, the screams of agony, however short, from man and beast." In between firefights, "We just sprawled next to the horses, face up to the sky, grateful to be alive and in one piece." Others were not so lucky, as he saw for himself. "We saw a large 60-tonner Russian tank. The turret was open. We walked cautiously around to the other side, and there was a dreadful sight, the result of a direct hit. The flames had burnt all the clothes off the driver's body ... and then we saw the woman, also burnt, hanging half-way out of the small side door ... the stench was unbearable." Exhausted and hungry, Kuhnert tucked into his iron rations, consisting of a small tin of meat with hard biscuits: "I opened the tin with my bayonet and was taking my first mouthful ... when I suddenly got a whiff of the tank. It was only about thirty feet away. I threw the tin away and tried to be sick ... for years to come whenever I tried to eat tinned pork I just couldn't."

Back with 299. *ID*, it was much the same for Hans Roth and his comrades: "Heavy night attacks from the Russians, they used those damn rifle grenades for the first time ... our morale has reached a low point." Even talk of reinforcements wasn't welcomed by the bedraggled *landsers*: "Someone has brought news from the rear that a thousand-man replacement column is marching towards us. We don't like that at all. We'd hoped that after the fall of Kiev we'd be sent back to Germany to regroup. According to rumours that has been the practice before – Scheisse!" As ever with soldiers, black humour helped keep them going. Roth recalled one such macabre incident after a VVS attack dropped a load of incendiary bombs on the valley they were fighting in. "We should be thankful to the Red devils. They have transformed the valley and its heaps of dead bodies into a crematorium. No stench of decay will now turn our stomachs ... Ribs, Kassel-style! Well-smoked as someone remarked!" The trapped Soviets fought on.

Max Kuhnert and his comrades ended up searching an abandoned factory complex: "I stumbled stupidly over some debris and, as I was holding my Schmeisser, I stretched my arms out in front of me so as not to damage it. I fell headlong to the floor and my face hit something round and jelly-like. It was the decaying face of a Russian corpse. Trying to wipe it off, all I did was smear the stuff all over my face ... I was sick." Günther von Scheven was nearing the end of his tether: "The last few days of combat are taking their toll of my courage ... they have placed a heavy burden on me. You cannot comprehend the annihilation of so much life. The wild despairing break-out attacks the Russians attempted, surprising even for us, right up to our front with tanks, infantry and Cossacks. I am too shattered to grasp it all." Another *landser* wrote of his enemy, "Expressionless, their dull eyes fixed into the distance as if fascinated by the rattle of our guns, they would run into our hail of fire ... everything about them was mechanical, without a soul. That was perhaps the most horrible of our experiences on the eastern front – mechanical dying."

This was no walk-over though, and German casualties were piling up, as one motorised infantry regiment found to its cost: "Russian tank forces, attempting a relief thrust on Kiev, hit the rear of the regiment ... Lacking the firepower to mount a defence against tanks, the infantry set fire to its own vehicles and set out on foot."[7] As one veteran of the pocket remarked, "Often you didn't know who was encircled, the bolsheviks or us ... the losses on our side are quite high." Erich Hager was in *17. Panzerdivision*:

> The gruesome day is over. The Russian attack started early. We were firing with all barrels ... now all hell is breaking loose ... *Feldwebel* Pusch, Krethner and Max are dead. Shot in the back. Grossmann shot in the lung ... now we've had it, there's no-one left on our right ... there's a one-kilometre gap where there are no Germans. All of a sudden a 52-ton tank attacks, it comes from the edges of the woods with a Russian assault-gun. Our flamethrowers clear off, what do we do? We run for our lives as never before ... everyone runs. *Leutnant* Meyer, the whole of second platoon ... we get out. In the village of Slout there are eight of us left.[8]

As so often before, the *landsers* found the Soviets refusal to give in infuriating. "The Russians behaviour in action is simply incomprehensible ... they are incredibly stubborn and refuse to budge even under the most powerful gunfire." The unknown soldier had written this in a letter home. It was found on his dead body.

The brutality of the fighting led seemingly inexorably to atrocities. The discovery of a group of German soldiers hung from trees by their hands, with their feet doused in petrol and then set alight – Stalin's socks as it was gruesomely termed – led to revenge killings. "At noon the next day an order was received by Division that all prisoners captured during the last three days were to be shot in reprisal ... the lives of 4,000 men were forfeit ... they lined up eight at a time, by the side of a large anti-tank ditch. As the first volley crashed, eight men hurled forward into the depths of the ditch ... already the next file was lining up."[9]

From the air, the pocket resembled a vast cauldron. Johannes Kaufmann remembered it well. With so many targets, Kaufmann and his fellow fliers made hay:

> At 1005hrs I took off again and headed for the area to the east of Kiev, it was here that the panzer spearheads had made contact. This was the final stage of a gigantic pincer movement, the largest and most ambitious of the campaign to date, which has surrounded the Ukrainian capital and trapped the greater part of fifty Red Army divisions. The

Soviets were now desperately trying to force a way into the Kiev *kessel* [cauldron] from the east to give those divisions an escape route out of the trap ... Our immediate task was to provide direct support to relieve the pressure on our thinly-stretched panzer divisions forming the eastern wall of the cauldron. We had been ordered to concentrate our attacks on the enemy's armour and artillery. But, as usual, the situation on the ground was one of total confusion.

The Soviet response to the appearance of the *Luftwaffe* was to fire at them with every single weapon to hand: "It required an awful lot of determination to grit one's teeth and dive down into that almost solid cloud of exploding flak shells, and even more luck to emerge in one piece. Then came the strafing runs. The watchwords were: show no hesitation – think and act quickly – short bursts of fire to keep their heads down, and keep jinking and weaving to spoil their aim." With four heavy 7.92mm machine-guns and twin 2cm cannon in the nose, Kaufmann's Bf 110 packed an awesome punch, and the strafing runs were deadly. "There was no shortage of targets. The Red Army were masters of camouflage but even they couldn't hide the mass of men and equipment they were throwing into the battle."

For the men of 6. *Armee* there was no rest, as the dreadful fighting in front of Kiev continued, until, "Finally, finally! You could shed tears of joy! This terrible trench war will be over ... The battle of Kiev has reached its climax." The order to attack the city had been given, and Hans Roth was elated. He was even more jubilant when he heard why the attack had been delayed so long. "An enormous encirclement has been achieved which is unprecedented in the history of war ... people will still be talking about it in a hundred years."

To the north of Roth's unit were the Austrians of 44. *Infanterie-Division*. They too had been slugging it out with the Soviets and had suffered terrible casualties, especially among their officers. One result of which was that during a visit by von Reichenau, the Army commander found himself having to personally lead a regimental attack for lack of other leaders. The fifty-six-year-old general later described the almost surreal experience to Jodl at OKH: "I didn't lead the assault out of any lust for adventure ... I led the assault for three kilometres, while literally not only with the first wave, but as the leading man in it. Enemy resistance was very stubborn, their mortar fire being particularly severe, and the only way to avoid it was to advance just as fast as we could ... the fighting has been really fierce, literally to the last drop of blood." Reichenau then ordered the division to cross the Dnieper north of Kiev via a pontoon bridge hastily erected by the engineers. Once on the eastern bank, the Austrians advanced to help seal the pocket's northern boundary.

By Friday 19 September, amid so much carnage, Soviet resistance finally began to crack. Max Kuhnert saw "the retreat of many thousands of Russian soldiers. The columns seemed not to end. Many of the poor fellows were wounded and limping. All were in tatters, their faces in utter despair. I thought, if I were in such a dreadful position what would I do? Why not run away?" On the same day, Kleist's *panzergruppe* reported taking 12,000 captives, along with four tanks and no fewer than 277 guns, and Roth and his comrades attacked Kiev itself. "We penetrated the heavily defended outer ring of fortifications. The enemy, not nearly as strong as we had thought, was defeated in bloody, close combat and by 0900hrs we'd already reached the western part of the city."

In the skies above them was Johannes Kaufmann: "Our first sortie was again in support of our troops in the field, and the second against the enemy's rail network to the east ... between the two we had just eighty-five minutes to get our aircraft refuelled – by hand – rearmed and have a fresh bomb load attached to the belly and wing-racks."

Expecting a tough fight, Roth was surprised when "by noon we were in the centre of the city, no more shots are heard, the wide streets and squares are abandoned. It's eerie. The silence is making us nervous." The *landsers* found that the biggest threat they faced wasn't from Red Army strongpoints but from "seemingly random objects that are of interest to all soldiers: watches, packs of cigarettes, bars of soap etc, all of them connected to a hidden detonator. If a soldier picks one up he detonates a mine, or even an entire field." They also came across "mine dogs; we shot about a dozen German shepherds alone ... The animals carry an explosive pack on their backs." Roth wrote that the Soviets were using dumdum bullets, and what he called fire-grenades – seemingly ordinary illuminating shells that exploded when the phosphorous filling was burnt out, inflicting terrible wounds: "These devilish projectiles are supposed to be banned under the Geneva Convention ... those who've seen the injuries caused by these monsters will never take any prisoners ever again." Roth wasn't the only German to be enraged at the possible use of banned munitions.

Gerhart Panning – a staff doctor in *6. Armee* – wanted to prove the Soviets were indeed using them when they were found in captured stocks. His solution was pure savagery. He requested Paul Blobel, the commander of *Sonderkommando 4a* of *SS-Einsatzgruppe C*, supply him with prisoners – mostly POWs and Jewish civilians – who Panning then had shot to demonstrate the effects of the banned ammunition on arms, legs, the torso and so on. He published the results of his grisly experiments in a scientific journal and went on to become a professor at Bonn University's Institute of Forensic Medicine in 1942.

As for the *Luftwaffe*, it was having a rare old time, although as Hermann Plocher – chief of staff for *V. Fliegerkorps* – admitted, there were massive logistics problems. "Repeated requests for timely and sufficient fuel supplies were futile ... the tremendous distances and inadequate available transport didn't allow a smoothly functioning supply system." Nevertheless, his *Korps* still managed to fly 1,422 sorties between 12 and 21 September, dropping some 567,560 kilos of bombs on the wretched Soviets trapped in the pocket. It was always difficult to accurately tally enemy losses during the confusion of a raid, even with the help of a gun camera, but Plocher's men were officially credited with destroying 2,171 motor vehicles, 107 aircraft, fifty-two trains, twenty-three tanks, and six anti-aircraft batteries during the battle. If accurate this was a remarkable success, particularly when its own casualties were fairly meagre at just seventeen aircraft shot down and another fourteen damaged, with twenty-seven men killed or listed missing.

In the middle of it all, Kaufmann and his unit moved once more. "Unlike our recent bases, where we'd lived and worked under canvas, Konotop was an established airfield." The very next day – a Sunday – they set off on their next mission. "The target was once again the Soviet units trapped to the east of Kiev. It was little more than a repetition of our earlier sorties against the pocket." Two days later, he was in the air attacking the VVS air base at Lebedin, a hundred miles southeast of Konotop. "First, we dive-bombed the hangars and technical sites, and then we went in low to strafe the few aircraft dispersed around the field. At 1250hrs on 22 September, after just sixty-five minutes in the air, I landed back at base." It was Kaufmann's swansong in the East – at least for a while. His unit was sent back to Germany to begin conversion to the replacement for the ageing Bf 110, the ill-fated Messerschmitt Me 210. It was a change Kaufmann was glad of. "Truth be told, the past three months campaigning on the Eastern Front had taken more of a toll on us – both mentally and physically – than many of us would care to admit."

He wasn't the only one feeling the strain, as one soldier in Hans von Tettau's *24. Infanterie-Division*, holding a southern section of the pocket, freely admitted: "To show fear no longer embarrasses people. Fear is no longer an unmentionable word."

The day before Kiev fell, a second envelopment was completed when *2. Armee* from the north and *17. Armee* from the south met at Yahotyn, a town roughly half-way between Romny and Kiev. The pocket was now split in two.

Sudden downpours turned swathes of the battlefield into a quagmire, as an *SS-Reich* trooper recalled: "We're soaked to the skin, we dig in and our slit trenches fill with water ... we lie down in them but are thirsty." Curzio Malaparte wrote of the deadly intimacy of it all: "There in front of us, concealed amid the corn and within the solid dense mass of the woods, the enemy sleeps. We can hear his hoarse breathing, we can discern his smell – a smell of oil, petrol and sweat." He laid the blame for the slaughter squarely on the shoulders of the Moscow leadership:

> During the fighting the words of Stalin, magnified to gigantic proportions by loudspeakers, rain down upon the men kneeling in holes ... the soldiers lying amid the shrubs, the wounded writhing in agony upon the ground. There is something diabolical, and at the same time terribly naïve, about these soldiers who fight to the death, spurred on by Stalin's speech on the Soviet constitution ... these dead who never surrender, these dead scattered all around me; about the final gestures, the stubborn, violent gestures of those men who died so terribly lonely a death on this battlefield amid the deafening roar of cannon and the ceaseless blaring of the loudspeaker.

Still the killing went on. Kurt Meissner and his gunners carried on hammering away at the milling throngs of Red Army soldiers, the horrendous effect of shot, shell and cordite making the young officer feel physically sick. "I was in a sweat, very hot and frightened." Then, as if a giant switch had been pulled, "the whole mass of surviving Russians – and there were still thousands of them – simply stopped dead about a kilometre from us, as if on order. We wondered what was happening ... they were discarding their equipment. Then they turned about to face us. All the enormous sacrifice they had made had been in vain. They simply sat down on the spot and we received orders to go in and round them up."[10] Red Army resistance – so strong for so long – simply fell away, and on Friday 26 September, ceased. All over the gargantuan battlefield, dispirited Soviet soldiers raised their hands and began to numbly file into German captivity.

As the shooting stopped, the similarly exhausted Germans could begin to survey what they had achieved; it was truly daunting. Wilhelm Moldenhauer in *17. Armee* wrote to tell his family, "A great new victory has been achieved here, which is still not being made public for understandable reasons." Despite the young infantryman's reticence, Nazi propaganda was lightning quick to leap on the Army's success, with *Signal* magazine publishing extensive coverage of the battle's aftermath under the headline of "Ruins as far as the eye can see". Back home a *Sondermeldung* (Special Broadcast) on the radio claimed the capture of 150,000 prisoners by 22 September, and the newspapers were filled with photographs of wrecked Soviet equipment and endless lines of dejected captives. The Nazi Party rag, the *Völkischer Beobachter*, called it "the greatest battle of annihilation of all time", and for once they could almost be forgiven the exaggeration. Wilhelm Prüller wrote in his diary,

"I can't describe how the enemy vehicles look ... and how many there are – at least two thousand. In a curve they were standing four abreast, apparently knocked out by Stukas. Hundreds of skeleton vehicles were sitting there, burned out right down to the iron frame." A Nazi newspaper report echoed Prüller's description: "1,500 Soviet vehicles are lying in chaotic confusion in the ring around Kiev ... tanks of all sizes from the light 15-tonner to the terrific monster weighing 52-tons were employed by the Soviets in the fight against the German units where their fate overtook them. As a result of the increasingly heavy blows dealt at Soviet industry, this figure represents an important part of the annual production in Soviet Russia."

Alongside the triumphal nature of the article, there seems to be an almost pleading tone – surely this victory spelt the end for the Soviet Union? "The amount of material of all arms either captured or destroyed in the great encirclement battle of Kiev will greatly weaken the enemy. These tremendous losses cannot be made good by deliveries from Great Britain and America." Eyewitnesses confirmed the massive haul, with one *landser* writing to his family, "The defeat of the enemy is huge ... the place is a giant arsenal of abandoned vehicles, wagons, weapons of all kinds, including heavy guns. Moreover, thousands of abandoned horses graze in the nearby area ... in the attempt to break out towards the north hundreds of Russians were mown down by machine-guns."[11]

For grieving families, identification of the dead was often impossible, as one *landser* explained. "The Russians had a sort of dog-tag around their necks, but because of their superstitious beliefs that if you wore them you'd get killed, many of them just threw them away." Among the piles of Soviet dead were many female soldiers, an inevitable consequence of Moscow's total war policy. The *landsers* called them rifle sluts and despised their presence on a battlefield they considered the sole preserve of men. Two soldiers were later secretly recorded discussing the subject:

"The women fought like wild beasts."

"What did you do with the women?"

"Oh, we shot them too."

Despite the callousness of the response, the majority of German soldiers shuddered to see women's corpses clad in earth brown uniforms and hideously mutilated by shells and machine-gun fire.

A medical officer in Model's *3. Panzerdivision* couldn't help but dwell on the appalling slaughter he saw all around him: "It is a picture of horror. Corpses of men and horses scattered among vehicles and equipment of all types. Ambulances are turned over ... it's chaos."[12] Max Kuhnert said of it: "We saw so many corpses lying by the roadside, and pieces of bodies, some of them scorched or charred from the heat of the guns or exploding shells." The cavalry NCO was clearly scarred by the sight of so much death. "One could actually become jealous of others who got wounded – not badly mind you – but just enough to get them home or at least away from this place of slaughter, stench and utter destruction."[13] The anonymous SS trooper was likewise astonished at the destruction: "We work our way through village after village, the enemy has abandoned great masses of vehicles and material." At the same time he could look on the bright side. "We reached Romny, and here for the first time we get a beer issue."

Battles and campaigns are measured by numbers as much as anything else, and in that regard Kiev was and is a statistician's paradise. However, the claims and counter-claims of two totalitarian dictatorships very happy to tell lies and falsehoods makes the job of accurately quantifying casualties a difficult task. What is undisputed is that Soviet losses in the encirclement were jaw-dropping, and of a scale not seen before or since. It was the Nazis who got their tallies in first, and it is their numbers which have become those quoted again and again ever since. On 28 September, Goebbels authorised another *Sondermeldung*, which gave the German people the following figures: 343 aircraft, 884 tanks and 3,718 guns captured or destroyed, and no fewer than 665,000 POWs taken, with another hundred thousand killed. Adding in the wounded, total Red Army casualties topped one million. Four entire Soviet armies were wiped off the Red Army's Order of Battle, and a further two were reduced to remnants.

The Soviets vigorously disputed these rather hastily produced numbers, and there is good reason to doubt them, although Moscow's claim that total losses were 616,000 – including killed and missing – looks on the low side. Much of the disparity almost certainly came from Soviet unwillingness to admit the scale of the catastrophe on one side, and the Germans' rather breezy way of estimating the prisoner haul on the other. One man who wasn't among the prisoners was Colonel-General Mikhail P. Kirponos – the pocket commander after Semyon Budenny was airlifted out – he had tried to break out with his men only to be killed along with his entire staff. His courageous leadership of the defence would be belatedly recognised after the war.

For Stalin and the STAVKA, Kiev was a mind-numbing defeat. The Southern and Southwestern Fronts – the largest field formations in the entire Red Army – had disappeared, and with them had gone most of Ukraine. The Crimea was under direct threat, and with it the home of the Soviet Black Sea fleet at Sevastopol. There was now very little standing in the way of Rundstedt's army group, and a path was open all the way to the far-off city of Rostov on Don – the gateway to the fabled Caucasus.

Morale back in the Reich soared, with internal Nazi Party reports detailing a huge uplift in the public mood, with all the talk once more being of final victory. At the front, too, Kiev was a major shot in the arm. Hans-Erdmann Schönbeck – a young officer in *11. Panzerdivision* – said: "The victory at Kiev made a deep impression on me. When they said, 'we've done it!' I felt an incredible sense of triumph. It was an overwhelming experience seeing the long lines of enemy prisoners going past."[14] Gustav Böker in *6. Armee* wrote home expressing a common view among *landsers* that surely there was no way the Red Army could continue the fight given the scale of its losses in the battle: "In just one day our Division took seven hundred prisoners. A large number of the prisoners were in new uniforms and had only been soldiers for two weeks. I think now that the Russian war will soon be over. My wildest hopes are that the war here will be over by mid-October and I can then celebrate my birthday in the peaceful East or even back in Germany. You can only hope and wish for the best."[15]

The Germans had smashed the door down, now all they had to do was walk through it – but how, and with what? German losses were nothing like those of the Red Army, but were enough to cripple an already wounded *Ostheer*. Mikhail Kirponos and his gallant defence had cost the Germans 26,856 dead, 100,000 wounded and 5,000 missing. As ever, it was the front-line companies that suffered disproportionately, with one *Obergefreiter* in *98. ID* noting that "we've had losses of 75 per cent in our *kompanie*". He had little faith in the promised reinforcements.

By the end of the battle, the *SS-Reich*'s *Deutschland Regiment* had lost 1,519 men killed, wounded or missing since the beginning of the campaign – its sister regiment, the mainly-Austrian *Der Führer*, about the same. That was half their manpower. Some replacements had indeed arrived, but nowhere near enough to fill the gaping holes in the ranks. One of those few was Walter Schminke, a young SS trooper trained as a mortarman, who described his bizarre introduction both to his new regiment, and to the Soviet Union itself, when he was dropped off by truck somewhere near the front after Kiev. "An *Oberschar* stood on a wooden box and called out names ... he came up to me and asked my age. 'Twenty, *Oberschar*!' 'Right then, you take this group to the motorcycle battalion. From here march straight for two kilometres, then turn left and march another three kilometres. Turn right and march another four kilometres. You'll come to a tree and there'll be a guide from the battalion to take you the rest of the way.' So, there we were, no weapons, no compass, no officer or NCO, told to march across Russia ... somehow, we found the tree and the guide. He was dressed in Russian clothing and I only recognised him because of the German pistol at his belt."

Schminke soon realised that the reality of the Eastern Front was nothing like the propaganda of the newsreels back home. "When we arrived we had a special meal; thick pea soup which tasted great ... the atmosphere in the *bataillon* was excellent, no parade ground bullshit ... we went down to the banks of the river and we thirty-six men sung the *bataillon* anthem. We heard applause coming from the other bank – it was the Russians – then they sang a song and we applauded, was this really what the front was like?"

The *SS-Reich* was lucky to get Schminke and his fellow replacements. Back in Germany the depots were near deserted, with only 46,000 men in training at the end of September. It wasn't just a manpower problem either, equipment was also in short supply, with the Army having lost 1,488 armoured fighting vehicles of all types and only having received a fraction of that number in return. But the *Ostheer*'s most cavernous gaps were to be found among its transport fleet. Trucks are not glamorous pieces of military kit. Trucks are work-a-day, functional items that inspire neither fear, awe nor martial pride – trucks are never at the forefront of any military parade. However, what they lack in kerb appeal they more than make up for in utility. Outside of the railways and horses, in the Soviet Union it was trucks that moved everything: men, ammunition, fuel, food, spares and every other item in the panoply of logistics that the *Ostheer* required. Unfortunately for that same *Ostheer*, trucks were not high on the priority list for German war production. This was something that Adolf von Schell understood only too well.

On the eve of Barbarossa, Adolf von Schell was probably the most important German officer almost no one has ever heard of. A native of Magdeburg in Saxony-Anhalt, he had fought in the First World War, winning both classes of Iron Cross, and had then served with the *Freikorps* before joining the *Reichswehr*. A stint in the US as an infantry instructor had opened his eyes to the benefits of military mechanization, and had also made him painfully aware of the chasm between modern American society – driven by oil and the internal combustion engine – and his own impoverished nation drowning under the economic tsunami of the Great Depression and hyperinflation.

He returned to Germany evangelising on military motorisation, and Berlin took note; in 1938 he was made undersecretary in the Ministry of Transport and the General Plenipotentiary for Motor Vehicles in Hermann Goering's macroeconomic Four-Year Plan. His brief was nothing less than the wholesale mechanization of the entire *Wehrmacht* – a task akin to the labours of Hercules. Like every military force, the *Wehrmacht* was to all intents and purposes a reflection of the society from which it was drawn. For von Schell that meant trying to mechanize an army when the country from which it sprang was in many ways almost pre-industrial. Nazi Germany – like fascist Italy – had élite motor companies, such as Mercedes-Benz and Audi, but little in the way of mass manufacturers; on Schell's accession to his new role the German automotive industry produced no fewer than 131 types of truck and fifty-two separate car models, and its only contender for mass market production, Ferdinand Porsche's Type 60 (which would become famous as the iconic VW Beetle), was still only a prototype. The building of the *autobahnen* had been a prestige project that had showcased the Nazis' desire for modernity, but it also highlighted the backwardness of German society – those self-same gleaming concrete lanes were conspicuously empty of vehicles – and no vehicles meant no garages or mechanics to maintain them or petrol stations to fill them up.

Von Schell was also handicapped by the industrial structure of the time. The Nazis may have believed that the State should have extensive and extraordinary powers in many aspects of German life, but not, it seems, in its industrial (or agricultural for that matter) base. This translated into a lack of executive authority delegated to Schell to force the multitude of producers to do as he wished – instead, Berlin advised him to use persuasion.

The result was the Schell Plan, submitted to government in March 1939 and approved on New Years Day 1940. The Plan had three major elements. The first was the compulsory requisitioning of half of all Germany's civilian truck fleet for military use. The second was the establishment of the Home Motor Pool Organisation, whereby all repair facilities and garages in the Reich would come under *Wehrmacht* control while remaining privately owned; the idea being that military needs would take precedence, but civilian use would still be allowed. Lastly – and most importantly – the plethora of car and truck models available in the country was drastically reduced, with car types almost halved, and the number of truck models cut down to just one-sixth of their pre-Plan total.

Despite these radical measures, Schell was pessimistic about the *Wehrmacht*'s ability to motorise, writing to Goering himself to complain about desperately needed raw materials being switched from truck production to other sectors of the war economy: "Once this has happened then an increase in production is unimaginable for several years. This would damage the motorisation of the *Wehrmacht*, the Reich and commerce, from which it would struggle to recover." Never keen on inconvenient truths, the Nazi leadership's response followed its usual pattern, with Schell at first promoted in an effort to shut him up. When that didn't work, he was compulsorily retired into the *Führerreserve*. The mild-mannered Schell's legacy was a job left unfinished. His efforts succeeded in significantly increasing the motor vehicle pool the *Wehrmacht* could draw upon, but left the great majority of divisions untouched by mechanisation, and still reliant on horses and the marching man.

As it was, the *Wehrmacht* could now rely on three truck types above all: Opel's Blitz 3.6, the Bogward B 3000 and the Mercedes-Benz L3000. All were simple designs, with the latter being more rugged than the others and using all-wheel drive as standard – a definite advantage on what passed for roads in the Soviet Union. The real problem was that there was never anywhere near enough of any of them. Opel only manufactured 130,000 of the *Blitz* in total – and many of them were made pre-war – while there were even fewer Bogward and Mercedes, with only about 30,000 built of each. That was a drop in the ocean compared to what was required. In fact, the peak production year for German-made trucks was 1943, when 109,000 rolled off the production lines. This was roughly the number the *Wehrmacht* would lose in the first half of that same year. By comparison, the US shipped the Soviet Union more than 400,000 trucks and jeeps during the war under the Lend-Lease programme – the majority of the former being big, heavy, four-wheel-drive workhorses.

To help fill the gap the Nazis turned to wholesale requisitioning, i.e. state theft, of any and every vehicle they could lay their hands on in the occupied countries. At first, this was restricted to the military vehicle parks of their defeated foes, but it was soon extended to include civilian vehicles as well, as troops stripped farms and businesses in France, Belgium, the Netherlands and Scandinavia – the knock-on effect in industry and food production was huge.

All of these stop-gap measures enabled the *Wehrmacht* to mechanize a minority of its combat formations for Barbarossa, but exposed more problems such as a lack of spare parts and maintenance expertise. This was the reason why Walther Nehring's *18. Panzerdivision* fielded over one hundred different truck models in its ranks as it crossed the Soviet border. Those same trucks – particularly the most common French Laffly and Berliet models – were totally unsuited for the primitive road conditions prevalent in the eastern campaign. The result was entirely predictable: a haemorrhaging of truck stocks as they broke down in the mud and sand.

A full month before the end of the Kiev battle, Eduard Wagner, the Quartermaster of the Army, was warning Halder that the truck situation was "beginning to become more difficult. Replacements only possible in exceedingly small quantities". Wagner himself, having warned Halder, proceeded to do very little about it. The German military system was one where the best officers were steered towards front-line units, and those of lesser ability tended to fill the ranks of the supply and service branches. In truth, Wagner was nothing more than part and parcel of a system that set the *Wehrmacht* up to fail in the East.

Wagner himself was originally an artillery officer who had served in the First World War, and then stayed on in the *Reichswehr*. A number of staff jobs ended with him taking up his post as Quartermaster, but he had no particular expertise or flair for the role. In the spring of 1941, the senior *Sicherheitsdienst* officer Walter Schellenberg worked with him to organise future Army service support for the SS murder squads created to follow the advancing troops during Barbarossa. Schellenberg found the general "calm and objective", and his boss – Reinhard Heydrich no less – described him as "an extremely clever and able man". 'Able' he may have been when it came to arranging the transport and supply of several thousand lightly armed killers behind the front, but in terms of ensuring the greatest invasion force ever assembled had enough motor transport, rations, suitable clothing, fuel and ammunition, to do the job given them, then he was woefully lacking. As early as the invasion's second day, Helmut Pabst reported that "for breakfast we had a slice of bread, and for lunch the four of us shared an inch-thick crust", and as they hurried to keep up with the forward troops, "We had a problem on our hands ... our observation post wireless cart – a high-wheeled monstrosity which used to be a French Army ration wagon – had run off the road, and one of the horses had done a somersault in the traces." Pabst and his comrades weren't alone, with an SS trooper recalling that "the next morning breakfast was brought up – if you can call one piece of dry bread per man breakfast – but we were so hungry we ate it anyway". This was not the mark of an Army with a smoothly functioning supply chain, and Eduard Wagner must take a large measure of responsibility for the results.[16]

Those results were that of the 600,000 non-armoured motor vehicles (the figure includes motorcycles, cars, all motorised transport) the Germans began Barbarossa with, around a third had been written off by the end of the Kiev fighting. Germany's factories could send just 3,500 forward as replacements, and occupied Europe had been picked clean – the cupboard was bare. The outcome was what the noted historian David Stahel termed the 'de-modernisation of the *Ostheer*'. The problem wasn't confined to the Army either. The *Luftwaffe* was just as dependent on motor transport for its day-to-day supply needs, as well as for constant leapfrogging forward to keep its front-line *staffeln* in touch with the ground troops they were supporting. Red Army stragglers would often attack the *Luftwaffe* convoys as easy prey, and if anything, the air force's fall-out rates were even higher than the Army's, with over 80 per cent of its 100,000 wheeled vehicles soon inoperable. The serviceability situation was only partially relieved by the fact that the *Luftwaffe* didn't have to maintain as many aircraft as it had at the beginning of the campaign, with only some one thousand or so flight-worthy at September's end, from a starting fleet of over two and half times that number – mechanics more used to working on aircraft engines now found themselves spending hours under the bonnets of formerly French, Dutch and Czech trucks and cars.

The reality for the Germans – and Rundstedt's army group typified the situation – was that they were too worn down to seize a war-winning advantage from the Kiev bloodbath. No trucks meant no rapid drive east, even as the shattered Red Army scrambled to form a new defensive line in front of the exhausted victors. Kiev was a masterpiece of the operational art of warfare at which the Germans excelled, but it wasn't a strategic success in terms of causing a general collapse of the Red Army, or even of convincing the Soviet populace that defeat was likely at some future point, as Stalingrad would be for the Germans. Kiev was a twentieth-century Cannae writ large, and little more, and some of the men who'd won it knew that. One *Unteroffizier* wrote, "I have strong reservations whether we will see an end to the war in Russia this year ... Russia's military might is certainly broken, but the land is too big, and the Russians are not thinking of surrender." Otto Kumm – a senior *Waffen-SS* officer and decorated commander of *Der Führer* said, "In spite of all our self-confidence, a feeling of isolation crept over us when we advanced into the endless expanses of Russia. We didn't share the unfounded optimism of many who hoped that they might spend Christmas at home." This feeling of entering another world was captured in the words of an Army photographer: "We have no more maps and can only follow the compass needle to the east."

Not all *landsers* felt the same. Some, like Hans Roth, were initially exhilarated. He and his comrades stayed in central Kiev, at first wandering around the city they had just conquered, until a series of deafening explosions shattered the calm. The Soviets had left behind booby-traps and mines on timers, some of which were massive. Roth recalled the aftermath of one blast: "A huge mushroom cloud of smoke hangs over the city ... The local command station housed in the largest hotel in Kiev blew up and with it more large administrative buildings. A whole quarter of the city is burning, and under the debris there are several thousand civilians." The German authorities were quick to blame bandits and saboteurs, and that catch-all – the Jews – a scapegoat Roth for one was happy to accept: "All Jews without exception have until noon on the 25th to report. Sure, only half of them will show up, but they won't evade us ... the revenge for our comrades who lost their lives in the mine attacks is beginning. Now, twenty-four hours later, 2,000 Hebrews have already been sent to Jehovah!"

However, even Roth was shocked when he fell into conversation with a member of the SS killing squads dealing with the 'Hebrews'. The young SS trooper – he told Roth he was nineteen – described to the former graphic designer the killing operation he had just taken part in.

'For two days they had to dig fifty-metre-long trenches, each trench was calculated to be able to hold 250 Jews ... then, on the third day, when the trenches were ready, everybody, from babies to the oldest had to strip naked. The first 250 have to step to the edge of the ditch, the throaty barking of two machine-guns – the next ones are herded forward, they have to climb into the trench and position the dead bodies next to each other, no room must be wasted – the large spaces are neatly filled with dead children – forward, forward, more than fifteen hundred must fit in! Then the machine-guns rip the air again, here and there somebody moans, they are finished off ... this continues through the evening, we have so little time, so many Jews inhabit this country!' At first, I cannot speak at all. This young man talks about it as if he was on a casual pheasant hunt. I can't believe it's true and tell him so. He just laughs and says I should take a look.

Sure enough, Roth and several of his comrades cycled out to a ravine that cut through an outlying part of the city – the natural cutting was called Babi Yar. "What I see there is terrible, this is a picture I will never forget. At the edge of the gorge there are Jews standing, the machine-guns are whipping into them, they fall over the edge – fifty metres. Whoever is on the edge is swept down ... My God, my God, without a word I turn and run more than walk back to the city." What Roth had witnessed first-hand was one of the biggest discrete mass murders of the entire Holocaust. In the space of two days some 33,771 Jewish civilians were butchered by a combination of SS extermination squads, reserve police units from Hermann Franz's *Polizei-Regiment Süd*, and Ukrainian auxiliaries, all under the command of Paul Blobel – the SS officer who had obligingly supplied Gerhart Panning with human guinea pigs for his dumdum bullet experiments. One of Wilhelm Moldenhauer's comrades in 296. *ID* wrote of Babi Yar and the events that preceded it. "There have been fires for days already, all lit by the Jews ... for that the Jews aged between fourteen and sixty have been shot, and the wives of the Jews are still being shot, otherwise there'll be no end to it."

Fritz Höfer was an Army truck driver in Kiev when he was detailed on a collection job:

I had a Ukrainian with me. It was about 10am. On our way, we passed Jews marching in columns in the same direction we were going. They were carrying their belongings. There were whole families ... There were piles of clothes in a wide, open field. My job was to fetch them. I stopped the truck nearby, and the Ukrainians standing around started loading it. From where I was, I saw other Ukrainians meeting the Jews who arrived, men, women and children, and directing them to the place where, one after another, they were supposed to remove their belongings; coats, shoes, outer garments and even their underwear. They were supposed to put all their belongings together in a pile. Everything happened very quickly, the Ukrainians hurried along those who hesitated by kicking and pushing them. I think it took less than a minute from the moment a person took off his coat before he was standing completely naked. No distinction was made between men, women and children ... Naked Jews were led to a ravine about one hundred and fifty metres long, thirty metres wide and fifteen metres deep ... When they got closer to the edge of the ravine, members of the *Schützpolizei* [German 'protection' police] grabbed them and made them lie down over the corpses of the Jews who had already been shot. It took no time. The corpses were carefully laid down in rows. As soon as a Jew lay down, a man with a sub-machine gun shot them in the back of the head ... The Jews who descended into the ravine were so frightened by this terrible scene that they completely lost their will. You could even see some of them lying down in the row on their own and waiting for the shot to come. Only two men did the shooting. One of them was working at one end of the ravine, the other started at the other end. I saw them standing on the bodies and shooting one person after another. It was an extermination machine that made no distinction between men, women and children. Children were kept with their mothers and shot with them. I didn't watch for long. When I approached the edge, I was so frightened I couldn't look at it for long ... It was beyond my comprehension to see bodies twitching in convulsions and covered with blood ... The Ukrainians paid no attention to the noise and just kept forcing people through the passages into the ravine ... I concluded that the Jews had no idea what was actually happening. Even today I wonder why the Jews did nothing to challenge what was going on. Masses of people were coming from town and they did not seem to suspect anything. They thought they were just being relocated.

Kurt Werner was one of Blobel's murderers.

It was all hands on deck ... There were countless Jews gathered there and a place had been set up where the Jews had to hand in their clothes and their luggage. I saw a large natural ravine. The terrain there was sandy ... As soon as I arrived at the execution area, I was sent down to the bottom of the ravine with some of the other men. It wasn't long before the first Jews were brought to us over the side of the ravine. The Jews had to lie face down on the earth by the ravine walls. There were three groups of marksmen down at the bottom of the ravine, each made up of about twelve men. Groups of Jews were sent down to each of these execution squads simultaneously. Each successive group of Jews had to lie down on top of those that had already been shot. The marksmen stood behind the Jews and killed them with a shot in the neck.

Werner was proud of his fortitude in carrying out such a task: "It's almost impossible to imagine what nerves of steel it took to carry out the dirty work down there ... I had to spend the whole morning down in the ravine. For some of the time I had to shoot continuously. Then I was given the job of loading sub-machine gun magazines with ammunition. While I was doing that, other comrades were assigned to shooting duty. Towards midday we were called away from the ravine and in the afternoon I, with some of the others up at the top, had to lead the Jews to the ravine."

Anton Heidborn was a fellow member of Werner's death squad, and he remembered the aftermath of the orgy of killing:

The third day after the executions we were taken back to the killing area. On our arrival we saw a woman sitting by a bush who had apparently survived the execution unscathed. She was shot by the SD man who was accompanying us ... We also saw someone waving their hand from among the pile of bodies, I don't know whether it was a man or a woman ... The same day work began to cover up the piles of bodies. Civilians were used for this task. The ravine walls were partly blown up ... The next few days were spent smoothing out banknotes belonging to the Jews that had been shot. I estimate these must have totalled millions. I don't know what happened to the money. It was packed up in sacks and sent off somewhere.

Most of the stolen money and valuables were handed to the local Nazi authorities. The same authorities who on 30 September closed off the city to food supplies from the surrounding countryside as part of Herbert Backe's Hunger Plan. Kiev's pre-war population of 850,000 had already been halved by conscription, refugee flight and the slaughter of its Jewish citizens, and now checkpoints were set up around the city to ensure no food could get in for the remainder.

Hans Roth, though, could leave the nightmare behind him as he and his division left to re-join the advance east: "On the road once more! ... the destruction of the surrounded Armies is complete ... their endless rows pass us; maybe they're the same guys we fought for weeks ... gunfire destroyed mercilessly those who were trapped, it was insanity not to surrender. The long line of Soviets passes." The sudden burst of humanity he seemed to feel at Babi Yar was fast fading as he stared at the columns of dejected captives trudging by on the roadside: "What kind of people are they? In their eyes and their demeanour is something strange, something dull, completely un-European, even un-human." His old racist views resurfaced. "It is not the personal courage of the individual who is called to sacrifice his life for a greater idea, but the instinctive defence against danger ... what looks like courage is brutality!"

Another *landser* said much the same to his father:

The pitiful hordes on the other side are nothing but felons who are driven by alcohol and the threat of pistols at their heads. They are nothing but a bunch of assholes! ... Having encountered these bolshevik hordes, and having seen how they live, it has made a lasting impression on me. Everyone, even the last doubter, knows today that the battle against these *untermenschen*, who've been whipped into a frenzy by the Jews, was not only necessary but came in the nick of time. Our *Führer* has saved Europe from certain chaos.

9

Germany's Shame

The murder of unarmed Red Army prisoners had been part and parcel of Barbarossa since day one. One German soldier wrote home at the beginning of the campaign describing his experiences of the fighting so far: "The Russian is a tough opponent ... we hardly take any prisoners, we shoot them all instead."[1]

This admission – shocking as it is – wasn't the exception. The killing was widespread and accepted. It was also common knowledge. Again and again in correspondence home, soldiers talked about shooting Red Army captives. With the sheer volume of letters home making censorship little more than perfunctory, the soldiery felt no fear in writing about what they'd seen and done. It is impossible to state with any real accuracy just how many Soviet prisoners were killed by front-line units at the point of their surrender or shortly afterwards, but given the sheer mountain of evidence, the number must run into the tens of thousands at the very least.

This sort of behaviour by members of the *Wehrmacht* did not start with Barbarossa. Since war had broken out in the autumn of 1939, German soldiers across multiple theatres had committed atrocities against the men they had taken captive; the massacres of Poles at Goworowo and Złoczew, and British POWs at Le Paradis and Wormhoudt, predated the invasion. There were reports of the killing of captured French colonial troops – black Africans prominent among them – seemingly on grounds of racial inferiority. The German historian Raffael Scheck identified that anywhere between one thousand and fifteen hundred French colonial soldiers were shot after surrendering in the June 1940 fighting. French authorities investigated after the war and a number of mass graves were found, including that of thirty-six Senegalese from the *4e Division d'Infanterie Coloniale*, or

4e DIC (4th Colonial Infantry Division), in a farmyard near the village of Erquinvillers, in the Oise.[2] Another historian, Robert Forcyk, unearthed an official French report that quoted an unnamed German officer discussing the killing of black African POWs: "An inferior race does not deserve to do battle with a civilized race such as the Germans." All these incidents were shocking, but they were also – thankfully – the exception rather than the norm.

Appalling as this was – and make no mistake it was – in the white heat of battle, and in its immediate aftermath, rage, fear and bloodlust sometimes got the better of individuals, and prisoners could be shot out of hand straight away; this is an abhorrent aspect of war, and not one limited to the German *Ostheer*. To mitigate against this potential savagery, militaries and governments the world over put in place checks and balances to prevent just such behaviour – starting with every level of command from the most junior NCO and upwards. For the *Wehrmacht*, Barbarossa saw the wholesale abandonment of that structure of safeguards. Kurt Meissner – the young anti-tank officer on the picket line at Kiev – described his own units behaviour during the first days of the campaign: "No prisoners were taken … if we felt we couldn't collect or care for prisoners then they were 'killed in action'."[3] The gunnery officer Siegfried Knappe saw it too: "Our soldiers went berserk … they took no prisoners and left no one alive in a trench or foxhole. I didn't try to stop them, nor did any other officer."[4]

As officers both Meissner and Knappe were culpable, but it was the *Wehrmacht*'s senior command who were setting the tone for what was acceptable. With the *Kommissarbefehl*, Germany's generals effectively licensed these aberrations to become the norm. Fuelling such acts was years of propaganda depicting bolsheviks and the peoples of the East as *untermenschen* whose racial inferiority made them unfit to live. In the weeks running up to the launch of Barbarossa the Army circulated a pamphlet to its soldiers containing the following passage:

> Anyone who has ever looked into the face of a Red commissar knows what the bolsheviks are. There is no need here for theoretical reflections. It would be an insult to animals if one were to call the features of these, largely Jewish, tormentors of people, beasts. They are the embodiment of the infernal, of the personified insane hatred of everything that is noble in humanity. In the shape of these commissars we witness the revolt of the subhuman against noble blood.

Rabid to the point of insanity as this appears today, this was par for the course at the time, and just one drop amidst the torrent of poison. There is no denying it had an effect.

The panzer gunner Karl Fuchs spoke for many *landsers* when he described the Soviets to his wife: "Hardly ever do you see the face of a person who seems rational and intelligent. They all look emaciated, and the wild, half-crazy look in their eyes makes them appear like imbeciles. And these scoundrels, led by Jews and criminals, wanted to imprint their stamp on Europe, indeed on the world. Thank God that our *Führer*, Adolf Hitler, is preventing this from happening."[5]

The Soviets were also only too capable of indulging in bestial behaviour, as Hermann Heiss knew only too well. Surrounded and forced to surrender along with some 180 of his comrades, Heiss and his fellow prisoners were herded into a nearby field of clover and ordered to strip naked. Red Army soldiers proceeded to help themselves to anything they considered of value: watches, rings and so on. When one wounded man was undressing too slowly for the liking of one of the guards, he was shot dead in front of Heiss. Panic spread among the half-dressed men, and that's when the massacre started: "A Russian soldier stabbed me in the chest with his bayonet, at which point I turned over. I was then stabbed seven times in the back. I didn't move any more. The Russians thought I was dead ... I heard my comrades cry out in pain and then I passed out."[6] Heiss, along with eleven other survivors, was found alive but badly injured by advancing German soldiers; everyone else was dead.

A *Leutnant* Leichtfuss with *Heeresgruppe Mitte* saw the aftermath of another slaughter: "I found six of our men who'd been nailed to a table through their tongues, ten more had been hung from meat hooks, and some more had been thrown down a well and stoned to death." Given what he'd seen, Leichtfuss saw no issue with retribution; "So, when we captured a small detachment of Russians – it was about ten to fifteen men ... they were locked in a room and three or four grenades were flung in through the window."[7]

Very quickly after the start of the invasion, every *landser* in the *Ostheer* had heard of Soviet atrocities and was only too aware of their fate if captured by the Soviets. "They shot at our convoys despite them having red crosses on them, and they killed wounded German soldiers as well as shooting many soldiers on the spot after surrendering." Over 9,000 German soldiers were reported as Missing in Action in the month of July, a further 7,830 in August and 4,900 in September, with the majority taken prisoner. However, only a tiny minority made it to the horrors of a Soviet POW camp, with an estimated nine out of ten being killed immediately on capture. Red Army unit records confirm this ugly truth. On 13 July 1941, the Red Army's 26th Rifle Division reported on the day's fighting to the west of the town of Slastena, near Pskov. It detailed that along with those it had killed in the fighting, "some eighty Germans had surrendered and were executed".

Savagery begat savagery, as each side justified its own behaviour in light of the other's actions. A young *Waffen-SS* recruit recalled listening to his platoon commander telling of his experiences during Barbarossa: "Our *Zugführer* said that in Russia they would assemble about a hundred prisoners and make them march over any minefields they found so they'd blow up their own mines."[8] Behaviour like this was common knowledge, as Gotthard Heinrici wrote to his family: "The Russian has behaved bestially towards our wounded, and now our people are clubbing and shooting to death anything in a brown uniform. Both sides are driving each other on so there are enough corpses to fill whole mausoleums." German divisional war diaries are filled with the truth of Heinrici's statement. *Heeresgruppe Nord*'s *61. Infanterie-Division* reported that three of its members were captured by the Soviets, and later found murdered. The divisional commander – Siegfried Haenicke – ordered ninety-three prisoners shot the next day in reprisal.

As touched upon earlier, ever since the war, a concerted effort has been made by apologists for the *Wehrmacht* that atrocities were almost solely the responsibility of Nazi thugs and functionaries, usually operating under the catch-all banner of the SS, that multitudinous octopus of an organisation that managed to insert its tentacles into almost every aspect of German life. In contrast, the various service branches of the *Wehrmacht* – and most notably the Army – were free from such stains. This is the myth of the clean *Wehrmacht*, and myth it is. Typical of the lie are the claims of one German infantry commander, who wrote in his much-publicised memoirs that all the battles fought by his men were "always fairly conducted, though tough and bitter". Such claims were widely believed not only in Germany but abroad, with the British military historian Captain Basil Liddell Hart writing that "the German Army in the field on the whole observed the rules of war better than in 1914–18".[9] The mass of evidence available strongly refutes this statement, in particular regarding one of the greatest crimes of the war: the murder of between two and a half and three and a half million unarmed Soviet POWs in makeshift camps over the summer and autumn of 1941. The aftermath of the Kiev battle put this horrific crime front and centre.

From the front seat of his signals truck, Wilhelm Moldenhauer wrote to his wife Erika as he watched prisoners begin their march west after the fall of Kiev. "The column of the defeated has no end. That an army thrown together from this mishmash of peoples can fight so hard is astonishing. It clearly only worked under the knout of the commissars."

Under the glare of the late summer sun, those endless columns were soon crazed with hunger and thirst, as Martin Meier told his father: "Many have only eaten berries during the last few days. When they saw green cucumbers, they fell upon them like wild animals ... Such is the situation."[10]

Another *landser* had a far more dreadful story to tell: "When they took the Russian prisoners back, they had nothing for them to eat for three to four days, and so they collapsed. Then a guard would go up to one, bash him on the head and he would be dead, and the others would set on him, cut him up and eat him." This might seem far-fetched, but the charge of cannibalism was repeatedly made. "When one of the prisoners died, the Russians often ate him while he was still warm. That's a fact."

None of these witnesses were die-hard Nazis. They weren't former concentration camp guards, or members of SS extermination squads, they were ordinary German soldiers; Meier was a doting husband and worked as a bank clerk back in Berlin, while Moldenhauer was a shop keeper from Hanover who still subscribed to his local paper. Yet all described the brutal mistreatment of unarmed prisoners as unremarkable, the only thing worthy of note being to what level a starving man would go in order to survive.

What they witnessed were snapshots of a war crime that has never received the attention it deserves – a killing spree of such magnitude it is hard to comprehend. This killing wasn't systematic – there were no gas chambers, no railway timetables taking the victims to their secret doom, nor was there a huge flurry of officially documented *Aktionen*. This was mass murder by starvation, by disease, by neglect. It was not, though, as has so often been claimed by *Wehrmacht* apologists, murder by accident. The horrific maltreatment of Soviet POWs was the result of policy, and it was a policy in which the *Wehrmacht* was fully complicit. The architect was *General der Infanterie* Hermann Reinecke, a fifty-three-year-old Saxon veteran of the First World War. As head of the General Office of the Armed Forces, he promulgated regulations for the treatment of Soviet POWs that stated:

> The Bolshevist soldier has lost all claim to treatment as an honourable opponent … ruthless and energetic action must be taken at the slightest indication of insubordination … active or passive resistance must be broken immediately by force of arms … Anyone carrying out this order who does not use his weapons, or does so with insufficient energy, is punishable … Prisoners of war attempting escape are to be fired on without previous challenge. No warning shot must ever be fired … The use of arms against POWs is as a rule legal.

This was the foundation stone for the largest POW death toll in history.

Since the war began, the *Wehrmacht* had taken masses of prisoners: 675,000 in Poland, 1.8 million in France (the majority after the Armistice), and over 300,000 each in Yugoslavia and Greece, to name just a few of their earlier campaigns. This meant that by the advent of

Barbarossa, the *Wehrmacht* was the most experienced force on earth when it came to handling prisoners of war. Disarming them, placing them in camps of varying quality and comfort, feeding them, and generally looking after their needs as per the established rules of conflict was a process the Germans had become expert at out of necessity.

For Barbarossa, German high command knew they were facing an infinitely larger military force than anything they had so far tackled, and one they were convinced they would rapidly defeat, *ergo* they would either have to kill millions of men in battle or those same men would become POWs. Given that Hitler's mantra was that the invasion would cause the Soviet system to quickly collapse – "You only have to kick in the door and the whole rotten structure will come crashing down" – it would seem rational for the Germans to plan on taking several million captives in a short space of time. This would be no small undertaking. Simply providing food, water, medical support and basic shelter for anything like this number of men would be a herculean task, and it was a task *Wehrmacht* high command totally failed to prepare for.

With frontline units short on numbers, and almost constantly on the move, commanders were unwilling – and unable – to release men and resources to move detainees out of harm's way, and then escort them rearwards to designated collection points for further processing as mandated by the rules of war. Max Siry – a *generalleutnant* and divisional commander – thought he'd hit upon a solution to the problem:

> In the East I suggested to Korps that with thousands of prisoners coming back and no one to guard them – because we didn't have anyone to do it – then in France what had worked well, as the French were so degenerate, was that you would tell them to go to a certain place to be rounded up and they would do it, but in Russia that distance was 50 to 80 kilometres away, that was the distance between the armoured spearheads and the following infantry, so a march of two to three days, and I said, 'That's no good, we must cut off one of their legs, or break a leg or the right forearm, that way they can't fight us for the next four weeks and we can round them up later.' There was an outcry about it.

Siry wasn't joking.

In reality, groups of prisoners marching to the rear soon became columns, which then became rivers of men – all trudging west under minimal guard; but trudging where, and to what?

The *Wehrmacht*'s answer was the *Befehlshaber des rückwärtigen Heeresgebietes* (Army Rear Area Command). This was the ever-growing zone directly behind the front that was under military jurisdiction. Split into three separate regions to correspond with the three army groups, each command was then allocated three *Sicherungs-Divisionen* – security divisions.

The *Sicherungs-Divisionen* were smaller than normal infantry divisions, having only two, or sometimes even just one, infantry regiment, with the gaps filled by local levies, most notably Ukrainians and native Russians. The German rank and file were usually older reservists, as were their officers, and most had no front-line combat experience. Meagrely equipped with small arms, they lacked heavy weapons, the few they did have usually being *beutewaffen*, often French or Soviet, salvaged from one or more of the encirclement battles. Even this fig leaf was often removed as the front took precedence, and heavy weapons were reallocated forward at a moment's notice, leaving the security units unsupported. The transport situation was the same; motor vehicles were in short supply, so the horse and cart took the strain. Given the fact that each division had to cover a truly vast territory, this was an incredibly difficult deficiency to overcome.

At thirty-seven years old, Berliner Kurt Miethke was a member of just such a security formation. Formally titled a *landsschütze,* a territorial type designation, Miethke was a former goldsmith, a profession in which he no doubt would have come across, and worked with members of Germany's Jewish community. Regardless, he made plain his disdain for Jews when he wrote to his wife about what he saw in Russia: "There is not much going on here, it is a dirty, dusty area with about 40,000 inhabitants, of whom two-thirds are Jews. You can't imagine what the Abraham's walking around here are like, so dirty and ragged."

The senior officers who led the likes of Miethke weren't the pick of the bunch either. The officer responsible for the entire rear area was none other than Eduard Wagner, the same Wagner who, as Quartermaster General, commanded the *Ostheer*'s under-performing logistics system. Of the three generals who reported to him on rear area security, one was Max von Schenckendorff, responsible for *Rückwärtiges Heeresgebiet Mitte* (Army Group Centre Rear Area). At sixty-seven years old, von Schenckendorff had had an undistinguished career, was overly fond of good food and long holidays back in the Reich, and was no one's idea of a young charger. Wagner's other commanders were two first cousins, Franz and Karl von Roques, responsible for the north and south respectively. All three would preside over vast tracts of occupied territory that would become charnel houses as they acted according to the regulations set out by their fellow general, Hermann Reinecke.

Hugely under-resourced, the Rear Area commands were nevertheless given an array of tasks, among which were the rounding up of slave labour, the mass theft of foodstuffs and the destruction of enemy partisans – the latter a programme initially entitled *Partisanenkrieg* – Partisan War – before becoming *Bandenbekämpfung*, or bandit fighting, a euphemism for the shooting of anyone the Nazis considered a potential threat or racial enemy, including Jews and Communist Party functionaries. One German soldier wrote home explaining his role in the *Bandenbekämpfung*: "I'm one of those who are reducing the number of partisans. I put them against the wall and they get a bullet in the head, a very merry and interesting job … My point of view – this nation deserves only the knout, only by such methods can they be educated. Yesterday I saw the shooting of forty partisans … I am convinced that we are the masters and they are all *untermenschen*."[11]

It was in the Rear Area zone, immediately behind the advancing front, that the majority of prisoners were first concentrated in makeshift collection points as their initial captors re-joined their units and continued the advance eastwards. Sometimes, even this rudimentary level of care was forsaken by overstretched frontline divisions. "Prisoners were simply sent to the rear unguarded as every available man was desperately needed at the front."[12]

Most prisoners were marched to the rear on foot, but some were put on trains, not a distinction that conferred any sort of preferential treatment, as Hans Reimann of *10. Panzerdivision* made clear to his *Luftwaffe* comrade, Georg Neuffer:

> It was gruesome. I was there when they transported Russian POWs from Korosten [in Ukraine] to just outside L'viv. They were driven like cattle from the rail trucks to drinking troughs and bludgeoned to keep in ranks … they rushed to them and drank like beasts. Then they were driven back into the wagons – there were sixty or seventy to each cattle truck. Each time the train halted ten of them were taken out dead from each cattle truck, having suffocated from lack of oxygen … I asked one of the guards, a *feldwebel*, how long this had been going on and he said 'Well, I've been doing this for four weeks, I can't stick it much longer, I have to get away.' I asked him if he had any food for them at all and he said, 'We haven't anything, nothing has been prepared at all.'

Reimann's revelation was no surprise to Neuffer: "I know, I often travelled along the route they took the prisoners on – the roadside ditches were full of shot Russians. Cars had even driven over them, it was ghastly."[13]

Hans von Luck saw one of the Army's rudimentary POW camps: "We were given a few days' rest, one of which I used to go to a makeshift collection camp for prisoners that had recently been set up. In it were penned thousands of Russian POWs in a closely packed space with no protection from the hot sun or torrential rain showers." His instinctive compassion was tinged with the Nazis' 'unfeeling animal horde' attitude: "They seemed apathetic, their faces without expression. Their uniforms, which were simple but practical, were dull and emphasised the impression of a grey mass. Because of the danger of lice their heads had been close-cropped. They seemed resigned to their fate … many of them called out to me for 'voda' – water, they were suffering terribly from thirst." Luck swiftly pinned the blame for the terrible conditions on the sheer numbers of prisoners, rather than looking past that to the criminal lack of preparation. "Our services behind the lines hadn't been prepared for so many prisoners. With the best intentions in the world they were quite unable to look after them and evacuate them quickly. I felt sorry for them, for they too were human beings like ourselves." Luck's sympathy was real no doubt, but unlikely to assuage the thirst of the wretched thousands.

The young panzer officer was one of many German witnesses to what was going on that long, hot summer. Franz Xaver Dorsch was a senior civil engineer in the paramilitary construction body, the *Organisation Todt*. On an official visit to Minsk on 10 July 1941, he visited a camp in the city: "The prisoners are packed so tightly together they can hardly move and have to relieve themselves where they stand … the small size of the guard unit – it was about 200-strong – means that it can only control the camp by using the most brutal level of force. The problem of feeding the prisoners is virtually insoluble. Some of them have been without food for six to eight days." The Minsk captives were among the hundreds of thousands of prisoners who were simply starving to death.[14] Not that this was a surprise. Erich von Manstein – so often cited as a paragon of the German officer caste – circulated an order to his own command that stated, "The food situation at home makes it essential that the troops should, as far as possible, be fed off the land and in enemy cities a large part of the population will have to go hungry. Nothing … may, out of a misguided sense of humanity, be given to prisoners or to the population unless they are in the service of the German *Wehrmacht*."

Not all *Wehrmacht* units followed this dictum. The *24. Infanterie-Division* went so far as to make a written complaint about the camps to Karl von Roques as the responsible officer, after it herded thousands of captives back from the Kiev fighting. In particular, its commander, Hans von Tettau, cited huge overcrowding at the Oleksandriya and Novoukrainka camps. However, von Tettau's moral stance was somewhat tarnished when he admitted that more than a thousand prisoners had been shot en route or died from exhaustion while under his division's tender care.[15] Max Kuhnert saw the misery: "The columns seemed not to end. Many of the poor fellows were wounded and limping. All were

in tatters, their faces in utter despair."[16] His divisional commander;
Generalleutnant Friedrich von Broich, was secretly recorded at the Trent
Park holding facility in north London telling his fellow prisoners what
he witnessed: "We marched down the road and a column of about 6,000
tottering figures went past, completely emaciated, helping each other
along. Every one to two hundred metres or so, two or three men would
collapse. Soldiers of ours on bicycles rode alongside them with pistols;
everyone who collapsed was shot and thrown into the ditch by the side
of the road ... At night they howled like wild beasts ... they hadn't got
anything to eat."

So the truth was that the *Wehrmacht* had made few – if any –
preparations to care for Soviet POWs. The small number of troops made
available to the Rear Area Commands were intended to primarily act
as a security force to police the *Wehrmacht*'s lines of communication
back to the Reich, and were only reluctantly detached from that role
to help administer the newly established system of camps. Into those
camps – most of them nothing more than a patch of land surrounded
by a barbed wire fence and nothing more – hundreds of thousands of
hapless prisoners were herded and left to rot from lack of space, shelter,
water, food and medical attention. This was no accident – this was policy.

As early as 8 July, an *OKW* order was sent to all units stating that
for POWs, "Russian medical personnel, doctors and medical supplies
are to be used first" – German medical services were to be reserved for
Germans. *Wehrmacht* transport was not to be used to move prisoners,
although *in extremis* badly wounded POWs could use the Soviet horse-
drawn cart – the *panje* wagon. Even then, German requirements were to
be paramount. On 6 August, the *OKW* then declared that Soviet POWs
capable of work were to receive 2,200 calories per day, and those not
capable of work 2,040 calories per day. This allocation was subsequently
slashed to 1,490 calories a day but rarely – if ever – provided. Eduard
Wagner would later declare to a meeting of his senior commanders that
"non-working prisoners of war in the camps are to starve". In reality this
exhortation extended to working prisoners as well. A German Red Cross
nurse arriving for her first eastern posting saw a nearby POW camp, the
occupants staring at her "like skeletal animals hanging on the barbed
wire fence".

Sanctioned neglect was the main killer in the camps, but it wasn't the
only one. A *Leutnant* Riebel – company commander in *Polizeibataillon
322* – reported to his superiors that "in the early morning hours of
10 August, the liquidation of the Jews lodged in the Bialowieza prisoner
collection camp was carried out by *3. Kompanie*. Seventy-seven
male Jews between sixteen and forty-five were shot. The *Aktion* was
performed without incident." Whether or not the murdered prisoners

were actually Jewish or not, is, of course, irrelevant. The fact was that by carrying out the killings, Riebel and his men were both fulfilling the Jewish extermination policy and reducing the number of captives the German authorities had to deal with.

The Germans' only real consideration regarding POWs was to prevent escape. Kurt Miethke wrote to his wife about his duties at a camp near Rovno in western Ukraine: "Today I have a guard shift again near a part of the camp where there are many graves, as many as two thousand. You wouldn't stay here for ten minutes. But this can no longer shake us, you get used to it. We are only bothered by the rain and the cold." He described conditions in the camp and its daily routine of horror. "The Russians are still so wild, but we don't let ourselves be disturbed and if there is no other way, then there is a bang (Miethke is talking about shooting prisoners). We still have ten to twelve thousand here today, and some twenty to thirty die every day." Miethke at one and the same time sympathised with his charges, while also being prepared to shoot them down in droves: "Fifteen hundred Russians arrived again. These were the most pitiful figures. We also take care of our safety, and we now have several machine-gun towers and if we need to then there will be a hail of blue beans (bullets, once again Miethke is referring to shooting prisoners)." Throughout, the former goldsmith peppers his letters with endearments to his wife and talk of mundane household issues. "It won't be long before we can be together again my darling. I think the war will end ... the Russians only have another four to five weeks, then it will all be over for them. Have you already paid for the insurance?" He also constantly updated his wife on the food he and his comrades were being provided with – "it's good and there's plenty of it" – while watching as thousands of men starved to death just yards away. This ghastly blindness – perhaps classified in modern terminology as dissociative identity disorder – is probably the best way to define men like Miethke who saw the horror with their own eyes but lived with it.

Many would fall back on what could, or would, happen to them if they didn't follow orders or objected in any way to what was going on – known as *Befehlnotstand*. Edmund Bonhoff was one who used that defence: "We all had to do our duty, or we'd have been punished. If any of us had said 'we don't want to fight' or anything like that then we'd have been shot ourselves, we all knew others who'd been shot, they did it often enough."[17] There is some truth in that. In the First World War, the Imperial German Army executed forty-eight men for desertion; during the Second that figure was 15,000, with another 5,000 condemned for 'defeatism' or 'subversion of national defence'. Most were shot, some were hanged, and a small number guillotined. In comparison, the Red Army had shot 10,201 deserters by October 1941 alone, while the

United States convicted 20,000 of its troops for desertion during the war, although only the incredibly unlucky Eddie Slovik was actually executed.

The fear of punishment – and the sense of shame a crime such as desertion would bring on the individual and their family – was a powerful force, as one junior German officer pointed out: "I must be clear, if I disobeyed orders I would have been put against the wall and executed – no doubt about that. Many men suffered that fate and were hanged in Germany."[18] Where this defence has far less validity was outside the specific military crime of desertion. Heinrich Einsiedel was clear about the rules of the time: "At the military academy we were told that we could refuse an order that was criminal or senseless. You didn't have to obey an order to jump from the fourth floor for example." As the historian Manfred Oldenburg noted in his 2004 book *Ideology & Military Calculation*, there were no known cases of action being taken against soldiers who had refused to take part in killings. Christopher Browning said the same in his revelatory book, *Ordinary Men*, about the involvement in mass murder of the reservists of *Polizeibataillon 101*: "No defence attorney or defendant in any of the hundreds of post-war trials has been able to document a single case in which refusal to obey an order to kill unarmed civilians resulted in the allegedly inevitable dire punishment."[19] Those men who didn't want to become killers found other ways of avoiding involvement, as Boris von Drachenfels recalled: "Every day about thirty men – sometimes as many as fifty to sixty – reported sick to get out of an *Aktion*." While it was true that men were derided by their superiors – and sometimes by their peers – for being weak and cowardly in their failure to take an active part in slaughter, it simply wasn't the case that your average German soldier was compelled on pain of death to play a role in the savagery.

Instead, they saw the officially sanctioned brutality all around them, and some took it as a licence to do as they pleased. Unsurprisingly this attitude was most prevalent among those involved day-to-day in the killing. SS death squad members would select pretty young Jewish girls from those marked for slaughter, and force them to have sex to stay alive. When the killer grew bored, or was moving to another area, the girls were shot in turn. Sexual violence wasn't limited to the SS by any means. One young Army officer recalled "a very stupid young *leutnant* from Frankfurt was talking about Russia, and he said 'We got hold of a female Russian spy in our area, we hit her on the head with a stick and flayed her backside with an unsheathed bayonet. Then we raped her, threw her out, shot at her and threw grenades at her. Every time one landed close she screamed. In the end she died, and we threw her body away.'"[20]

Two junior *Luftwaffe* NCOs talked about their duties in Ukraine: "Everywhere we saw women doing compulsory labour service."

"How frightful."

"They were employed on road-making – extraordinarily lovely girls; we drove past, simply pulled them into the armoured car, raped them and threw them out again, and did they curse!"

German soldiers would press-gang prisoners – sometimes even the wounded – into carrying out tasks they couldn't or wouldn't do, such as digging latrines or carrying extra ammunition, until they dropped from exhaustion – whereupon they'd be shot and another one grabbed to take their place. The line between violence as a necessity of war, and violence for its own sake, became increasingly blurred.

In a village in Russia there were partisans, and we obviously had to raze it to the ground without considering the casualties. We had one man called Brosicke from Berlin, he was only aged nineteen and a half or maybe twenty, anyway, if he saw anyone in the village he took them behind a house and shot them. The order was given that every tenth man in the village should be shot, but Brosicke said 'To hell with that, every tenth man', it's obvious that the whole village should be wiped out.' We filled beer bottles with petrol and put them on the tables in the houses, and then, as we left, we just threw hand-grenades behind us. Straightaway everything was burning – all the roofs were thatched – the women and children were shot, everyone was shot, only a few were partisans.[21]

The effect on any soldier's state of mind can be imagined.

Willy Peter Reese was a bespectacled young private soldier from the smoke-stack Ruhr city of Duisburg. Nicknamed 'pudding' at school due to his liking for desserts and a resulting rotund appearance, he was drafted into the Army and found himself playing his part in Barbarossa. Quickly understanding how the war was changing him, he began to write a diary, often including his own poetry. He wrote of marching past a makeshift gallows in a Russian village, with several supposed partisans hanging from it: "Their faces swollen and bluish, contorted into grimaces. The flesh was coming away from the nails on their tied hands … one soldier took a picture, another gave them a swing with his stick." On capturing a town they found an abandoned train in a siding filled with food and alcohol: "We whooped and skipped over the rails and danced in the cars laughing, firing shots into the air … we made a Russian woman prisoner dance naked for us, greased her tits with boot polish and got her as drunk as we were." Reflecting on why they behaved the way they did, he wrote that

We were forever drinking … our camaraderie arose from our forced dependency on each other, our humour was cruel towards others, black, satiric, obscene, biting and angry ... the fact that we were soldiers was enough to justify any crimes and corruption. We were of no significance, and neither were starvation, frostbite, typhus, dysentery, people freezing to death or being crippled or killed ... we could die without a care ... we are the war.[22]

Reese was right in many ways. According to the standards of Barbarossa, brutality was conformist while humane behaviour was almost deviant. It was into this context that somewhere between 5.3 and 5.7 million Soviets became POWs during the fighting in the East – the majority during that first summer and autumn of 1941. Their chances of survival were slim. Given the paucity of German records, estimates are the only viable means of assessing the horror, and they make for grim reading. Some two million are believed to have perished in the areas under military jurisdiction, with another half million dying in Poland's occupied *Generalgouvernement*, many murdered in Nazi death camps in the region. A further 360,000 to 400,000 died as forced labour in the Third Reich proper. The majority of deaths occurred in the first six months of the invasion. Barely one prisoner in three survived.

As for the men who presided over the slaughter, Eduard Wagner threw in his lot with the anti-Nazi resistance, and shot himself on 23 July 1944 as the *Gestapo* closed in. Max von Schenckendorff died of a heart attack in 1943 on a walking holiday, while Karl von Roques was convicted of war crimes in 1948 and sentenced to twenty years. He died in prison in 1949. Hermann Reinecke was convicted at the same Generals Trial as Karl von Roques and sentenced to life imprisonment. He was quietly released in 1954 and lived another nineteen years. Franz von Roques was questioned six times by the Allied authorities, but inexplicably never arrested. He ended up living out his retirement in peace, until passing away at home in 1967. Max Siry – he of the 'chop a prisoner's leg off' suggestion – was captured by the British, survived the war and died in Fulda aged seventy-five.

10

The End of Barbarossa

Kiev was the last hurrah for Barbarossa. By the end of the battle, the *Ostheer* was in possession of most of Ukraine, and had annihilated a sizeable chunk of the Red Army – but it hadn't won the campaign. The German victory had been breathtaking, but Moscow's 'rotten structure' had not come crashing down. The Red Army was still at least the size of the *Ostheer*, even after Bialystok-Minsk, Smolensk, Uman and Kiev. The Germans faced the question: what now?

Even as the fighting in Ukraine was still bleeding two dozen of his divisions, Hitler sought to answer that overwhelming conundrum with *Führerbefehl Nr. 35*. Signed and distributed on 6 September, it belatedly set the *Wehrmacht*'s sights on the Soviet capital, with an operation entitled *Taifun* (Typhoon). The panzer and mobile formations previously dispersed south and north would return to Bock and be launched like a spear to the east. Almost in desperation, some *landsers* still spoke of final victory: "The *Führer* recently made a very big announcement that the war against Russia will end this year ... as soon as the capital falls, it can be assumed that Stalin will disappear to America with those of his generals who haven't yet been shot in the neck ... we will soon no longer need to fight."[1]

Yet – as so often in Nazi military planning – the temptation to grab at every shiny bauble on the tree, rather than ruthlessly focus on one overarching goal, was just too strong to be resisted. Hence, the directive also tasked *Heeresgruppe Nord* with meeting up with the Finns, pushing on to the Volkhov River, and to "encircle Leningrad more closely, in particular in the east, and, should weather permit, a large scale air attack (on the city)". Rundstedt didn't escape this diversionary overload either: "The offensive against the Crimea from the lower Dnieper River will continue, with support from *Luftflotte 4*." With reinforcements lacking and logistics faltering, all three army groups were expected to continue attacking – it was pure folly, especially, as time itself was now firmly against the Germans.

The nights were getting distinctly colder, and the unique Russian phenomenon of the *rasputitsa* – literally the 'time without roads' – was almost upon them, when heavy seasonal rains would transform the already-primitive road network into an impassable quagmire of glutinous mud often several feet deep. Curzio Malaparte described the onrushing weather: "All of a sudden it starts to rain. At first it's a gentle shower ... but soon it develops into a regular hurricane, a veritable cloudburst ... around me I hear a chorus of yells and oaths. The artillery-trains come to an abrupt halt, the horses slither about in the mud that has formed as if by magic, and the lorries skid on the slippery surface."

Luciano Mela, a junior cavalry officer in the Italian *Eugenio di Savoia*, described another problem for the advance: "The Soviets only leave ruins. When leaving a village without bridges to blow up, or roads to wreck, but only trails like the ones they have here, tractors follow them with ploughs making large zigzag ruts. This doesn't seem like it amounts to much, but afterwards on such a trail our trucks can't go more than eight to ten kilometres per hour."

While the weather and the Soviets scorched earth policy caused havoc in the south, it was the strength of Soviet resistance that was proving more of an issue in the north. Leeb's army group had been far from idle while the Kiev drama was playing out. The smallest of the three German invasion forces, *Heeresgruppe Nord* was forever trying to stretch its thin resources to meet the military challenges it faced. As elsewhere with the *Ostheer*, it was the paucity of motorised formations, and the relatively slow pace of the following infantry, that was causing most of the problems.

Having forged ahead from the Daugava bridgehead, Manstein found himself and his panzers enduring another period of paralysis as they neared Leningrad. Moscow's response – even as the Kiev catastrophe unfolded – was to launch a series of vicious counter-attacks against 8. *Panzerdivision*, which succeeded in cutting the formation off from the rest of the army group for several days. Forced to rely on resupply by air to keep his men fed and fighting, Brandenberger's division took heavy losses until the troopers of the *SS-Totenkopf Division* were able to re-establish a link with the exhausted tankers and push the attacking Soviets back.

The *Totenkopf*'s Max Simon cast an expert eye over the Soviet positions he and his men had to fight through to reach Manstein's men:

This is defence in depth – protected by wire entanglements and numerous minefields. The Russians blend themselves into the terrain and could dig themselves in in an amazingly short time. Their defensive positions were simple and effective. Machine-guns are skilfully sited, and the snipers ... were given the best positions. Trench mortars are available in all calibres and flame-throwers – often fitted with remote control – are used in conjunction with mortars so that the attacking troops run into a sea of flames. Well-concealed tanks stand by to take part in counter-attacks or are dug in at intervals.

SS-Oberscharführer Wieninger remembered: "We had a thunderstorm, like nothing I'd ever experienced, and then came the enemy's shells, the Russians fired an incredible amount at us, and there was strike after strike. The crashing of the shells and the storm merged into a single constant roar."

It wasn't much easier behind the lines in the so-called cleared areas: "German officers driving through seemingly deserted villages ... and follow-up troops would find themselves facing a fortified position defended by an infantry regiment reinforced by all-arms. The position had been so well-camouflaged, and the Soviet soldiers had remained so still, that the officers had noticed nothing as they drove through."

With Manstein and his panzers rescued, *Heeresgruppe Nord* prepared for its part in Hitler's new directive. But the Soviets refused to allow the Germans any breathing space, repeating their attacks on *8. Panzerdivision* across Leeb's entire front. Wilhelm Lübbecke was in the forefront of the action: "At Lake Peipus we reached the old Estonian/ Russian border. There was heaving fighting there, infantry fighting – panzers were there too – but it was much more about infantry. That was tough, the Russians were tough ... We took a lot of casualties ... For the first time since the start of the campaign we were being confronted with stiff enemy opposition."

The army group was running out of steam. In the first fortnight of the invasion it had advanced an astonishing 280 miles – and was just 150 miles short of Leningrad – but then, in the following month, the pace fell to less than 20 miles a week, leaving them still over 70 miles shy of the city as their strength ebbed away. Nevertheless, it was tantalisingly close.

Now was the time to concentrate their fighting power, use their bridgeheads over the River Luga as a springboard, and drive for the city. Walter Krüger's *1. Panzer-Division* was chosen as the spearhead – the forty-nine-year-old *generalmajor* having taken over command from his fellow Saxon, Friedrich Kirchner, a few weeks previously. However, from its original 155 panzers, the division could muster just forty-four runners, with almost half of those being obsolete Mark IIs. Its infantry complement was equally weakened, standing at two understrength battalions, the men tired and in need of rest as well as reinforcement. Orders were orders though, and Krüger was able somehow to push on, advancing at the stately pace of around 6 miles a day to finally get within 25 miles of Leningrad by 21 August.

Frustrated at the delay, Hoepner badgered Leeb to reinforce him with the bulk of *18. Armee* to get the job done, but the ever-cautious army group commander instead insisted that Georg Küchler's men finish clearing out the Soviets from Estonia first, and so protect what he regarded as a wide-open flank.

Securing the smallest of the three Baltic states meant taking its capital, the port city of Tallinn on the country's north coast. German infantry and artillery battered away, and by late August the STAVKA made the decision to evacuate the city and the Soviet Red Banner Baltic fleet anchored within. In an attempt to blockade the harbour, the *Kriegsmarine* and the Finnish navy, the *Merivoimat*, laid over 2,400 mines in the sea lanes off Tallinn, with both navies readying fast torpedo boats to intercept any withdrawal. On the morning of 28 August, as German troops began fighting their way into the city, the first of seven Soviet convoys slipped their moorings and headed out to sea. This first packet consisted of thirty-two ships under the command of Captain N. Bogdanov. Another 132 ships were readying to follow – many of them being former Estonian and Latvian naval vessels – all of them packed with over 28,000 Soviet military and civilian personnel, as well as 10,000 Estonians who had thrown in their lot with the occupiers and were desperate to escape the vengeance of their countrymen. Clearing the harbour entrance, the Soviet convoys had to run the gauntlet of attacking aircraft and torpedo boats, as well as German shore-based guns on the Juminda peninsula and the lurking danger of the newly sown minefields. Ship after ship was hit, many smaller vessels being blown to pieces while larger ones were set ablaze in the waves. Given the situation, it was nigh on impossible for undamaged ships to stop and pick up survivors, leaving thousands to drown or die of hypothermia in the freezing Baltic. As night fell, the flashes of explosions and the flames from burning ships created an eerily horrifying scene, until at last – when nearing the massive Soviet naval base at Kronstadt – the attacks finally abated. The toll on the fleet was huge; some sixty-five vessels were sent to the bottom – almost half of those that had set out – and with them went 16,000 souls, including the families of many Party officials and functionaries.

To complete the job in Estonia, Siegfried Haenicke's *61. ID* launched *Unternehmen Beowulf* on 8 September to occupy the islands of Vormsi, Saaremaa, Hiiumaa and Muhu, off the west coast. The 24,000-strong Soviet garrison was crushed, with 19,000 surrendering. Haenicke lost one man in four killed, wounded or missing.

The Red Banner Baltic fleet suffered another loss on 23 September when the *Luftwaffe* launched a raid on Kronstadt, during which the 23,600-ton battleship *Marat* was hit several times, with Hans-Ulrich Rudel's Stuka delivering the coup de grâce with a bomb into the forward magazine of the stricken ship that blew her bow off. She sank in shallow water.

With the fall of Tallinn and the capture of Estonia, much of the Baltic had now become a German pond, and tens of thousands more Soviet soldiers marched into the brutal captivity of the *Wehrmacht*. But the opportunity to take Leningrad had gone. Moscow used the time it took for the Germans to subdue Estonia to rush troops to defend the city, so when the attack finally came it was simply too weak to break through Soviet defences. On 8 September, as the Kiev pocket was being closed, Walter Broschei and his comrades were only 10 miles from Leningrad city centre: "It pulsed with life ... but now we only had twenty-eight soldiers left from the 120 we normally had in the *kompanie*, and we'd been gathered into so-called '*kampfgruppen*' – totally unsuitable with our reduced strength for attacking Leningrad." Wilhelm Lübbecke reflected on his own unit's situation: "While our heavy weapons *kompanie* of about 300 men had only lost perhaps ten to fifteen over the preceding three months, the toll had been far more costly for our infantry *kompanien*. From their initial strength of about 180 men each, they had typically been reduced down to between fifty and seventy-five men." Hans Pichler, a medical officer in the *SS-Polizei*, wrote that "in the last twelve days our Division has lost a thousand men killed ... in every regiment the third *bataillon* has been dissolved to provide replacements for the others". The casualties included the divisional commander himself, Arthur Mülverstedt, killed by artillery fire.

Hans Simon was a twenty-one-year-old Mecklenburger from Rostock on the north German coast. After graduating from high school, he had completed his Labour Service and then been drafted. Joining Walther von Seydlitz-Kurzbach's *12. Infanterie-Division*, he fought in Poland and France before the launch of Barbarossa. Marching from East Prussia through the Baltic states, he had initially been swept along on a wave of optimism: "The Russians in front of us are disintegrating. They leave behind cannons and armoured cars, many are killed or taken as prisoners." But as he neared Leningrad the veteran *landser*'s tone changed dramatically:

The roads are such that I cannot describe them. You have to fight your way through mud, metre by metre. It has rained a lot in the last few days ... Wet boots and clothes for days, and then the cold nights ... from early in the morning to late in the evening, and often on into the dark night, we have to build roads and drag the vehicles through the ankle-deep mud. We have had no hot food for six days ... Hopefully we don't have to stay here for the winter.

Erich Drohl was another young member of *Heeresgruppe Nord*, but unlike Simon wasn't a front-line infantryman, but an anti-aircraft gunner. He wrote home and couldn't hide his relief at no longer being in the thick of the action. "I'm in the city of Velikiye Luki. There's not much shooting here and we're no longer with the infantry. We protect the crossing over the Lovat, a river as wide as the Nidda near Frankfurt ... Hopefully we will stay here a little longer." For young Drohl, the worsening weather was now the biggest enemy. "It's gotten cold and we're freezing, and it definitely won't make my runny nose any better. I will go to the doctor one day because now it stings in my ear. Hopefully, the war will be over soon, because living in a tent won't make you healthier in this weather. But for now, we have to be patient." The gunner – like Simon a veteran of the western campaigns – recognised that Barbarossa was different.

The Russian campaign is arguably the hardest and toughest that we have had to date. The country is too big, and the Russian is tough as leather. Our troops are much further east on other fronts, that's the only consolation. The infantry all believe that the war will be over by mid-September. I'm not so optimistic ... There has been as much death here in Russia as in all other previous campaigns taken together. You should see how bad the infantry look, mind you that's no surprise if you had to lie in a hole in the ground for over fourteen days in all weathers and you're constantly being shot at.

By late September *Heeresgruppe Nord* were over the Volkhov River, and in among the Valdai Hills, but had been forced into a siege of their main objective – Leningrad. Wilhelm Lübbecke spoke of the frustration felt by many *landsers* at the situation: "Just 7 or 8 miles away central Leningrad's high-rises and tall smokestacks stood silhouetted against the horizon. While feeling no sense of euphoria in the midst of combat, we had every expectation that the capture of the city and victory over Russia was within reach ... a few days later we learned that Hitler had ordered a siege of the city rather than an attempt to take it by storm."

The dictator had indeed ordered a siege, and made a point of telling anyone who would listen that he had never intended to capture the city outright and that it was always his plan to starve and bomb it into oblivion, but his protestations rang hollow. Not all *landsers* were disappointed at the decision not to attack the city. The forward artillery observer Hans Mauermann was glad of the respite: "Then suddenly it was halt – which was actually met with some satisfaction. Every day it had been attack with all its uncertainties and not knowing what might happen ... the emotion swung between shame that we hadn't pulled it off, to thanking God we didn't have to go in there."[2]

As for the *Ostheer*'s supposed allies, the Finns, having reached their pre-Winter War frontier, they had continued their advance but pointedly refused to join up with the Germans and co-ordinate an offensive against Peter the Great's city. The fighting would now become a grim struggle, dominated inside the city by bombardment and the haunting spectre of starvation, and outside by miles and miles of mud and water-filled trenches reminiscent of the First World War's Western Front.

Georg Fulde's Heinkel He 111 *staffel* was assigned the task of bombing the besieged Leningrad, and having not been in touch with his married sister for quite some time, he wrote to her on 29 September giving her his news:

As you may already know, I am a pilot and commanding officer in a battle squadron in Russia. I have been here for eight weeks, have carried out about thirty missions and on many nights I've dropped my bombs over Russia. Soon I will hopefully have the Iron Cross 1st and 2nd class ... I've had to fight hard for these medals on some missions ... but my bombs have never missed their target. Many Russian train stations have already been blown up, and sometimes my machine has been hit, but I always come home ... Yesterday morning at 6am, after I had blown up a large barracks outside Leningrad, three enemy fighters attacked me. One cannon shell came from behind me through my left cabin window, some ten centimetres past my head. That Russian was then shot down by one of our fighters; it was a great dogfight ... Fourteen days ago I got a direct hit in the right engine over Leningrad, and the engine started to burn, but I brought her home safely. That's how it works more often than not ... That night I blew up a fuel dump in Leningrad, the detonation was indescribable! There were terrible fires. Tonight we're going back to Leningrad.

He was keen to draw a distinction between his own bombing and that of RAF Bomber Command, which was attacking his home town of Berlin at the time: "We only attack militarily important targets. Not like the Tommy who drops his bombs onto houses and then hurries away again. I even drop a flare after the bomb is gone to see if my bombs have hit their proper target."

Leningrad wasn't Fulde's first bombing objective: "I bombed Moscow in August ... lots of searchlights and a lot of flak, but the Russians can be bluffed by constant deception so they miss. Of course, some experience is required. I have an impeccable crew and we understand each other ... When we get home we have hot soup, coffee, eggs, etc. We don't lack for anything. But you need it … when we attacked Moscow for the first time we flew there from Königsberg … that's ten hours. You may not be able to imagine what a ten-hour mission means! We were completely exhausted! It was like that every night."

If anything, Fulde was seriously under-playing Moscow's air defences, which were comparable at the time to London's. Organised by altitude, everything from five hundred to 3,000 metres up was covered by interlocking waves of fire, giving the impression to the crews of having to fly into seemingly solid walls of smoke, shot and flame. As it was, the *Luftwaffe* would launch a total of seventy-six air raids on Moscow before the end of the year, with all but seventeen being harassing sorties of ten aircraft at most, with many composed of just a trio of bombers, almost ignored by the city's deadly air defences. The only raids of any real import came on the night of 21/22 July 1941 when 127 aircraft attacked the Soviet capital, followed by 115 the next night, dropping to just a hundred the night after as casualties and serviceability issues further enfeebled the *Luftwaffe*'s already overstretched bomber arm. By way of comparison, even the dog ends of the London blitz in October the previous year beat that pathetic tally, especially on the 15th of the month when some 400 bombers had hit the rather underwhelmed British capital.

Even with the *Luftwaffe*'s efforts shrinking day by day, Fulde still had much the same derogatory view of his Soviet enemy as Hans Roth: "Russia is a miserable desert, you can't imagine it … These are not people at all, they are completely different." He also refused to see their continued resistance as anything other than an act of criminality. "There are still shootings in the hinterland every night. Motorists are gunned down on lonely country roads and murdered, cars shot at … we were shot at on the way home late one morning … we ran over five of the rascals and I killed another three of them with a submachine gun … But that's nothing new any more, it's just war and it will be over here soon." Like so many airmen, Fulde had a very different view of the fighting from several thousand feet up in his cockpit: "It is a horribly beautiful picture when you fly over the front at night. It looks like everything is burning, there are fires all over the Russian side; entire cities, towns and villages all ablaze. The sky glows red." He ended with every flier's mantra: "The aircraft is often hit, but you have to be lucky."

Many of Fulde's bomber comrades clearly didn't have his luck. By the time the letter reached his sister, the *Luftwaffe* had lost 536 bombers destroyed and a further 337 damaged so badly they had to be returned to Germany for repair. Since the *Luftwaffe* only fielded some 510 operational bombers on invasion day, that meant in only three months it had lost almost double its original strength. As for Georg

Fulde, his luck ran out just over one month later when he was shot down and killed – he was one of the 126 *Luftwaffe* bomber crewmen lost that month in Russia.[3]

Back in the Reich, Fulde's sister mourned him no doubt, and she wasn't alone in her grief at losing a family member. Bridget von Bernstoff – a Briton married to a German aristocrat and living in Hamburg – wrote in her diary that "One sees so many people in black, it's very depressing." One of her husband's friends, Felix von Schaffgotsche, was serving in the *Ostheer*: "Felix has been shot in the lung and is lying in a cowshed in southern Russia being eaten by bugs." At least Felix was alive, which was more than could be said for so many *landsers*, as another German housewife – Hildegard Gratz – realised for herself after Kiev; " ... everything changed. The radio carried on broadcasting news of victories. But the daily papers carried endless columns of death notices."

The mood back home in the Reich would have been even darker had the civilian population known the true state of their enemy. Kiev had sounded the death knell of the pre-Barbarossa Red Army. Soviet losses had been so huge that almost three-quarters of the army that started the campaign had been lost by the time the Kiev battle was over – and yet. Even as Bock readied his men for *Taifun*, the Red Army could still put over three million men in the field and outnumbered the Germans in guns by more than three to one, and tanks by two to one.[4] This was despite German intelligence reporting that since the invasion began the *Ostheer* had destroyed 35 Red Army tank divisions, and an additional thirty had been disbanded owing to the scale of their losses.[5]

The Germans, meanwhile, were beginning to run on empty, as Max Kuhnert knew only too well: "It was nearly the end of September, and Kiev had fallen. After counting the losses in men, horses and equipment we realised that we had to change our arrangements." These *arrangements* included disbanding whole cavalry squadrons, and amalgamating others. It could have been worse though, as Kuhnert's friend Erich Helm acknowledged: "Mind you, our losses are as nothing compared to the poor devils in the *bataillonen* ... replacements were out of the question."[6] The young medical officer Berndt Tessen von Heydebreck saw it for himself when he arrived in September at his posting with 7. *Infanterie-Division*: "Immense casualties. I found out that of a whole *kompanie* only twenty men were left, and among the wounded was the *kompanie* commander." The state of the survivors was little better. "The men are covered with dirt from head to foot. Their uniforms are in tatters and their faces unshaven." Heydebreck's unit wasn't the only one in such a parlous state. By the time Kiev fell, some fourteen Barbarossa divisions had suffered more than 4,000 casualties each, forty had suffered more than 3,000, and another thirty over 2,000 – mostly in the front-line companies.

Helmut Paulus's *198. Infanterie-Division* fought at Kiev and was one of the formations hardest hit. It reported suffering 1,025 casualties in just three days of battle, and two of its nine battalions were disbanded as a result. Hans-Adolf von Arenstorff's *60. Infanterie-Division (mot.)* lost the same in just over a week. One of Paulus's comrades, Helmut Schiebel, wrote: "Everywhere there are bangs, shots, hits, ricochets. A comrade suddenly screams or keels over, and you don't even know where the bullet came from."

Having lost momentum, the Germans were given no respite by the Red Army or the weather. Horst Slesina was a member of Goebbels' Propaganda Ministry, covering Bock's *Heeresgruppe Mitte*: "One *bataillon* commander spoke about Flanders back in the First World War. The features of our current situation have many similarities with that time. Wet and dirt, the sodden ground, the heavy artillery battles, the fighting in trenches and bunkers – it is the worst form of war ... hard days are coming."[7]

The Germans were still capable of hitting their enemy hard, but none of it was decisive, no matter how bloody. Ernst Guicking was a *feldwebel* in Gustav Höhne's *8. Infanterie-Division*. He wrote to his wife in late September telling her of his latest mission:

> Our job was to storm the enemy-occupied village, take prisoners, and come back scot-free if possible. So, it started at 2.30 in the morning ... A railway line ran through the centre of the village. Forty men went left of the railway line and forty men went right of it. At 4.20am our artillery started hammering away. The last shell fell at 5am. Now the way was clear for us. In the dark we managed to get within 200 metres of the first houses without being noticed ... Then the machine-guns and grenades went in. The infantrymen reached the first houses. A shootout began. The Russians shot wildly all over the place ... they didn't know what to do, much less where to shoot. You see, a surprise attack is a big advantage. You should have seen their stupid faces. Such a surprise must be terrible ... by 7:00am we were done with our work. We retreated so the Russian artillery couldn't get us ... on the way back the three of us alone counted ninety dead Russians. The Russians lost 150 prisoners and just as many dead in this action.[8]

Willi Betz was a twenty-five-year-old Bavarian serving in Herbert Loch's *17. Infanterie-Division*. Writing to a friend back home, he described the ferocity of the fighting. "Yesterday we managed to cut off some retreating Russians ... fifteen trucks fully loaded with Russian infantry. We let them come to within 100 metres of us and then opened a murderous fire on them with our cannons. The impact was devastating. The majority of the fifteen trucks were immediately on fire. The Russians rolled off them, largely wounded and burning. In total, the Russians had to leave more than forty dead and thirty-six seriously wounded. We captured another ninety-four after a heavy gun battle ... It was a terrible scene with so many dead and wounded."[9] Betz was a *leutnant*, one of the 1,625 officers the training academies were graduating every month. The problem was – as Franz Halder noted in his diary on 26 September 1941 – the *Ostheer* was losing some 5,880 per month.

Stripped of its armour, *Heeresgruppe Mitte* had gone from being the strongest German army group to being the weakest, and as the Kiev battle raged, the Soviets had stepped up the pressure on Bock's remaining infantry formations. The Yel'nya bridgehead, held at such great cost for so long, was abandoned, as Bock struggled to keep his forces from disintegrating. Franz Frisch was an Austrian gunner in an artillery unit in the salient:

Officially it was called a 'planned withdrawal', and a 'correction of the front lines' ... it was so much bullshit. The Russians were kicking us badly and we had to regroup ... we on the front-line were running back like rabbits in front of the fox ... I remember the retreat well. We had nearly exhausted our supplies of artillery ammunition. I remember we didn't receive a resupply of shells until days later when the front settled ... nobody knew where the battery commander was, and I guess he didn't know where his guns were.[10]

Taifun changed everything. The *panzergruppen* were coming back to *Heeresgruppe Mitte* and Bock would command Nazi Germany's most powerful field force once more. Only this time, that force was fragile. Its infantry were exhausted and in need of reinforcements, its panzers ground down by the hundreds of miles they'd driven to north and south. The *Luftwaffe*'s serviceability rates had deteriorated even further, and the supply problem was becoming chronic.

As Guderian's weary panzer crews headed back north to Bock's assembly areas, Rundstedt's men once more headed east. "The battle of annihilation around Kiev has ended, we are on our way again, heading east. We have already rattled down innumerable kilometres ... Only those who know the infinite vastness of Russia and have been involved from the start can judge what it's like here ... we have already travelled so far, and it always goes on. The misery, the dirt and the miserable houses ... terrible streets, nothing but mud and filth."[11]

Tasked to continue the advance, *Heeresgruppe Süd* was reduced to relying on Kleist's dwindling forces for mobility and, increasingly, on Berlin's allies. Those same allies were beginning to regret their decision to become involved in Barbarossa.

Even before the Kiev victory, Romania had achieved its war goals having taken back the provinces it had been forced to cede to Moscow in 1940. Hitler, however, persuaded Bucharest to stay in the fight with the promise of a massive slice of former Soviet land to be called Transnistria. As Guderian began his drive south towards Romny, the Romanians prepared to attack the Black Sea port city of Odessa. Hellmuth H., a veteran *landser* with Karl-Adolf Hollidt's *50. ID*, served alongside the Romanians and was appreciative of their courage: "The Romanians fight very bravely, contrary to expectations, and went singing into the fire in double ranks." Starting on 28 August the under-equipped and poorly trained Romanians strove to break through the concentric defence lines built around Odessa. The offensive was a disaster, and their losses horrific, over 30,000 in the first two weeks alone. Metre by metre the Romanians battered their way forward, paying with lakes of blood for a city most couldn't place on a map. By the time the Soviets evacuated their garrison by sea on 16 October, Romanian casualties stood at almost 100,000 men killed, wounded or missing. Bucharest could claim victory, but its forces would never recover from Odessa.

As for the Italians, on the same day the Romanians began their ill-fated attack on the Black Sea, Mussolini made one of his rare appearances at the front, flying in with Hitler, with whom he had been staying for the previous few days, to visit his troops in Ukraine. Watched by the two dictators and an apathetic Rundstedt, elements of the Italian expeditionary force marched by a makeshift dais, saluting a beaming Mussolini. Afterwards, Giovanni Messe sought to bring to his master's attention the parlous state of his units, explaining to *Il Duce* how short they were of motorised transport and heavy weaponry in particular. Messe also detailed the lack of suitable boots, the paucity of food, fuel and even ammunition. Mussolini's only reply was, "I am sure you deserve the trust which the *Führer* places in Italian troops." He then returned to Hitler's side and the two men were whisked away for their return flight. Messe's footsore men trudged on. The arrival of autumn with its rains, mud and increasingly cold nights spelt agony for the Italians. Luciano Mela raved: "I've had it! ... We're without food, with broken boots, uniforms in tatters, with only a little ammunition issued to each individual, since the rest is on trucks stranded without fuel some 200 kilometres away."

As for the Hungarians, they had sat on the Dnieper's western bank during the Kiev fighting, but once it was over they were ordered to cross and push onwards towards the far-off River Donets. Suffering from all the same shortages as the Italians and Romanians, the Magyars were desperate to head home, but unable to find a way out of the hole they'd dug for themselves.

With so much of Rundstedt's army group depleted and exhausted, his men simply stumbled on into the endless vastness of the interior. After hoping that their victory at Kiev would be the last act in the struggle, they soon realised their folly. Gottlob Bidermann wrote: "Our lines of supply became more strained with each day's advance, and as our momentum slowed to a crawl we continued to experience ever-increasing sporadic shelling ... The depth of our penetration into Russia began to take its toll, and ammunition rationing served as the first indication of the shortages we were to encounter."

Even the supposedly ideologically committed warriors of the *Waffen-SS* were dismayed by the grinding conditions they were forced to endure, as one SS trooper noted:

There is very little water and what there is, is salty. Coffee is salt-flavoured, the soup is over-salted ... this is true desert country. Movement is visible for miles; clouds of choking red brown dust hang over our moving columns and pinpoint our exact positions ... the only signs of life are the dead tree trunks of telegraph poles. Without them it would be difficult to orientate yourself. Sometimes we find a melon field and gorge ourselves, but the unripe ones have unhappy effects![12]

Nevertheless, the fighting went on. This was no Railway Offensive as, somehow, Moscow managed to scrape up enough reserves to form a defensive front and force the Germans to fight for every yard of ground, as Edgar Steuerwald recalled:

Our *kompanie* made an attack ... The first *kompanie* was to our right and the third to our left. The natural boundary between our *kompanien* was a railway embankment. All of a sudden, to our amazement, we saw that the Russians were marching towards us on a road dead ahead of us. He had teams of artillery and anti-tank guns with him. We were only assigned a 3.7cm PAK gun and a light tank. We received the order to open fire. Almost every shot was hitting because the distance was only about 400 metres. The Russians immediately counterattacked. In terms of numbers, they were far superior to us ... the other *kompanien* to our right and left retreated, but our commander didn't give us the order for the time being as he still hoped it would work out ... we got very heavy fire from the front, right and left ... our *kompanie* leader saw that it was getting very hot and gave the order to retreat.

Steuerwald was wounded in the withdrawal. "I got a knock on the left leg. At first I was in a lot of pain, but it was fine after medical treatment. Now the wound, which is not too big, has already healed. I can walk perfectly again." Having reassured his parents as to his condition, he continued: "The number of deaths that we had in the battle was fifty-four ... It's a shame about those boys. Many of them were only wounded and were then murdered by the Russians. But we took our revenge. In a subsequent attack with heavy tanks, we took almost no prisoners, everyone was cold and brutal. We didn't spare ammunition. Every shot was a hit. Let the Russians see what they will get for murder."

Rudolf Oehus was a farmer's son from Lower Saxony and was now serving in an artillery regiment as it trudged forward: "Our Division was completely encircled by the enemy. The greatest danger for us was tanks, a total of forty tanks attacked, but twenty-nine of them were destroyed, and we took eleven hundred prisoners ... Russian radio had already announced that we were going to be annihilated, but we quickly put an end to that."

Klaus Becker was, like Oehus, an artilleryman but unlike him, at thirty-eight years of age, was one of the oldest men in his unit. A member of the Party and proud of it, his early letters home to his wife mocked the enemy and poured scorn on the civilian population. In the aftermath of Kiev, the tone of his writing changed. All his earlier talk of a heady advance disappeared, to be replaced by blunt acceptance of reality: "We're stuck here right now. It's been raining for two days ... there is terrible mud so that the roads are hardly passable, at least not for our heavy vehicles. Of course, everyone suffers from this, not only the motorized units, but also marching troops and supplies. But somehow progress is made." He even began to show some small signs of sympathy for the civilian population he met along the way.

> You cannot imagine how sad life is for Russian people ... Farmers without cattle and hardly the bare necessities for food and drink ... There is nothing pleasant here. It's always the same picture in Russia; crumbling houses, dirty villages, poor people and nowhere cheerfulness and sunshine. But there is also nothing at all that could bring joy here ... Many houses were abandoned by their residents even before the campaign, without anyone caring about them. They crumbled even more than the inhabited houses.

He was clear where the blame for this lay: "That's what communism looks like."

Helmut Paulus, having survived the crossing of the Prut back in June and the Kiev fighting, had one overriding obsession: "Our feet have had it ... You can't stand for five minutes without getting pain in your feet and calf muscles. It's not just like that for me but for all my comrades ... food, post, leave. Everyone is dreaming day and night of leave." One of

Paulus's fellow *landsers* spoke for many when he wrote on 22 September, "Three months ago today the campaign against Russia began. Everybody thought at the time that the bolsheviks would be ripe for capitulation within no more than eight to ten weeks. That assumption, however, was based on a widespread ignorance of Russian war materiel ... Russia is almost inexhaustible!"[13]

A few days later, Helmut Pabst remarked, "When I got up today there was hoar-frost everywhere. I found thick lumps of ice in the watering bag. Winter isn't far off."[14]

11

Where Did It All Go Wrong?

Today, it is a commonly accepted view among students of military history that the reason for Germany's defeat at the hands of the Russian giant was the fact that she made no attempt to carry out strategic air warfare.

This astonishing claim was made after the war in a staggeringly long twelve-volume analysis by the United States Air Force Historical Support Division of why the once-mighty *Luftwaffe* disintegrated during the war. It would, perhaps, be understandable if this supposition had been made by the likes of Curtis LeMay or Carl Spaatz – America's greatest wartime exponents of strategic bombing – but its authorship lay instead with a coterie of former high-ranking *Luftwaffe* officers. These men – Hermann Plocher, Paul Deichmann, Klaus Uebe and so on – had all held senior appointments in the *Luftwaffe* and been intimately involved with Barbarossa and the subsequent Russo-German struggle. As such, they could reasonably be expected to have useful insights into the German failure, and while an emphasis in any post-war study on the importance of their own service branch might be expected, to boil down a number of complex issues to one overriding theme is over-simplified to say the least, and smacks of post-war rationalisation. In the study the authors illustrated their argument with the example of Soviet versus German tank production. They explained that during the war the Soviet Union manufactured a colossal 150,000 tanks, while Nazi Germany only managed a meagre 25,000. They then lauded the incredible success of the *Luftwaffe*'s foremost ground-attack *Experte*, Hans-Ulrich Rudel, in destroying 510 of those Soviet tanks, while pointing out that this was a mere drop in the ocean, their argument being that "a single, successful air attack on the Russian tank factories would have destroyed the product of several weeks' work all at once … It is difficult to stop a rushing stream; its source, however, can be dammed up with relatively little effort."

Maybe they were playing to their employers' prejudices. Of all countries, America is the keenest to be told that a war can be won by bombing alone, and that air power is all-masterful. Regardless, what can be said with certainty is that the largest invasion in history did not fail just for want of a strategic bomber fleet; after all, the Anglo-Americans possessed the most powerful bomber force of the war and it still wasn't enough to win the conflict on its own, no matter how fervently the likes of Britain's Arthur Bomber Harris may have wished it could.

More useful would be to look at tank production from another angle as a litmus test for the failure of Barbarossa. In 1941 some 3,790 panzers rolled out of factories in Nazi Germany, of which 815 were produced in the critical months of June through to August. The Reich also built 11,200 artillery pieces and heavy guns, and 11,776 aircraft that crucial year. The Soviet Union, by contrast, built 15,735 aircraft, 42,300 guns and 6,590 tanks – all while losing vast swathes of her industrial base in western Russia and having to evacuate much of what was left thousands of kilometres away beyond the Urals.[1] Continuing this theme of lack of industrial punch as a core reason for the failure of Barbarossa, back in the late autumn of 1939 – when the *Wehrmacht* was busy subjugating Poland – there had been a cold snap across much of northern Europe. Consequently, there was a surge in demand for coal from the German population desperate to keep the home fires burning. Germany's mines stepped up production and churned out huge amounts of the black stuff, so there shouldn't have been a problem – except there was. Germany's rail system was busy supplying the war effort, and simply didn't have the capacity to do the two things at once. The result was a systems failure; coal piled up at the pit heads, homes went cold, schools were closed, and people got used to wearing coats indoors. The stark truth these production figures and economic failures illustrate so vividly was that Nazi Germany's economy was nowhere near strong enough to defeat the Soviet Union, let alone conquer a global empire. The economic provisions stemming from the Nazi–Soviet Non-Aggression Pact proved that; Berlin was willing to trade modern weapon designs and prototypes and cutting-edge technology in exchange for the food, raw materials and fuel it couldn't produce itself but desperately needed to keep its people and war machine fed, clothed and mobile.

So under-powered was the Germany economy that even after receiving a direct order from their *Führer* that all Mark IIIs in the *panzerwaffe* be equipped with the latest heavy cannon, the Army Ordnance Department instead had the majority fitted with the obsolete L/42 gun, purely because they had plenty of them in stock and couldn't produce enough of the newer model. Hitler reacted badly when he found out, as Heinz Guderian attested: "I was present at a demonstration of armoured equipment on 18 April 1941 which Hitler attended. He noticed that the Panzer III had been re-equipped with the 50mm L/42 cannon instead of the 50mm L/60 as he had ordered ... this infuriated him."[2] The German tank crews suffered the consequences of this deficiency when they came face to face with the magnificent T-34 during Barbarossa.

The dearth of weapons and resources needed to make the campaign a success was mirrored by the Nazis' lack of knowledge about their enemy. Hitler himself said before Barbarossa that "at the beginning of every campaign one pushes a door into a dark, unseen room. One can never know what is hiding inside." There is an element of truth in this statement, but not much. In essence, the Nazi dictator was paraphrasing Helmuth von Moltke the Elder's famous moniker, 'No plan survives contact with the enemy.' However, in the spring of 1941 arguably no country on earth knew the Soviet Union better than Germany. Both outcasts of the established world order after the First World War, the two nations had formed strong bonds, which included Soviet support for early German rearmament programmes; German pilots were trained at Lipetsk air base to bypass Versailles Treaty restrictions, and joint military commissions would regularly attend and observe each other's training exercises. The Soviet Union even had its own German minority, some two million ethnic Germans spread over several regions, with the majority living on the banks of the southern Volga River in their own Autonomous German Republic of the Volga, with their regional capital in Engels.[3] The German spearheads were often astounded to come across communities of German-speakers seemingly caught living in a time capsule, as Manfred von Plotho mused in a letter home:

What contrasting images does this war bring? Recently we came across some Volga Germans; poor people who still speak the genuine Swabian dialect ... almost all blue-eyed and light-haired. At first we were amazed when someone answered the questions of our interpreter with 'I don't understand Russian.' We have also come through areas of Volhynian German settlements. Often there was hardly a man left in these villages. They had all been kidnapped by the Bolsheviks, never to be seen or heard of again. The brain simply cannot grasp this accumulation of human suffering.

Viewed and treated by Moscow as a fifth column, Berlin had never made any systematic attempt to utilise the priceless knowledge of their erstwhile countrymen.

German diplomats and politicians knew the country well, too. Not long before the invasion the well-connected *Luftwaffe* officer Werner Baumbach found himself at a drinks reception at the German Embassy in Moscow. Talking to the ambassador – von der Schulenberg – as well as Ernst Köstring (the senior Military Attaché) and Heinrich Aschenbrenner, the Air Attaché, Baumbach remembered that "Aschenbrenner believes Russia's strength is in her system, which isn't going to collapse overnight".[4] Yet this was precisely what Berlin envisaged with Barbarossa – an invasion that committed the *Wehrmacht* to hugely ambitious goals with no real regard as to the resources available to achieve them.

As for Barbarossa itself, it was, quite simply, a poor plan. Erich Marcks – militarily brilliant in some ways – originated a folly. Success across Europe, and over France in particular, blinded the Germans as to the reality of their military capability. Heinz Rahe fought in the French campaign and believed wholeheartedly in the supremacy of German arms. An experienced NCO, he wrote home to his wife Ursula as late as the beginning of September that "I still believe that for us this campaign will end in four, at the most six, weeks. By then we will have reached the most important goals: Petersburg, Moscow and the Donets Basin – and the mass of the Russian army will be destroyed ... The main thing is if the weather allows us to end the campaign quickly." A week later he was still talking about "maybe eight days until Petersburg is taken".

Rahe wasn't alone, it seemed to many in Berlin's high command that the universal underpinnings for modern twentieth-century military operations had ceased to apply to them. Through a combination of luck and judgement the *Wehrmacht* had hit upon the ultimate war-winning doctrine of its time in blitzkrieg, and this new concept – still so little understood by anyone outside a few true believers – would carry them to ultimate victory. This was a view shared by the majority of the rank and file in the Army, of whom the young panzer officer Hans-Erdmann Schönbeck was typical: "We were fast and our panzer forces could cover huge distances, and once we'd broken through the enemy's defences our orders were not to worry about threats to our flanks but to keep going ... We would strike his rear installations, communication units and supply depots. It was a new way of fighting – highly mobile and flexible – and it was difficult to anticipate. It brought fear and panic to our opponents."[5] Kurt Meyer – who would go on to become the youngest divisional commander in the *Wehrmacht* – agreed with Schönbeck about how to make the new theory work: "The one thing not to do was stop – just continue to move and take advantage of the enemy's confusion!"

The *Wehrmacht*, however, was fundamentally unable to sustain – either physically or mentally – the type of campaign that Schönbeck and Meyer articulated with such fervour. Marck's plan for Barbarossa called for the Army to advance in lightning fashion to an imaginary line on the map anchored on the port city of Arkhangelsk in the north and ending in fabled Astrakhan on the shores of the Caspian Sea in the south. This would entail the leading invasion units covering some 1,100 miles from their start lines – it was 500 miles to Leningrad, and 750 to Moscow alone. Geography meant that the initially huge frontage for the invasion would increase exponentially with the advance and would have doubled at the point of success. This epic would be achieved by a military that had never done anything like it before in terms of scale and, despite all the propaganda to the contrary, was still dominated by the horse and marching infantry.

In essence, Barbarossa had a lot more in common with Napoleon's 1812 disaster and Charles XII's 1708 debacle than any German involved cared to admit. While it was true that the *Wehrmacht* had cut through France in record time, France was a minnow when compared to the Soviet Union. In 1940, conquering Paris was the key to defeating the French republic, and, at the time, the distance from the German border to Paris was 200 miles. Two hundred miles from the German border in the east would find a *landser* from *Heeresgruppe Nord* standing in Madona, Latvia, a town of some 3,000 citizens which got its first train station in 1903. For *Heeresgruppe Mitte*, it would mean reaching the tiny Belarussian village of Bialiou, and for Rundstedt's forces it would be a place now called Yuzhnoukrayinsk in Ukraine, which didn't even exist in 1941 having only been founded in 1976 to service a nearby nuclear power plant. The sort of distances that Barbarossa demanded be reached were simply unachievable for the German Army. Almost three-quarters of the invasion force were foot-slogging infantry units with a minimum of motorised transport, and while they could – and indeed would – achieve miracles during the early days of the campaign, they couldn't sustain the pressure or speed.

Generalleutnant Kurt Herzog's Prussian Masurians of *291. Infanterie-Division*, for example, advanced an astounding 44 miles in the first thirty-four hours of the offensive, but couldn't hope to keep up that blistering pace. They weren't alone. The average German advance before Bialystok-Minsk was 40 miles a day, after that victory it dropped to just 12. The dreadful state of the roads, the harsh weather, swarms of insects and plain exhaustion were as big an enemy as the Red Army. Gottlob Bidermann wrote of it all: "We experienced a severe shortage of water, and the few deeply dug wells and cisterns not poisoned by the enemy contained brackish water that varied from bad-tasting to undrinkable. The horses and soldiers developed an unquenchable thirst as they laboured under the tormenting heat, and for the horses it meant that even the strongest and healthiest had to be rotated out of the harness." The *Waffen-SS* suffered the same problems, as the *SS-Reich*'s Heid Ruehl made clear: "Crossing the swamp was very difficult as we had to jump from one clump of grass to another, and often had to put down our rifles and pull ourselves out of the swamp so we didn't get sucked under. That wasn't the only problem though – we were also attacked by huge clouds of voracious mosquitoes ... and the lack of proper roads slowed our advance."

The sheer scale and doggedness of Soviet resistance wasn't taken into account in Marck's plan either. One *landser* accurately described the chasm between each side's behaviour on the battlefield: "When we attacked we would spread out over a large area, then, randomly, a couple of soldiers would jump up, run forward and drop down again. Before the Russian machine-gunner could even aim his target was out of sight. By doing this we would advance with a minimum of casualties." Not so their Soviet opponents: "The Russians would attack as one big group of screaming and shouting men, running into the fire of our mortars and machine-guns. This strategy could only be successful if you didn't care about your own casualties and you had enough soldiers to do it – and both of those applied to the Russians ... a Russian life had no value to Stalin." The cliché of the 'Red horde' only became a cliché because there was a lot of truth in it.

Again, as with the issue of distance, the model for Barbarossa was the victory over France, where the enemy would surrender en masse when their position became untenable – this was not how the Red Army fought, as Ruehl pointed out. It was clear that this was a very different enemy to any the Germans were used to, and not just in the way they fought but in every aspect of their existence:

> The Russians avoided being drawn into direct action and instead withdrew into the almost impenetrable forests, which meant we had frequent brushes with Soviet units that had been bypassed ... That night, the first vehicles of our column had just passed a small hollow when a single shot from an enemy anti-tank gun hit and destroyed our prize 5,000 litre petrol bowser. From all sides came the chilling cry of 'Urrah!' and then a storm of small arms fire ... we were soon in action putting down a heavy barrage and throwing grenades just like infantry veterans. A Russian grenade flew through the air and landed next to Kindl, I shouted at him to watch out and he rolled away. It was a dud ... no help came until the morning when Nr. 7 battery moved forward ... they thought we'd all been wiped out ... we found some Russian iron rations; a piece of hard brown bread the size of a fist and a similarly large piece of cane sugar. Together the two produced a feeling of fullness that our own iron rations never achieved.[6]

Given these limiting factors, the success of Barbarossa – whether the Nazi leadership and the *Wehrmacht* wanted to acknowledge it or not – relied almost wholly on the previously winning combination of armour, air power and well-trained, well-equipped motorised infantry. The main problem with this approach was that German high command was fundamentally split between those officers who believed in the campaign-winning potential of the *panzerwaffe* and the new maxims, and those – the majority – who still clung to an orthodox military approach that emphasised a steady, methodical advance, the protection of flanks and the importance of set-piece battles, upon whose outcomes political leaders would make rational decisions on whether to continue the fight or not. For the latter, the definition of success was the physical annihilation of the Soviet armed forces; for the former, it was more about their paralysis and the destruction of their ability to resist. As that master of armoured warfare George S. Patton would later say to one of his divisional commanders in Normandy in 1944: "Let me worry about your flanks, you just worry about your objectives."

The dilemma for Barbarossa was that its only hope of success was in a messianic embracing of blitzkrieg, while the men who would command it – including Hitler himself – were still wedded to orthodox military philosophy. As it was, the Germans sent four powerful but brittle *panzergruppen* into the Soviet Union. Half the vehicles they had were war booty designed for western Europe's metalled roads, supplies of engine oil and tyres were nowhere near sufficient, spare parts were impossible to get hold of, and as the number of vehicles in the field plummeted – with a fifth of trucks and a third of all other wheeled vehicles written off by early September – the *Wehrmacht* couldn't even bring up enough fuel to keep them going. Franz Halder himself admitted that of the ninety trainloads of fuel per day the *Ostheer* needed they were only receiving around seventy.[7] Günther Blumentritt explained that "nearly all transport consisted of wheeled vehicles, which couldn't move off the roads, or move on them if the sand turned to mud. An hour or two of rain reduced the panzer forces to stagnation. It was an extraordinary sight, with groups of men strung out over a hundred miles, all stuck until the sun came out and dried the ground."

The panzers themselves were in no better shape. Wilhelm von Thoma – latterly the commander of 6. *Panzerdivision* – wrote of his own unit on its withdrawal from the campaign for a much-needed refit: "Repairs can only be made by cannibalising other panzers because there are no longer any spare parts. This means that after the retrieval of the panzers that are scattered all over the surrounding terrain, a maximum of ten can actually be repaired out of the forty-one reported as requiring repair. In short the vast majority of my *PzKpfw 35 (t)*s can no longer be rebuilt or maintained as all the components are worn out. To be practical, perhaps the armoured hulls are still useable." As one commentator suggested, "It was perhaps the Soviet Union's lack of an adequate westernised road system that was her most effective defence against the German onslaught."[8]

If the *panzergruppen* weren't up to the mark, what about the *Luftwaffe*? Could it be the hammer in the sky Barbarossa so desperately needed? In Poland, to an extent, but especially in France, the *Luftwaffe* had begun to establish a modus operandi: hit the enemy air force hard in the very first days, try to destroy as much of it as possible on the ground, then concentrate on crushing the remainder in the air before unleashing a hailstorm of firepower on enemy troops in support of the Army. The opening weeks of Barbarossa were the zenith for this approach, the carnage on the ground and in the air almost beyond belief. Yet still the VVS fought on, retreating into the interior, sending hundreds of barely trained pilots into the air in often obsolete aircraft as a stopgap, and paying a massive blood price; but they were still there. A *Luftwaffe* that had lost 1,814 aircraft conquering France, and a further 2,000 losing *die Luftschlacht um England* (the Battle of Britain), and was still having to fight in North Africa, the Mediterranean and across the English Channel at the same time as Barbarossa, was rapidly worn down. An invasion force of fewer than 3,000 aircraft with an anaemic supply of replacements could never hope to be decisive when faced with the Soviet Union's almost limitless space; in the summer of 1944 the Anglo-Americans fielded an aerial armada of almost 10,000 aircraft post-D-Day to fight a far smaller battle in terms of square mileage.

An uninformed member of Walther Nehring's *18. Panzerdivision* said, "In the weeks before our attack we constantly saw Russian bombers and fighters, but now they seem to have been blown away. Either the enemy is frightened or he hasn't got any planes left, and the last few are being held for the fellows in the Kremlin's towers." In contrast, Hermann Plocher, then Chief of Staff for *V. Fliegerkorps*, wrote in his diary: "The mass of equipment of the Soviets amazes us again and again." By the end of the Kiev encirclement the *Luftwaffe* was reduced to shuttling forces up and down the front to try and achieve local superiority in at least one operational area at a time – as a tactic it worked, but it ground down men and machines, with bomber serviceability dropping from 70 per cent in June to less than 40 per cent by late September, and fighters not much better off at 50 per cent. That meant that on any given day more than half of all German aircraft on the Eastern Front were unfit to fly. When Erhard Milch inspected his front-line *staffeln* in late August he found hundreds of inoperable aircraft littering makeshift airfields, unable to fly from lack of spare parts and adequate maintenance.

Ever since the end of the war, much has been made of the role played by time in the failure of Barbarossa, and more specifically Hitler's decision to delay the invasion to strike out and conquer Yugoslavia and Greece in April. The theory goes that this deprived the *Wehrmacht* of two whole months of campaigning time that it could have used to defeat the Red Army and end the war in the East. But time was surely not Barbarossa's biggest enemy, rather it was the *Ostheer*'s own weaknesses that proved the campaign's undoing. Nazi Germany's truck doyen – Adolf von Schell – wrote that "the Balkan campaign left a large hole in the stock of supplies, because the vehicles of the motorised troops that took part had suffered badly in the mountainous terrain, and they had to be re-equipped for action in the East in four weeks". This was only part of the story – but it was a big part.

The truth was that by early August, after just six weeks or so of combat, the greatest invasion force ever assembled was running out of steam, and it then spent much of that same month – arguably the best in the summer campaigning season – marking time. At that point the Germans had charged forward some 300–500 miles across their vast frontage, and that was exactly the same distance that their entire operational effort was geared to achieve. In other words, Barbarossa succeeded in attaining the objectives the *Wehrmacht* could realistically be expected to reach – in fact, it had achieved more, but that 'more' wasn't nearly enough against the enemy Hitler had set it to defeat.

Kiev, then, resembled almost a last, powerful punch by a fighter fast approaching exhaustion, and when that astounding victory wasn't followed by a Soviet collapse, Barbarossa had effectively ended. *Taifun*, with its massing of all available forces on a single axis while relegating the bordering army groups to subsidiary actions, simply acknowledged that fact.

The invasion's failure was then masked by another series of stunning victories. The later encirclements at Bryansk and Vyazma were operational masterpieces that together netted even more prisoners and booty than Kiev: some 673,000 men and over 1,300 tanks. A senior Communist Party official wrote to Stalin, "The retreat has caused blind panic. Many soldiers throw away their weapons and go home." The flip side of this coin was expressed by none other than the *Waffen-SS* firebrand Kurt Meyer when he said, "In general the Russian will to resist does not seem to have been broken ... for the moment one has the impression that the war will go on ... even if Moscow is taken, somewhere in the depths of this endless land." His fellow *Leibstandarte* officer – and son of Nazi Germany's Foreign Minister – Rudolf von Ribbentrop concurred: "It must have been quite early on – in my opinion November 1941 at the latest – that the realisation dawned on Hitler that the attack on Russia was a critical mistake ... the obvious erroneous estimation of Russian strength and the environmental conditions under which the *Wehrmacht* had to wage war in Russia were a profound shock."

Back in Berlin, the entry for 11 September in Joseph Goebbels' diary reads: "In my opinion the nation now has a right to know what is and what will be, above all that the progress of the eastern operation is not what we had actually wished for and what the people had also imagined it would be." Stark words from a man who a mere three months earlier had confided to his diary just prior to the invasion: "Bolshevism will collapse like a house of cards. We stand on the cusp of a victorious advance without equal. We must act ... Our operation is as well prepared as is humanly possible."

In a five-week period, the defeats at Kiev, Bryansk and Vyazma cost the Red Army a jaw-dropping one and a half million casualties, but the factories shipped east were beginning to churn out tanks, aircraft and guns, and German intelligence reports were noting the arrival at the front for the first time of Anglo-American Lend-Lease equipment. Even worse for Berlin, the Red Army was not only fighting back but even now was still as big as the *Ostheer* in terms of overall numbers. That same *Ostheer* was badly fraying, with one in six of the original invaders already a casualty, and correspondingly massive losses in equipment that weren't being made up by a German economy structurally unable to deliver what an attritional war in the East required. Even Berlin's allies were beginning to understand their folly, with the Finns refusing to move forward, the Romanians burnt out after Odessa, Budapest readying to pull its exhausted troops home, and the Slovaks and Italians in desperately poor shape.

Dr Franz Wertheim joined the *Ostheer* after the launch of Barbarossa and expressed a common view among the ranks: "Our armies marched to within 70 kilometres of Moscow. The great hope that the Russian people were waiting to be delivered from communism and would end the war of their own accord didn't materialise ... it meant that you couldn't see an end to a war which we had already thought to be finished."[9] Wertheim alludes to a campaign-winning philosophy that accepted the belief that given the Soviet Union's sheer size, military victories weren't enough. What was needed was a collapse in the country's government as in 1917, brought on by the actions of the people themselves. Only this approach would overcome the immense power of the Stalinist state. If the Germans failed to channel popular discontent within the country, then Moscow would be able to rely on its unequalled ability to trade space and human beings for time, and effectively turn a war of movement that it couldn't win into a war of attrition that it could. Hitler's real failing lay in the racism that disbarred the *Wehrmacht* from adopting such an approach – a racism that wasn't just an adjunct to Barbarossa but lay at its very heart. The Nazis didn't just want to win, they wanted to win on their terms rather than at any cost, even to their own beliefs. Perhaps the dictator realised this failure, as from then on, as young Rudolf von Ribbentrop noted, "He appeared less and less in public, and not at all at mass rallies – using the bogus excuse of not wanting to expose an audience to possible air attack, but he also didn't visit troops at the front any more."

Hitler and his generals based their entire campaign and, ultimately, the outcome of the war, on a philosophy that couldn't accommodate anything other than the victory of *superior blood* – a delusion shared by many of the men they sent East, including educated officers like Manfred von Plotho: "Was the victory in the West a victory of superior leadership with revolutionary tactics, combined with better armament and training? If so victory in the East can only be achieved through the superiority of the German soldier as a fighter with a different ideological background." The *SS-Totenkopf* NCO Wieninger was one of those *superior German soldiers*, although he didn't feel like it when he wrote home to his wife, "I have to tell you that I'm losing my hair – it's happening to all of us – and if the war goes on much longer I'll have to come home with a damned bald head."

The failure of the master race delusion would be felt – among so many – by a young German girl called Annerose, who wrote a letter to her sweetheart on 1 December 1941: "Oh, sometimes I ask myself: why did everything have to come to this? But can you ask like that? ... Is there no prospect of leave at all? It has been a year now since you were last at home. When will we see each other again dear Willi?" The object of her affections, the young anti-tank officer Willi Betz, was already dead as she put pen to paper, killed in action a few days before.

With Barbarossa a failure and *Taifun* still grinding on, Heinz Guderian wrote to his wife on 9 November 1941, touching upon his deepest fears: "We have seriously underestimated the Russians; the extent of the country and the treachery of the climate. This is the revenge of reality."

Manfred von Plotho would look that reality straight in the eye, and even though he would ultimately survive the war, he wouldn't return to Germany from his Soviet gulag until 1955. A devoted husband and prolific letter writer to his wife Ingrid before his capture at Stalingrad, his early letters from Barbarossa talk of impending victory and the superiority of German culture and blood: "The men fight very courageously, but unfortunately the battles cost a lot of good German blood, which isn't really worth it for this mixture of Asian peoples." Later, as the campaign ground on remorselessly, with victory seemingly getting further and further away, he was forced to confront the very human cost of the invasion:

The ranks of old comrades from the West Wall campaign are thinning. My old comrade Siekmann fell. Bad luck really, while eating he got a direct hit in the back. I happened to be around and so helped bury him. He was the man with whom I had the strongest camaraderie in the old *kompanie*. As early as '37 in the *Wehrmacht* field training manoeuvres, Siekmann was in my group, and when we were based in Quedlinburg we were in the same room. Then the time at the border in the Palatinate forest, our first attack where he did so well … He was always the first to go forward, in the whole western campaign, and so it was here in the East. And then to be picked out so indiscriminately by the hand of the god of war.

Heinrich Haape and Martin Meier were more prosaic than their aristocratic Prussian comrade. Haape – so mesmerised at the invasion's launch he almost shouted with joy – was now reduced to confiding in his diary: "I don't want to be a soldier. I'd go home and marry Martha (his fiancée, the opera singer Martha Arazym) tomorrow."

Meier was even briefer. "Will the war end this year? I don't believe it will."

Maps

The following are mostly campaign maps drawn up by the Staff of the German Army for use during the Barbarossa invasion. I am grateful to the United States Library of Congress for permission for their use. Germany. Heer. Generalstab, C. (1942) Der Feldzug gegen Sowjet-Russland: Band I. Operationen Sommer-Herbstvom 21. Juni-6. Dezember. [Berlin?: Generalstab, ?] [Map] Retrieved from the Library of Congress, https://www.loc.gov/item/map51000141/.

The initial set-up for Operation Barbarossa.

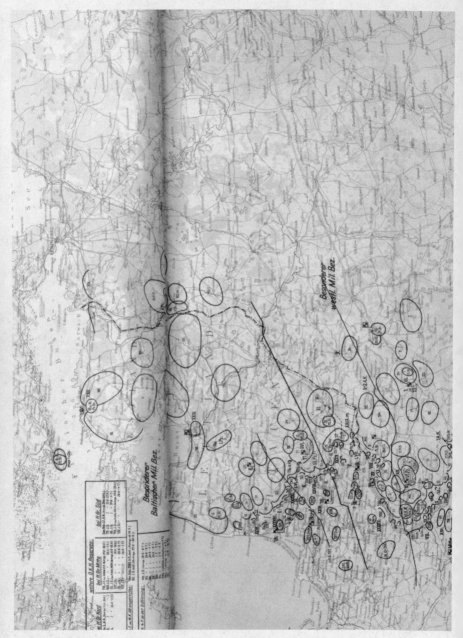

German positions on invasion day. (Courtesy of the Library of Congress)

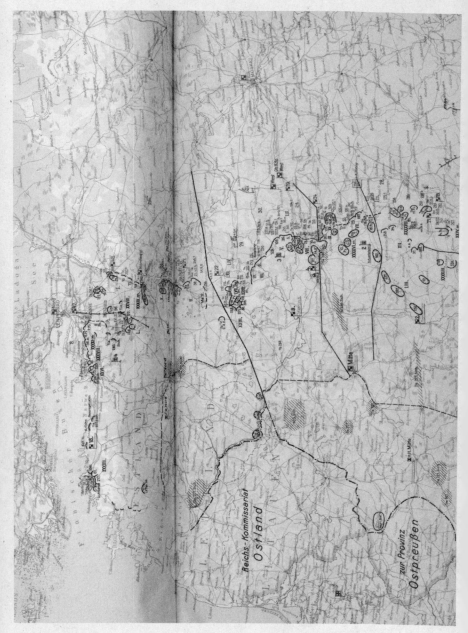

First day of the Kiev offensive drive by Guderian's forces. (Courtesy of the Library of Congress)

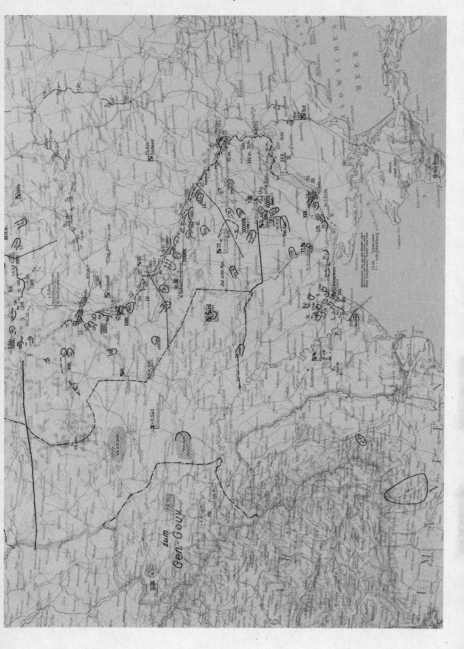

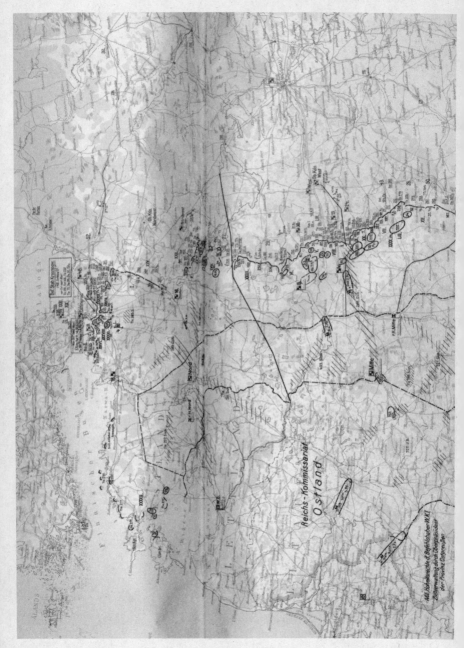

Aftermath of the German linkup sealing Kiev Pocket. (Courtesy of the Library of Congress)

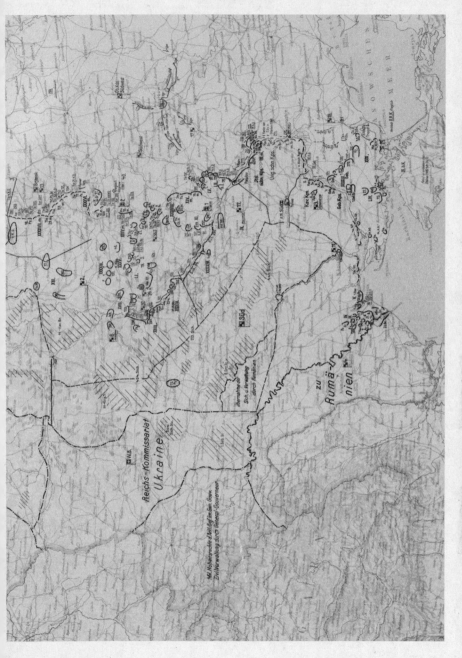

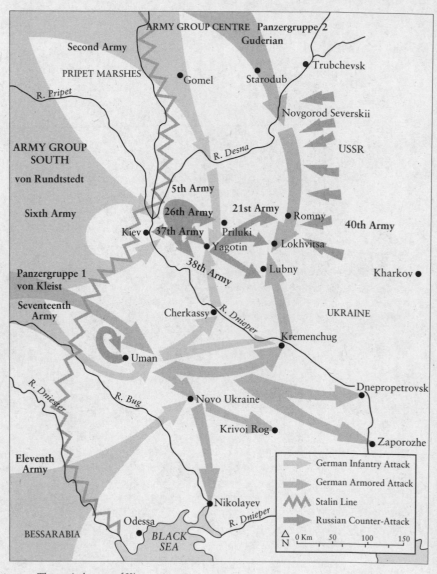

The encirclement of Kiev.

APPENDIX A

The following is a list of a few of the German soldiers who are quoted in the text in an effort to provide the reader with some additional biographical details.

Ernst Guicking was born in Altenburschla, Thuringia, in 1916. Married with two children, he became a professional soldier in the mid-1930s, enlisting in *8. Infanterie-Division*. He fought in France and then in the Soviet Union, rising to the rank of *feldwebel*. He survived the war and returned home in 1945.

Helmut Nick was born in the Westphalian town of Langenberg near Gütersloh. Married, he completed a banking apprenticeship after leaving school. A member of the Nazi Party, he joined the Army in 1939, serving in France and then the Soviet Union. Reaching the rank of *Spiess*, he survived the war.

Anton Böhrer was from the north Baden village of Höpfingen. Born in 1915, Böhrer was a gardener by profession. Drafted into the *Wehrmacht* at the beginning of 1941, he served in the artillery regiments of the *221.* and *294. Infanterie-Divisionen*. Eventually becoming a *Spiess*, Böhrer was reported as missing in action in August 1944.

Franz Siebeler initially trained as an apprentice in a bank before joining the military in October 1940. A gunner in *14. Panzerdivision*, Siebeler was killed in action near Stalingrad in June 1942.

Born in Potsdam in 1908, Manfred Freiherr von Plotho was married and a landowner before joining the Army in 1937. Serving in *71. Infanterie-Division*, he fought in Belgium, France and then the Soviet Union. As part of the doomed *6. Armee*, *Leutnant* von Plotho went into Soviet captivity at the end of the battle of Stalingrad. Imprisoned by the Soviets, he finally returned home in 1955.

Elmar Gustav Lieb, a member of the *Ulm Pioneers*, fell in action in early 1942, as did the *60. Infanterie-Division (mot.)*'s Edgar Steuerwald.

Rudolf Kurth was born in 1913 in Zehdenick in Brandenburg. A clerk in civilian life, Kurth was married before being drafted into *23. Infanterie-Division* in July 1939.

Hellmuth H., born in Cologne in 1904, was married and a Nazi Party member. As a soldier in *50. Infanterie-Division*, he fought in Poland, France, Greece and the Soviet Union. A *feldwebel*, he died in combat in southern Russia in February 1943.

Gerhard Kunde was born in Berlin in 1914. He worked in the legal profession before his service. Initially a member of *68. Infanterie-Division*, he latterly became a junior officer in *Ost-Bataillon 441* – a unit recruited from former Red Army POWs. He was captured by the Soviets.

Gustav Böker from Oberg in Lower Saxony served in *111. Infanterie-Division*. He was killed in Russia in July 1943.

Heinz Rahe was born in Heiligendorf near Wolfsburg in 1912. A Protestant pastor in civilian life, Rahe was married and had completed his obligatory military service in 1935. Recalled in 1939, he served in *13. Infanterie-Division*, fighting in France, before the unit's conversion to become *13. Panzerdivision*. He fought in Ukraine, reaching the rank of *feldwebel*, before being transferred back to France in 1943. Eventually he was taken prisoner by the Americans in 1945, before being released home.

Kurt Marlow, the flower shop owner born on the Baltic Sea island of Usedom in 1914, served as a medic – a *Sani* – in *68. Infanterie-Division* until 1942 when he was posted to a military hospital in Guben, Brandenburg. When the Anglo-Americans landed in France in June 1944, he was sent to the static *719. Infanterie-Division* in the Dordrecht area of the Netherlands. Promoted to *feldwebel*, Marlow fought with the division in the Battle of the Scheldt, where the unit was almost destroyed. Withdrawn back to Germany, the division fought in the Saar, where Marlow was posted as missing at the end of April 1945.

The two Catholic Youth pen pals from Gelsenkirchen, Hans Albring and Eugen Altrogge, continued to serve as infantrymen in Russia for the rest of 1941 and through 1942. Selected for officer training, Altrogge was promoted to *leutnant*, only to go missing in action in January 1943. *Gefreiter* Hans Albring was killed almost exactly a year later in Belarus.

Kurt Miethke continued to guard Soviet POWs across Ukraine until he was posted missing in September 1944.

APPENDIX B

Waffen-SS, German Army and Comparable British Army Ranks, 1941

Waffen-SS	German Army	British Army
SS-Schütze	Schütze	Private
SS-Oberschütze	Oberschütze	Private
SS-Sturmmann	Gefreiter	Lance-corporal
SS-Rottenführer	Obergefreiter	Corporal
SS-Unterscharführer	Unteroffizier	Lance Sergeant (only used in the British Brigade of Guards)
SS-Scharführer	Unterfeldwebel	Sergeant
SS-Oberscharführer	Feldwebel	Colour/Staff Sergeant
SS-Hauptscharführer	Oberfeldwebel	Sergeant-Major – Warrant Officer Class 2
SS-Sturmscharführer	Hauptfeldwebel	Sergeant-Major – Warrant Officer Class 1
SS-Untersturmführer	Leutnant	Second-Lieutenant
SS-Obersturmführer	*Oberleutnant*	Lieutenant
SS-Hauptsturmführer	Hauptmann	Captain
SS-Sturmbannführer	Major	Major
SS-Obersturmbannführer	*Oberstleutnant*	Lieutenant-Colonel
SS-Standartenführer	Oberst	Colonel
SS-Brigadeführer	Generalmajor	Brigadier
SS-Gruppenführer	Generalleutnant	Major-General
SS-Obergruppenführer	General	Lieutenant-General
SS-Oberstgruppenführer	Generaloberst	General
	Generalfeldmarschall	Field-Marshal

Endnotes

1 Food & Hatred

1. Guderian, Heinz, Panzer Leader, p150.
2. Entitled Konto 5, a secret fund was used to bribe the *Wehrmacht*'s senior leadership by paying them large, regular, tax-free sums. As a general, Guderian would have received 2,000 *Reichsmarks* a month on top of his 24,000 *Reichsmarks* a year salary, plus Aufwandsentschädigungen (compensation for expenses) payments. Guderian was also given a 2,000-acre estate at Deipenhof (now Głębokie) in the annexed Warthegau area of Poland. When asked by Manstein how he came by his new home, Guderian told him that "he had been given a list of fine Polish properties which he had viewed over a few days before deciding on the most suitable", he also told Manstein he had no idea what had happened to the former owners, but after the war Guderian changed the dates and circumstances of the theft in his memoirs to try and present the seizure as a legitimate retirement gift.
3. Boyd, Julia, Travellers in the Third Reich, p278.
4. Hagen, Louis, Ein Volk, Ein Reich, p164.
5. Holmes, Richard, World At War, p180.
6. Guderian, Heinz, Panzer Leader, p142.
7. Holmes, Richard, World At War, p181.
8. Wrench, Sir Evelyn, Editor of The Spectator magazine 1925-1932.
9. Hagen, Louis, Ein Volk, Ein Reich, p29.
10. Letter from Gerhard Kunde written to his mother – 15 June 1941.
11. Hagen, Louis, Ein Volk, Ein Reich, p17.

2 The *Wehrmacht* – the World's Finest

1. Stahel, David, Kiev 1941, p29.
2. Guderian, Heinz, Panzer Leader, p143.
3. Steiger, Rudolf, Armour Tactics in the Second World War, p127.
4. Recorded interview with Wilhelm Lübbecke in the United States several decades after he emigrated to the country and changed his name to William Lubbeck.
5. Rosen, Richard von, Panzer Ace: Memoirs of an Iron Cross Panzer Commander, p11.
6. Forty, George, Tank Warfare in World War II, p45.
7. Boyd, Julia, Travellers in the Third Reich, p279.
8. Ibid – p185.
9. Hagen, Louis, Ein Volk, Ein Reich, p64.
10. Interview with Andreas Fleischer.
11. Hagen, Louis, Ein Volk, Ein Reich, p199. Lebensborn
12. Kuhnert, Max, Will We See Tomorrow – A German Cavalryman At War, p2.
13. Kershaw, Robert, War Without Garlands, p22.
14. Ibid – p40.
15. Hagen, Louis, Ein Volk, Ein Reich, p122.
16. Eriksson, Patrick G., Alarmstart East, p26.
17. Carruthers, Bob, Voices from the *Luftwaffe*, p7.
18. Neitzel, Sönke and Welzer, Harald, Soldaten, p312.
19. Kistemaker, Henk, Wiking, p48.

3 The Build-up

1. Kaufmann, Johannes, An Eagle's Odyssey, p97.
2. Eriksson, Patrick G., Alarmstart East, p49.
3. Verton, Hendrik, In the Fire of the Eastern Front, p71.
4. Kershaw, Robert, War Without Garlands, p13.
5. Rosen, Richard von, Panzer Ace: Memoirs of an Iron Cross Panzer Commander, p31.
6. Kershaw, Robert, War Without Garlands, p14
7. Rowehl would retire from the *Luftwaffe* in December 1943 and devote himself to bringing up his daughter after his wife was killed in an Allied bombing raid.
8. Eriksson, Patrick G., Alarmstart East, p50. Like many of his contemporaries, Scholz had served in Nazi Germany's Condor Legion during the Spanish Civil War. Before his death in 2014 he was the last living veteran of that unit.
9. Luck, Hans von, Panzer Commander, p65.

10. Baumbach, Werner, Broken Swastika, p114-115.
11. Letter from Anton Böhrer to his father, (3,2002,0889).
12. Kershaw, Robert, War Without Garlands, p37.
13. Lucas, James, Das Reich, p56.
14. Landau, Sigmund Heinz, Goodbye, Transylvania, p20.
15. Knoke, Heinz, I Flew for the Führer, p43-49.
16. Letter from Franz Siebeler to his parents, (3,2002,1285).
17. Beevor, Antony, The Second World War, p192.
18. Holmes, Richard, The World At War, p182.
19. Guderian, Heinz, Panzer Leader, p153.
20. Pabst, Helmut, The Outermost Frontier, p11.
21. Herrmann, Hajo, Eagle's Wings, p129.

4 Invasion Day

1. Kershaw, Robert, War Without Garlands, p23.
2. Ibid – p155.
3. Eriksson, Patrick G., Alarmstart East, p48.
4. Kaufmann, Johannes, An Eagle's Odyssey, p98.
5. Mahlke, Helmut, Memoirs of a Stuka Pilot, p219.
6. Eriksson, Patrick G., Alarmstart East, p50.
7. Ibid – p50.
8. Faber, Harold, *Luftwaffe*, p227.
9. Faber, Harold, *Luftwaffe*, p227.
10. Bekker, Cajus, The *Luftwaffe* War Diaries, p221.
11. Eriksson, Patrick G., Alarmstart East, p48.
12. Knoke, Heinz, I Flew for the Führer, p46.
13. Kershaw, Robert, War Without Garlands, p127.
14. Neulen, Hans Werner, In the Skies of Europe, p95.
15. Bernad, Dénes, Karlenko, Dmitry and Roba, Jean-Louis, From Barbarossa to Odessa, p140.
16. Leutnant Heinz Döll, 18-Panzerdivision.
17. Lucas, James, Das Reich, p56.
18. De Giampietro, Sepp, Blood & Soil, p1.
19. Buttar, Prit, Between Giants, p75.
20. Roth, Hans, Eastern Inferno, p26.
21. Knappe, Siegfried, Soldat, Dell War.
22. Guderian, Heinz, Panzer Leader, p153. Guderian crossed with his personal command and control staff consisting of two radio vans, an armoured car, several kubelwagen and a few motorcycle despatch vehicles.
23. Pabst, Helmut, The Outermost Frontier, p12.
24. Kershaw, Robert, War Without Garlands, p127.

25. Lucas, James, Hitler's Mountain Troops, p89.
26. Carruthers, Bob, Voices from the *Luftwaffe*, p46.
27. Panzerkampfwagen 38(t)'s, or Pz. 38(t)'s for short, with the (t) standing for tschechisch, the German word for Czech. Small – it weighed under ten tonnes, had relatively thin armour, was reliable, manoeuvrable and fast, being able to reach speeds of 30mph on roads. Its biggest drawback was its main gun; the 37mm KwK 38(t) L/47.8, which was obsolete by 1940 and would prove disastrously under-powered in Barbarossa.
28. Evans, Richard J., The Third Reich At War, p189.
29. Hagen, Louis, Ein Volk, Ein Reich, p35.
30. Ibid – p50.
31. Baumbach, Werner, Broken Swastika, p119.
32. Hermann, Hajo, Eagle's Wings, p129.
33. Evans, Richard J., The Third Reich At War, p189.
34. Williamson, Gordon, Loyalty is my Honor, p22.
35. Meyer, Kurt, Grenadiers, p71.
36. Collier, Richard, 1941, p133.
37. Boyd, Julia, Travellers in the Third Reich, p385.
38. Beevor, Antony, The Second World War, p192.

5 Germany on the March!

1. Letter from Hans-Joachim S. to his wife, (3.2002.1214).
2. Buttar, Prit, Between Giants, p79.
3. Von Leeb's book was entitled Die Abwehr – The Defence.
4. Buttar, Prit, Between Giants, p84.
5. Carrell, Paul, Hitler's War on Russia, p23.
6. Letter from Adolf Dick, (3.2002.1288).
7. De Giampietro, Sepp, Blood & Soil, p143.
8. Bellamy, Chris, Absolute War, p188.
9. Kershaw, Robert, War Without Garlands, p189.
10. Haape, Heinrich, Moscow Tram Stop, p20.
11. Letter from Rudolf Kurth to his wife, (3.2002.0867).
12. Letter from Elmar Gustav Lieb to his parents, (3.2002.7255).
13. Neitzel, Sönke and Welzer, Harald, Soldaten, p92. Recording of landser Faller.
14. Prüller, Wilhelm, Diary of a German Soldier, p78.
15. Letter from Gustav Böker to his parents, (3.2002.7255).
16. Lucas, James, Hitler's Mountain Troops, p93.
17. Letter from Alois Breilmann to his sister, (03/2009 0714).
18. Neitzel, Sönke and Welzer, Harald, Soldaten, p92. Recording of Hoeschler.

19. Jones, Michael, The Retreat, p13.
20. Ibid – p14.
21. Kershaw, Robert, War Without Garlands, p144.
22. Evans, Richard J., The Third Reich At War, p179.
23. Letter from Manfred von Plotho, (3.2008.2195).
24. Pabst, Helmut, The Outermost Frontier, p15
25. Jones, Michael, Leningrad, p22.
26. Forty, Simon, German Infantryman, p55
27. Stahel, David, Kiev, p73.
28. Bellamy, Chris, Absolute War, p188.
29. Signal magazine – 2 August 1941.
30. Lucas, James, Hitler's Mountain Troops, p90.
31. Ochsenknecht, Ingeborg, Als ob der Schnee alles zudeckte.

6 Murderers & Liberators

1. Buttar, Prit, Between Giants, p103.
2. Landau, Sigmund Heinz, Goodbye, Transylvania, p20.
3. Knappe, Siegfried, Soldat, Dell War.
4. Bellamy, Chris, Absolute War, p22.
5. Named after the senior NKVD secret police officer, Ivan Serov. Serov also played a major role in the Katyn Massacre of thousands of former Polish Army officers, and a number of other infamous Soviet atrocities.
6. Letter from Adolf Dick to his father, (3.2002.1288).
7. Günter, Helmut, Hot Motors, Cold Feet: A Memoir of Service with the Motorcycle Battalion of SS-Division 'Reich' 1940-1941, p150.
8. Michael Melnyk interview with M. Dobrianskyj, 15 October 1992.
9. Stargardt, Nicholas, The German War, p163.
10. Lutsk was captured by the Germans on 25 June 1941. Two days earlier the inmates of the city prison were offered amnesty by the authorities and ordered to exit the building immediately. Upon which they were massacred. Estimates vary, but as many as 4,000 inmates – many being ethnic Poles and Ukrainians, were murdered.
11. Villani, Gerry, Voices of the *Waffen-SS*, interview with Kurt Schmidt, p189.
12. Letter from reserve policeman Hermann Gieschen.
13. Letter from Wilhelm Moldenhauer to his wife.
14. Evans, Richard J., The Third Reich At War, p192.
15. Letter from Alois Breilmann, (03/2009 0714).
16. Letter from RB to his brother, (3.2002.7227).
17. Letter from Martin Meier to his wife, (3.2002.0904).
18. Haape, Heinrich, Moscow Tram Stop, p20.

19. Lucas, James, Hitler's Mountain Troops, p89.
20. Knoke, Heinz, I Flew for the Führer, p20.
21. Letter from RB to his brother, (3.2002.7227).
22. Kershaw, Robert, War Without Garlands, p195.
23. Buttar, Prit, Between Giants, p103.
24. Rees, Laurence, The Nazis: A Warning from History, p179.
25. Rhodes, Richard, Masters of Death, p42.
26. Ibid – p39.
27. Excerpt from an interview carried out by Laurence Rees for his TV series.
28. Excerpt from the 2009 French TV series; Einsatzgruppen.
29. L'viv museum, archive 2019-01-15, Wayback, Natalia A. Feduschak, CDVR. 2010.
30. Quote from Joachim Schoenfeld. Schoenfeld later wrote the seminal works 'Shtetl Memoirs' and 'Holocaust Memoirs: Jews in the Lwow Ghetto.'
31. Littmann, Sol, Pure Soldiers or Sinister Legion, p27.
32. Rees, Laurence, The Nazis: A Warning from History, p187.
33. Lower, Wendy, Hitler's Furies, p95.
34. Neitzel, Sönke and Welzer, Harald, Soldaten, p97. Recording of Gericke.
35. Westermann, Edward B., Hitler's Police Battalions: Enforcing Racial War in the East, p17.
36. Neitzel, Sönke and Welzer, Harald, Soldaten, p139.
37. Browning, Christopher, Ordinary Men, p14.
38. Rhodes, Richard, Masters of Death, p63. Deposition to post-war Nuremburg trials.
39. Rees, Laurence, The Nazis: A Warning from History, p195.
40. Excerpt from the 2009 French TV series; Einsatzgruppen, secret filming of interview with Wulfes in his home.

7 Uncharted Territory

1. Jones, Michael, The Retreat, p6.
2. Bellamy, Chris, Absolute War, p206.
3. Lucas, James, Hitler's Mountain Troops, p108.
4. Ibid – p115.
5. Neulen, Hans Werner, In the Skies of Europe, p206.
6. Tsouras, Peter, Fighting in Hell, p182.
7. Lucas, James, Storming Eagles, p104
8. Lucas, James, Hitler's Mountain Troops, p88
9. Lubbeck, William, At Leningrad's Gate, p85.
10. Kershaw, Robert, War Without Garlands, p211.

11. Jones, Michael, The Retreat, p6.
12. Carrell, Paul, Hitler's War on Russia, p53.
13. Holmes, Richard, The World At War, p186.
14. Tsouras, Peter, Fighting in Hell, p193.
15. Rosen, Richard von, Panzer Ace, p104.
16. Kaufmann, Johannes, An Eagle's Odyssey, p113.
17. Eriksson, Patrick G., Alarmstart East, p55.
18. Jones, Michael, The Retreat, p2.
19. Kershaw, Robert, War Without Garlands, p216.
20. Neitzel, Sönke and Welzer, Harald, Soldaten, p268.
21. Jones, Michael, The Retreat, p7.
22. Ibid – p9.
23. Scheuer, Alois, Letters from the Field: 1941-1942, Wassermann Verlag 2001.
24. Kershaw, Robert, War Without Garlands, p229.
25. Carruthers, Bob, Voices from the *Luftwaffe*, p10. 19-year-old Hamburg apprentice Benedikt Sieb.
26. Bellamy, Chris, Absolute War, p245.
27. Villani, Gerry, Voices of the *Waffen-SS*, interview with Kurt Schmidt, p189.
28. Baumbach, Werner, Broken Swastika, p117/
29. Eberhard Kinzel was the Abwehr officer in Fremde Heere Ost (FHO – Foreign Armies East) responsible in January 1941 for producing an assessment of Red Army strength.
30. The Invisible Flag, by Peter Bamm (the pen name of Curt Emmerich), Frank Herrmann (translator), Penguin 1962.
31. Lucas, James, Hitler's Mountain Troops, p100.
32. Letter from Karl Nünninghoff to his parents, (3.2008.1388).
33. Lucas, James, Das Reich, p61.
34. Ibid – p63.

8 Kiev

1. Instituted on 23 June 1941, the STAVKA was the highest military authority in the Soviet Union and was chaired by Stalin himself.
2. In all previous campaigns the *Wehrmacht* had taken 218,109 casualties, with 97,000 of that number killed.
3. Lucas, James, Das Reich, p67.
4. Kuhnert, Max, Will We See Tomorrow?, p96.
5. Kershaw, Robert, War Without Garlands, p353.
6. Lucas, James, War on the Eastern Front 1941-1945, p193.
7. Tsouras, Peter, Fighting in Hell, p183.
8. Stahel, David, Kiev 1941, p297.

9. Kern, Erich, Dance of Death, p60.
10. Kershaw, Robert, War Without Garlands, p353.
11. Stahel, David, Kiev 1941, p291.
12. Ibid – p263.
13. Kuhnert, Max, Will We See Tomorrow?, p97.
14. Jones, Michael, The Retreat, p27.
15. Letter from Gustav Böker to his parents, (3.2002.0966).
16. Wagner was also made responsible for security in the rear areas behind the frontlines. The mass of Soviet POWs also came under his responsibility, and the failure to provide for them which led to mass starvation, can be laid at his door.

9 Germany's Shame

1. Beevor, Antony, The Second World War, p195.
2. Scheck, Raffael, Hitler's African Victims, p2.
3. Stahel, David, Kiev 1941, p306.
4. Ibid – p305.
5. Kershaw, Robert, War Without Garlands, p295.
6. Ibid – p298.
7. Neitzel, Sönke and Welzer, Harald, Soldaten, p91. Recording of Leutnant Leichtfuss.
8. Ibid – p309.
9. Evans, Richard J., In Hitler's Shadow: West German Historians and the Attempt to Escape the Nazi Past, p55-56.
10. Letter from Martin Meier to his father, (3.2002.0904).
11. Kochanowski, Jerzy & Zaremba, Marcin, Niemiecke listy ze wschodu.
12. Bidermann, Gottlob, In Deadly Combat, p44.
13. Neitzel, Sönke and Welzer, Harald, Soldaten, p95.
14. Evans, Richard J., The Third Reich At War, p184.
15. United Nations War Crimes Commission – 1997. Law Reports of Trials of War Criminals: Selected and prepared by the UN War Crimes Commission Volumes XI-XV.
16. Kuhnert, Max, Will We See Tomorrow?, p99.
17. Carruthers, Bob, Voices from the *Luftwaffe*, p10.
18. Forty, Simon, German Infantryman: The German Soldier 1939-45 – Operations Manual, p10.
19. Browning, Christopher, Ordinary Men, p170.
20. Neitzel, Sönke and Welzer, Harald, Soldaten, p173.
21. Ibid – p81. Recording of landser Müller.
22. Reese would be Killed in Action on 22 June 1944, aged 23, on the opening day of the Soviet Bagration offensive.

10 The End of Barbarossa

1. Letter from Anton Böhrer to his sister, (3.2002.0889).
2. Jones, Michael, Leningrad, p39.
3. Letter from Georg Fulde to his sister, (3.2002.0202).
4. At the beginning of Taifun, the Red Army still had 2,715 tanks and some 20,580 guns, despite its previous losses.
5. Cooper, Matthew & Lucas, James, Panzer, p42.
6. Kuhnert, Max, Will We See Tomorrow?, p98.
7. Slesina wrote a book about his experiences; Soldaten Gegen Tod und Teufel (Soldiers Against Death and the Devil).
8. Letter from Ernst Guicking to his wife, (3.2002.0349).
9. Letter from Willi Betz to a friend, (3.200.0257).
10. Kershaw, Robert, War Without Garlands, p156.
11. Jakob Geimer was a Saarlander, born in Neunkirchen in 1911.
12. Ailsby, Christopher, *Waffen-SS*: The Unpublished Photos, p115.
13. Stahel, David, Kiev 1941, p298.
14. Pabst, Helmut, The Outermost Frontier, p28.

11 Where Did It All Go Wrong?

1. Davies, Norman, Europe At War, p43.
2. Guderian, Heinz, Panzer Leader, p143. The heavier 5cm L/60 gun fired a 2.25kg armour-piercing shell at 1189 meters per second, while the smaller 5cm L/42 only fired a 2.18kg shell at 685 meters per second.
3. Evans, Richard, J. The Third Reich At War, p197. Mainly Hessian Lutherans, the settlers were invited to Russia by Czarina Catherine the Great at the end of the Seven Years War and given land on the virgin steppe of the Saratov region. There, they built over a hundred farming centres and several large towns, including their capital, Engels. Using a plan originally drawn up in the early days of the First World War, Moscow issued a Decree of Banishment on 28 August 1941, and enacted it three days later. The region's young men were drafted into the Soviet Labour Army, the young women were sent to service elsewhere, and everyone else was packed into cattle wagons and sent east to the Altai mountains on the frontier between western Siberia and Kazakhstan. On arrival they were assigned to 'closed' stations with only indigenous people and similarly banished ethnic Poles as neighbours. Fifteen thousand NKVD secret police were involved in deporting the first 50,000 people from the Volga region, followed by another 240,000 by the end of the year. By the end

of 1942 some 1.2m had been expelled, with 175,000 dying from starvation, disease and brutality.

4. Baumbach, Werner, Broken Swastika, p113.
5. Jones, Michael, Retreat, p6. Schönbeck would go on to become a member of the anti-Hitler resistance after the Stalingrad disaster.
6. Lucas, James, Das Reich, p58.
7. Forty, Simon, German Infantryman, p8.
8. Cooper, Matthew & Lucas, James, Panzer, p48.
9. Hagen, Louis, Ein Volk, Ein Reich, p51

Select Bibliography

Alexander, Christine (editor) & Kunze, Mason (editor), *Eastern Inferno – Journals of a German Panzerjäger on the Eastern Front 1941-1943*, Casemate 2010

Arthur, Max, *Forgotten Voices of the Second World War*, Ebury 2004

Bartmann, Erwin (translated by Derik Hammond), *Für Volk and Führer*, Helion 2013

Baumbach, Werner (translated by Frederick Holt), *Broken Swastika, The defeat of the Luftwaffe*, Robert Hale 1986

Bekker, Cajus (translated by Frank Ziegler), *The Luftwaffe War Diaries*, MacDonald 1966

Bidermann, Gottlob (translated & edited by Derek S. Zumbro), *In Deadly Combat: A German Soldier's Memoir of the Eastern Front*, University Press of Kansas 2000

Bishop, Chris, *SS: Hell on the Western Front*, Spellmount 2003

Blosfelds, Mintauts (edited by Lisa Blosfelds), *Stormtrooper on the Eastern Front – Fighting with Hitler's Latvian SS*, Pen & Sword 2008

Buttar, Prit, *Between Giants: The Battle for the Baltics in World War II*, Osprey 2015

Carell, Paul (translated by Ewald Osers), *Hitler's War on Russia*, George G. Harrap 1964

Carruthers, Bob, *Voices from the Luftwaffe*, Pen & Sword 2012

Chiariello, Dan & Scheja, Oskar, *The Man in the Black Fur Coat: A Soldier's Adventures on the Eastern Front*, CreateSpace 2014

Cooper, Matthew & Lucas, James, *Panzer – The armoured force of the Third Reich*, Book Club 1979

Davies, Norman, *Europe At War 1939-1945: No Simple Victory*, Macmillan 2006

Eriksson, Patrick G., *Alarmstart East: The German Fighter Pilot's Experience on the Eastern Front, 1941–1945*, Amberley 2018

Evans, Richard J., *The Third Reich At War*, Allen Lane 2008

Evans, Richard J., *In Hitler's Shadow – West German Historians and the Attempt to Escape the Nazi Past*, Pantheon 1989

Fischer, Wolfgang (edited & translated by John Weal), *Luftwaffe Fighter Pilot – Defending the Reich*, Grub 2010

Forty, George, *Tank Warfare in World War II – First-hand accounts from Allied and Axis soldiers*, Magpie 2004

Forty, Simon, *German Infantryman: The German Soldier 1939-45 – Operations Manual*, Haynes 2018

Friesen, Bruno, *Panzer Gunner*, Helion 2008

Galland, Adolf, *The First and the Last*, Blurb 2018

Guderian, Heinz (translated by Constantine Fitzgibbon), *Panzer Leader*, Michael Joseph 1952

Günter, Helmut, *Hot Motors, Cold Feet. A Memoir of Service with the Motorcycle Battalion of SS-Division 'Reich' 1940-1941*, Winnipeg 2004

Haape, Heinrich Dr, *Moscow Tram Stop: A Doctor's Experiences with the German Spearhead in Russia*, Stackpole 2020

Hagen, Louis, *Ein Volk, Ein Reich – Nine Lives Under the Nazis*, Spellmount 2011

Holmes, Richard, *The World at War*, Ebury 2007

Holmes, Richard, *Battlefields of the Second World War*, BBC 2003

Holmes, Tony (editor), *Dogfight – the greatest air duels of World War II*, Osprey 2011

Hooton, E. R., *Eagle in Flames – The Fall of the Luftwaffe*, Arms & Armour 1997

Jones, Michael, *The Retreat – Hitler's First Defeat*, John Murray 2009

Jones, Michael, *Leningrad – State of Siege*, John Murray 2008

Kaufmann, Johannes (translated by John Weal), *An Eagle's Odyssey; My Decade as a pilot in Hitler's Luftwaffe*, Greenhill 2019

Kern, Erich, *Dance of Death*, Collins 1951

Kistemaker, Henk, *Wiking: A Dutch SS-soldier on the Eastern Front*, Just Publishers 2019

Klapdor, Ewald, *Viking Panzers: The German 5th SS Tank Regiment in the East in World War II*, Stackpole 2011

Knappe, Siegfried (translated by Ted Brusaw), *Soldat: Reflections of a German Soldier, 1936-1949*, Bantam Doubleday Dell 1999

Knoke, Heinz (translated by John Ewing), *I Flew for the Führer; The Story of a German Airman*, Evans Brothers 1953

Korschorrek, Günter K. (translated by Olav R. Crome-Aamot), *Blood Red Snow, The Memoirs of a German soldier on the Eastern Front*, Greenhill 2011

Kuhnert, Max, *Will We See Tomorrow? A German Cavalryman At War 1939-42*, Leo Cooper 1993

Landau, Sigmund Heinz, *Goodbye Transylvania – A Romanian Waffen-SS Solider in WWII*, Stackpole 2015

Lowe, Keith, *Savage Continent*, Viking 2012

Lower, Wendy, *Hitler's Furies: German Women in the Killing Fields*, Vintage 2014

Lubbeck, William (contributor David B. Hurt), *At Leningrad's Gates: The Story of a Soldier with Army Group North*, Casemate 2010

Lucas, James, *Storming Eagles – German airborne forces in World War II*, Cassell 1988

Lucas, James, *Kommando – German special forces in World War II*, Cassell 1985

Lucas, James, *Das Reich*, Cassell, 1991

Luck, Hans von, *Panzer Commander: The memoirs of Colonel Hans von Luck*, Cassell 1989

Luther, Craig W. H., *The First Day on the Eastern Front: Germany invades the Soviet Union June 22, 1941*, Stackpole 2019

Mahlke, Helmut, *Memoirs of a Stuka Pilot*, Frontline 2013

McNab, Chris, *The Luftwaffe 1933-45, Hitler's Eagles*, Osprey 2012

Meyer, Kurt (translated by Michael Mendé and Robert J. Edwards), *Grenadiers*, J.J. Fedorowicz 2001

Michaelis, Rolf, *Cavalry Divisions of the Waffen-SS*, Schiffer 2010

Michaelis, Rolf, *Panzer Divisions of the Waffen-SS*, Schiffer 2013

Michaelis, Rolf, *Panzergrenadier Divisions of the Waffen-SS*, Schiffer 2010

Mitcham, Samuel W. Jr, *Eagles of the Third Reich*, Stackpole 1988

Mitcham, Samuel W., *Hitler's Legions: German Army Order of Battle World War II*, Leo Cooper 1985

Munk, Jan, *I was a Dutch Volunteer*, self-published 2010

Murray, Williamson, *Strategy for Defeat – The Luftwaffe – 1933-1945*, Chartwell 1986

Neitzel, Sönke and Welzer, Harald, *Soldaten*, Simon & Schuster 2012

Nowarra, Heinz, *Heinkel He111 – A Documentary History*, Jane's 1980

Ochsenknecht, Ingeborg, *Als ob der Schnee alles zudeckte* ('As if the snow covered everything'), Econ Verlag 2004

Pabst, Helmut, (translated by Andrew & Eva Wilson), *The Outermost Frontier – A German Soldier in the Russian Campaign*, William Kimber 1957

Perrett, Bryan, *Knights of the Black Cross*, Robert Hale 1986

Pöppel, Martin (translated by L. Willmott), *Heaven and Hell: The War Diary of a German Paratrooper*, Spellmount 1988

Prüller, Wilhelm, *Diary of a German Soldier*, Faber 1963

Reese, Willy Peter (translated by Michael Hofmann), *A Stranger to Myself: The inhumanity of war – Russia 1941-1944*, Farrar, Strauss and Giroux 2005

Reynolds, Michael, *The Devil's Adjutant – Jochen Peiper, Panzer Leader*, Spellmount 1995

Ribbentrop, Rudolf von, *My father Joachim von Ribbentrop*, self-published 2015

Richardson, Horst Fuchs, *Your Loyal And Loving Son: The Letters of Tank Gunner Karl Fuchs, 1937-1941*, Potomac 2003

Roland, Paul, *The Nazis: The rise and fall of history's most evil empire*, Arcturus 2019

Rosen, Richard Freiherr von (translated by Geoffrey Brooks), *Panzer Ace: The Memoirs of a Panzer Commander*, Greenhill 2018

Scheck, Raffael, *Hitler's African Victims: The German Army Massacres of Black French Soldiers in 1940*, Cambridge University 2010

Snyder, Timothy, *Blood Lands; Europe Between Hitler and Stalin*, Vintage 2010

Stahel, David, *Kiev 1941: Hitler's Battle for Supremacy in the East*, Cambridge University Press 2012

Stargardt, Nicholas, *The German War: A Nation Under Arms, 1939-45*, Vintage 2015

Umbrich, Friedrich (translated by Anna M. Wittmann), *Balkan Nightmare*, Columbia University Press, 2000

Verton, Hendrik C. (translated by Hazel Toon-Thon), *In the fire of the Eastern Front – The experiences of a Dutch Waffen-SS volunteer on the Eastern Front 1941-45*, Helion 2007

Villani, Gerry, *Voices of the Waffen-SS*, self-published 2015

Voss, Johann, *Black Edelweiss – A memoir of combat and conscience by a soldier of the Waffen-SS*, Aberjona 2002

Wacker, Albrecht, *Sniper on the Eastern Front – The Memoirs of Sepp Allerberger*, Pen & Sword 2005

Werner, Herbert, *Iron Coffins*, Da Capo Press 2002

Williamson, Gordon, *Loyalty is my Honor*, Motorbooks 1997

Index

Also available from Amberley Publishing

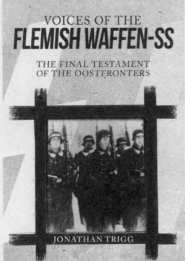

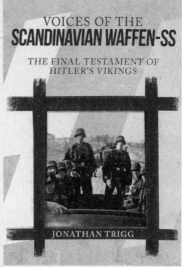